MARK WAID VERONICA FISH
THOMAS PITILLI RYAN JAMPOLE

ARCHIE®

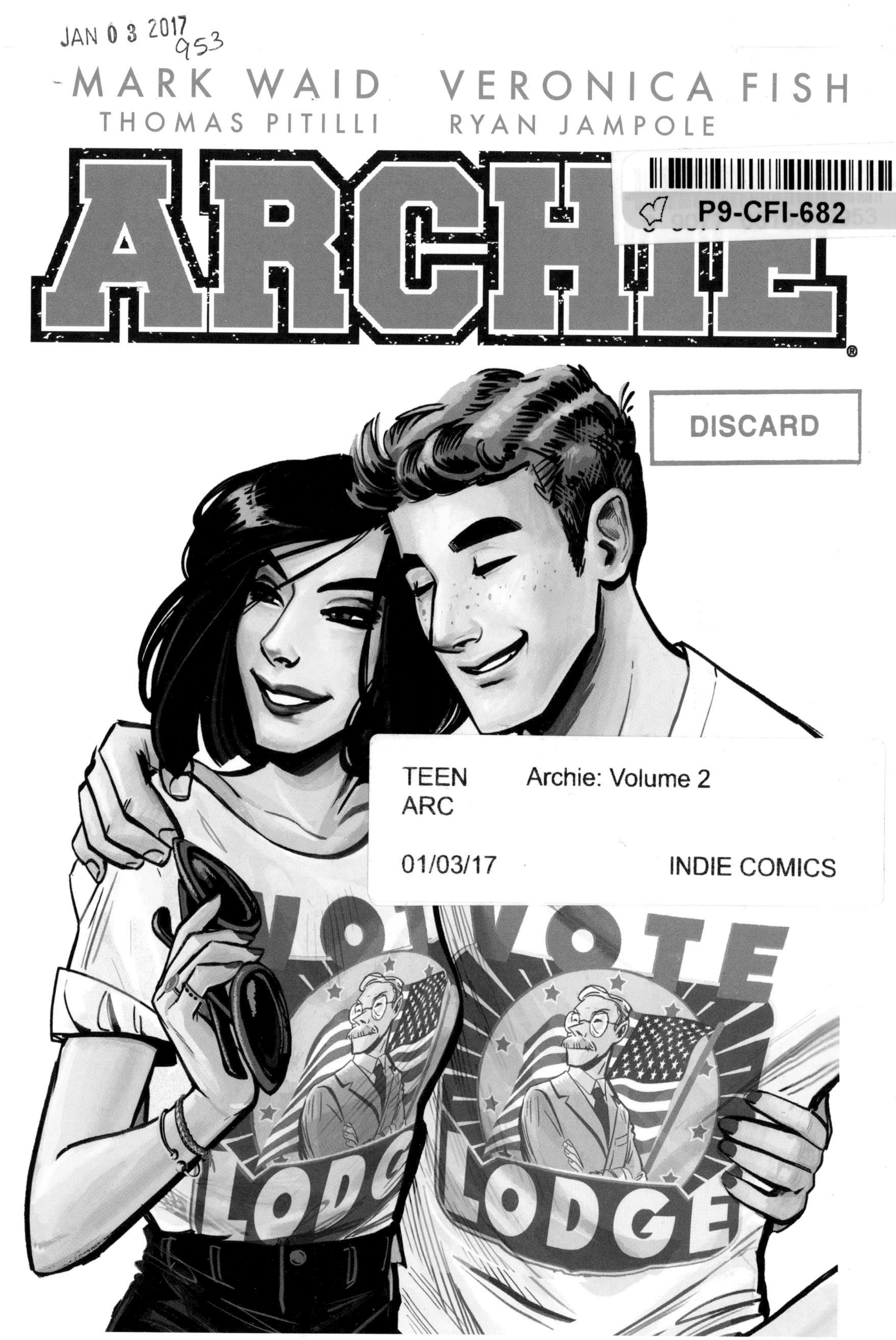
VOTE
LODGE
VOTE
LODGE

VOLUME TWO

STORY BY
MARK WAID

ART BY
VERONICA FISH
(ISSUES 7-10)

FINISHES BY
THOMAS PITILLI
(ISSUES 11-12)

BREAKDOWNS BY
RYAN JAMPOLE
(ISSUES 11-12)

COLORING BY
ANDRE SZYMANOWICZ
WITH JEN VAUGHN (ISSUE 7)

LETTERING BY
JACK MORELLI

EDITOR
MIKE PELLERITO

ASSOCIATE EDITOR
STEPHEN OSWALD

ASSISTANT EDITOR
JAMIE LEE ROTANTE

EDITOR-IN-CHIEF
VICTOR GORELICK

GRAPHIC DESIGN BY
KARI McLACHLAN

PUBLISHER
JON GOLDWATER

THE ONLY CONSTANT IS CHANGE

ARCHIE®

by MIKE PELLERITO

In 1941 (that's 75 years ago!), a lot changed in the world, and even more was to come. Also in that year, a little company called MLJ Comics that created superhero comics after years of publishing pulp novels introduced a brand new character: seemingly out of the blue, a red-headed everyday teen character showed up in their comics… and everything changed.

The teen, named Archie Andrews, was so influential on the company that MLJ actually changed its name to Archie Comics! (Well, *technically* Archie Comic Publications, Inc., but you get the idea!) Archie, the character, lived in the perfect any town known as "Riverdale," which for the past 75 years has remained the same—while simultaneously changing and evolving, just like the world around us. Thanks to comic book magic, you are now holding in your hands the latest documented change that Archie and his hometown of Riverdale has undergone. (Aaaand the history part is over. No test either!)

There's something to be said for making a 75-year-old character fresh and new. Fighting the zombie apocalypse (have you read the hit comic *Afterlife with Archie*? I'm sure you'll love it. Once you pick up the first volume in trade paperback, you might even be *dying* to read more—shameless plug) or marrying Archie off to BOTH Betty AND Veronica and creating two different universes (check out the *Archie: Married Life* graphic novel series) are a great start.

Seriously, both of these are stories we actually printed. We even killed Archie once in the *Death of Archie* graphic novel (available in finer bookstores and comic shops now—shameless plugs all around!) We got some great press and a lot of people picked up on something new going on with Archie—both the character AND the company. All the while, we have continued to put out the traditional Archie adventures in our Double Digests at grocery checkout aisles, not to mention the *Best of Archie* collections, massive 1000 page compilations and more (all well worth a shameless plug).

Archie was changing as a company, but keeping true to the characters at the same time—which was very cool, but not easy. And in 2015, we made our biggest change yet when we relaunched the main *Archie* comic series after well over 600 issues. What writer Mark Waid and the ever-changing group of brilliant artists: Fiona Staples, Annie Wu, Veronica Fish, Thomas Pitilli, Ryan Jampole, Andre Szymanowicz, Jen Vaughn and Jack Morelli, have put together are some of the best new stories we could have hoped for with the timeless teenagers of Riverdale.

So what's next? Starting in the first year of our next 75 years as a company, a new live-action TV series called *Riverdale* is coming to the CW. It's another huge step in the ever-changing, ever-evolving Archie-verse. But what's most important is you, yes you, the fearless readers at the forefront of the next 75 years. Imagine the changes yet to come!

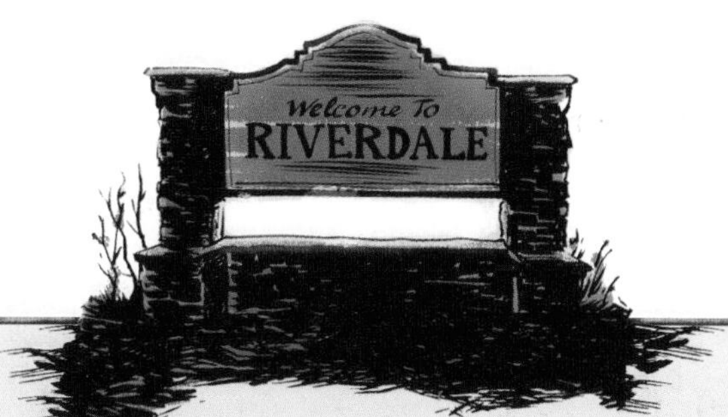
Welcome To
RIVERDALE

ISSUE SEVEN

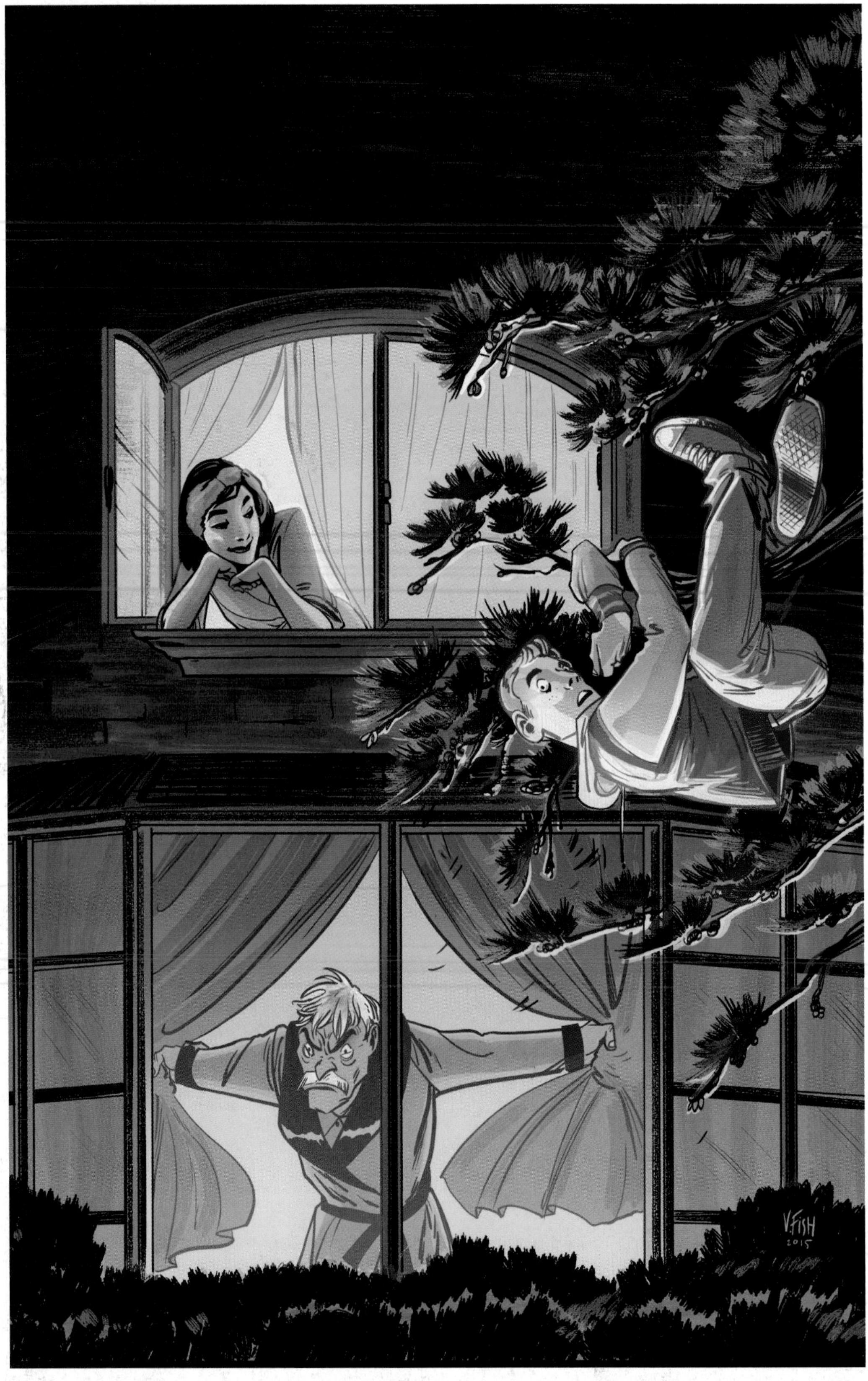
V.FISH
2015

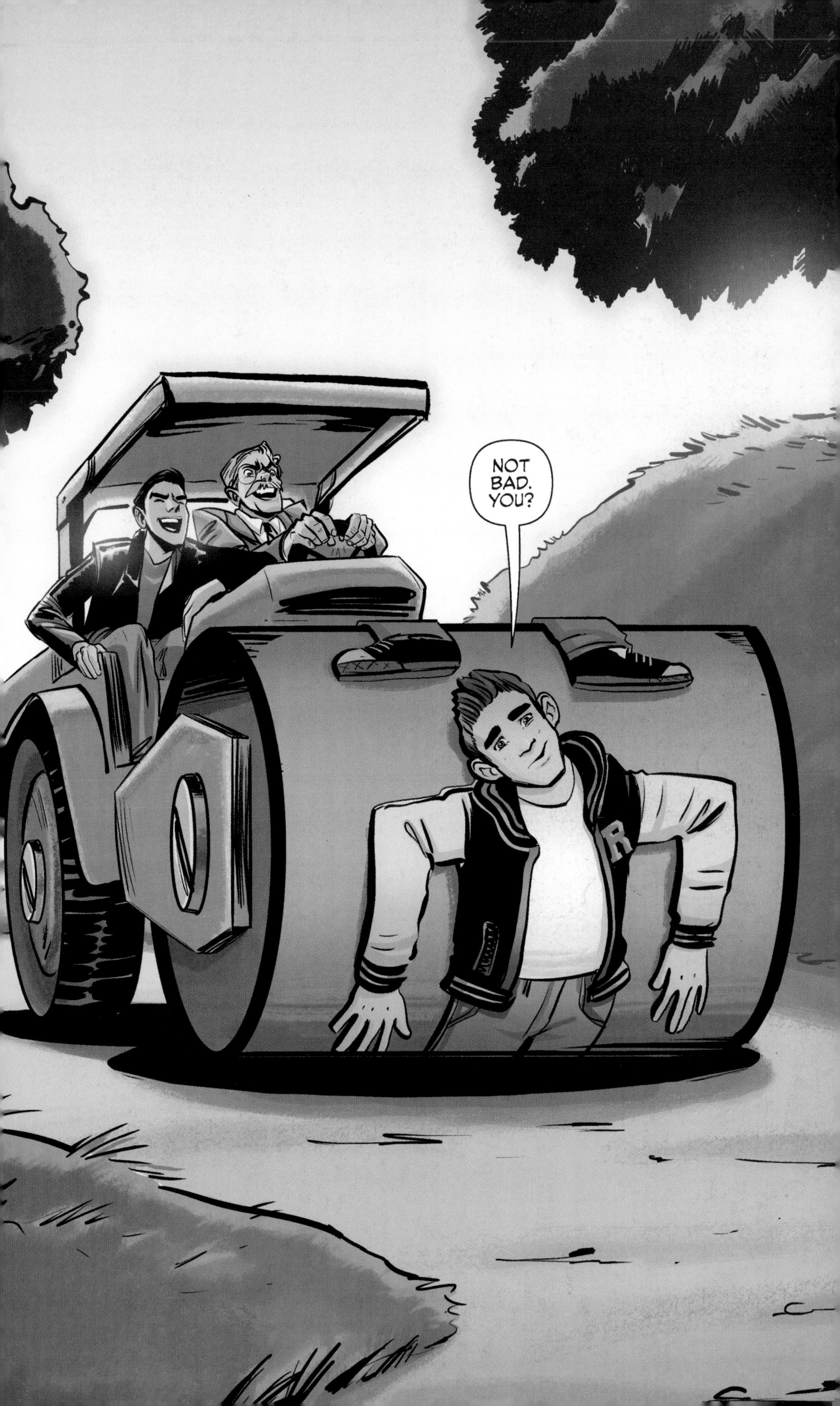
NOT BAD. YOU?

CHAPTER ONE: FAMILY TIME!

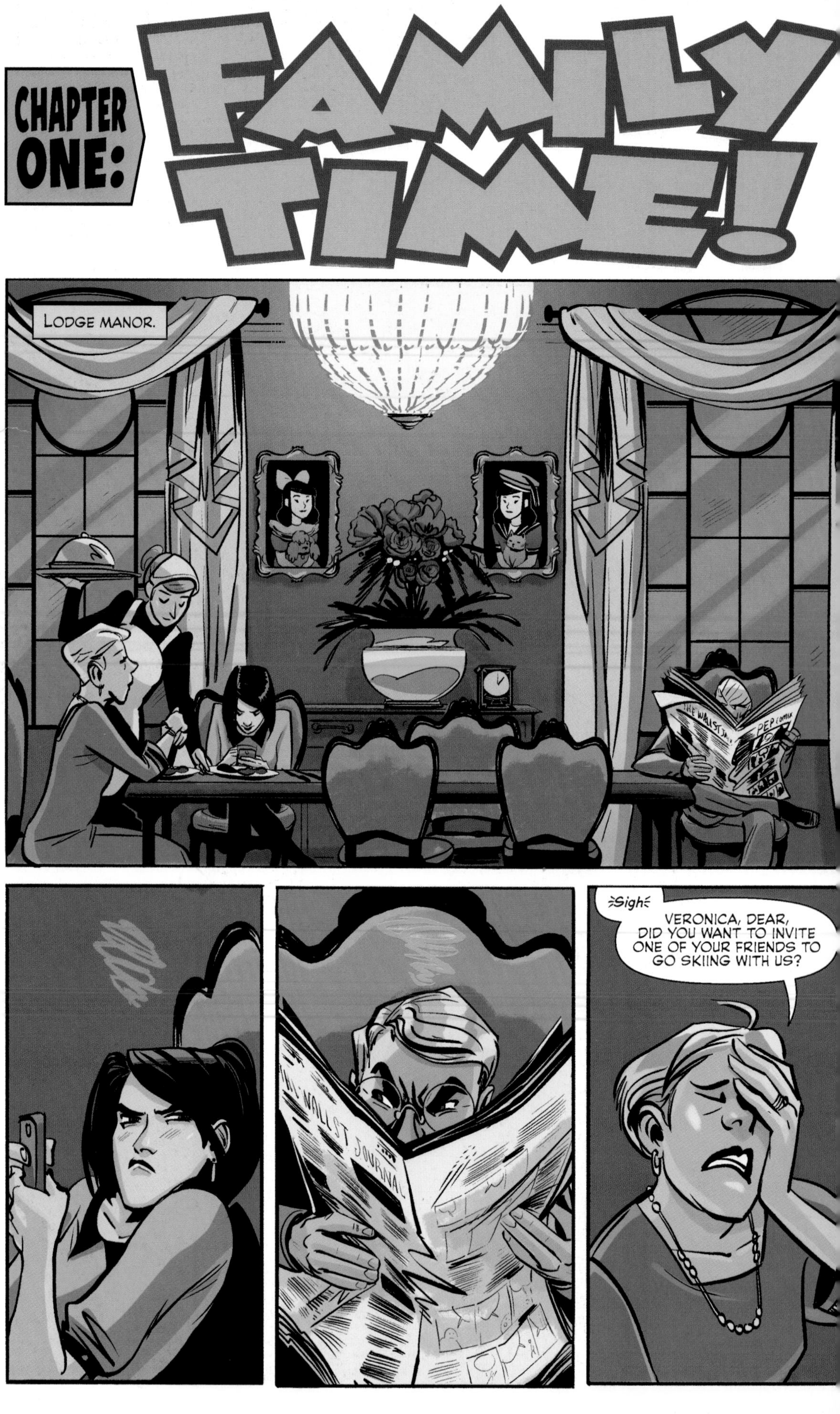
LODGE MANOR.
Sigh
VERONICA, DEAR, DID YOU WANT TO INVITE ONE OF YOUR FRIENDS TO GO SKIING WITH US?

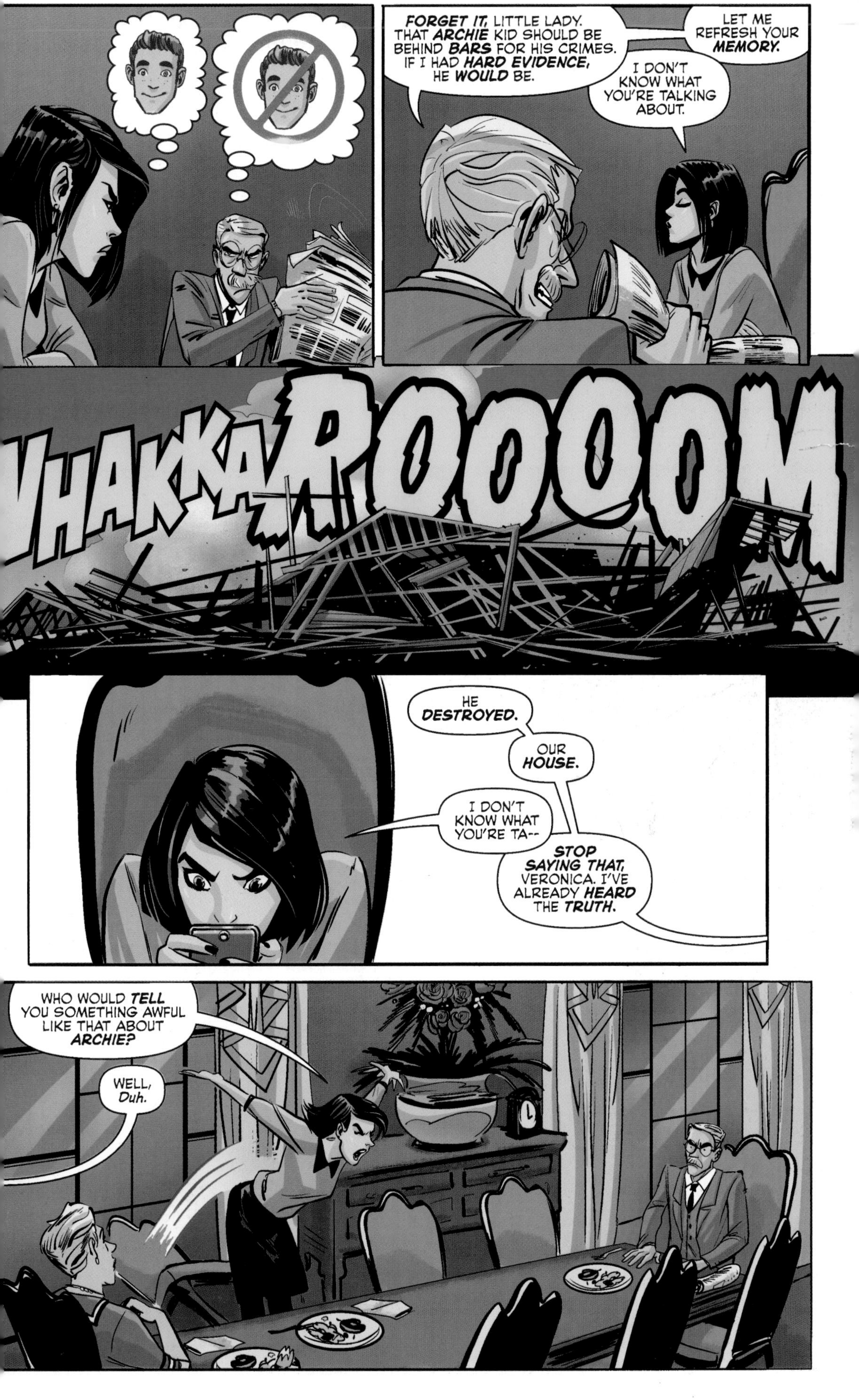
FORGET IT, LITTLE LADY. THAT ARCHIE KID SHOULD BE BEHIND BARS FOR HIS CRIMES. IF I HAD HARD EVIDENCE, HE WOULD BE.
LET ME REFRESH YOUR MEMORY.
I DON'T KNOW WHAT YOU'RE TALKING ABOUT.
VHAKKAROOOOM
HE DESTROYED.
OUR HOUSE.
I DON'T KNOW WHAT YOU'RE TA--
STOP SAYING THAT, VERONICA. I'VE ALREADY HEARD THE TRUTH.
WHO WOULD TELL YOU SOMETHING AWFUL LIKE THAT ABOUT ARCHIE?
WELL, Duh.

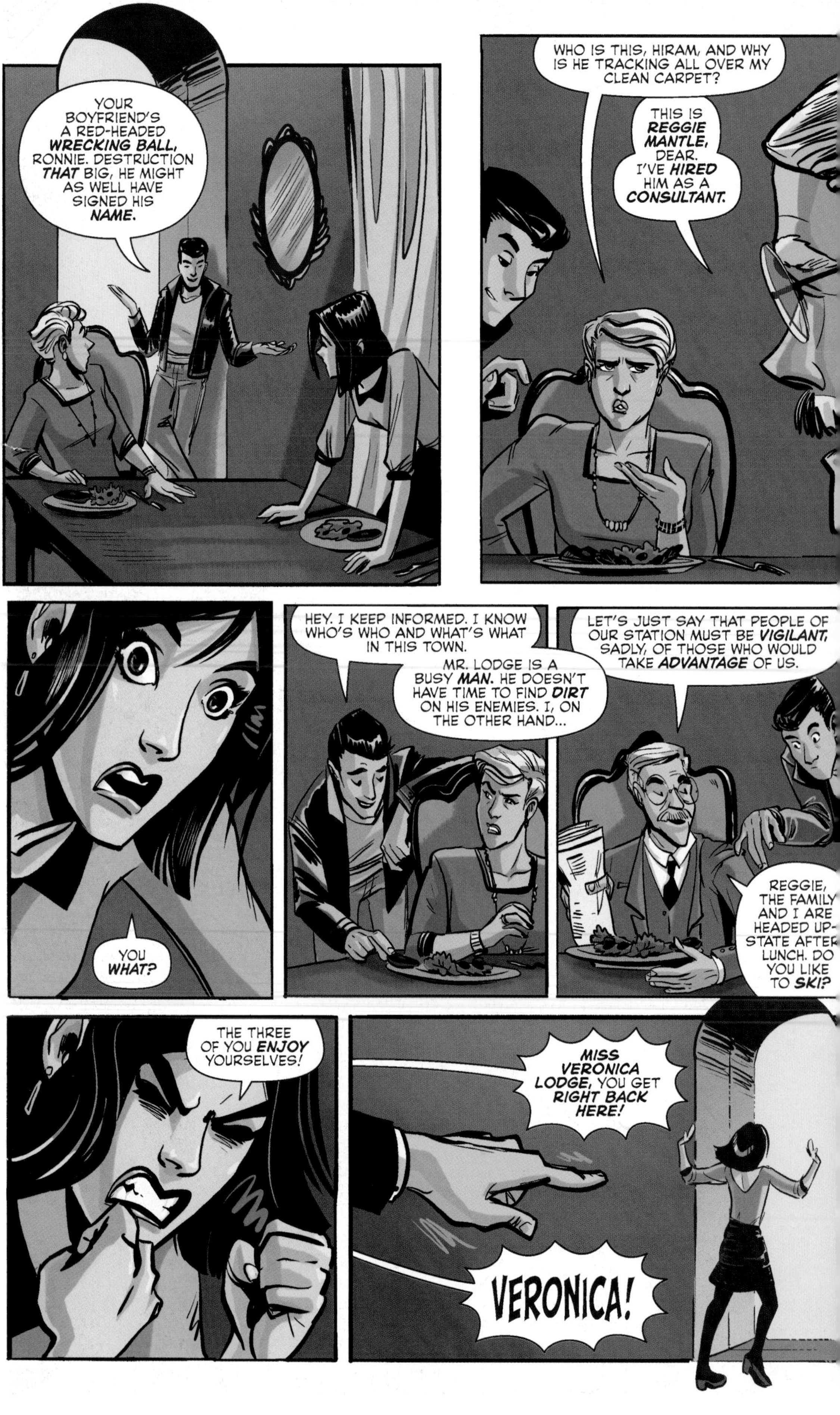

YOUR BOYFRIEND'S A RED-HEADED WRECKING BALL, RONNIE. DESTRUCTION THAT BIG, HE MIGHT AS WELL HAVE SIGNED HIS NAME.
WHO IS THIS, HIRAM, AND WHY IS HE TRACKING ALL OVER MY CLEAN CARPET?
THIS IS REGGIE MANTLE, DEAR. I'VE HIRED HIM AS A CONSULTANT.
YOU WHAT?
HEY. I KEEP INFORMED. I KNOW WHO'S WHO AND WHAT'S WHAT IN THIS TOWN.
MR. LODGE IS A BUSY MAN. HE DOESN'T HAVE TIME TO FIND DIRT ON HIS ENEMIES. I, ON THE OTHER HAND...
LET'S JUST SAY THAT PEOPLE OF OUR STATION MUST BE VIGILANT, SADLY, OF THOSE WHO WOULD TAKE ADVANTAGE OF US.
REGGIE, THE FAMILY AND I ARE HEADED UP-STATE AFTER LUNCH. DO YOU LIKE TO SKI?
THE THREE OF YOU ENJOY YOURSELVES!
MISS VERONICA LODGE, YOU GET RIGHT BACK HERE!
VERONICA!

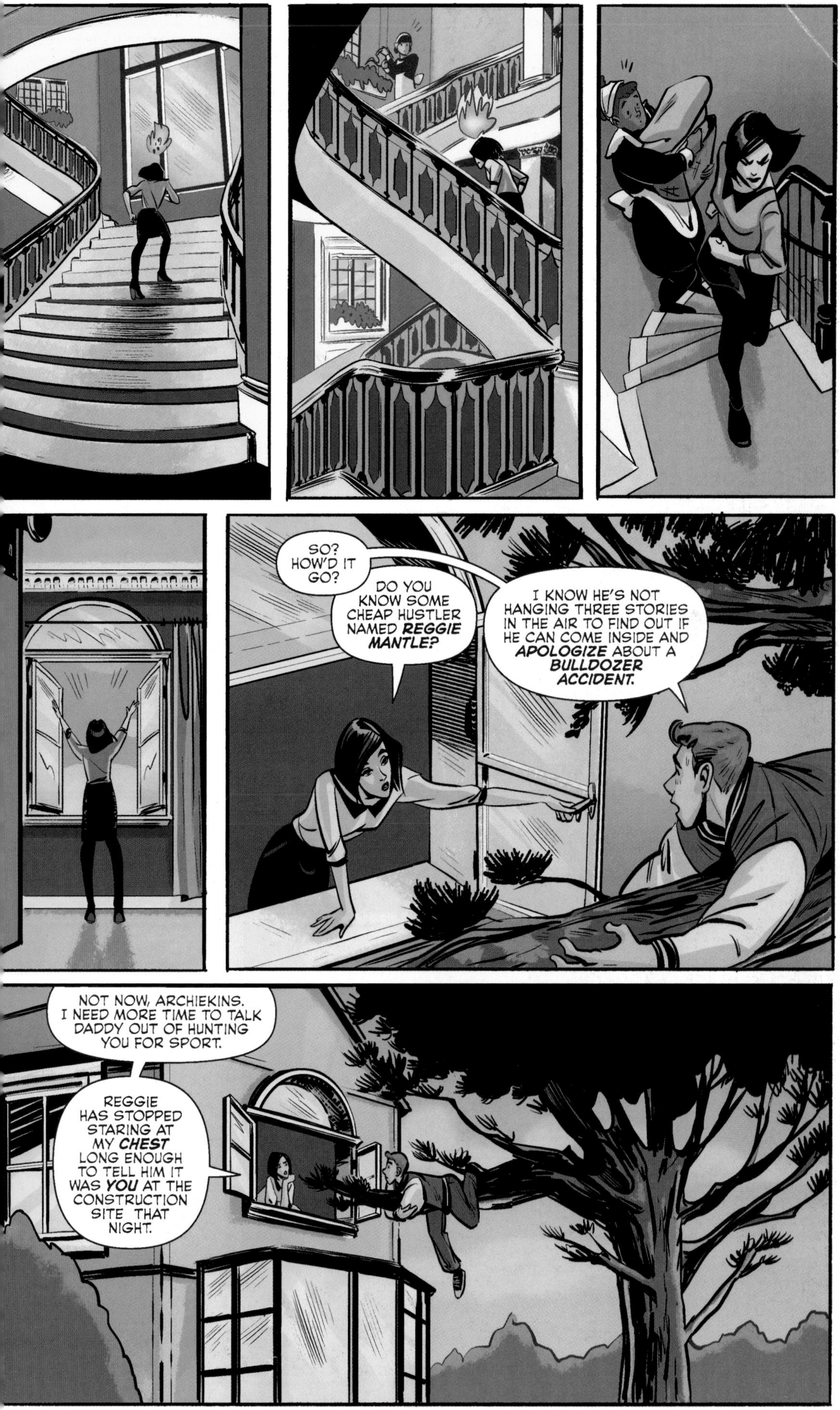
SO? HOW'D IT GO?
DO YOU KNOW SOME CHEAP HUSTLER NAMED REGGIE MANTLE?
I KNOW HE'S NOT HANGING THREE STORIES IN THE AIR TO FIND OUT IF HE CAN COME INSIDE AND APOLOGIZE ABOUT A BULLDOZER ACCIDENT.
NOT NOW, ARCHIEKINS. I NEED MORE TIME TO TALK DADDY OUT OF HUNTING YOU FOR SPORT.
REGGIE HAS STOPPED STARING AT MY CHEST LONG ENOUGH TO TELL HIM IT WAS YOU AT THE CONSTRUCTION SITE THAT NIGHT.

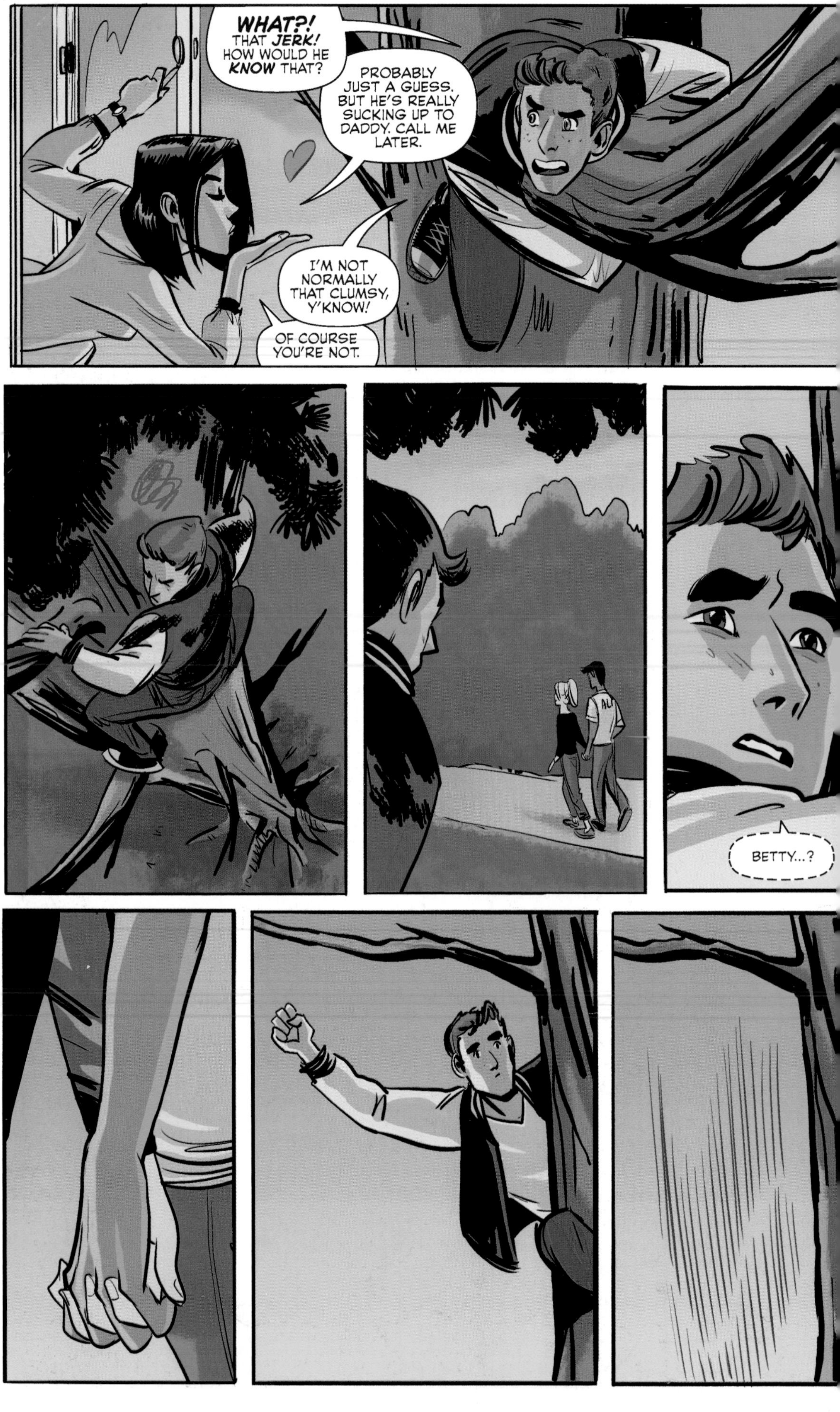
WHAT?! THAT JERK! HOW WOULD HE KNOW THAT?
PROBABLY JUST A GUESS. BUT HE'S REALLY SUCKING UP TO DADDY. CALL ME LATER.
I'M NOT NORMALLY THAT CLUMSY, Y'KNOW!
OF COURSE YOU'RE NOT.
BETTY...?

CHAPTER TWO: SACRED TRUST

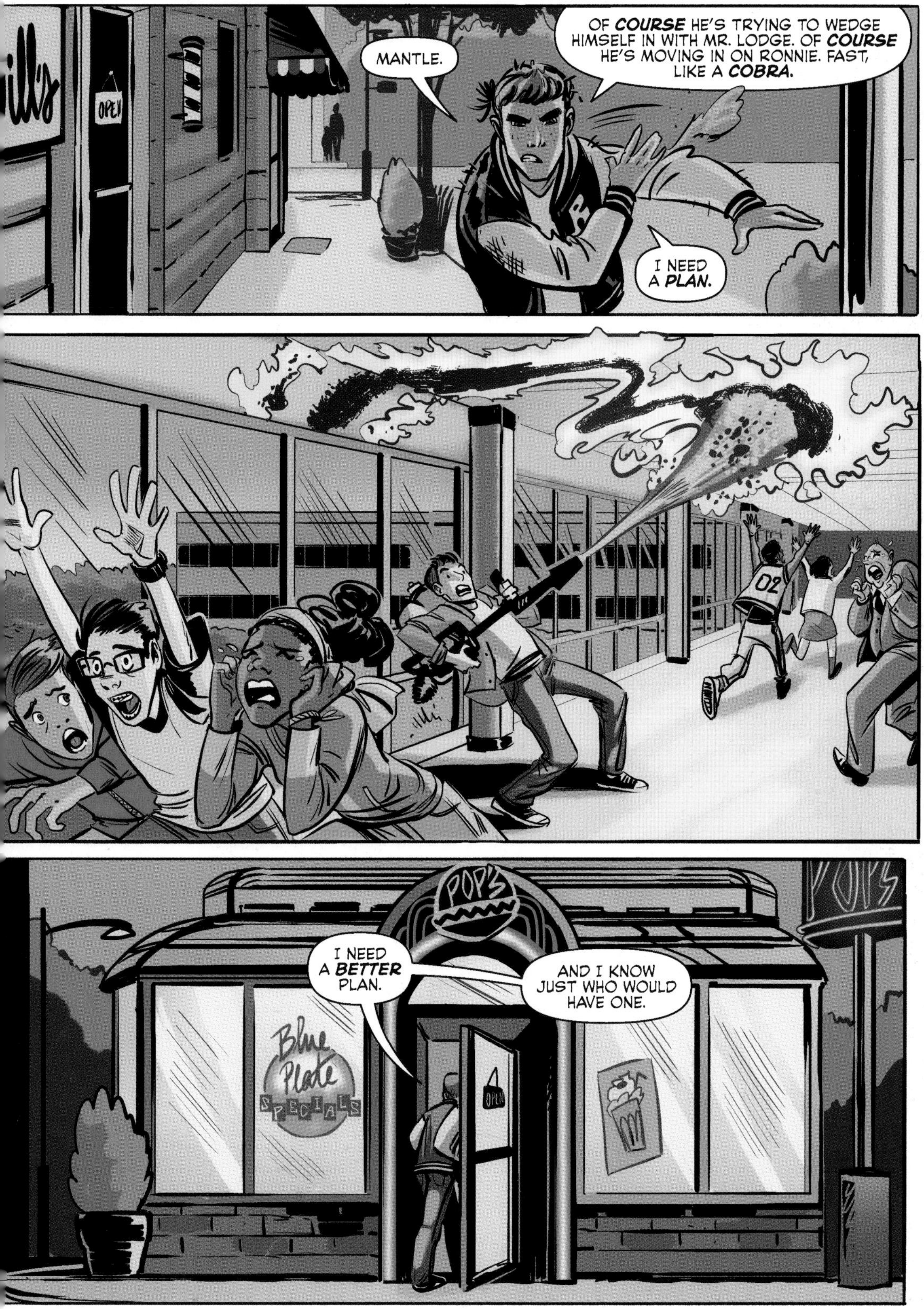

OPEN
MANTLE.
OF COURSE HE'S TRYING TO WEDGE HIMSELF IN WITH MR. LODGE. OF COURSE HE'S MOVING IN ON RONNIE. FAST, LIKE A COBRA.
I NEED A PLAN.
02
POP'S
POP'S
I NEED A BETTER PLAN.
AND I KNOW JUST WHO WOULD HAVE ONE.
Blue Plate SPECIALS
OPEN

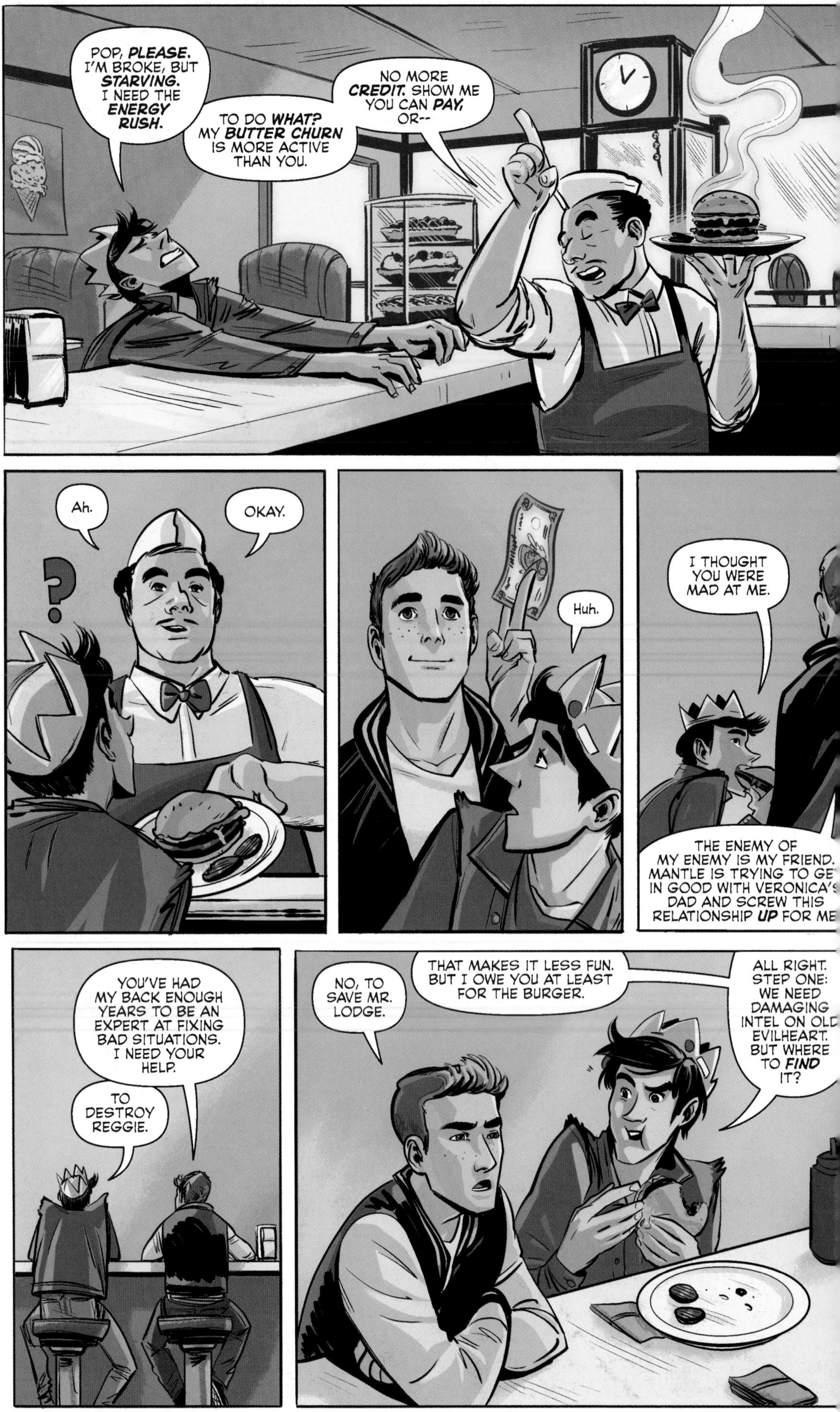
POP, PLEASE. I'M BROKE, BUT STARVING. I NEED THE ENERGY RUSH.
TO DO WHAT? MY BUTTER CHURN IS MORE ACTIVE THAN YOU.
NO MORE CREDIT. SHOW ME YOU CAN PAY, OR--
Ah.
OKAY.
Huh.
I THOUGHT YOU WERE MAD AT ME.
THE ENEMY OF MY ENEMY IS MY FRIEND. MANTLE IS TRYING TO GE IN GOOD WITH VERONICA'S DAD AND SCREW THIS RELATIONSHIP UP FOR ME
YOU'VE HAD MY BACK ENOUGH YEARS TO BE AN EXPERT AT FIXING BAD SITUATIONS. I NEED YOUR HELP.
TO DESTROY REGGIE.
NO, TO SAVE MR. LODGE.
THAT MAKES IT LESS FUN. BUT I OWE YOU AT LEAST FOR THE BURGER.
ALL RIGHT. STEP ONE: WE NEED DAMAGING INTEL ON OLD EVILHEART. BUT WHERE TO FIND IT?

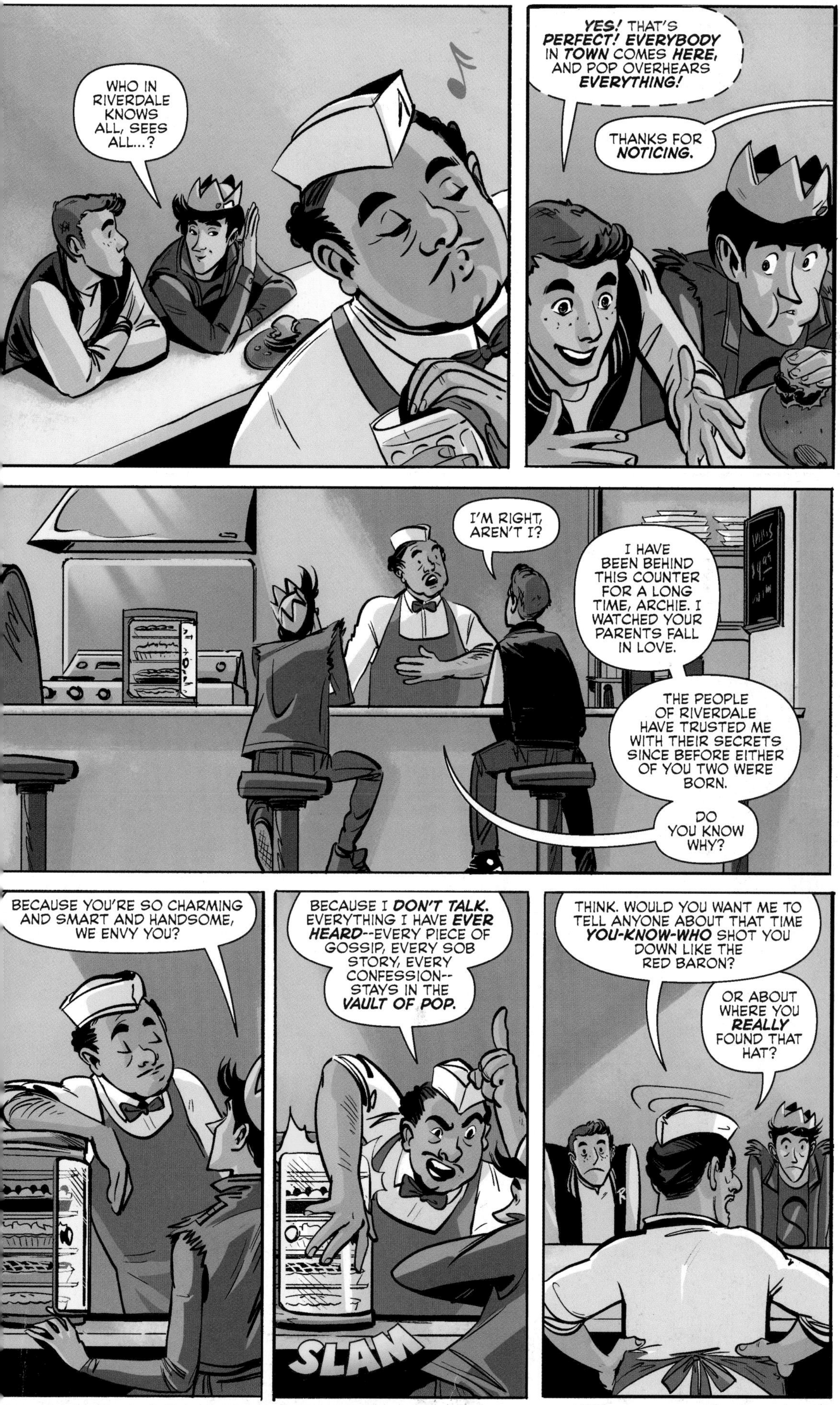
WHO IN RIVERDALE KNOWS ALL, SEES ALL...?
YES! THAT'S PERFECT! EVERYBODY IN TOWN COMES HERE, AND POP OVERHEARS EVERYTHING!
THANKS FOR NOTICING.
I'M RIGHT, AREN'T I?
I HAVE BEEN BEHIND THIS COUNTER FOR A LONG TIME, ARCHIE. I WATCHED YOUR PARENTS FALL IN LOVE.
THE PEOPLE OF RIVERDALE HAVE TRUSTED ME WITH THEIR SECRETS SINCE BEFORE EITHER OF YOU TWO WERE BORN.
DO YOU KNOW WHY?
BECAUSE YOU'RE SO CHARMING AND SMART AND HANDSOME, WE ENVY YOU?
BECAUSE I DON'T TALK. EVERYTHING I HAVE EVER HEARD--EVERY PIECE OF GOSSIP, EVERY SOB STORY, EVERY CONFESSION--STAYS IN THE VAULT OF POP.
SLAM
THINK. WOULD YOU WANT ME TO TELL ANYONE ABOUT THAT TIME YOU-KNOW-WHO SHOT YOU DOWN LIKE THE RED BARON?
OR ABOUT WHERE YOU REALLY FOUND THAT HAT?

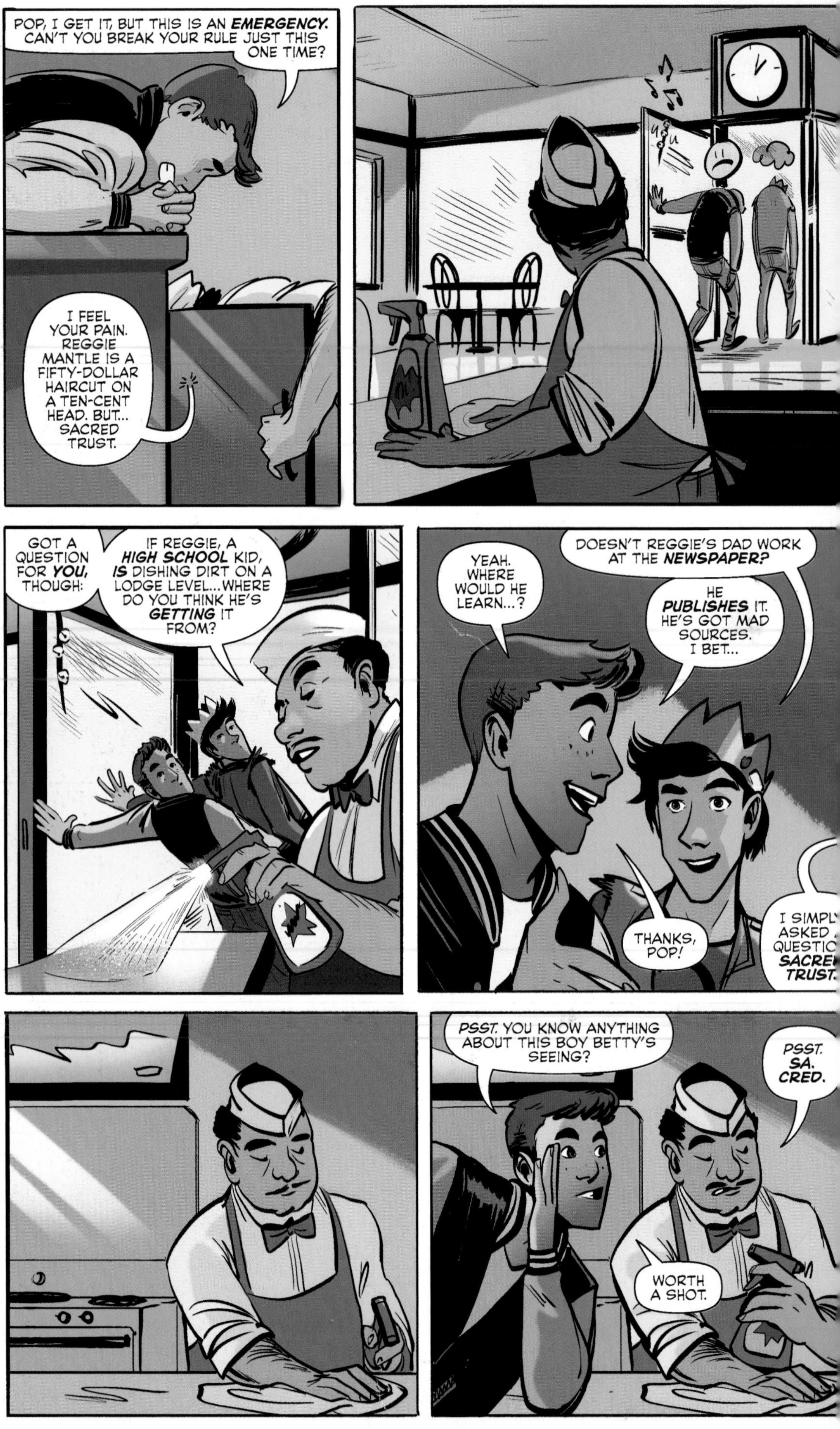

POP, I GET IT, BUT THIS IS AN ***EMERGENCY.*** CAN'T YOU BREAK YOUR RULE JUST THIS ONE TIME?
I FEEL YOUR PAIN. REGGIE MANTLE IS A FIFTY-DOLLAR HAIRCUT ON A TEN-CENT HEAD. BUT... SACRED TRUST.
GOT A QUESTION FOR ***YOU,*** THOUGH:
IF REGGIE, A ***HIGH SCHOOL*** KID, ***IS*** DISHING DIRT ON A LODGE LEVEL...WHERE DO YOU THINK HE'S ***GETTING*** IT FROM?
YEAH. WHERE WOULD HE LEARN...?
DOESN'T REGGIE'S DAD WORK AT THE ***NEWSPAPER?***
HE ***PUBLISHES*** IT. HE'S GOT MAD SOURCES. I BET...
THANKS, POP!
I SIMPLY ASKED A QUESTIO... ***SACRE... TRUST.***
PSST. YOU KNOW ANYTHING ABOUT THIS BOY BETTY'S SEEING?
PSST. SA. CRED.
WORTH A SHOT.

CHAPTER THREE: STOP THE PRESSES

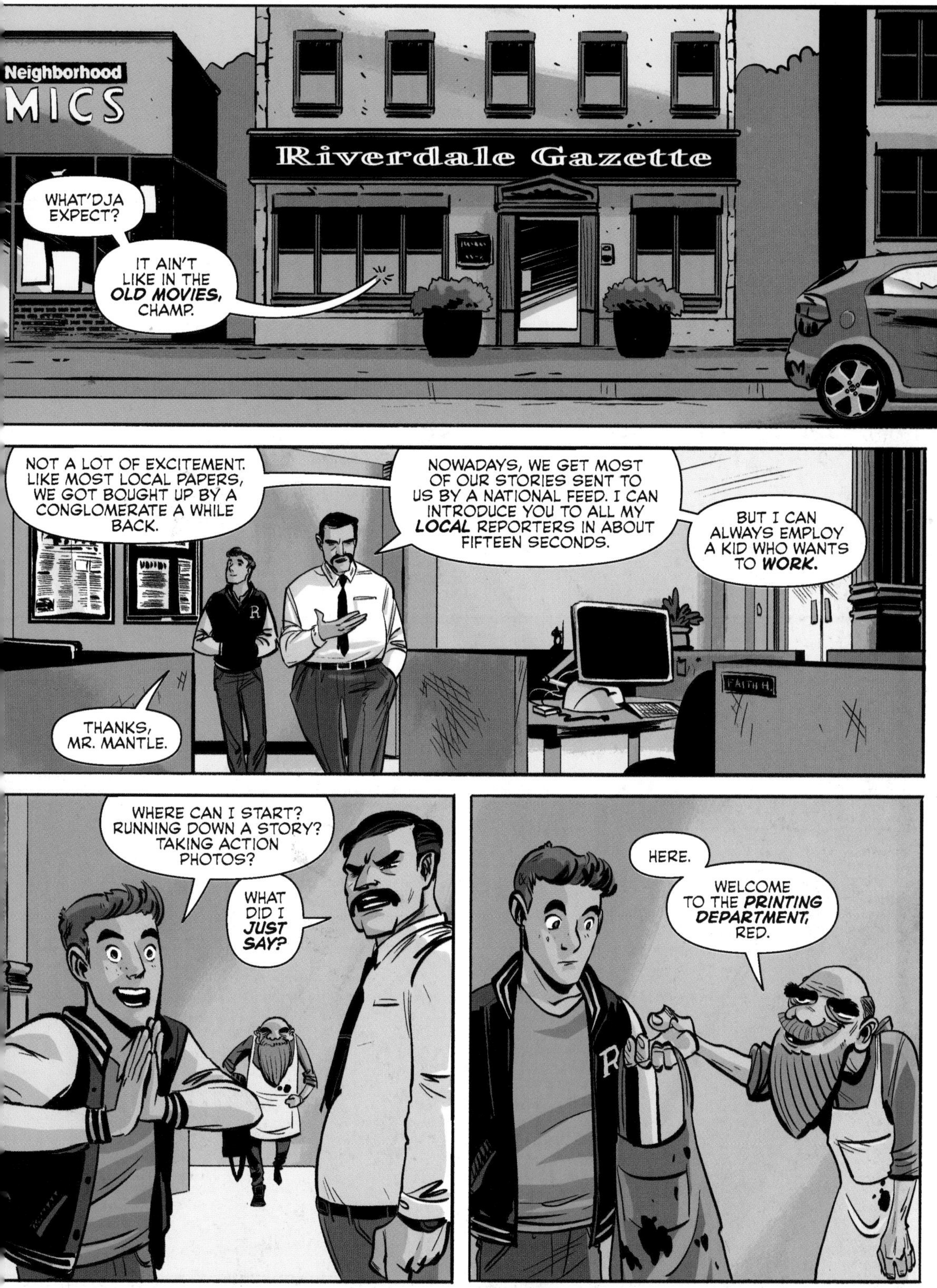
Neighborhood
MICS
Riverdale Gazette
WHAT'DJA EXPECT?
IT AIN'T LIKE IN THE OLD MOVIES, CHAMP.
NOT A LOT OF EXCITEMENT. LIKE MOST LOCAL PAPERS, WE GOT BOUGHT UP BY A CONGLOMERATE A WHILE BACK.
NOWADAYS, WE GET MOST OF OUR STORIES SENT TO US BY A NATIONAL FEED. I CAN INTRODUCE YOU TO ALL MY LOCAL REPORTERS IN ABOUT FIFTEEN SECONDS.
BUT I CAN ALWAYS EMPLOY A KID WHO WANTS TO WORK.
THANKS, MR. MANTLE.
FAITH H.
WHERE CAN I START? RUNNING DOWN A STORY? TAKING ACTION PHOTOS?
WHAT DID I JUST SAY?
HERE.
WELCOME TO THE PRINTING DEPARTMENT, RED.

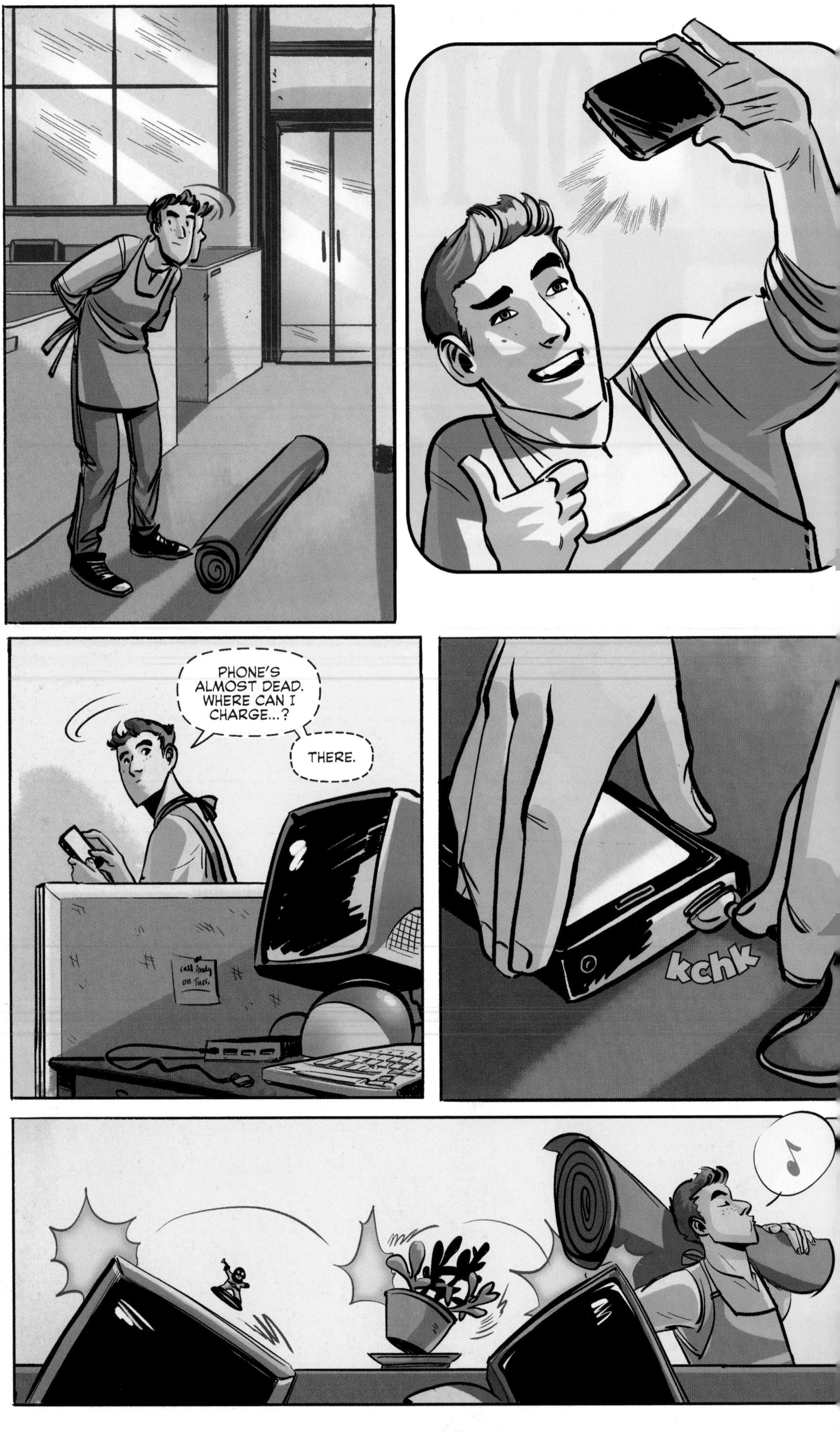

PHONE'S ALMOST DEAD. WHERE CAN I CHARGE...?
THERE.
call Andy on Tues.
kchk

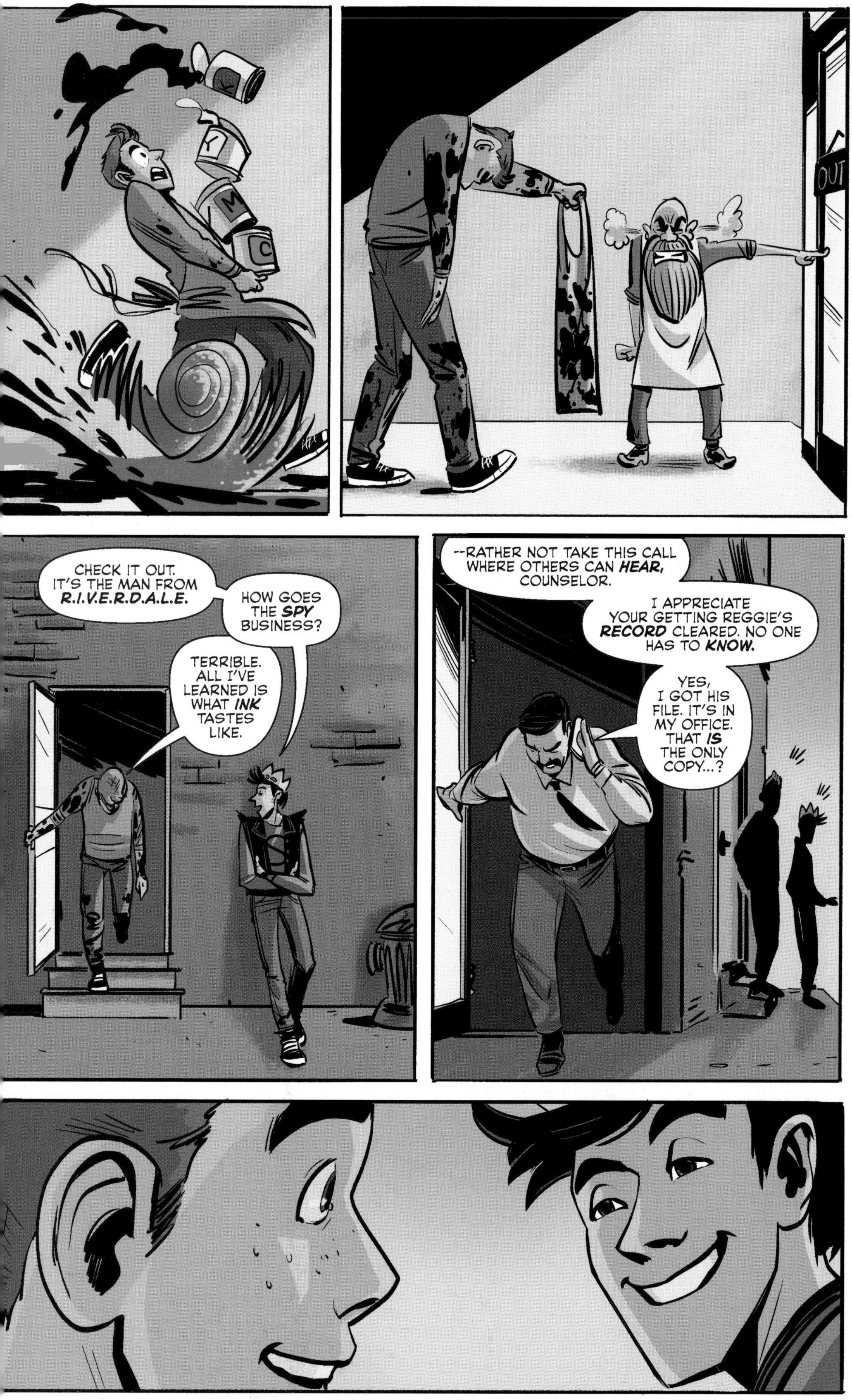
OUT
CHECK IT OUT. IT'S THE MAN FROM R.I.V.E.R.D.A.L.E.
HOW GOES THE SPY BUSINESS?
TERRIBLE. ALL I'VE LEARNED IS WHAT INK TASTES LIKE.
--RATHER NOT TAKE THIS CALL WHERE OTHERS CAN HEAR, COUNSELOR.
I APPRECIATE YOUR GETTING REGGIE'S RECORD CLEARED. NO ONE HAS TO KNOW.
YES, I GOT HIS FILE. IT'S IN MY OFFICE. THAT IS THE ONLY COPY...?

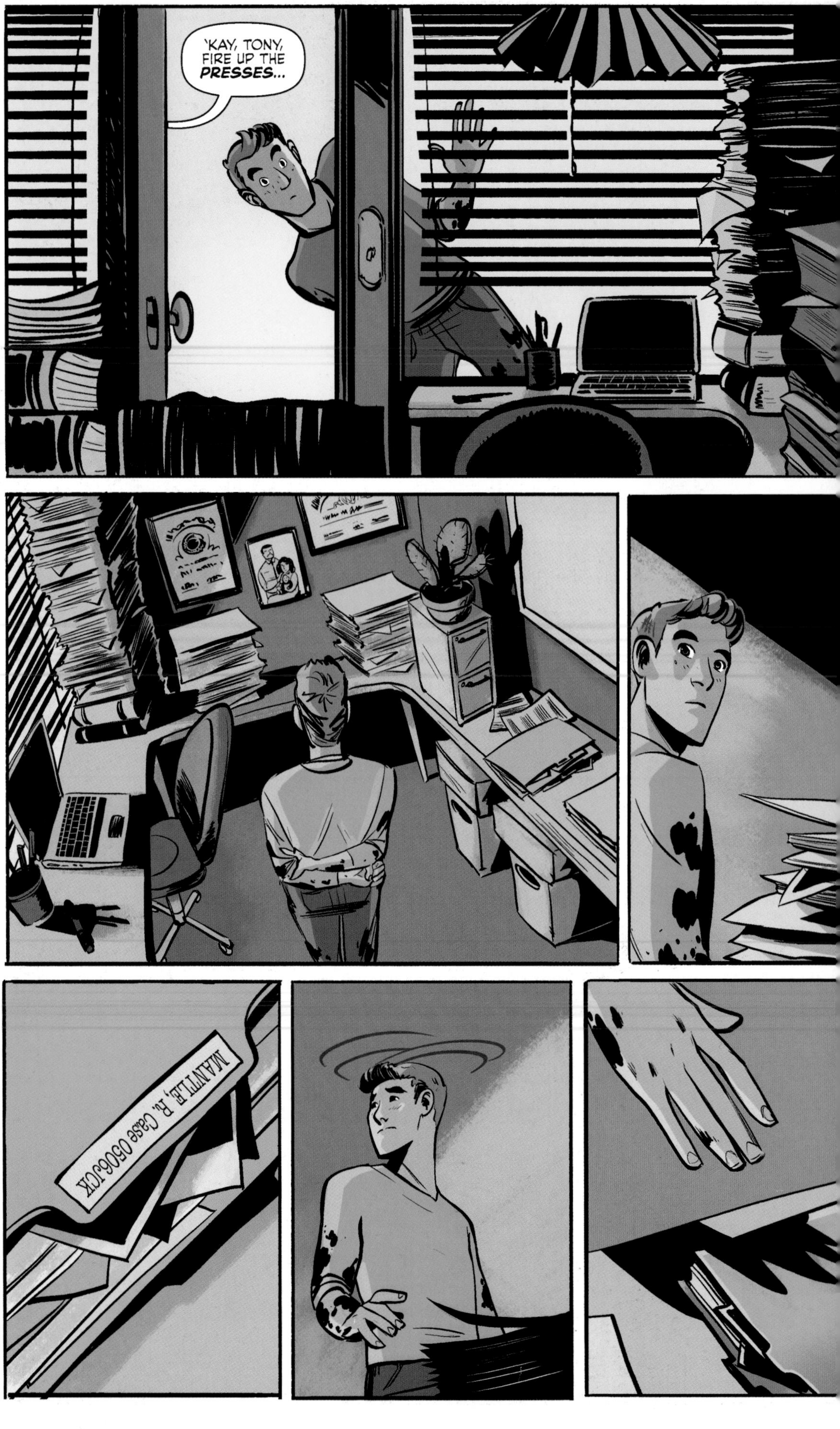
'KAY, TONY, FIRE UP THE PRESSES...
MANTLE, R. Case 0506JCK

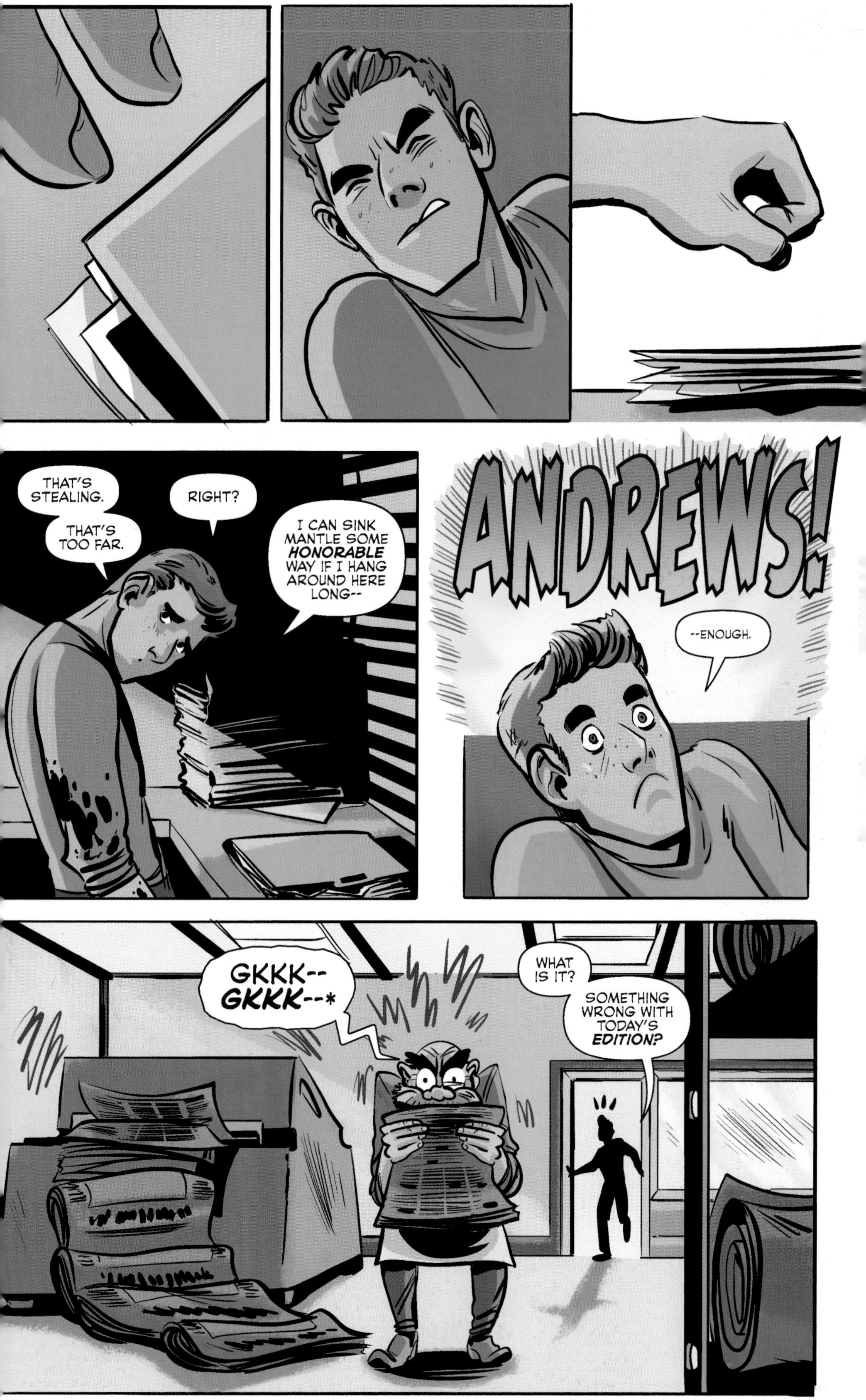

THAT'S STEALING.
THAT'S TOO FAR.
RIGHT?
I CAN SINK MANTLE SOME **HONORABLE** WAY IF I HANG AROUND HERE LONG--
ANDREWS!
--ENOUGH.
GKKK-- GKKK--*
WHAT IS IT?
SOMETHING WRONG WITH TODAY'S **EDITION?**

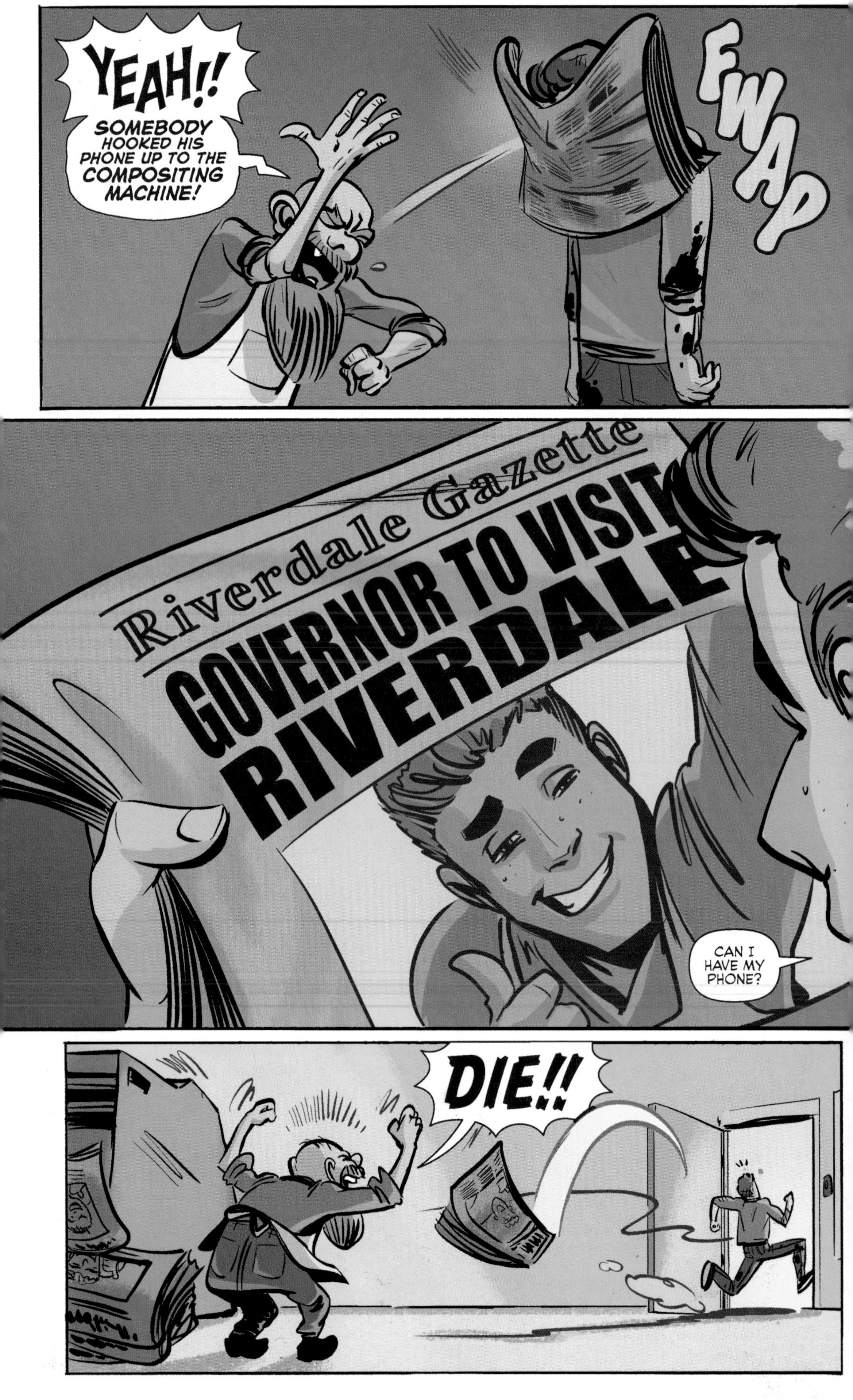
YEAH!! SOMEBODY HOOKED HIS PHONE UP TO THE COMPOSITING MACHINE!
FWAP
Riverdale Gazette
GOVERNOR TO VISIT RIVERDALE
CAN I HAVE MY PHONE?
DIE!!

CHAPTER FOUR: Since When Do You Call Me "Richard"?

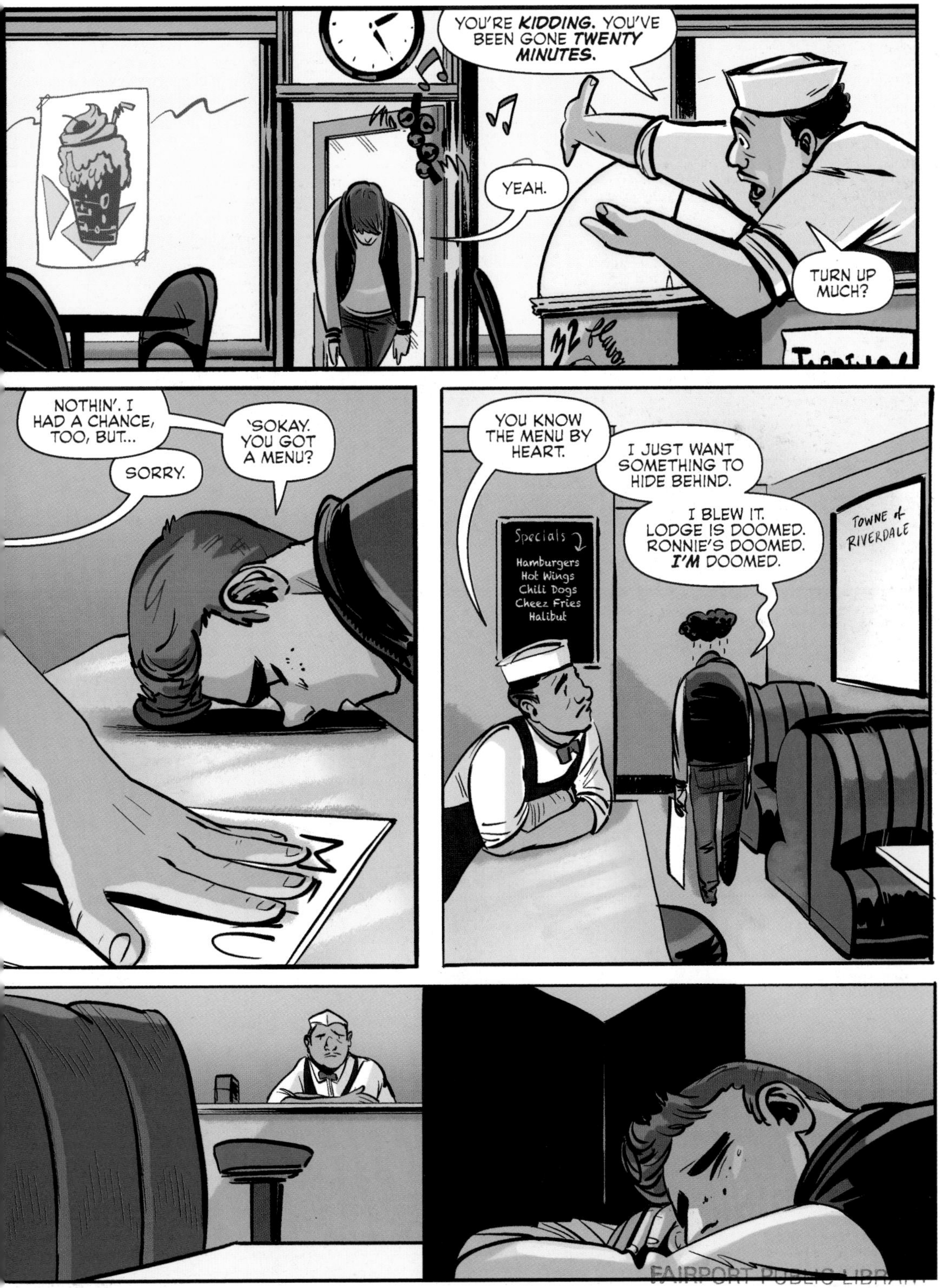
YOU'RE *KIDDING.* YOU'VE BEEN GONE *TWENTY MINUTES.*
YEAH.
TURN UP MUCH?
NOTHIN'. I HAD A CHANCE, TOO, BUT...
'SOKAY. YOU GOT A MENU?
SORRY.
YOU KNOW THE MENU BY HEART.
I JUST WANT SOMETHING TO HIDE BEHIND.
I BLEW IT. LODGE IS DOOMED. RONNIE'S DOOMED. *I'M* DOOMED.
Specials
Hamburgers
Hot Wings
Chili Dogs
Cheez Fries
Halibut
Towne of Riverdale

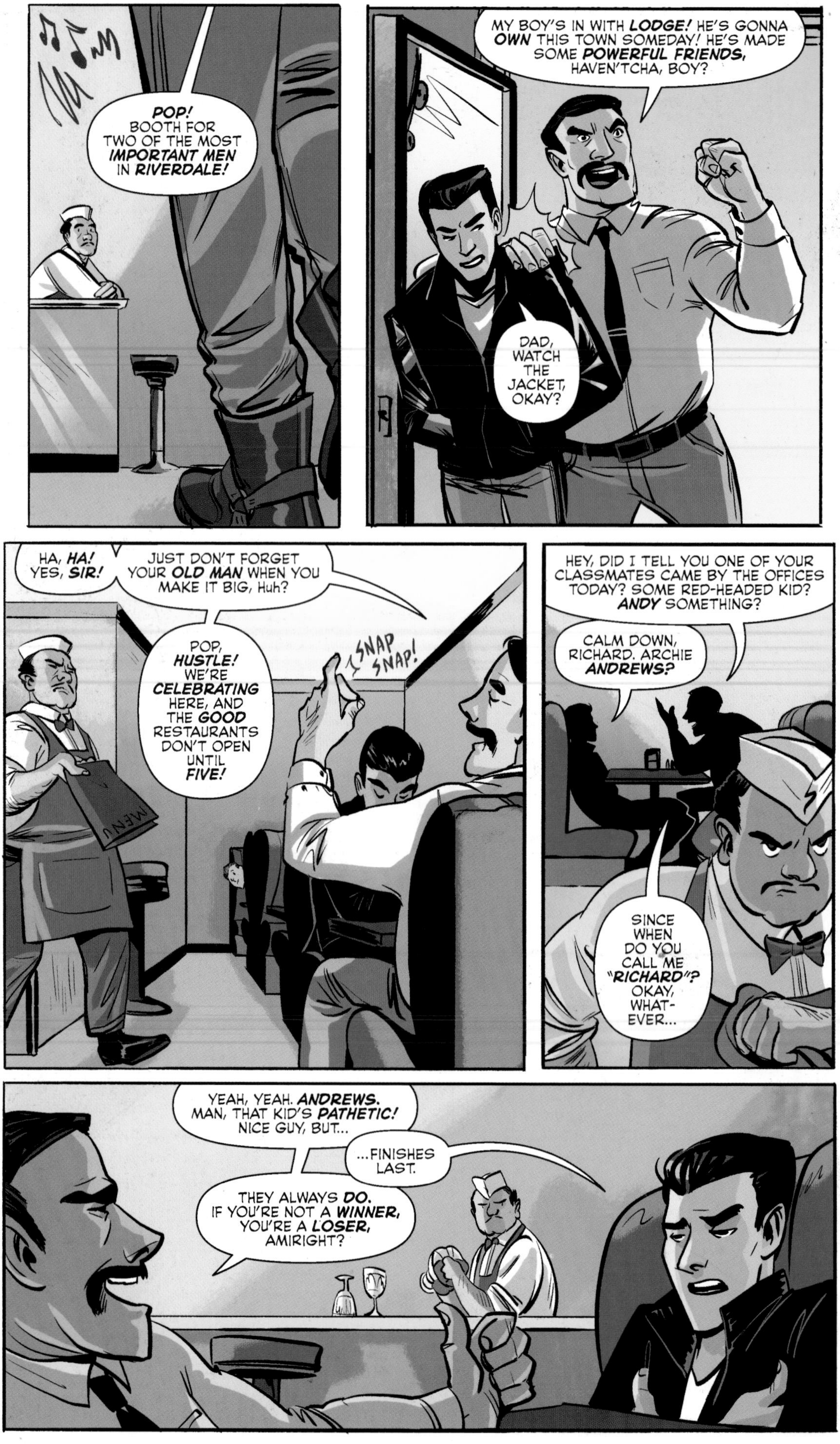
POP! BOOTH FOR TWO OF THE MOST IMPORTANT MEN IN RIVERDALE!
MY BOY'S IN WITH LODGE! HE'S GONNA OWN THIS TOWN SOMEDAY! HE'S MADE SOME POWERFUL FRIENDS, HAVEN'TCHA, BOY?
DAD, WATCH THE JACKET, OKAY?
HA, HA! YES, SIR!
JUST DON'T FORGET YOUR OLD MAN WHEN YOU MAKE IT BIG, Huh?
POP, HUSTLE! WE'RE CELEBRATING HERE, AND THE GOOD RESTAURANTS DON'T OPEN UNTIL FIVE!
SNAP SNAP!
MENU
HEY, DID I TELL YOU ONE OF YOUR CLASSMATES CAME BY THE OFFICES TODAY? SOME RED-HEADED KID? ANDY SOMETHING?
CALM DOWN, RICHARD. ARCHIE ANDREWS?
SINCE WHEN DO YOU CALL ME "RICHARD"? OKAY, WHAT-EVER...
YEAH, YEAH. ANDREWS. MAN, THAT KID'S PATHETIC! NICE GUY, BUT...
...FINISHES LAST.
THEY ALWAYS DO. IF YOU'RE NOT A WINNER, YOU'RE A LOSER, AMIRIGHT?

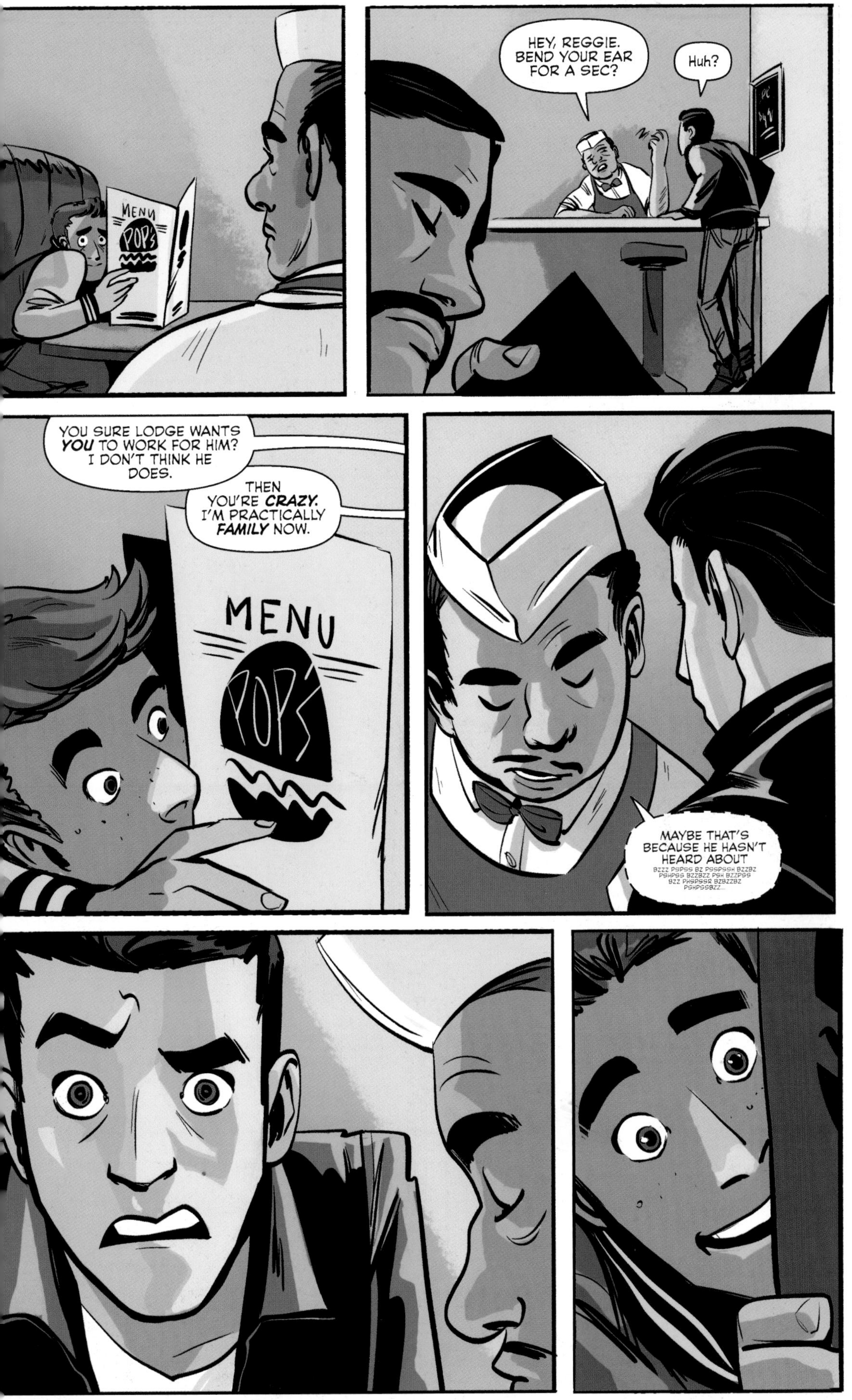
MENU
POP'S
HEY, REGGIE. BEND YOUR EAR FOR A SEC?
Huh?
YOU SURE LODGE WANTS **YOU** TO WORK FOR HIM? I DON'T THINK HE DOES.
THEN YOU'RE **CRAZY.** I'M PRACTICALLY **FAMILY** NOW.
MENU
POP'S
MAYBE THAT'S BECAUSE HE HASN'T HEARD ABOUT
BZZZ PSPSS BZ PSSPSSH BZZBZ PSHPSS BZZBZZ PSH BZZPSS BZZ PHSPSSR BZBZZBZ PSHPSSBZZ...

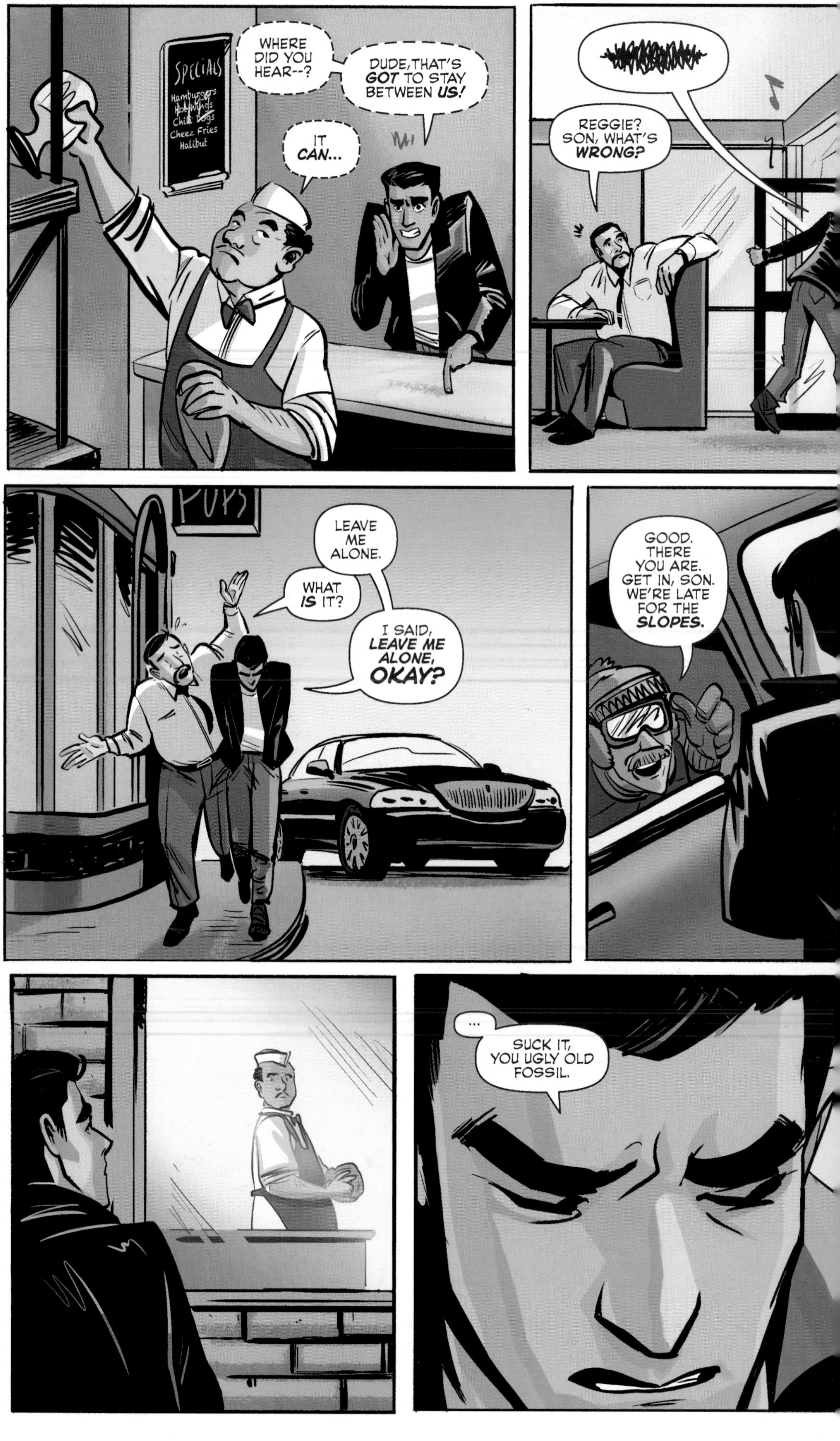

SPECIALS
Hamburgers
Hot Wings
Chili Dogs
Cheez Fries
Halibut
WHERE DID YOU HEAR--?
DUDE, THAT'S GOT TO STAY BETWEEN US!
IT CAN...
REGGIE? SON, WHAT'S WRONG?
POPS
LEAVE ME ALONE.
WHAT IS IT?
I SAID, LEAVE ME ALONE, OKAY?
GOOD. THERE YOU ARE. GET IN, SON. WE'RE LATE FOR THE SLOPES.
...
SUCK IT, YOU UGLY OLD FOSSIL.

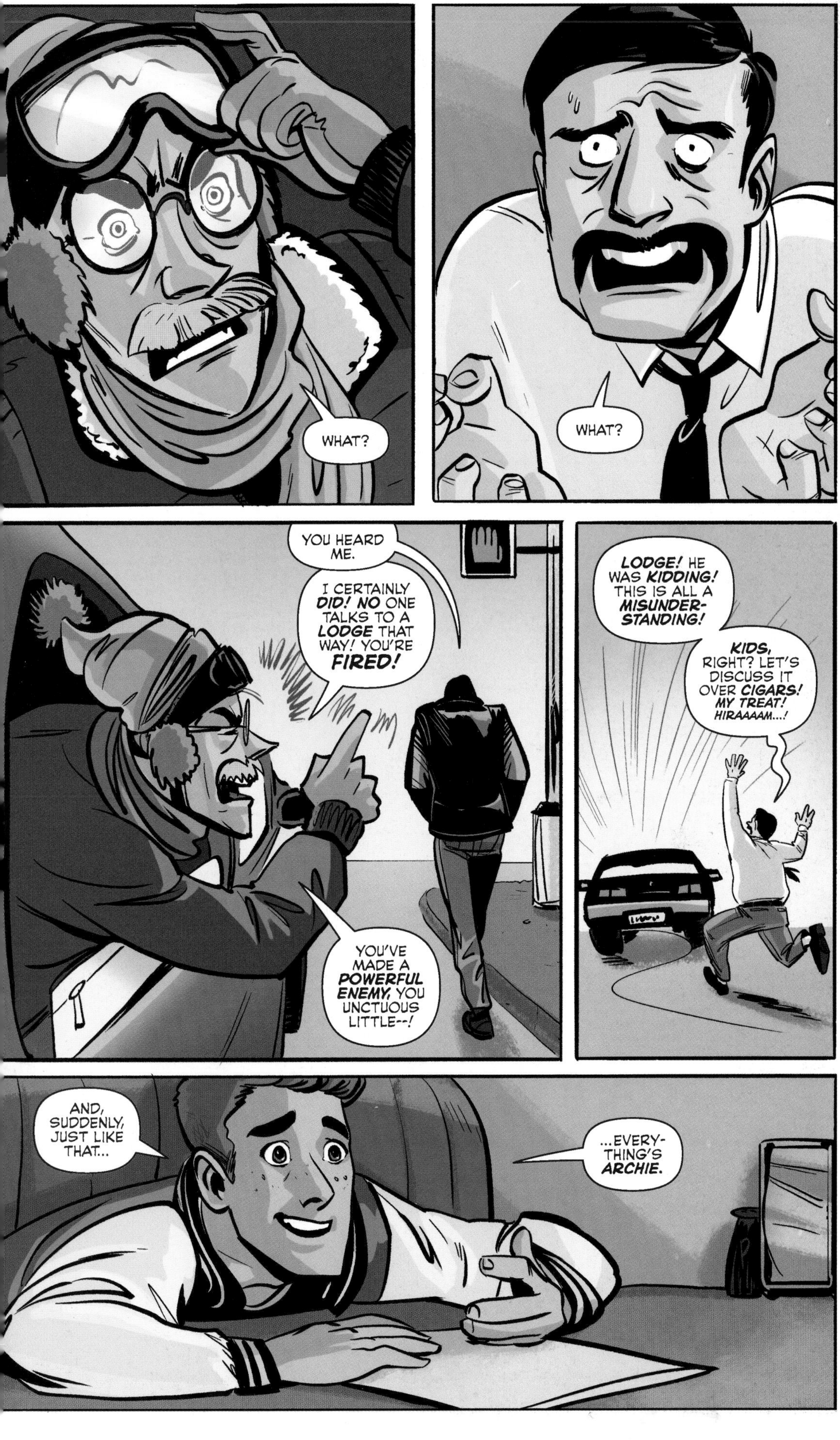
WHAT?
WHAT?
YOU HEARD ME.
I CERTAINLY DID! NO ONE TALKS TO A LODGE THAT WAY! YOU'RE FIRED!
YOU'VE MADE A POWERFUL ENEMY, YOU UNCTUOUS LITTLE--!
LODGE! HE WAS KIDDING! THIS IS ALL A MISUNDER-STANDING!
KIDS, RIGHT? LET'S DISCUSS IT OVER CIGARS! MY TREAT! HIRAAAAM...!
AND, SUDDENLY, JUST LIKE THAT...
...EVERY-THING'S ARCHIE.

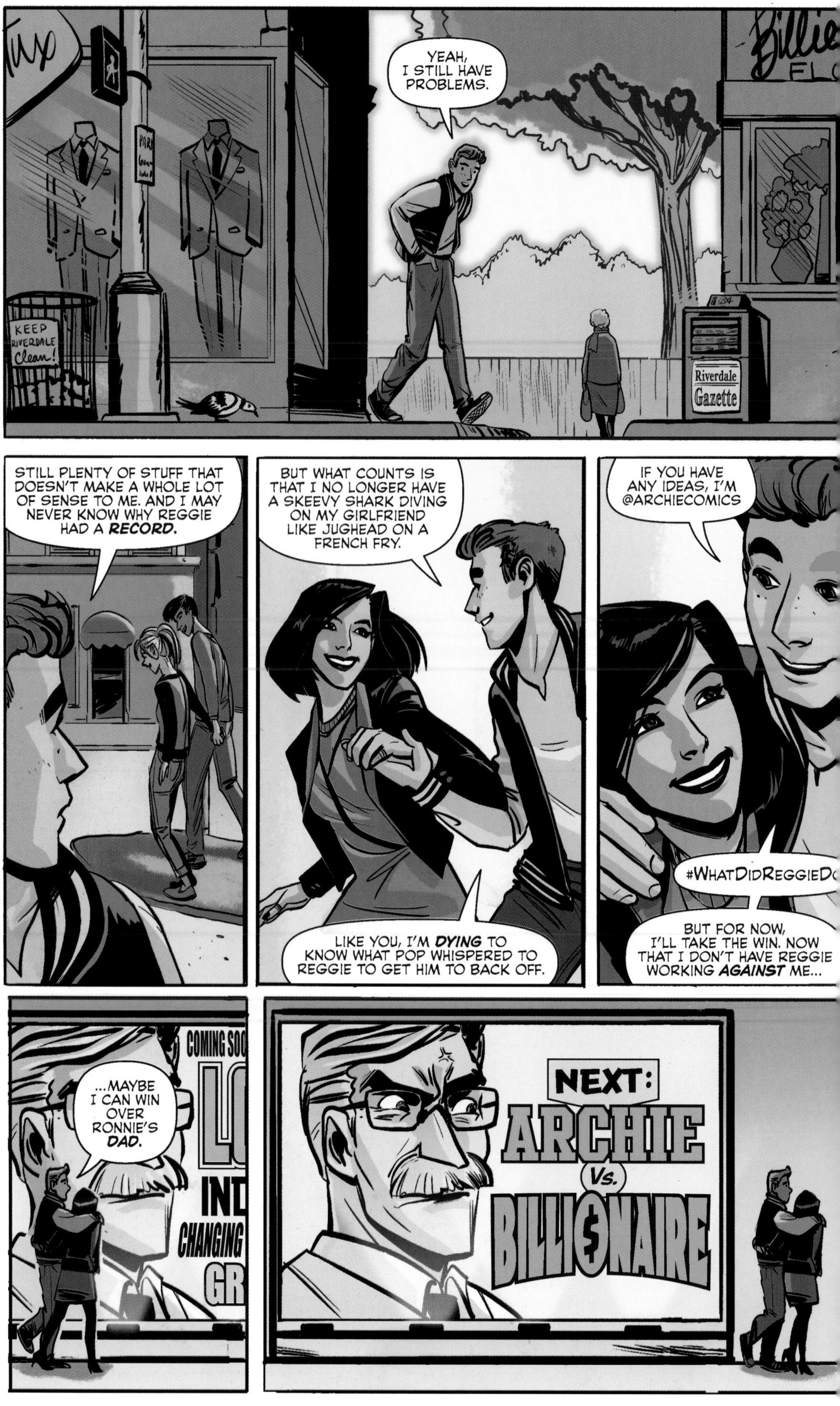

Tux
PARK
KEEP RIVERDALE Clean!
Billie
FL
YEAH, I STILL HAVE PROBLEMS.
Riverdale Gazette
STILL PLENTY OF STUFF THAT DOESN'T MAKE A WHOLE LOT OF SENSE TO ME. AND I MAY NEVER KNOW WHY REGGIE HAD A **RECORD.**
BUT WHAT COUNTS IS THAT I NO LONGER HAVE A SKEEVY SHARK DIVING ON MY GIRLFRIEND LIKE JUGHEAD ON A FRENCH FRY.
LIKE YOU, I'M **DYING** TO KNOW WHAT POP WHISPERED TO REGGIE TO GET HIM TO BACK OFF.
IF YOU HAVE ANY IDEAS, I'M @ARCHIECOMICS
#WHATDIDREGGIED
BUT FOR NOW, I'LL TAKE THE WIN. NOW THAT I DON'T HAVE REGGIE WORKING **AGAINST** ME...
COMING SOO
...MAYBE I CAN WIN OVER RONNIE'S **DAD**.
CHANGING
NEXT:
ARCHIE
Vs.
BILLI$NAIRE

TO BE CONTINUED...

ISSUE EIGHT

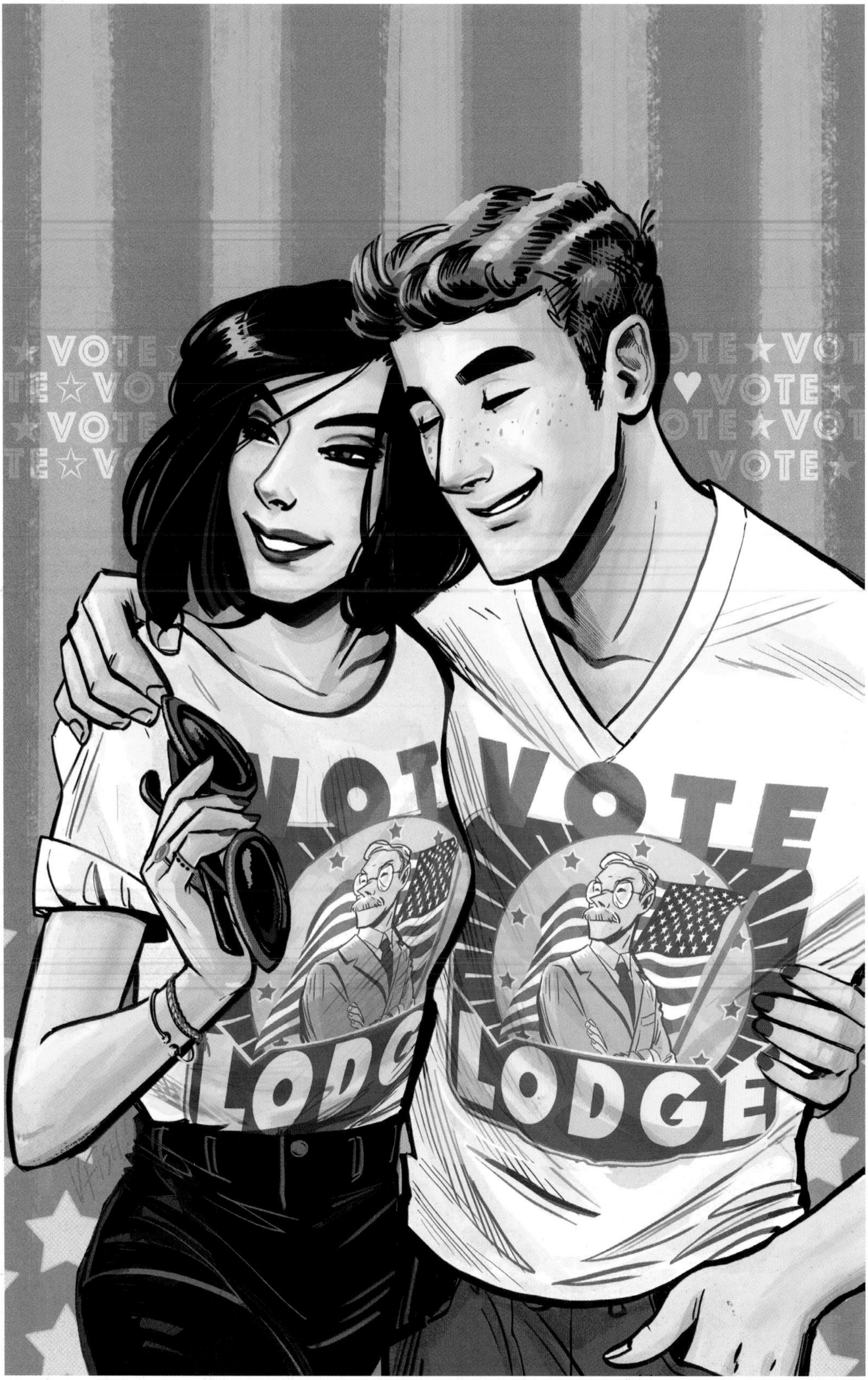
VOTE
VOTE
VOTE
VOTE
VOTE
LODGE
VOTE
LODGE

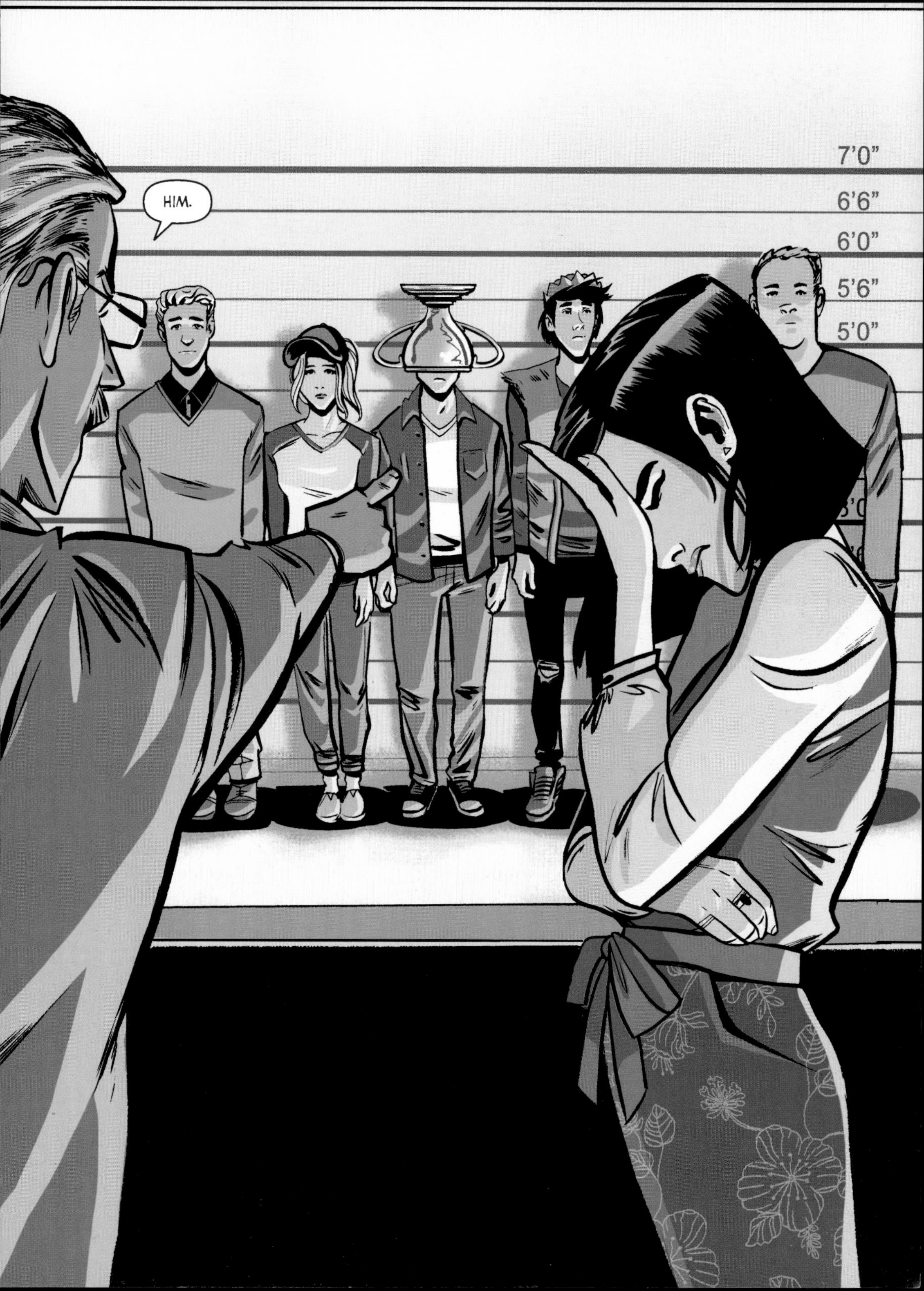
HIM.
7'0"
6'6"
6'0"
5'6"
5'0"

CHAPTER ONE: 2 KITTENS AND A PUPPY

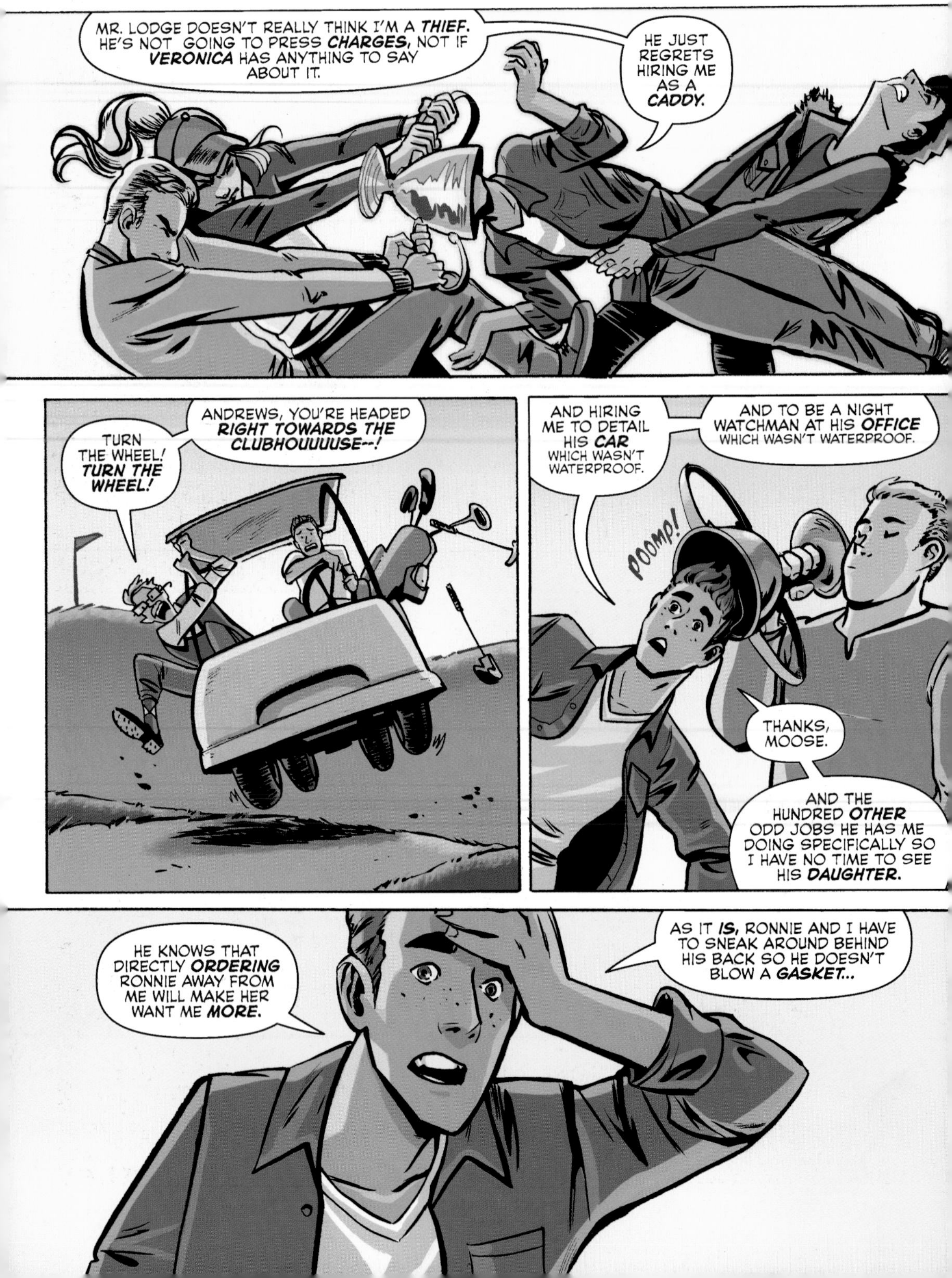
MR. LODGE DOESN'T REALLY THINK I'M A THIEF. HE'S NOT GOING TO PRESS CHARGES, NOT IF VERONICA HAS ANYTHING TO SAY ABOUT IT.
HE JUST REGRETS HIRING ME AS A CADDY.
TURN THE WHEEL! TURN THE WHEEL!
ANDREWS, YOU'RE HEADED RIGHT TOWARDS THE CLUBHOUUUUSE--!
AND HIRING ME TO DETAIL HIS CAR WHICH WASN'T WATERPROOF.
AND TO BE A NIGHT WATCHMAN AT HIS OFFICE WHICH WASN'T WATERPROOF.
POOMP!
THANKS, MOOSE.
AND THE HUNDRED OTHER ODD JOBS HE HAS ME DOING SPECIFICALLY SO I HAVE NO TIME TO SEE HIS DAUGHTER.
HE KNOWS THAT DIRECTLY ORDERING RONNIE AWAY FROM ME WILL MAKE HER WANT ME MORE.
AS IT IS, RONNIE AND I HAVE TO SNEAK AROUND BEHIND HIS BACK SO HE DOESN'T BLOW A GASKET...

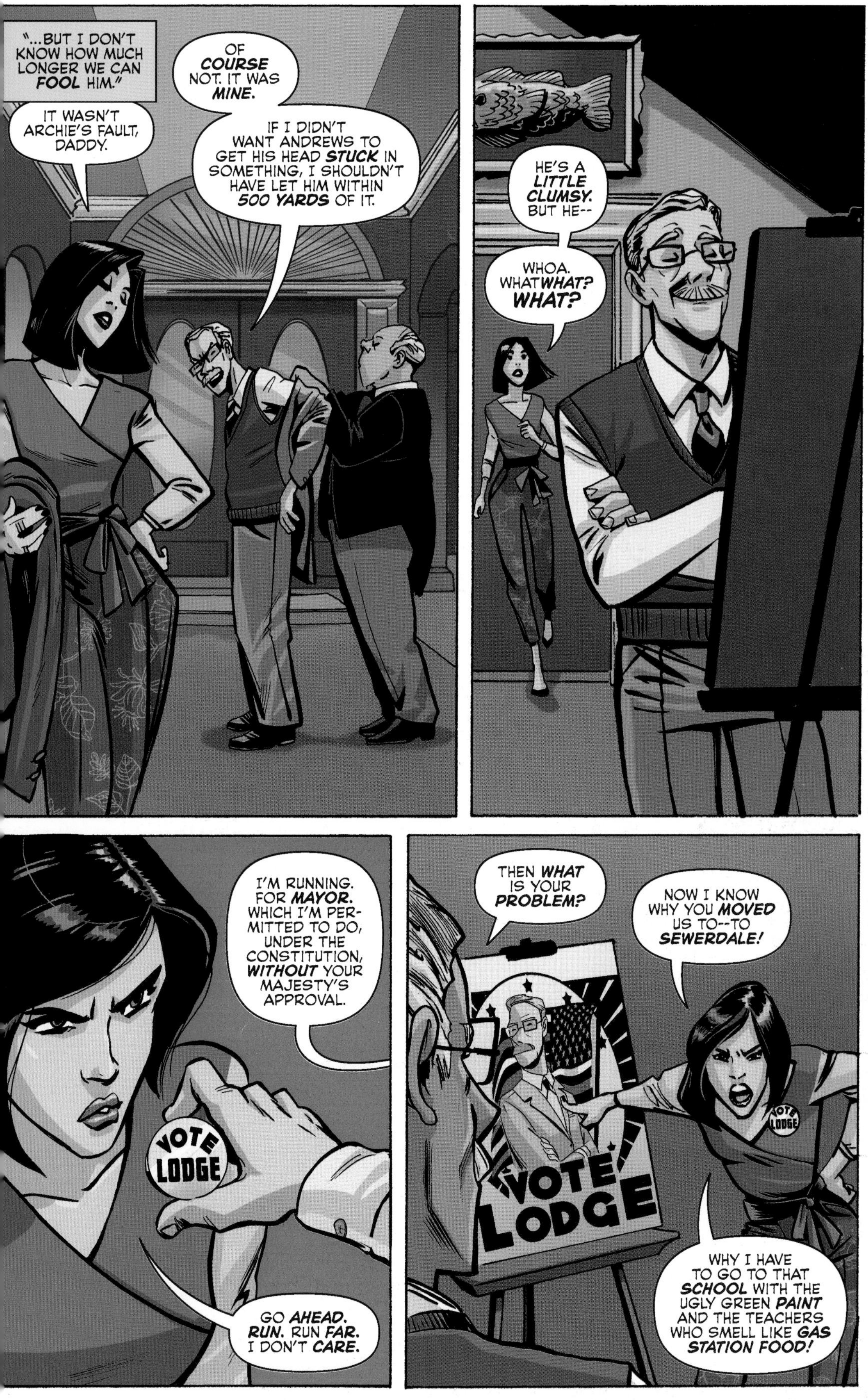
"...BUT I DON'T KNOW HOW MUCH LONGER WE CAN FOOL HIM."
IT WASN'T ARCHIE'S FAULT, DADDY.
OF COURSE NOT. IT WAS MINE.
IF I DIDN'T WANT ANDREWS TO GET HIS HEAD STUCK IN SOMETHING, I SHOULDN'T HAVE LET HIM WITHIN 500 YARDS OF IT.
HE'S A LITTLE CLUMSY. BUT HE--
WHOA. WHAT WHAT? WHAT?
I'M RUNNING. FOR MAYOR. WHICH I'M PERMITTED TO DO, UNDER THE CONSTITUTION, WITHOUT YOUR MAJESTY'S APPROVAL.
VOTE LODGE
GO AHEAD. RUN. RUN FAR. I DON'T CARE.
THEN WHAT IS YOUR PROBLEM?
NOW I KNOW WHY YOU MOVED US TO--TO SEWERDALE!
VOTE LODGE
VOTE LODGE
WHY I HAVE TO GO TO THAT SCHOOL WITH THE UGLY GREEN PAINT AND THE TEACHERS WHO SMELL LIKE GAS STATION FOOD!

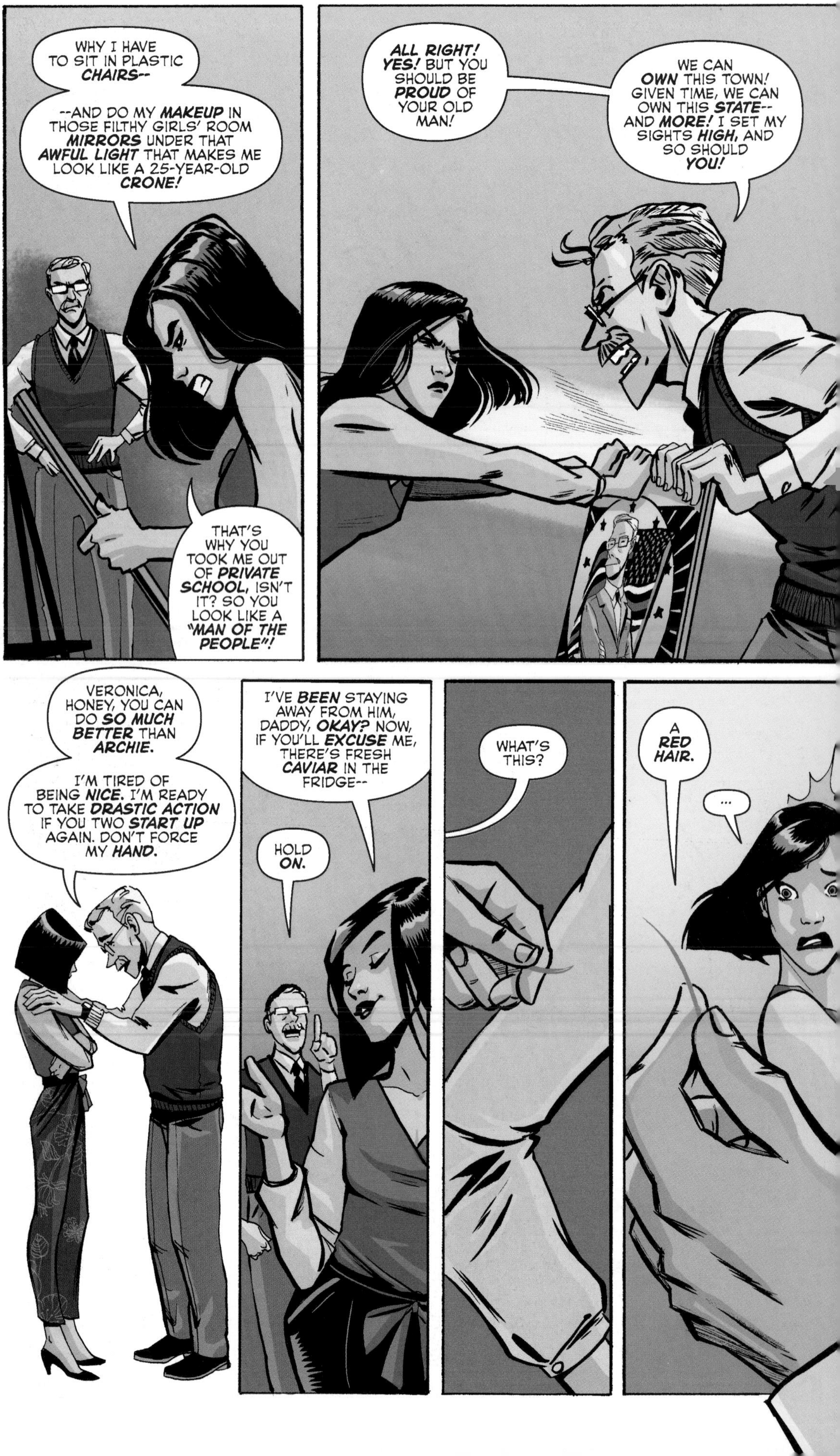
WHY I HAVE TO SIT IN PLASTIC CHAIRS--
--AND DO MY MAKEUP IN THOSE FILTHY GIRLS' ROOM MIRRORS UNDER THAT AWFUL LIGHT THAT MAKES ME LOOK LIKE A 25-YEAR-OLD CRONE!
THAT'S WHY YOU TOOK ME OUT OF PRIVATE SCHOOL, ISN'T IT? SO YOU LOOK LIKE A "MAN OF THE PEOPLE"!
ALL RIGHT! YES! BUT YOU SHOULD BE PROUD OF YOUR OLD MAN!
WE CAN OWN THIS TOWN! GIVEN TIME, WE CAN OWN THIS STATE-- AND MORE! I SET MY SIGHTS HIGH, AND SO SHOULD YOU!
VERONICA, HONEY, YOU CAN DO SO MUCH BETTER THAN ARCHIE.
I'M TIRED OF BEING NICE. I'M READY TO TAKE DRASTIC ACTION IF YOU TWO START UP AGAIN. DON'T FORCE MY HAND.
I'VE BEEN STAYING AWAY FROM HIM, DADDY, OKAY? NOW, IF YOU'LL EXCUSE ME, THERE'S FRESH CAVIAR IN THE FRIDGE--
HOLD ON.
WHAT'S THIS?
A RED HAIR.
...

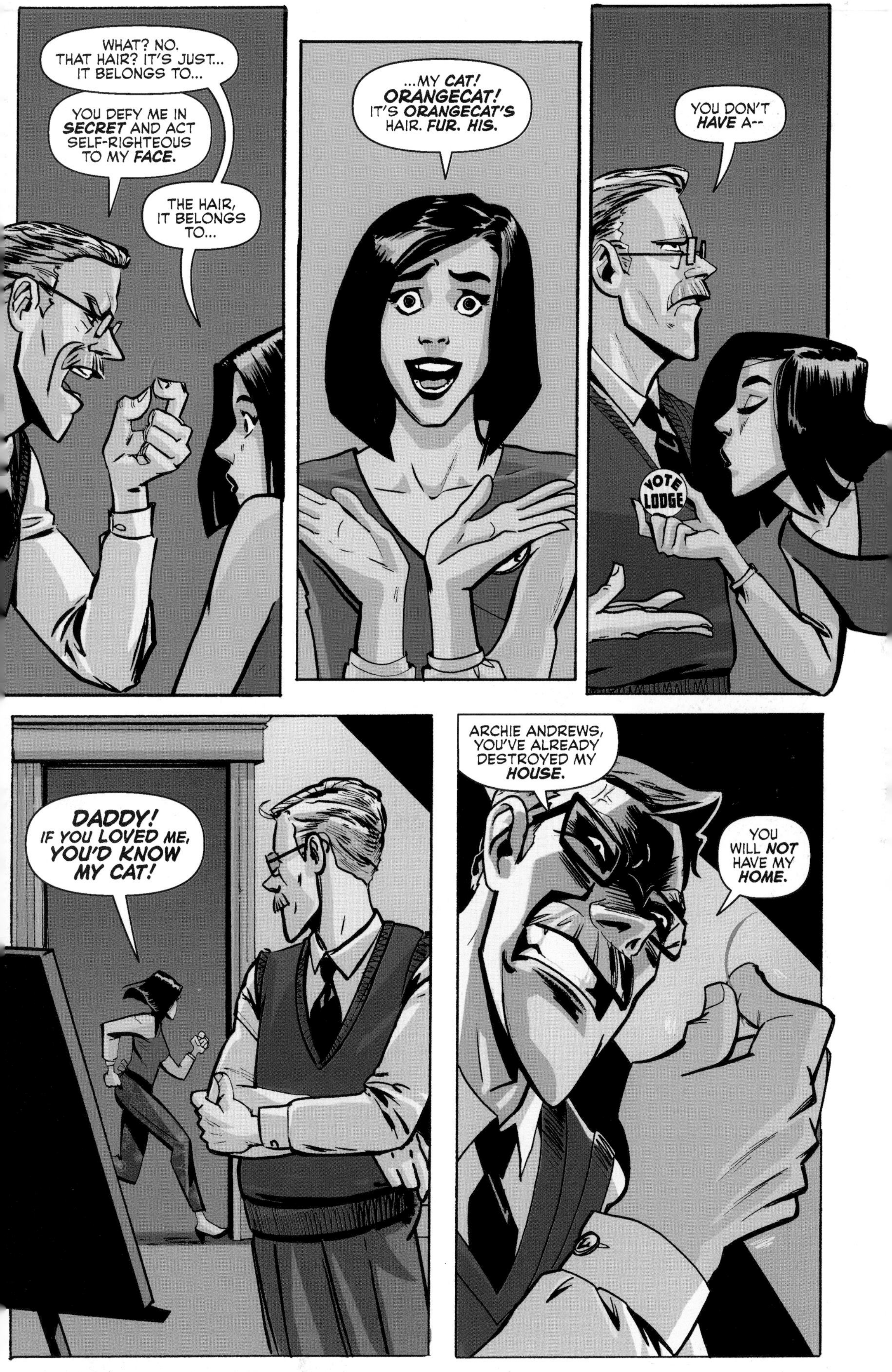
WHAT? NO. THAT HAIR? IT'S JUST... IT BELONGS TO...
YOU DEFY ME IN SECRET AND ACT SELF-RIGHTEOUS TO MY FACE.
THE HAIR, IT BELONGS TO...
...MY CAT! ORANGECAT! IT'S ORANGECAT'S HAIR. FUR. HIS.
YOU DON'T HAVE A--
VOTE LODGE
DADDY! IF YOU LOVED ME, YOU'D KNOW MY CAT!
ARCHIE ANDREWS, YOU'VE ALREADY DESTROYED MY HOUSE.
YOU WILL NOT HAVE MY HOME.

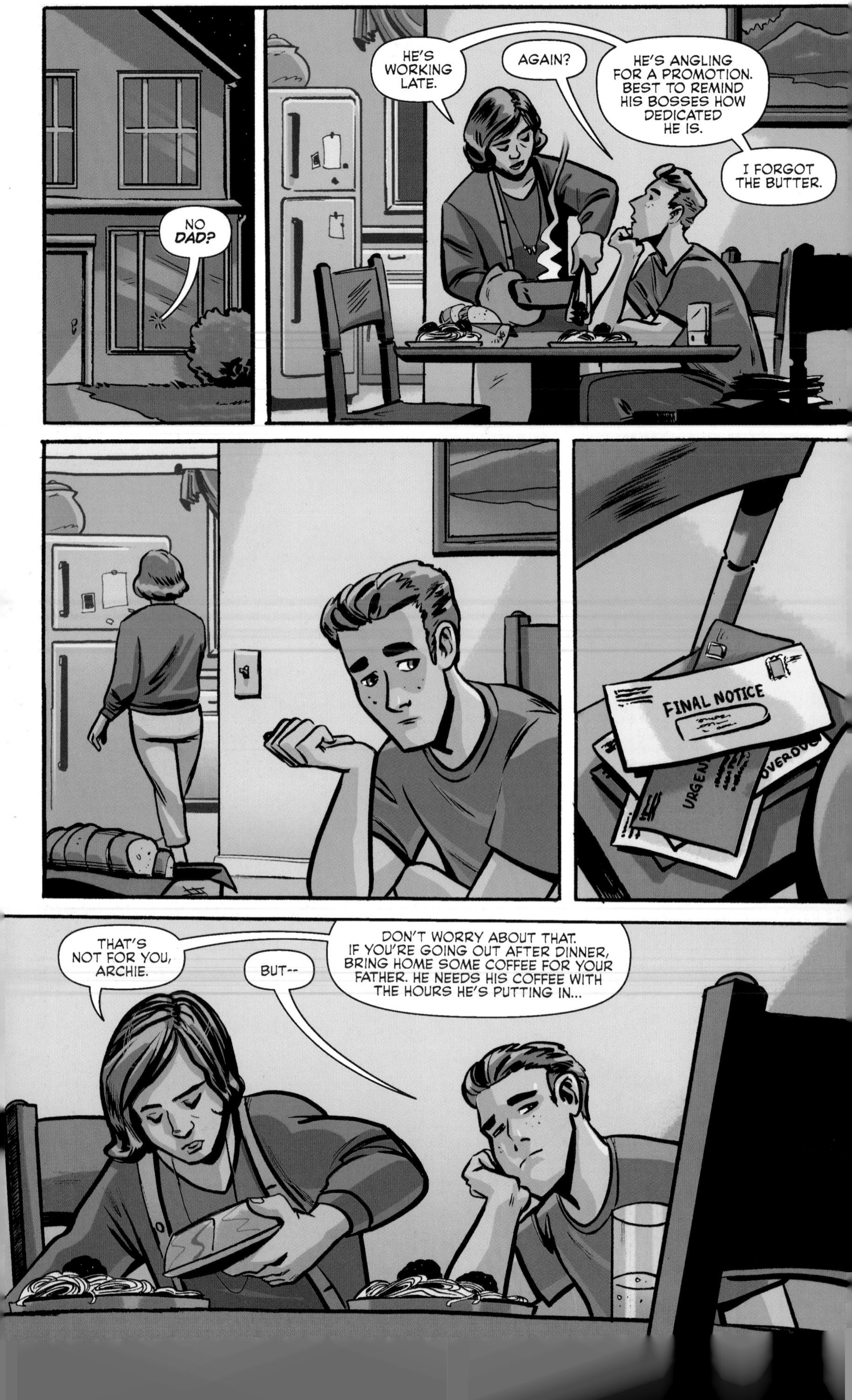
NO DAD?
HE'S WORKING LATE.
AGAIN?
HE'S ANGLING FOR A PROMOTION. BEST TO REMIND HIS BOSSES HOW DEDICATED HE IS.
I FORGOT THE BUTTER.
FINAL NOTICE
URGENT
OVERDUE
THAT'S NOT FOR YOU, ARCHIE.
BUT--
DON'T WORRY ABOUT THAT. IF YOU'RE GOING OUT AFTER DINNER, BRING HOME SOME COFFEE FOR YOUR FATHER. HE NEEDS HIS COFFEE WITH THE HOURS HE'S PUTTING IN...

RIVERDALE PET EMPORIUM

BUT I THOUGHT WE WERE HEADED TO *POP'S*.

TALK TO ME WHEN HE STARTS SERVING *MARBLED KOBE BEEF WELLINGTON*.

WE'RE GOING *SHOPPING*.

VERONICA...

DON'T USE MY NAME IN PUBLIC. IF IT GETS BACK TO DADDY-- HE'S TOO SUSPICIOUS AS IT IS.

HOLD STILL.

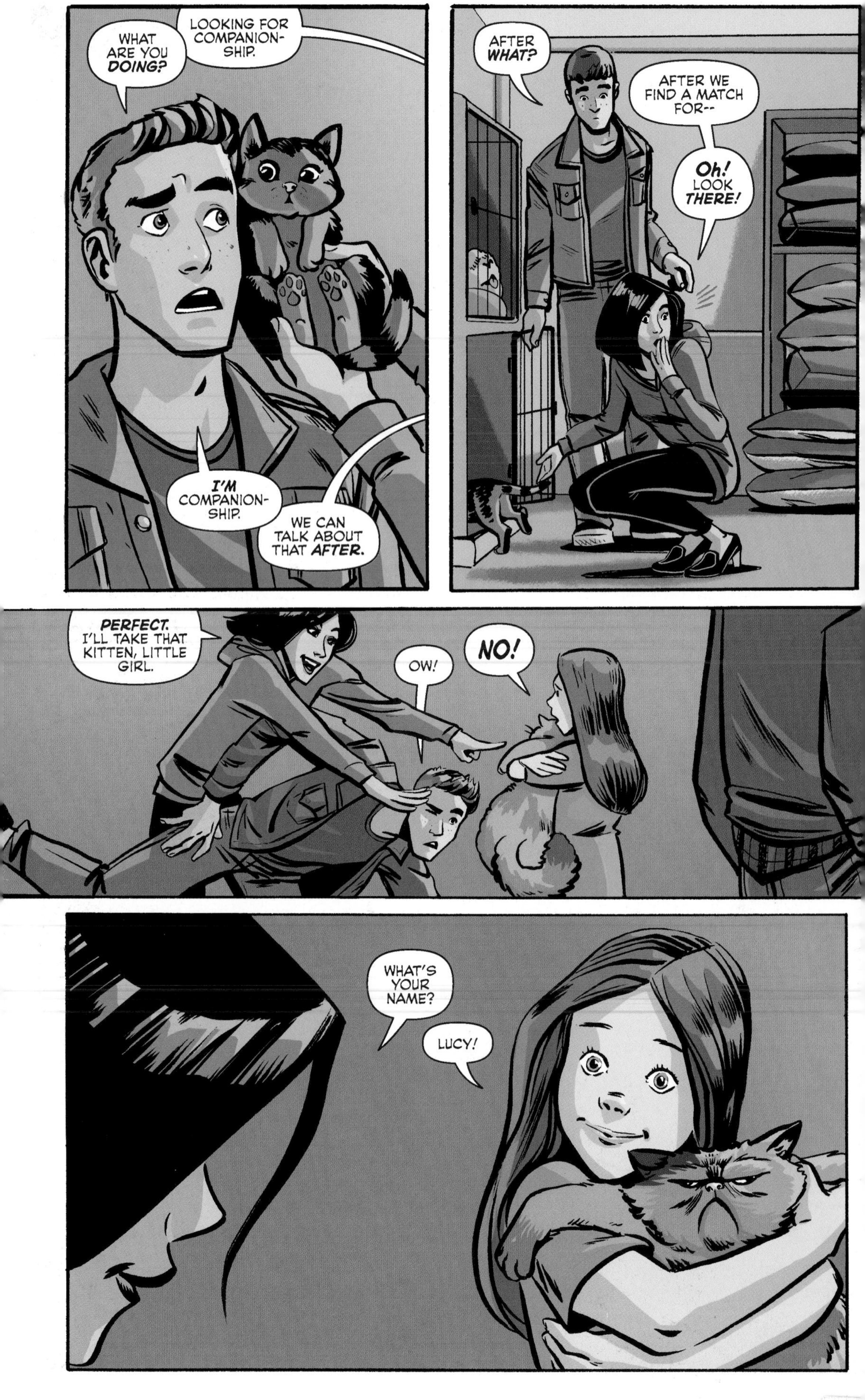
WHAT ARE YOU DOING?
LOOKING FOR COMPANION-SHIP.
I'M COMPANION-SHIP.
WE CAN TALK ABOUT THAT AFTER.
AFTER WHAT?
AFTER WE FIND A MATCH FOR--
Oh! LOOK THERE!
PERFECT. I'LL TAKE THAT KITTEN, LITTLE GIRL.
OW!
NO!
WHAT'S YOUR NAME?
LUCY!

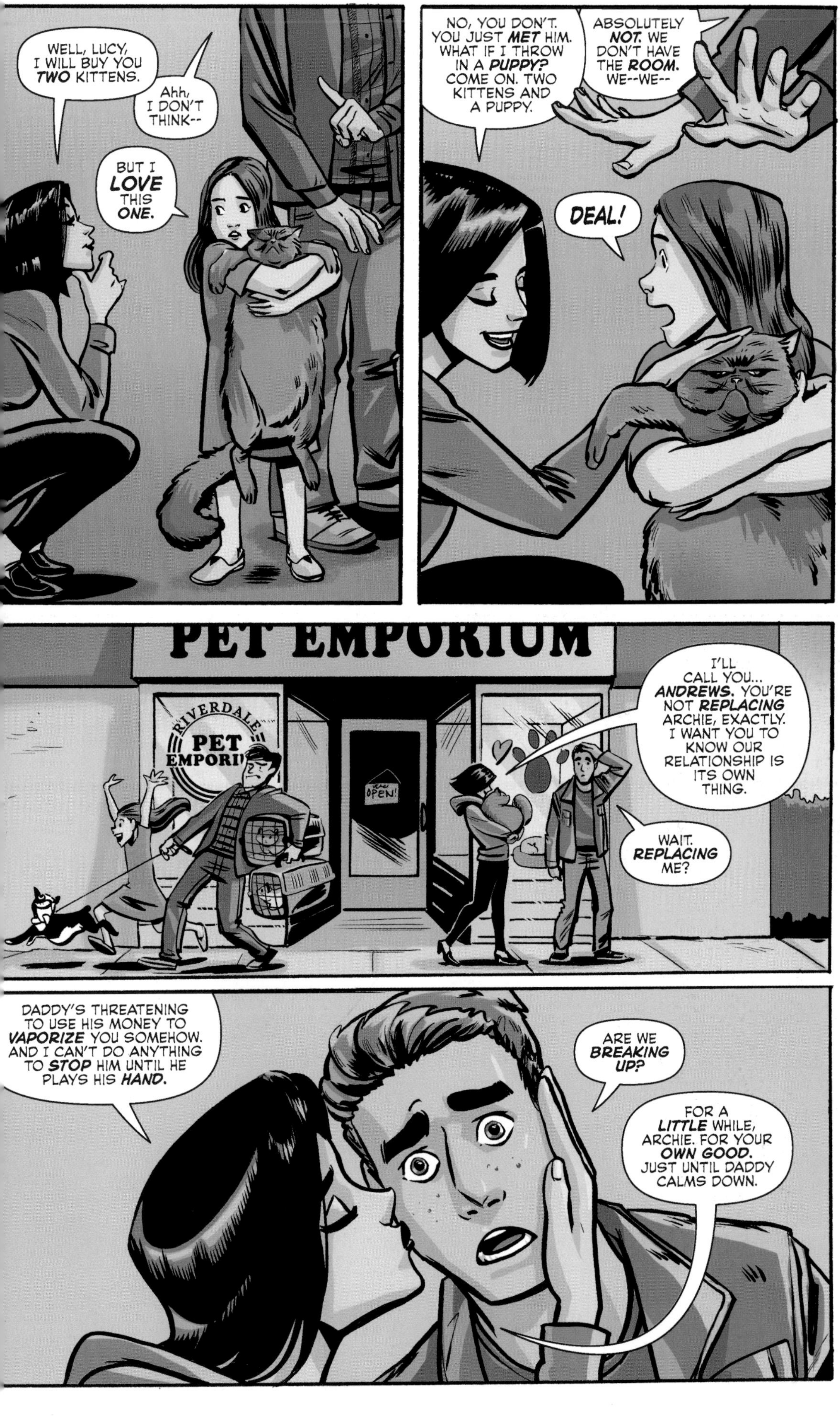
WELL, LUCY, I WILL BUY YOU **TWO** KITTENS.
Ahh, I DON'T THINK--
BUT I **LOVE** THIS **ONE.**
NO, YOU DON'T. YOU JUST **MET** HIM. WHAT IF I THROW IN A **PUPPY?** COME ON. TWO KITTENS AND A PUPPY.
ABSOLUTELY **NOT.** WE DON'T HAVE THE **ROOM.** WE--WE--
DEAL!
PET EMPORIUM
RIVERDALE PET EMPORI
OPEN!
I'LL CALL YOU... **ANDREWS.** YOU'RE NOT **REPLACING** ARCHIE, EXACTLY. I WANT YOU TO KNOW OUR RELATIONSHIP IS ITS OWN THING.
WAIT. **REPLACING** ME?
DADDY'S THREATENING TO USE HIS MONEY TO **VAPORIZE** YOU SOMEHOW. AND I CAN'T DO ANYTHING TO **STOP** HIM UNTIL HE PLAYS HIS **HAND.**
ARE WE **BREAKING UP?**
FOR A **LITTLE** WHILE, ARCHIE. FOR YOUR **OWN GOOD.** JUST UNTIL DADDY CALMS DOWN.

CHAPTER TWO: GOOD NEWS!

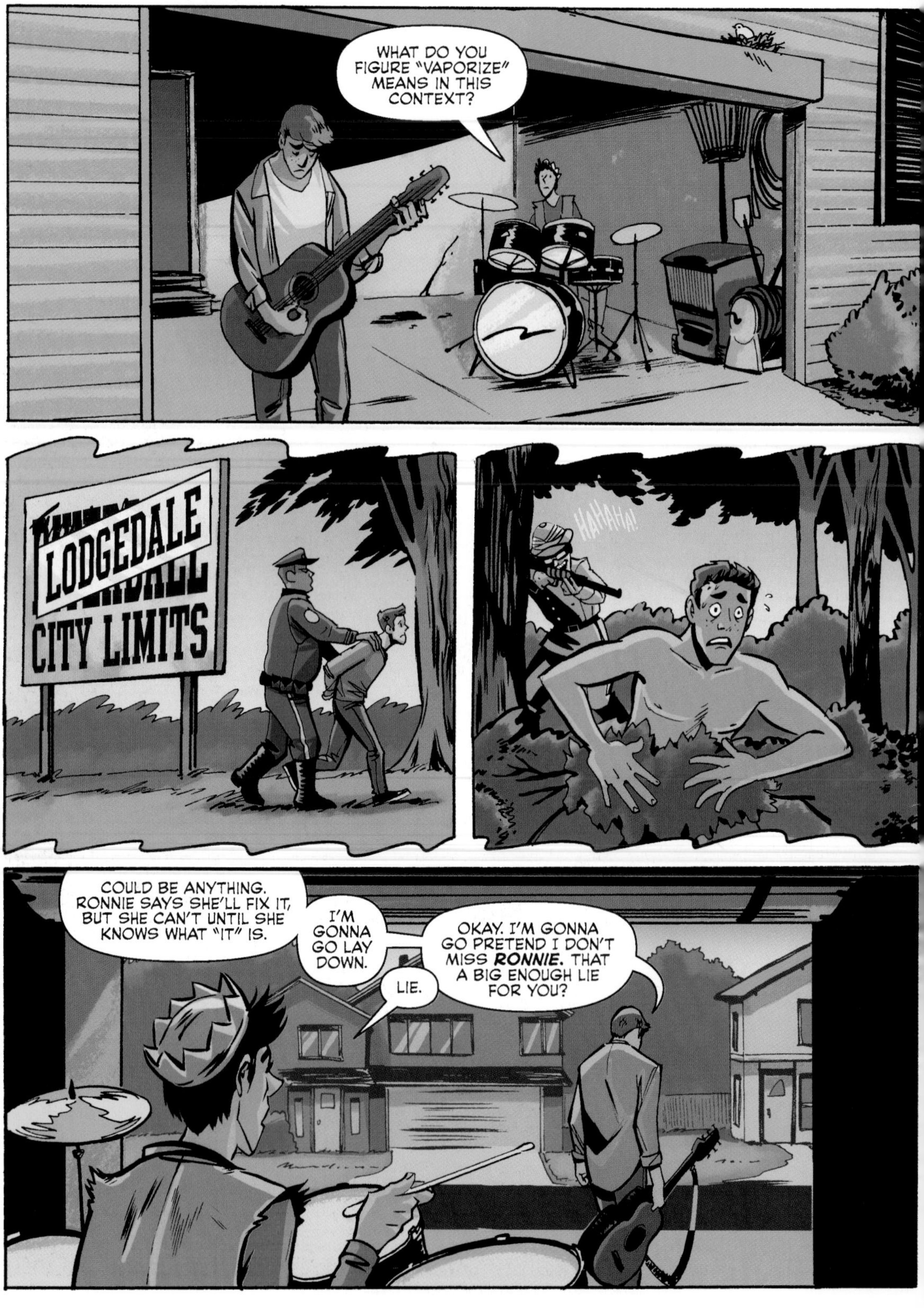
WHAT DO YOU FIGURE "VAPORIZE" MEANS IN THIS CONTEXT?
LODGEDALE
CITY LIMITS
HAHAHA!
COULD BE ANYTHING. RONNIE SAYS SHE'LL FIX IT, BUT SHE CAN'T UNTIL SHE KNOWS WHAT "IT" IS.
I'M GONNA GO LAY DOWN.
LIE.
OKAY. I'M GONNA GO PRETEND I DON'T MISS **RONNIE.** THAT A BIG ENOUGH LIE FOR YOU?

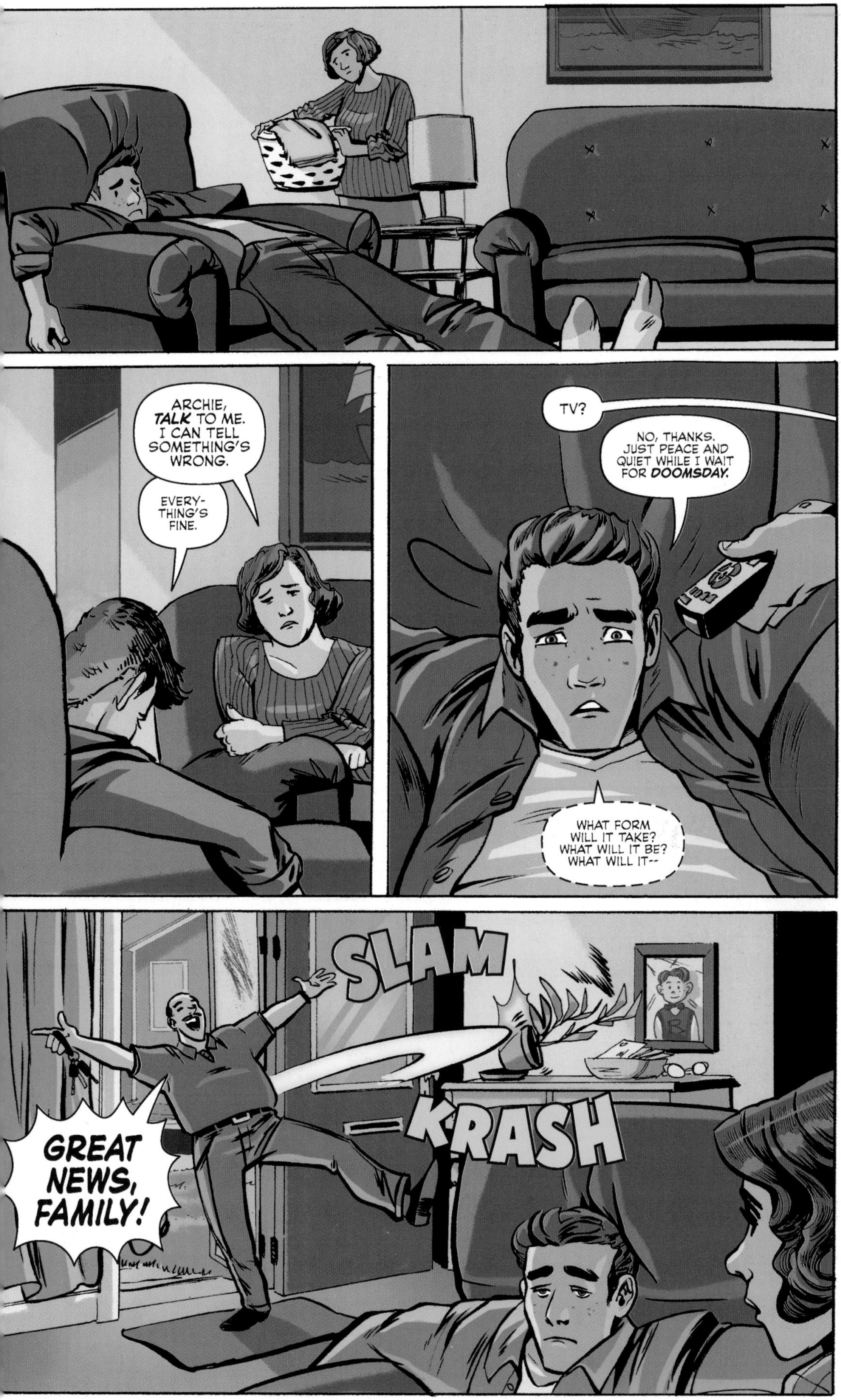

ARCHIE, TALK TO ME. I CAN TELL SOMETHING'S WRONG.
EVERY-THING'S FINE.
TV?
NO, THANKS. JUST PEACE AND QUIET WHILE I WAIT FOR DOOMSDAY.
WHAT FORM WILL IT TAKE? WHAT WILL IT BE? WHAT WILL IT--
SLAM
KRASH
GREAT NEWS, FAMILY!

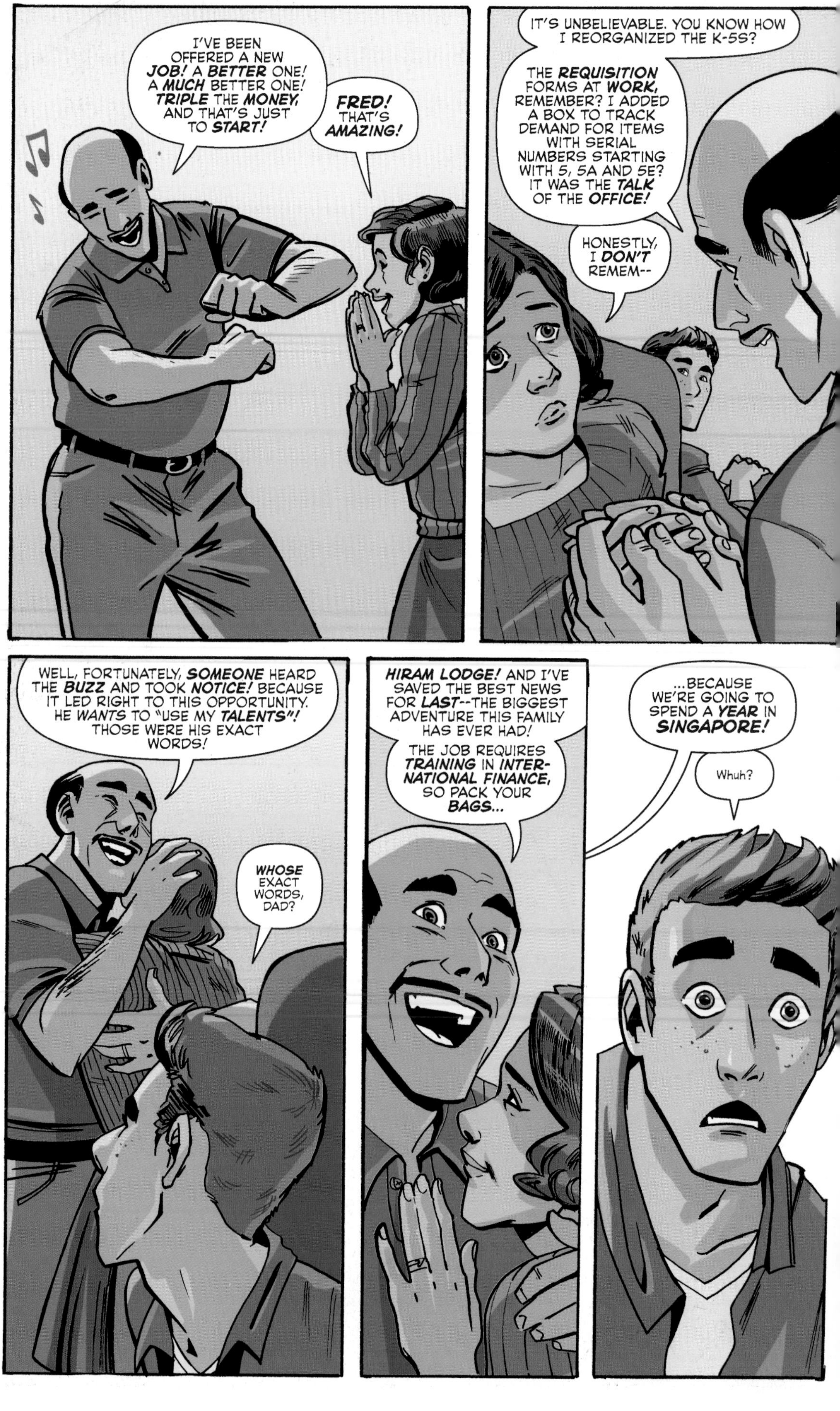
I'VE BEEN OFFERED A NEW JOB! A BETTER ONE! A MUCH BETTER ONE! TRIPLE THE MONEY, AND THAT'S JUST TO START!
FRED! THAT'S AMAZING!
IT'S UNBELIEVABLE. YOU KNOW HOW I REORGANIZED THE K-5S?
THE REQUISITION FORMS AT WORK, REMEMBER? I ADDED A BOX TO TRACK DEMAND FOR ITEMS WITH SERIAL NUMBERS STARTING WITH 5, 5A AND 5E? IT WAS THE TALK OF THE OFFICE!
HONESTLY, I DON'T REMEM--
WELL, FORTUNATELY, SOMEONE HEARD THE BUZZ AND TOOK NOTICE! BECAUSE IT LED RIGHT TO THIS OPPORTUNITY. HE WANTS TO "USE MY TALENTS"! THOSE WERE HIS EXACT WORDS!
WHOSE EXACT WORDS, DAD?
HIRAM LODGE! AND I'VE SAVED THE BEST NEWS FOR LAST--THE BIGGEST ADVENTURE THIS FAMILY HAS EVER HAD!
THE JOB REQUIRES TRAINING IN INTERNATIONAL FINANCE, SO PACK YOUR BAGS...
...BECAUSE WE'RE GOING TO SPEND A YEAR IN SINGAPORE!
Whuh?

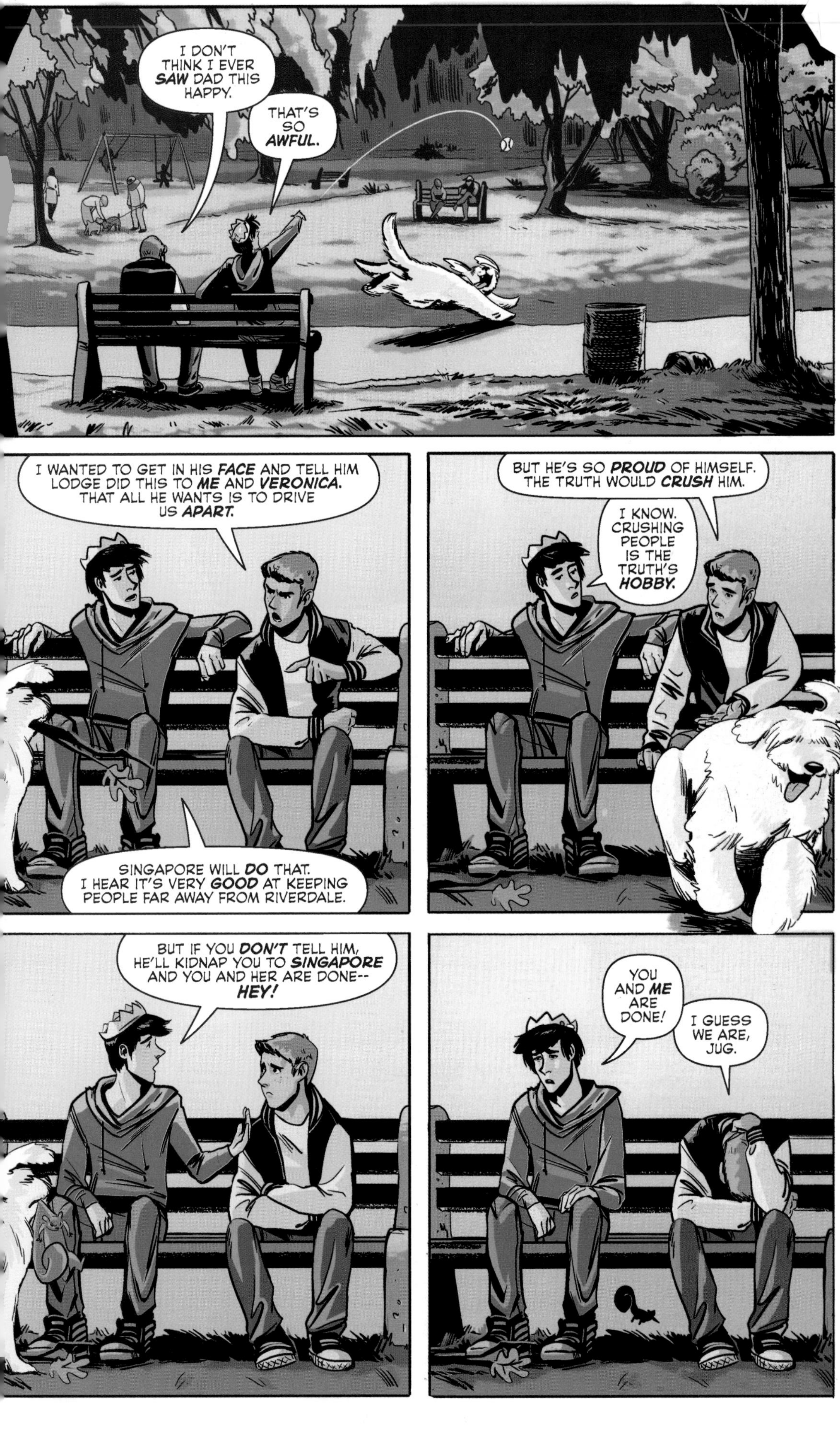
I DON'T THINK I EVER SAW DAD THIS HAPPY.
THAT'S SO AWFUL.
I WANTED TO GET IN HIS FACE AND TELL HIM LODGE DID THIS TO ME AND VERONICA. THAT ALL HE WANTS IS TO DRIVE US APART.
SINGAPORE WILL DO THAT. I HEAR IT'S VERY GOOD AT KEEPING PEOPLE FAR AWAY FROM RIVERDALE.
BUT HE'S SO PROUD OF HIMSELF. THE TRUTH WOULD CRUSH HIM.
I KNOW. CRUSHING PEOPLE IS THE TRUTH'S HOBBY.
BUT IF YOU DON'T TELL HIM, HE'LL KIDNAP YOU TO SINGAPORE AND YOU AND HER ARE DONE-- HEY!
YOU AND ME ARE DONE!
I GUESS WE ARE, JUG.

CHAPTER THREE: CONDOS!

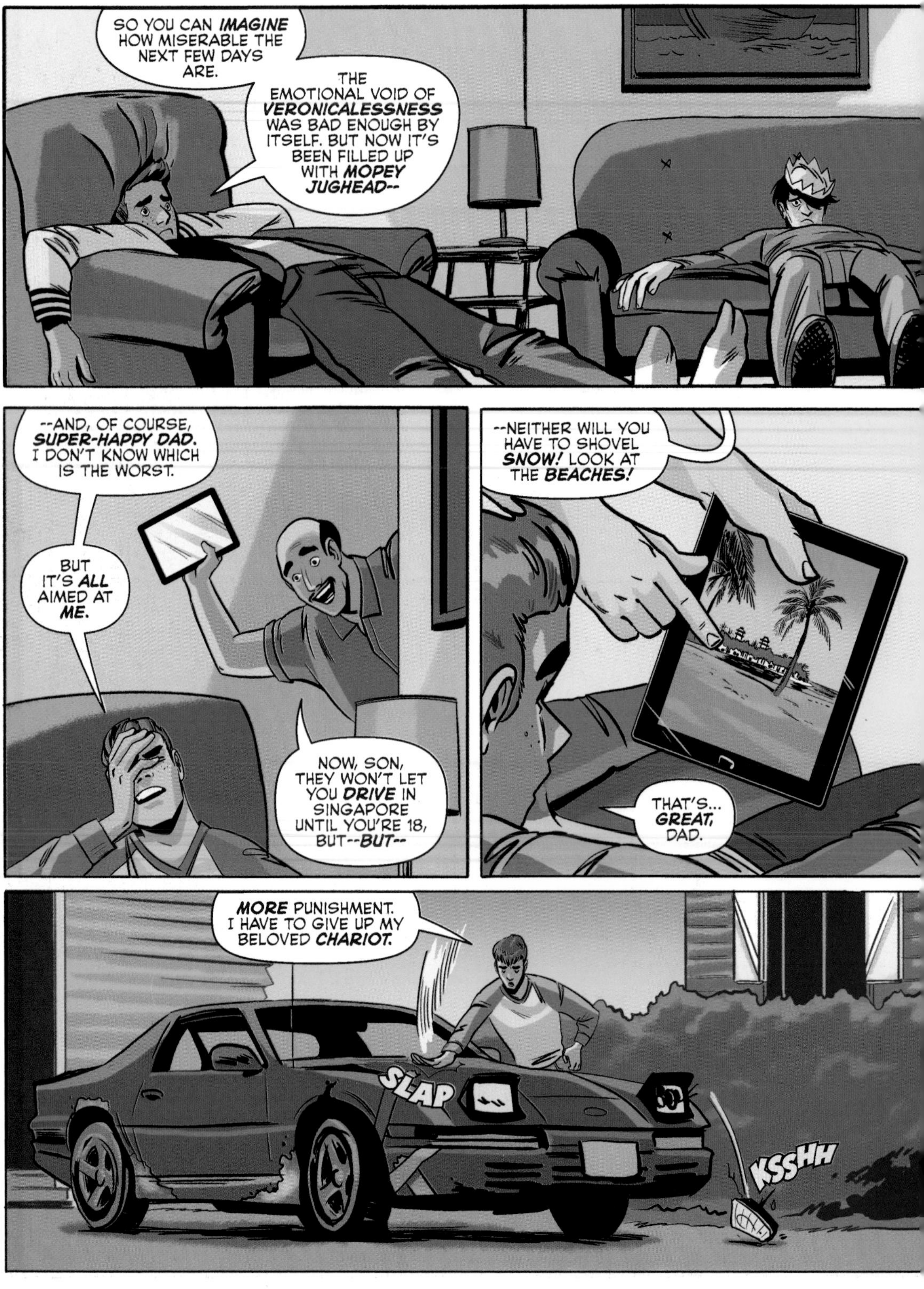

SO YOU CAN IMAGINE HOW MISERABLE THE NEXT FEW DAYS ARE.
THE EMOTIONAL VOID OF VERONICALESSNESS WAS BAD ENOUGH BY ITSELF. BUT NOW IT'S BEEN FILLED UP WITH MOPEY JUGHEAD--
--AND, OF COURSE, SUPER-HAPPY DAD. I DON'T KNOW WHICH IS THE WORST.
BUT IT'S ALL AIMED AT ME.
NOW, SON, THEY WON'T LET YOU DRIVE IN SINGAPORE UNTIL YOU'RE 18, BUT--BUT--
--NEITHER WILL YOU HAVE TO SHOVEL SNOW! LOOK AT THE BEACHES!
THAT'S... GREAT, DAD.
MORE PUNISHMENT. I HAVE TO GIVE UP MY BELOVED CHARIOT.
SLAP
KSSHH

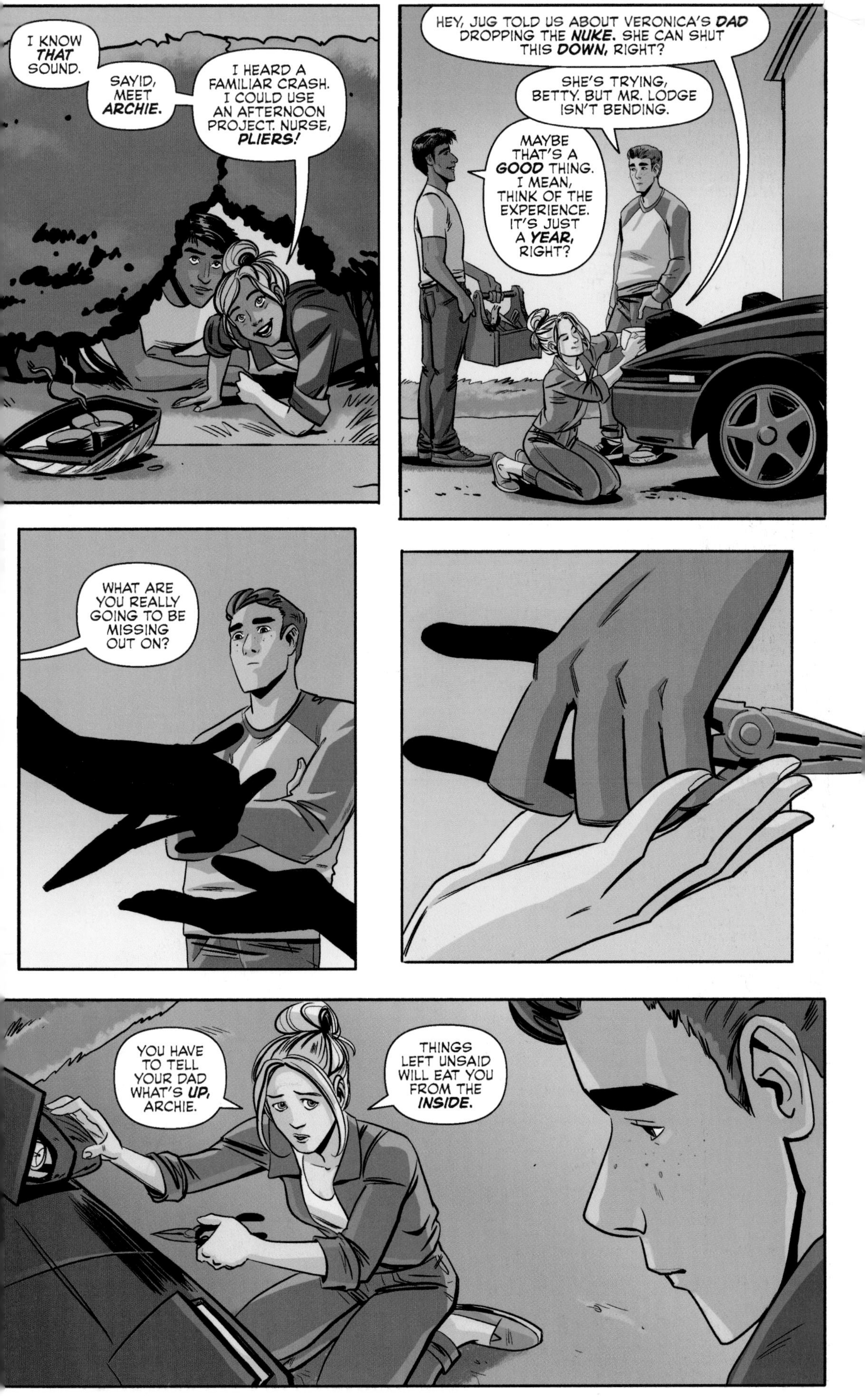

I KNOW THAT SOUND.
SAYID, MEET ARCHIE.
I HEARD A FAMILIAR CRASH. I COULD USE AN AFTERNOON PROJECT. NURSE, PLIERS!
HEY, JUG TOLD US ABOUT VERONICA'S DAD DROPPING THE NUKE. SHE CAN SHUT THIS DOWN, RIGHT?
SHE'S TRYING, BETTY. BUT MR. LODGE ISN'T BENDING.
MAYBE THAT'S A GOOD THING. I MEAN, THINK OF THE EXPERIENCE. IT'S JUST A YEAR, RIGHT?
WHAT ARE YOU REALLY GOING TO BE MISSING OUT ON?
YOU HAVE TO TELL YOUR DAD WHAT'S UP, ARCHIE.
THINGS LEFT UNSAID WILL EAT YOU FROM THE INSIDE.

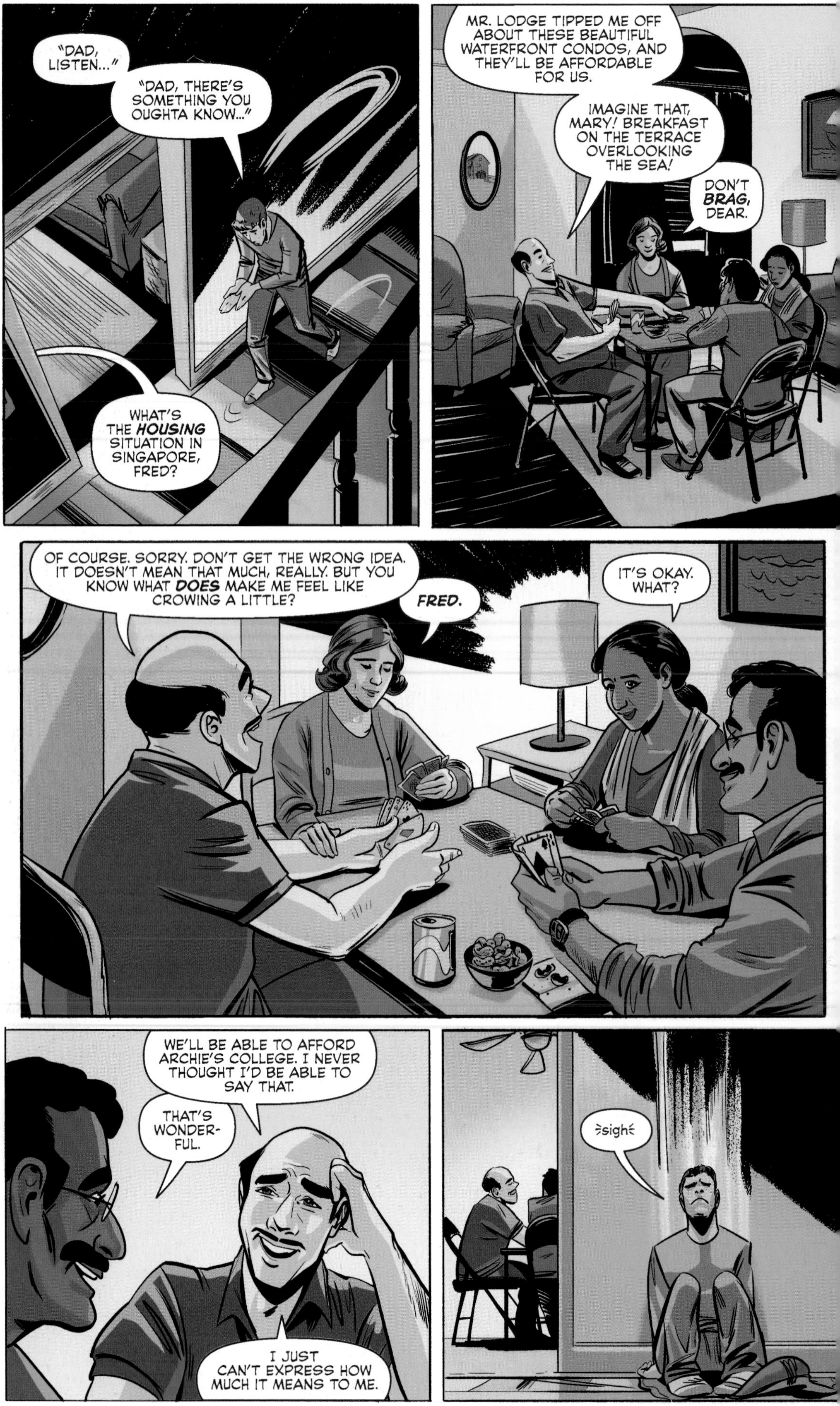
"DAD, LISTEN..."
"DAD, THERE'S SOMETHING YOU OUGHTA KNOW..."
WHAT'S THE **HOUSING** SITUATION IN SINGAPORE, FRED?
MR. LODGE TIPPED ME OFF ABOUT THESE BEAUTIFUL WATERFRONT CONDOS, AND THEY'LL BE AFFORDABLE FOR US.
IMAGINE THAT, MARY! BREAKFAST ON THE TERRACE OVERLOOKING THE SEA!
DON'T **BRAG**, DEAR.
FRED.
OF COURSE. SORRY. DON'T GET THE WRONG IDEA. IT DOESN'T MEAN THAT MUCH, REALLY. BUT YOU KNOW WHAT **DOES** MAKE ME FEEL LIKE CROWING A LITTLE?
IT'S OKAY. WHAT?
WE'LL BE ABLE TO AFFORD ARCHIE'S COLLEGE. I NEVER THOUGHT I'D BE ABLE TO SAY THAT.
THAT'S WONDER-FUL.
I JUST CAN'T EXPRESS HOW MUCH IT MEANS TO ME.
sigh

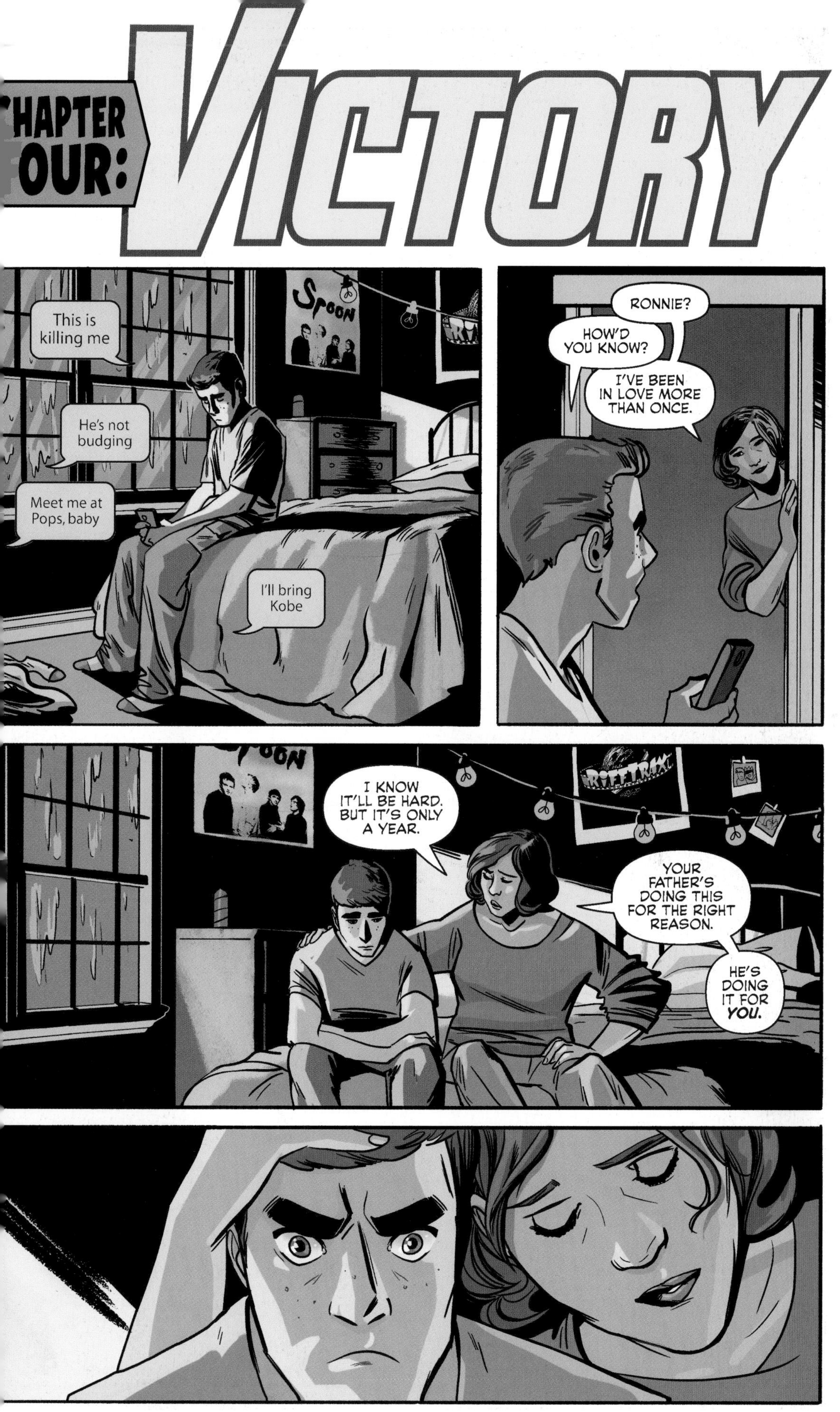

CHAPTER FOUR:
VICTORY
This is killing me
He's not budging
Meet me at Pops, baby
I'll bring Kobe
SPOON
RONNIE?
HOW'D YOU KNOW?
I'VE BEEN IN LOVE MORE THAN ONCE.
SPOON
RIFFTRAX
I KNOW IT'LL BE HARD. BUT IT'S ONLY A YEAR.
YOUR FATHER'S DOING THIS FOR THE RIGHT REASON.
HE'S DOING IT FOR ***YOU.***

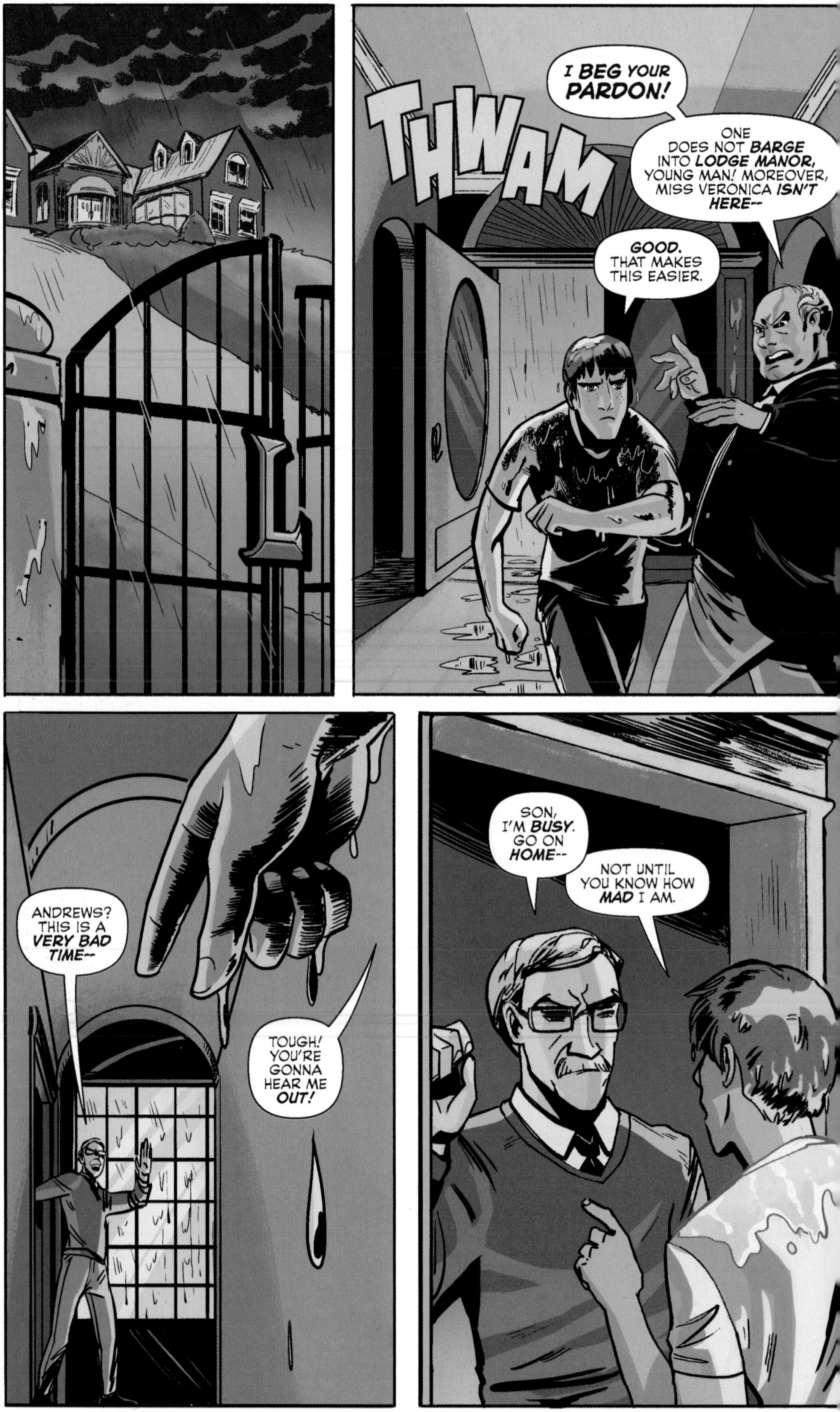
THWAM
I BEG YOUR PARDON!
ONE DOES NOT BARGE INTO LODGE MANOR, YOUNG MAN! MOREOVER, MISS VERONICA ISN'T HERE--
GOOD. THAT MAKES THIS EASIER.
ANDREWS? THIS IS A VERY BAD TIME--
TOUGH! YOU'RE GONNA HEAR ME OUT!
SON, I'M BUSY. GO ON HOME--
NOT UNTIL YOU KNOW HOW MAD I AM.

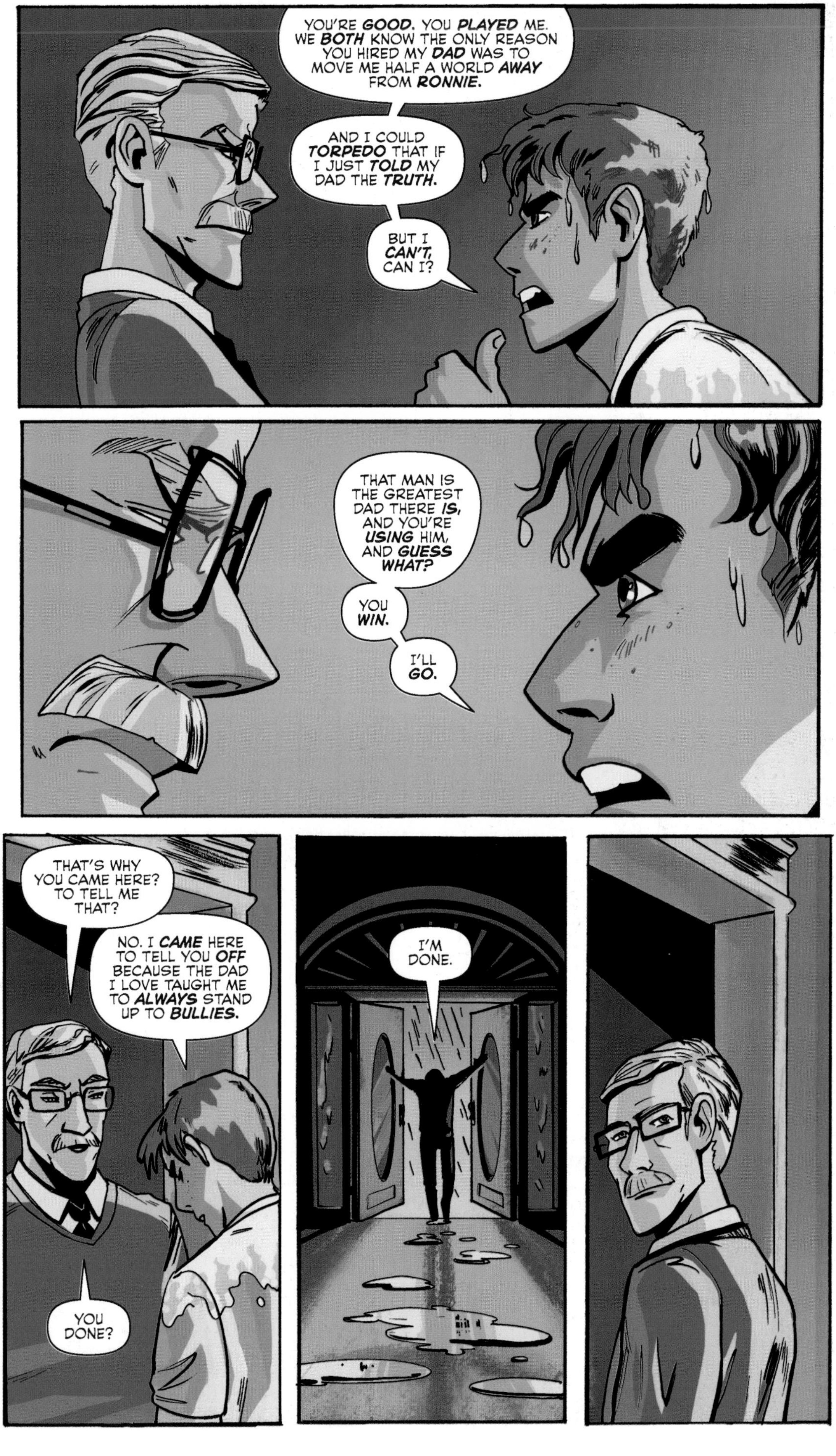

YOU'RE GOOD. YOU PLAYED ME. WE BOTH KNOW THE ONLY REASON YOU HIRED MY DAD WAS TO MOVE ME HALF A WORLD AWAY FROM RONNIE.
AND I COULD TORPEDO THAT IF I JUST TOLD MY DAD THE TRUTH.
BUT I CAN'T, CAN I?
THAT MAN IS THE GREATEST DAD THERE IS, AND YOU'RE USING HIM, AND GUESS WHAT?
YOU WIN.
I'LL GO.
THAT'S WHY YOU CAME HERE? TO TELL ME THAT?
NO. I CAME HERE TO TELL YOU OFF BECAUSE THE DAD I LOVE TAUGHT ME TO ALWAYS STAND UP TO BULLIES.
YOU DONE?
I'M DONE.

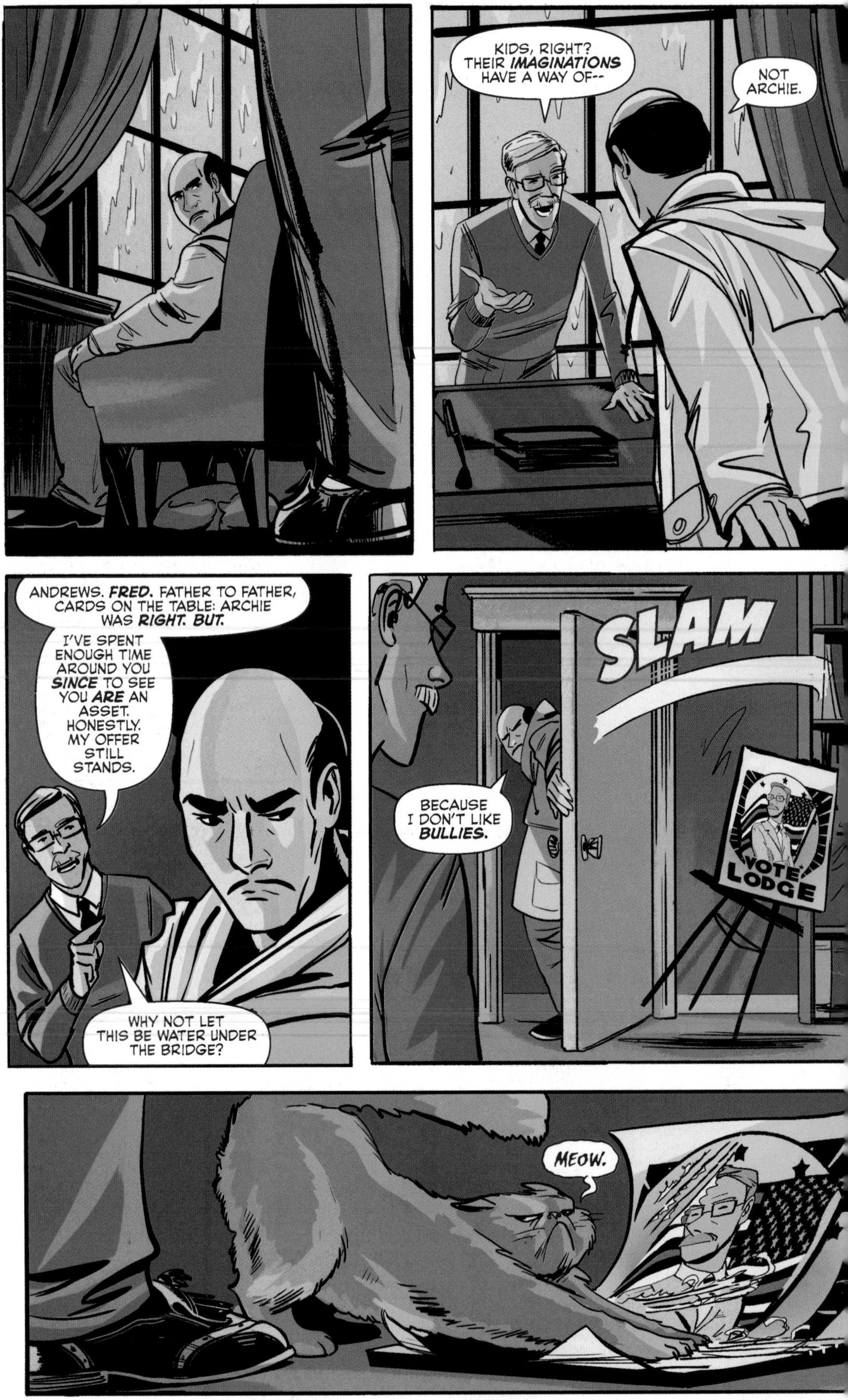
KIDS, RIGHT? THEIR IMAGINATIONS HAVE A WAY OF--
NOT ARCHIE.
ANDREWS. FRED. FATHER TO FATHER, CARDS ON THE TABLE: ARCHIE WAS RIGHT. BUT.
I'VE SPENT ENOUGH TIME AROUND YOU SINCE TO SEE YOU ARE AN ASSET. HONESTLY. MY OFFER STILL STANDS.
WHY NOT LET THIS BE WATER UNDER THE BRIDGE?
BECAUSE I DON'T LIKE BULLIES.
SLAM
VOTE LODGE
MEOW.

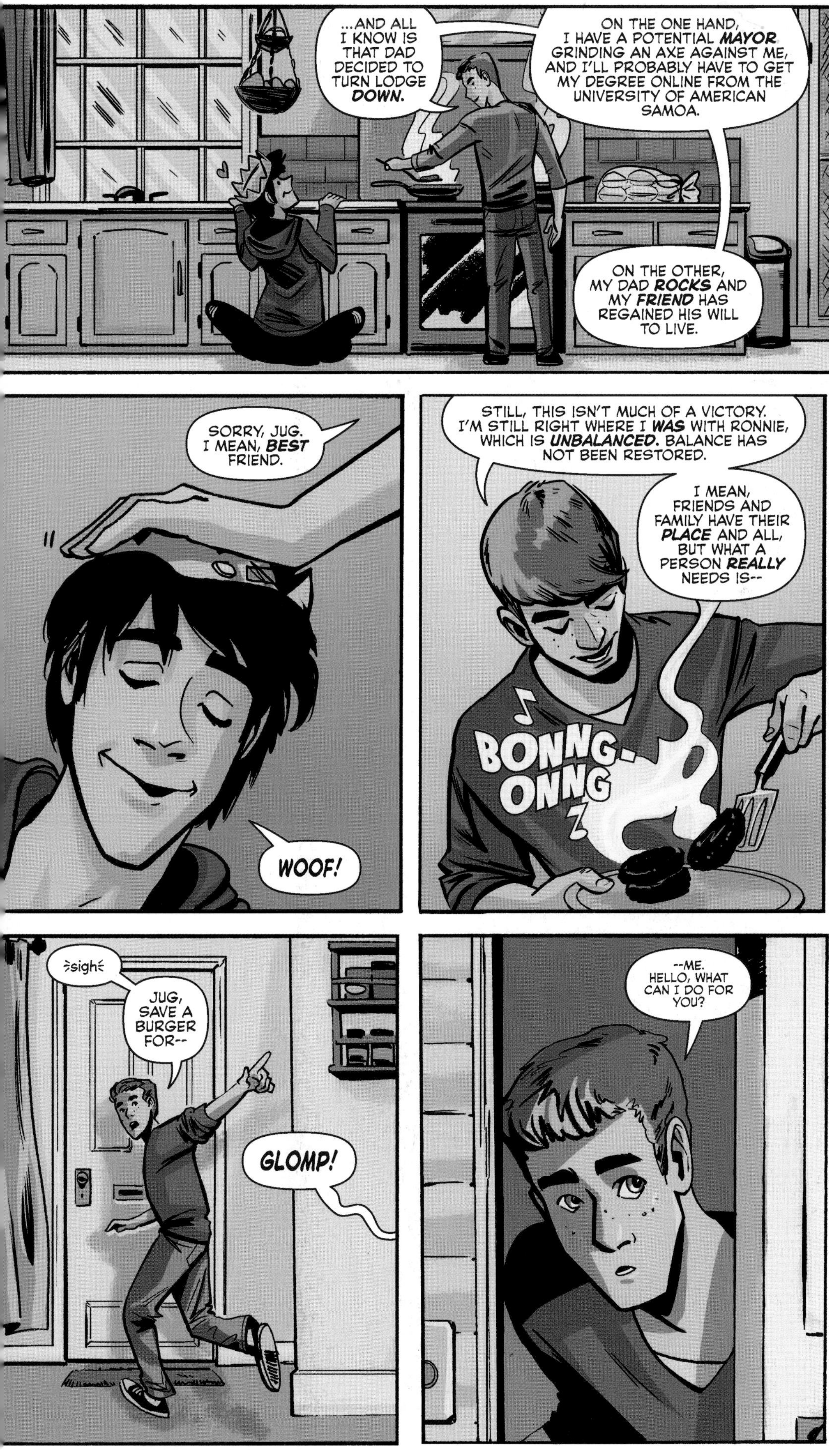
...AND ALL I KNOW IS THAT DAD DECIDED TO TURN LODGE DOWN.
ON THE ONE HAND, I HAVE A POTENTIAL MAYOR GRINDING AN AXE AGAINST ME, AND I'LL PROBABLY HAVE TO GET MY DEGREE ONLINE FROM THE UNIVERSITY OF AMERICAN SAMOA.
ON THE OTHER, MY DAD ROCKS AND MY FRIEND HAS REGAINED HIS WILL TO LIVE.
SORRY, JUG. I MEAN, BEST FRIEND.
WOOF!
STILL, THIS ISN'T MUCH OF A VICTORY. I'M STILL RIGHT WHERE I WAS WITH RONNIE, WHICH IS UNBALANCED. BALANCE HAS NOT BEEN RESTORED.
I MEAN, FRIENDS AND FAMILY HAVE THEIR PLACE AND ALL, BUT WHAT A PERSON REALLY NEEDS IS--
BONNG-ONNG
sigh
JUG, SAVE A BURGER FOR--
GLOMP!
--ME. HELLO, WHAT CAN I DO FOR YOU?

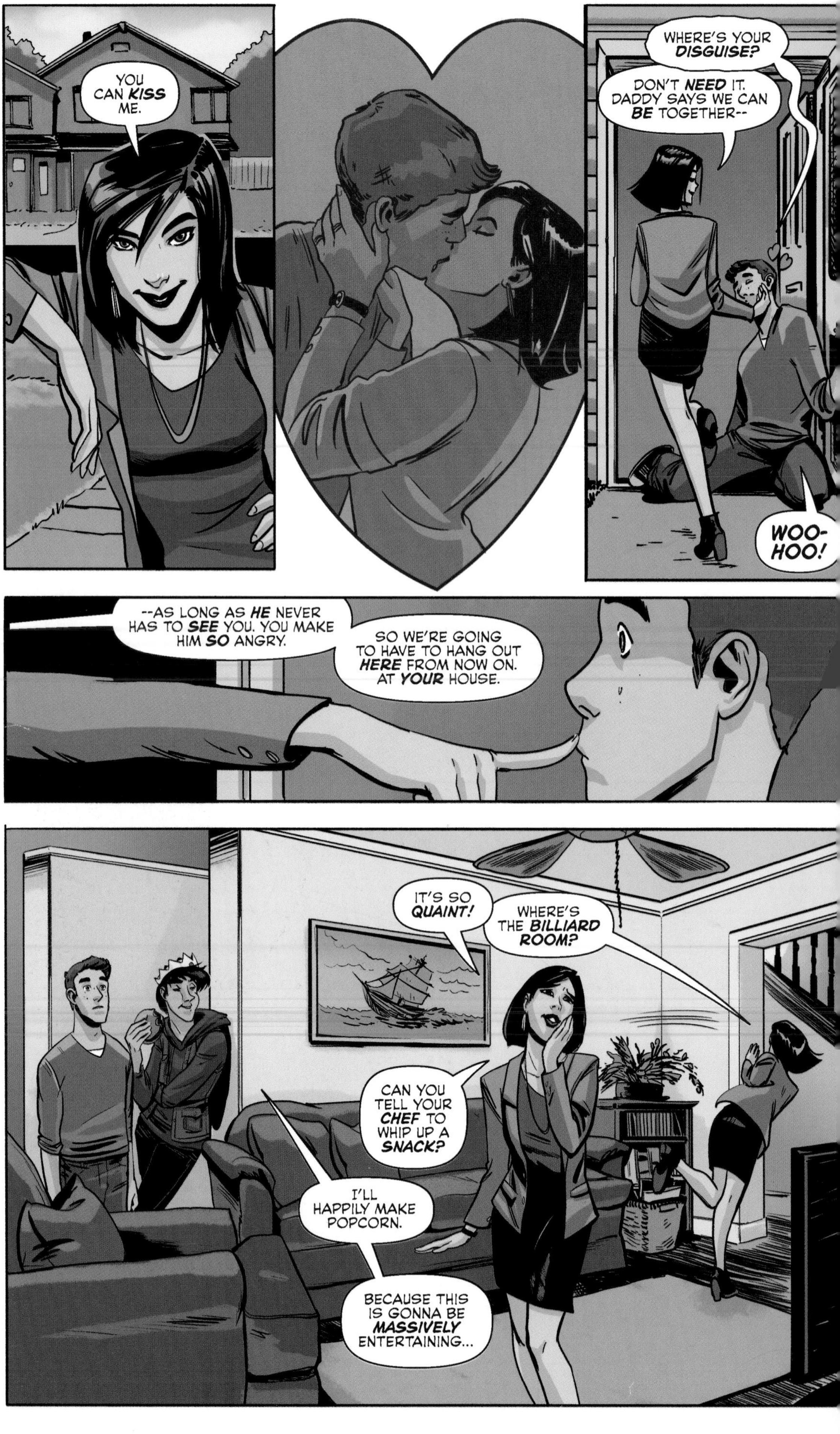
YOU CAN KISS ME.
WHERE'S YOUR DISGUISE?
DON'T NEED IT. DADDY SAYS WE CAN BE TOGETHER--
WOO-HOO!
--AS LONG AS HE NEVER HAS TO SEE YOU. YOU MAKE HIM SO ANGRY.
SO WE'RE GOING TO HAVE TO HANG OUT HERE FROM NOW ON. AT YOUR HOUSE.
IT'S SO QUAINT!
WHERE'S THE BILLIARD ROOM?
CAN YOU TELL YOUR CHEF TO WHIP UP A SNACK?
I'LL HAPPILY MAKE POPCORN.
BECAUSE THIS IS GONNA BE MASSIVELY ENTERTAINING...

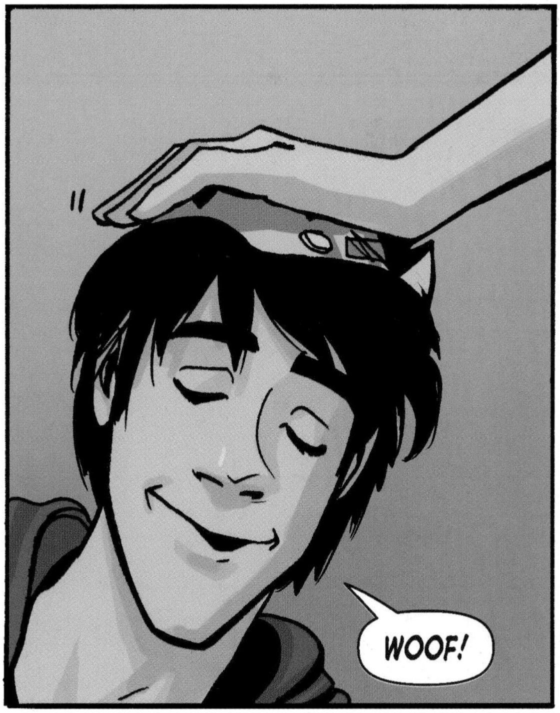
WOOF!

TO BE CONTINUED...

ISSUE NINE

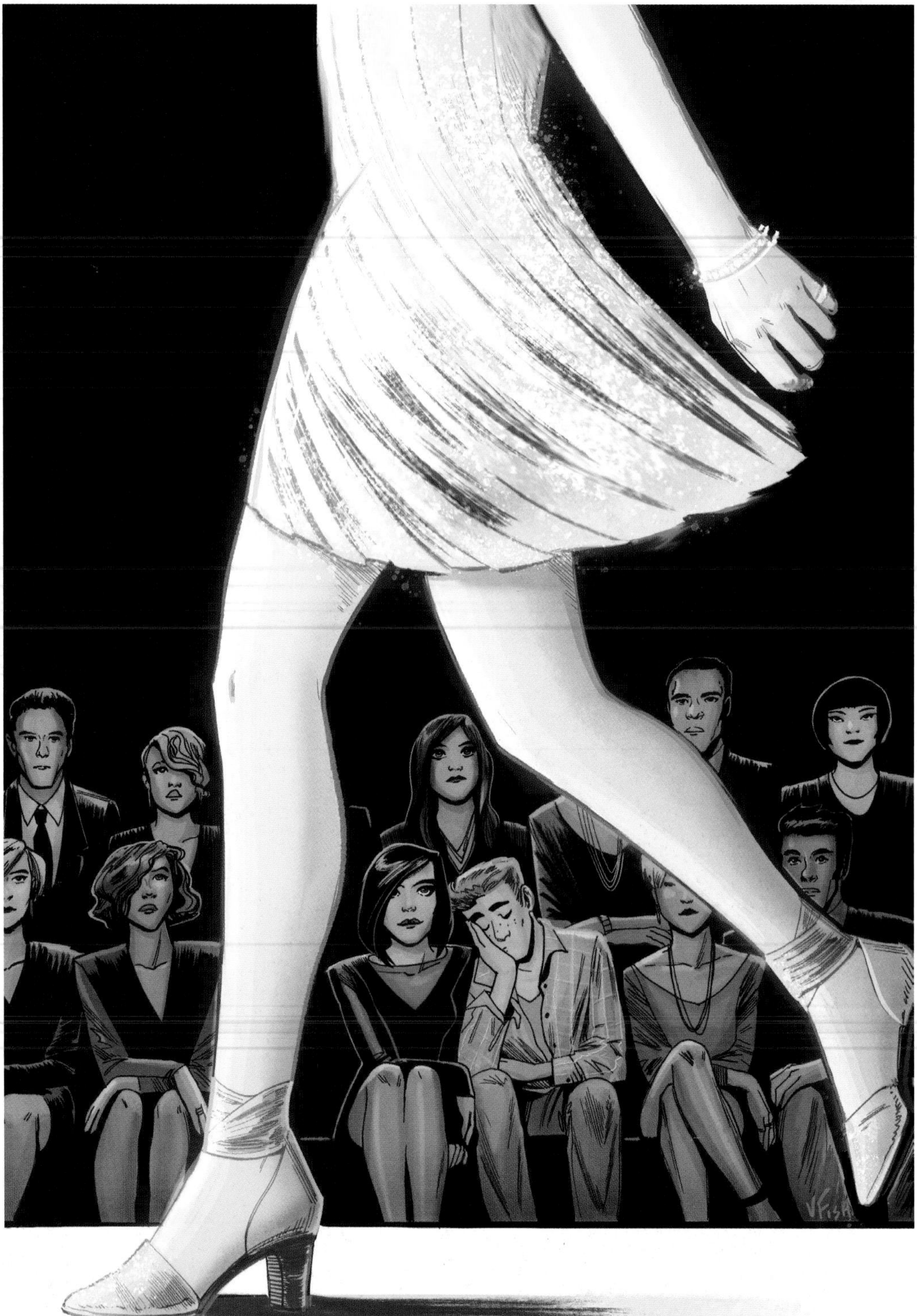

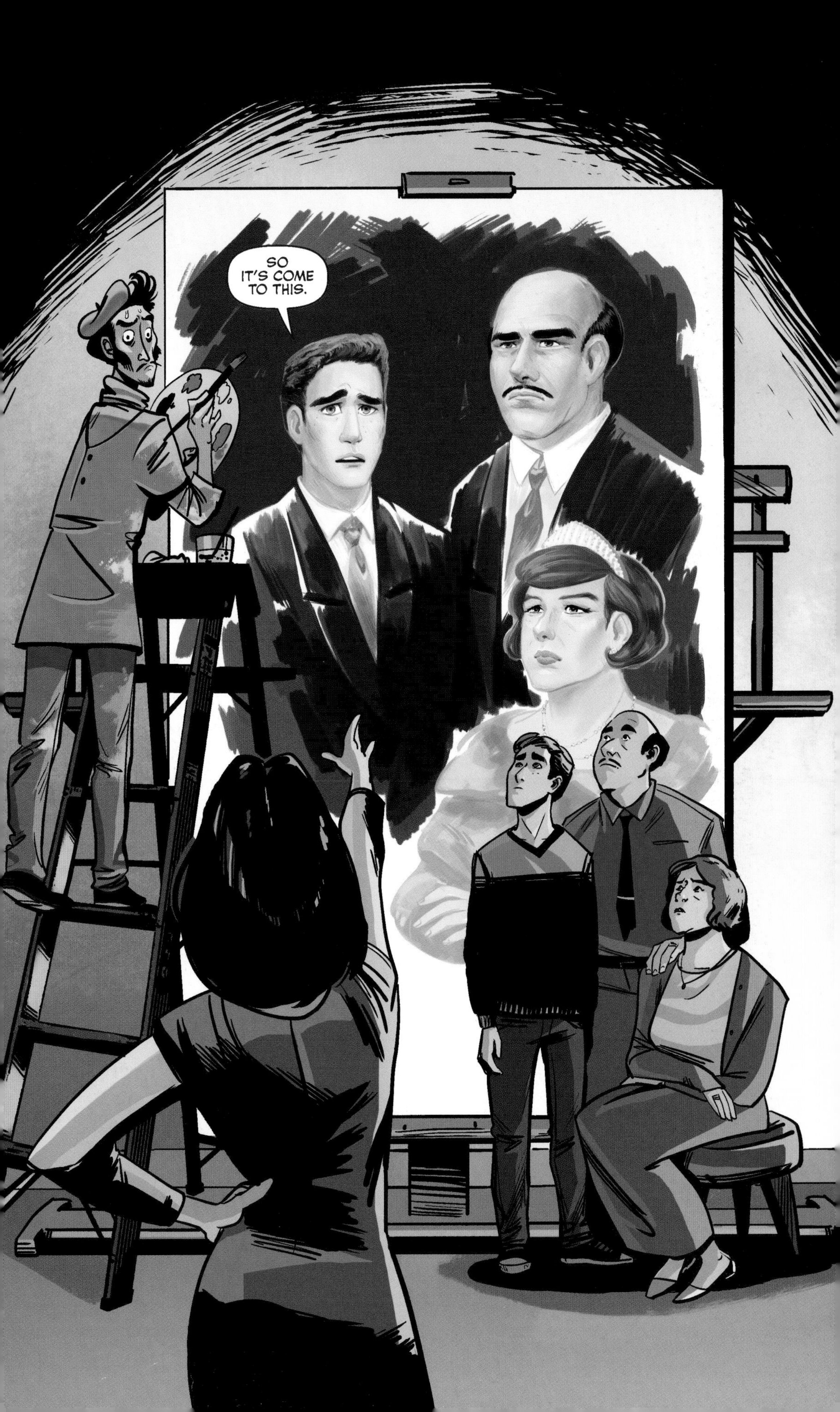
SO IT'S COME TO THIS.

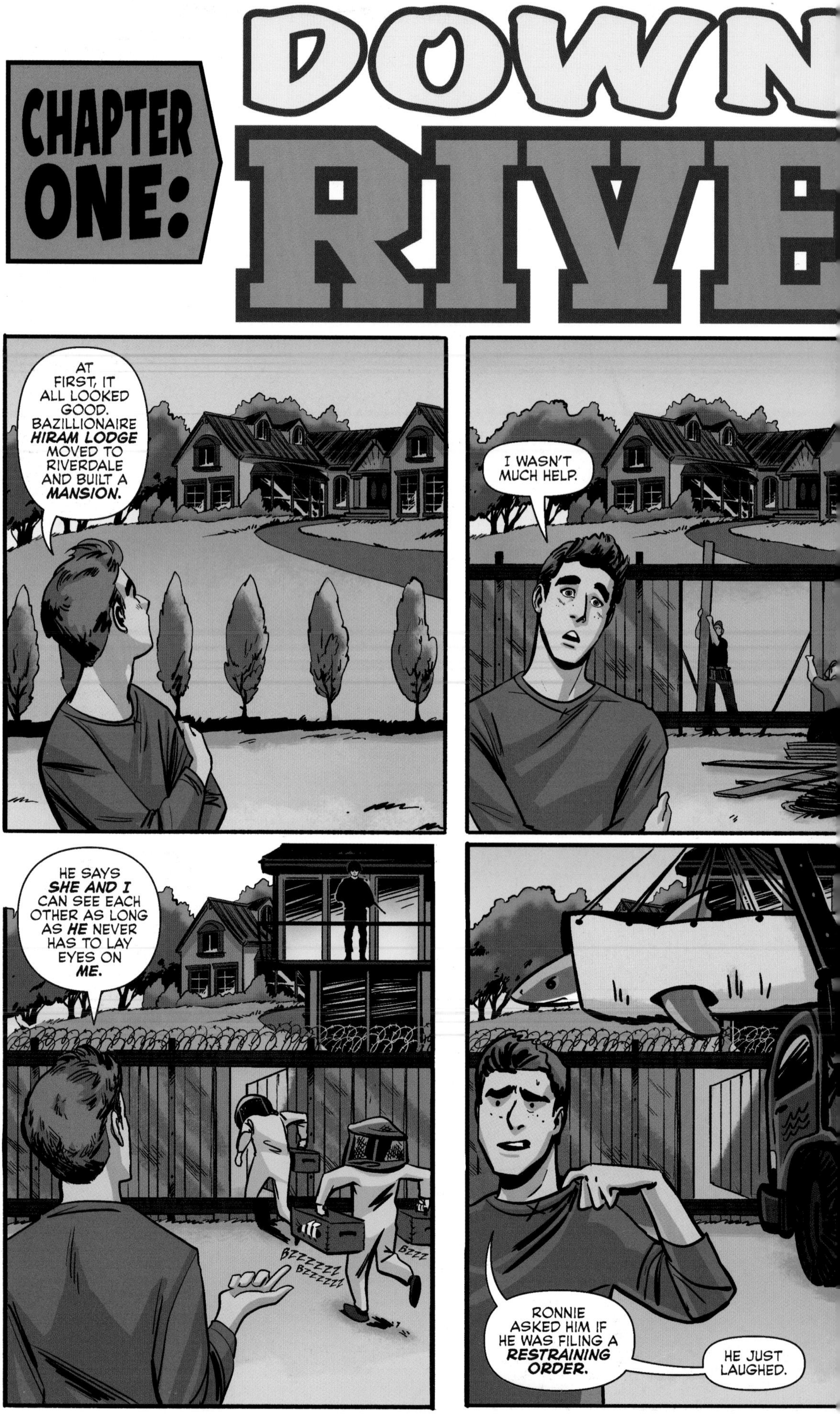
CHAPTER ONE:
DOWN
RIVE
AT FIRST, IT ALL LOOKED GOOD. BAZILLIONAIRE HIRAM LODGE MOVED TO RIVERDALE AND BUILT A MANSION.
I WASN'T MUCH HELP.
HE SAYS SHE AND I CAN SEE EACH OTHER AS LONG AS HE NEVER HAS TO LAY EYES ON ME.
BZZZZZZ BZZZZZZ
BZZZ
RONNIE ASKED HIM IF HE WAS FILING A RESTRAINING ORDER.
HE JUST LAUGHED.

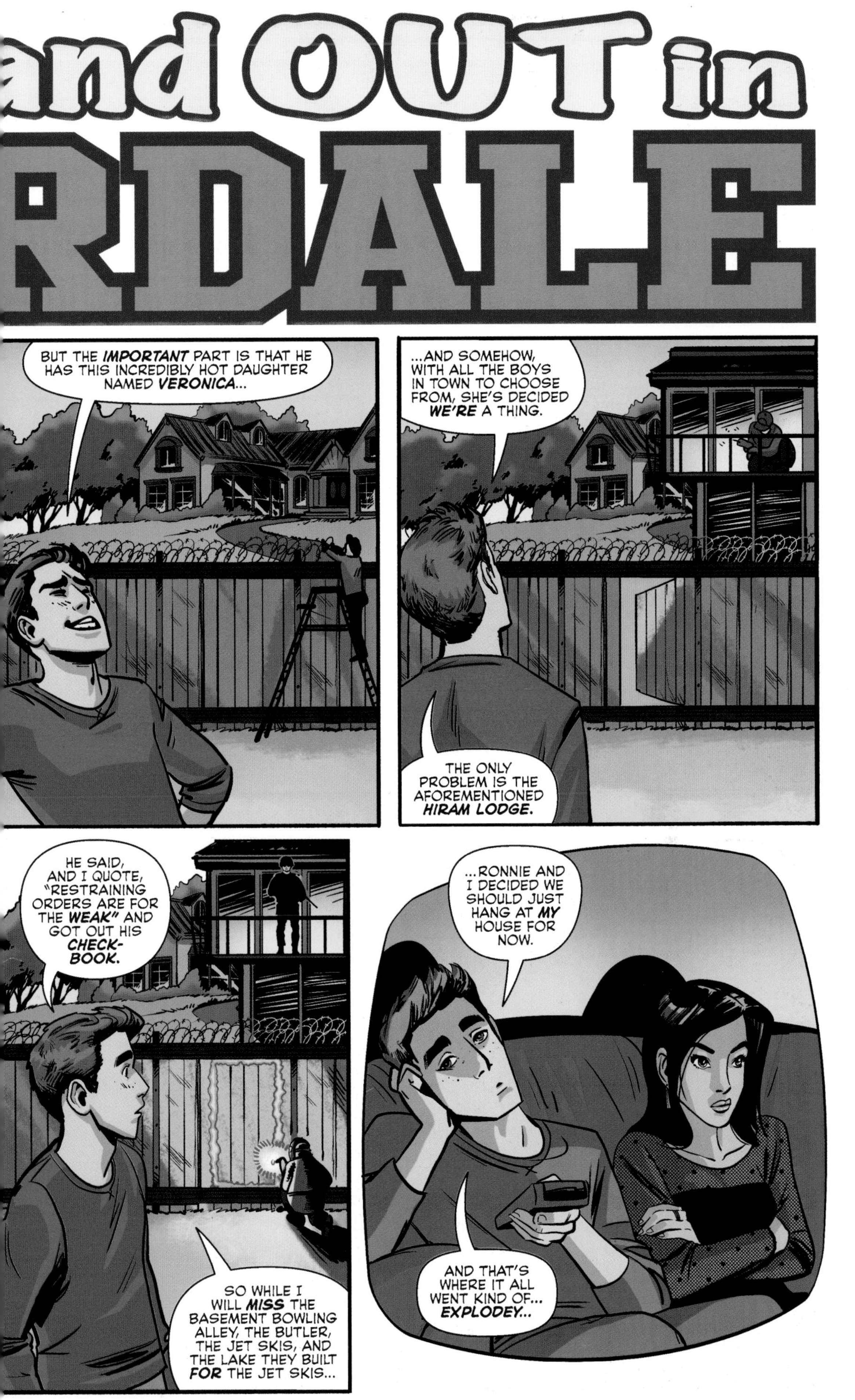
and OUT in
RDALE
BUT THE IMPORTANT PART IS THAT HE HAS THIS INCREDIBLY HOT DAUGHTER NAMED VERONICA...
...AND SOMEHOW, WITH ALL THE BOYS IN TOWN TO CHOOSE FROM, SHE'S DECIDED WE'RE A THING.
THE ONLY PROBLEM IS THE AFOREMENTIONED HIRAM LODGE.
HE SAID, AND I QUOTE, "RESTRAINING ORDERS ARE FOR THE WEAK" AND GOT OUT HIS CHECK-BOOK.
SO WHILE I WILL MISS THE BASEMENT BOWLING ALLEY, THE BUTLER, THE JET SKIS, AND THE LAKE THEY BUILT FOR THE JET SKIS...
...RONNIE AND I DECIDED WE SHOULD JUST HANG AT MY HOUSE FOR NOW.
AND THAT'S WHERE IT ALL WENT KIND OF... EXPLODEY...

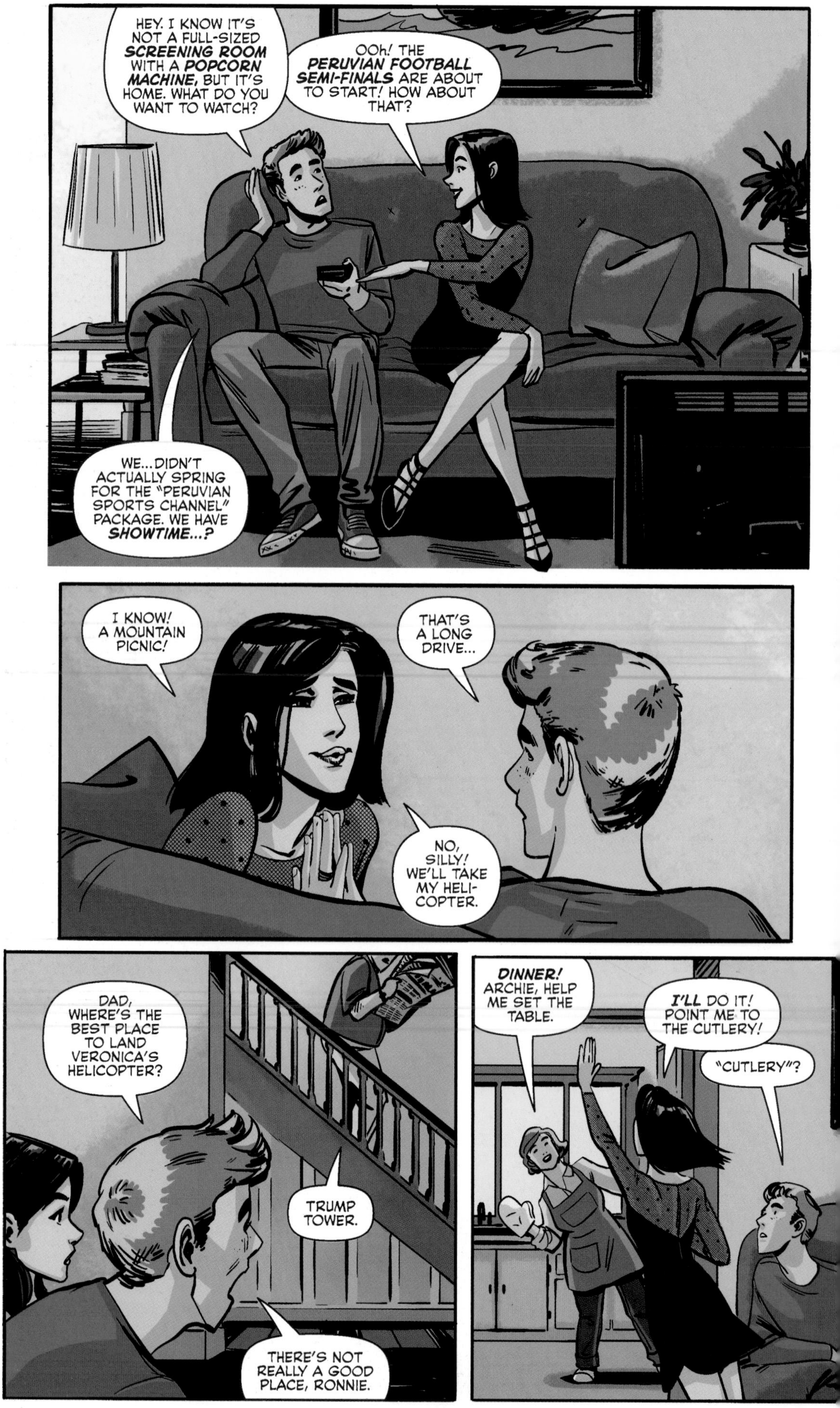
HEY. I KNOW IT'S NOT A FULL-SIZED **SCREENING ROOM** WITH A **POPCORN MACHINE,** BUT IT'S HOME. WHAT DO YOU WANT TO WATCH?
OOh! THE **PERUVIAN FOOTBALL SEMI-FINALS** ARE ABOUT TO START! HOW ABOUT THAT?
WE...DIDN'T ACTUALLY SPRING FOR THE "PERUVIAN SPORTS CHANNEL" PACKAGE. WE HAVE **SHOWTIME...?**
I KNOW! A MOUNTAIN PICNIC!
THAT'S A LONG DRIVE...
NO, SILLY! WE'LL TAKE MY HELI-COPTER.
DAD, WHERE'S THE BEST PLACE TO LAND VERONICA'S HELICOPTER?
TRUMP TOWER.
THERE'S NOT REALLY A GOOD PLACE, RONNIE.
DINNER! ARCHIE, HELP ME SET THE TABLE.
I'LL DO IT! POINT ME TO THE CUTLERY!
"CUTLERY"?

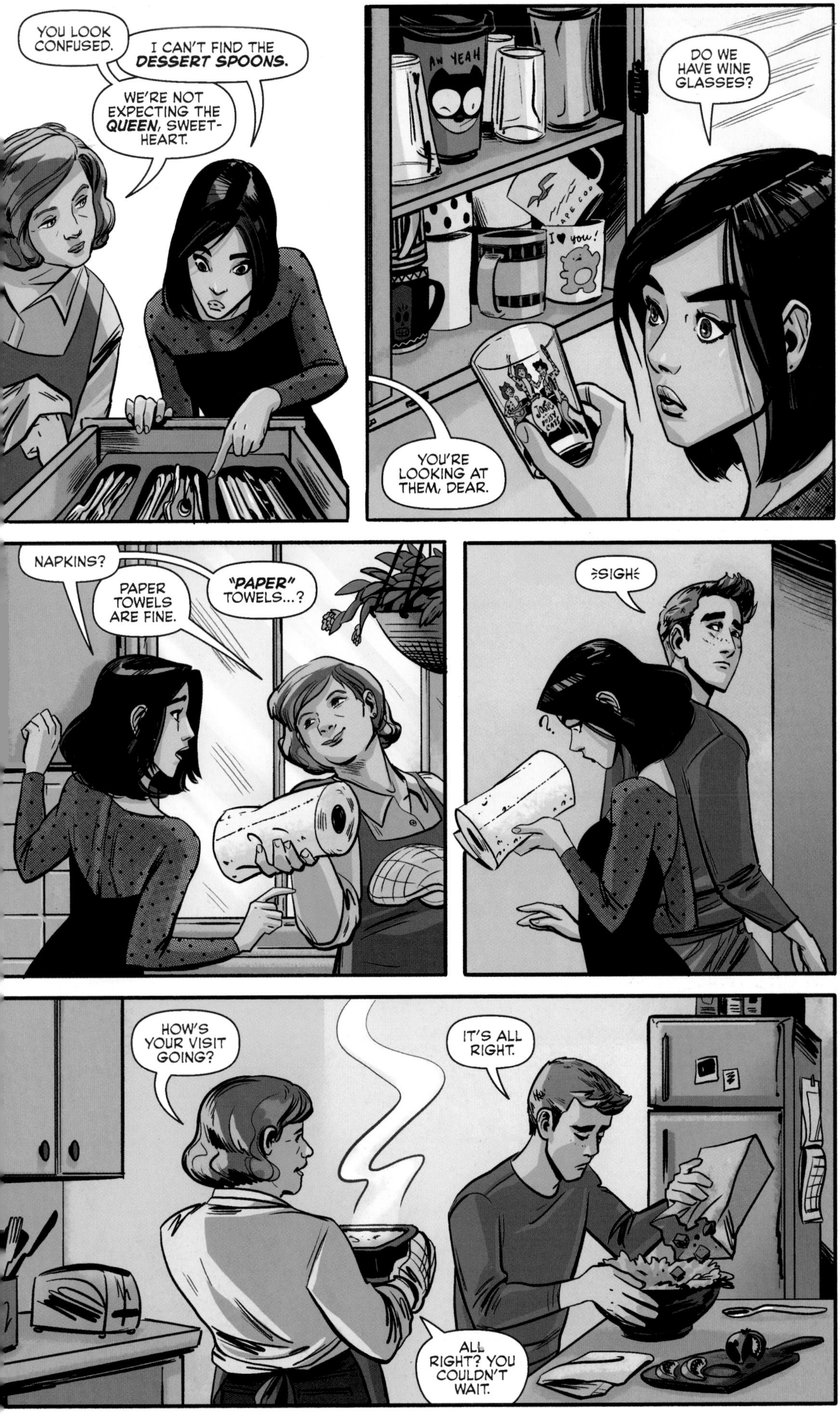
YOU LOOK CONFUSED.
I CAN'T FIND THE ***DESSERT SPOONS.***
WE'RE NOT EXPECTING THE ***QUEEN***, SWEET-HEART.
DO WE HAVE WINE GLASSES?
YOU'RE LOOKING AT THEM, DEAR.
NAPKINS?
PAPER TOWELS ARE FINE.
"PAPER" TOWELS...?
SIGH
HOW'S YOUR VISIT GOING?
IT'S ALL RIGHT.
ALL RIGHT? YOU COULDN'T WAIT.

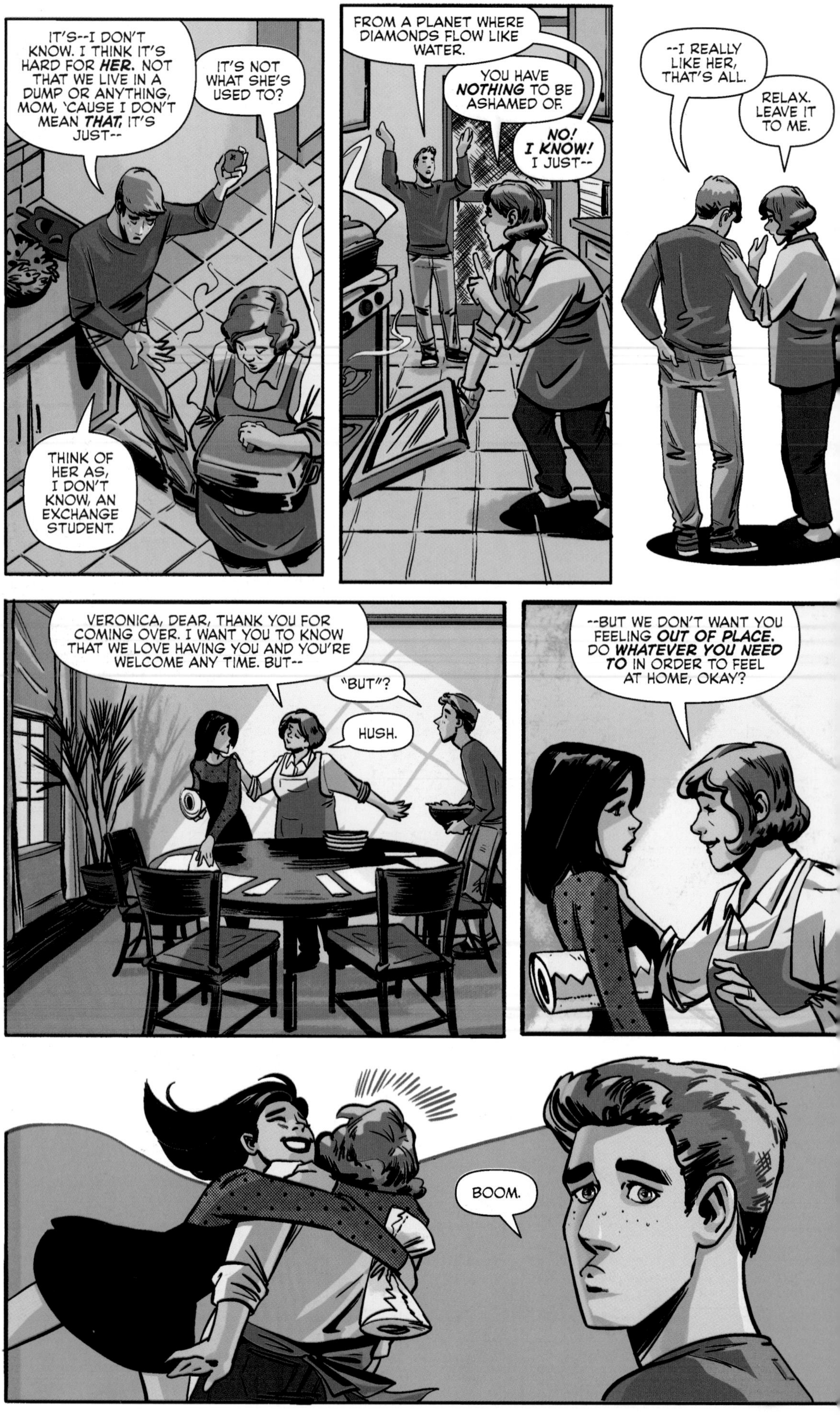
IT'S--I DON'T KNOW. I THINK IT'S HARD FOR **HER.** NOT THAT WE LIVE IN A DUMP OR ANYTHING, MOM, 'CAUSE I DON'T MEAN **THAT,** IT'S JUST--
IT'S NOT WHAT SHE'S USED TO?
THINK OF HER AS, I DON'T KNOW, AN EXCHANGE STUDENT.
FROM A PLANET WHERE DIAMONDS FLOW LIKE WATER.
YOU HAVE **NOTHING** TO BE ASHAMED OF.
NO! I KNOW! I JUST--
--I REALLY LIKE HER, THAT'S ALL.
RELAX. LEAVE IT TO ME.
VERONICA, DEAR, THANK YOU FOR COMING OVER. I WANT YOU TO KNOW THAT WE LOVE HAVING YOU AND YOU'RE WELCOME ANY TIME. BUT--
"BUT"?
HUSH.
--BUT WE DON'T WANT YOU FEELING **OUT OF PLACE.** DO **WHATEVER YOU NEED TO** IN ORDER TO FEEL AT HOME, OKAY?
BOOM.

HAPTER WO: Simple Comforts

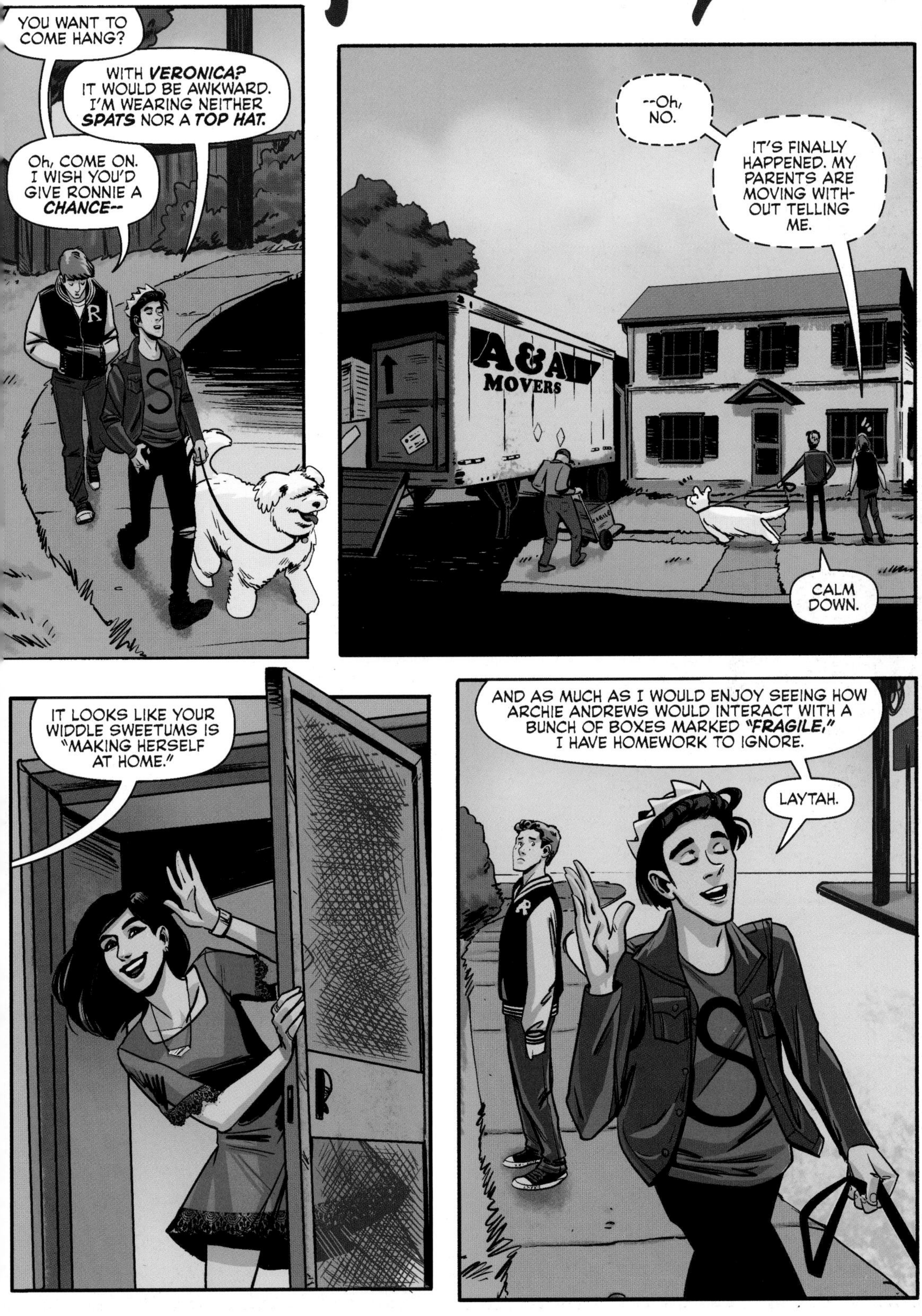

YOU WANT TO COME HANG?
WITH *VERONICA?* IT WOULD BE AWKWARD. I'M WEARING NEITHER *SPATS* NOR A *TOP HAT.*
Oh, COME ON. I WISH YOU'D GIVE RONNIE A *CHANCE--*
--Oh, NO.
IT'S FINALLY HAPPENED. MY PARENTS ARE MOVING WITH-OUT TELLING ME.
A&A MOVERS
CALM DOWN.
IT LOOKS LIKE YOUR WIDDLE SWEETUMS IS "MAKING HERSELF AT HOME."
AND AS MUCH AS I WOULD ENJOY SEEING HOW ARCHIE ANDREWS WOULD INTERACT WITH A BUNCH OF BOXES MARKED *"FRAGILE,"* I HAVE HOMEWORK TO IGNORE.
LAYTAH.

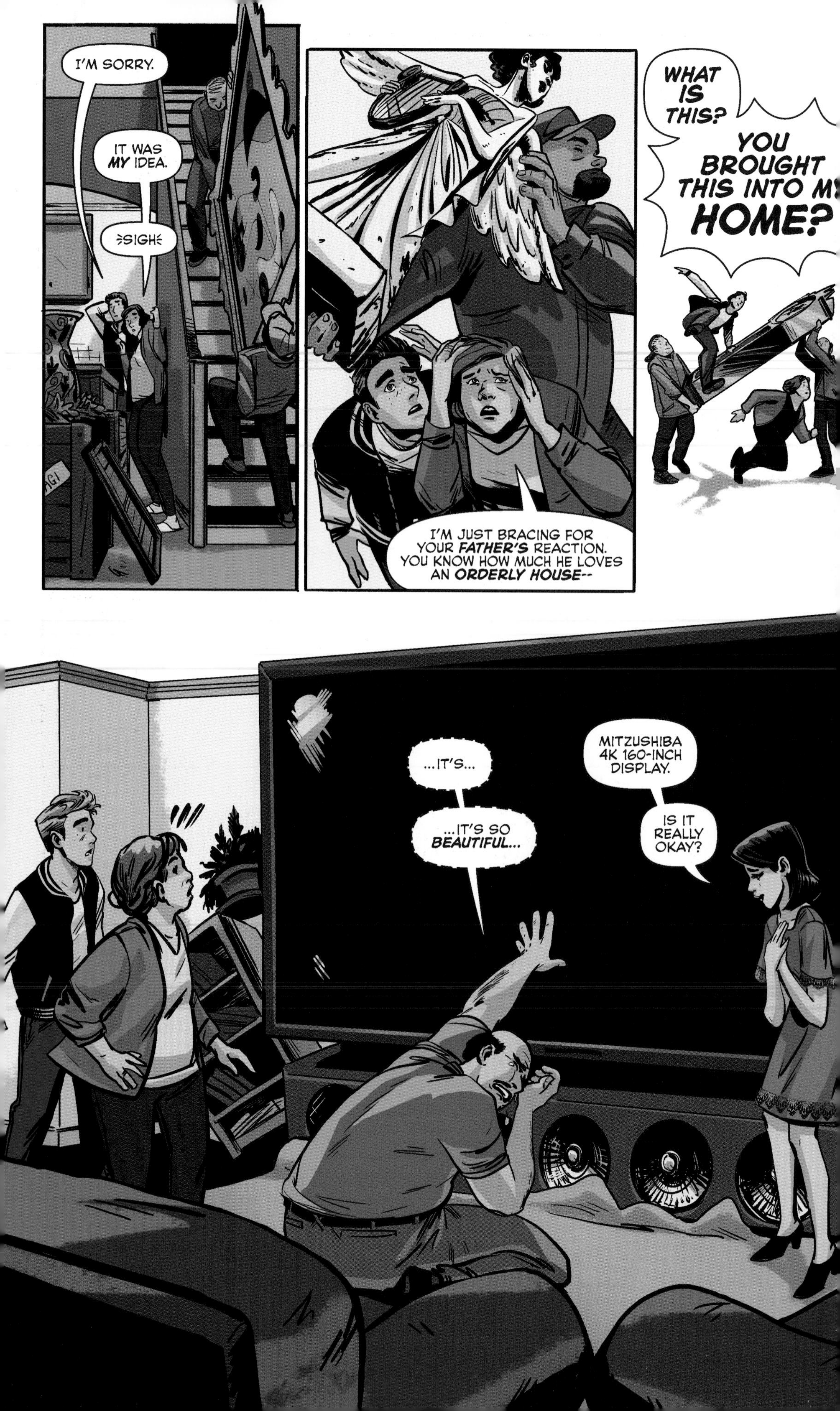
I'M SORRY.
IT WAS MY IDEA.
SIGH
I'M JUST BRACING FOR YOUR FATHER'S REACTION. YOU KNOW HOW MUCH HE LOVES AN ORDERLY HOUSE--
WHAT IS THIS?
YOU BROUGHT THIS INTO MY HOME?
...IT'S...
...IT'S SO BEAUTIFUL...
MITZUSHIBA 4K 160-INCH DISPLAY.
IS IT REALLY OKAY?

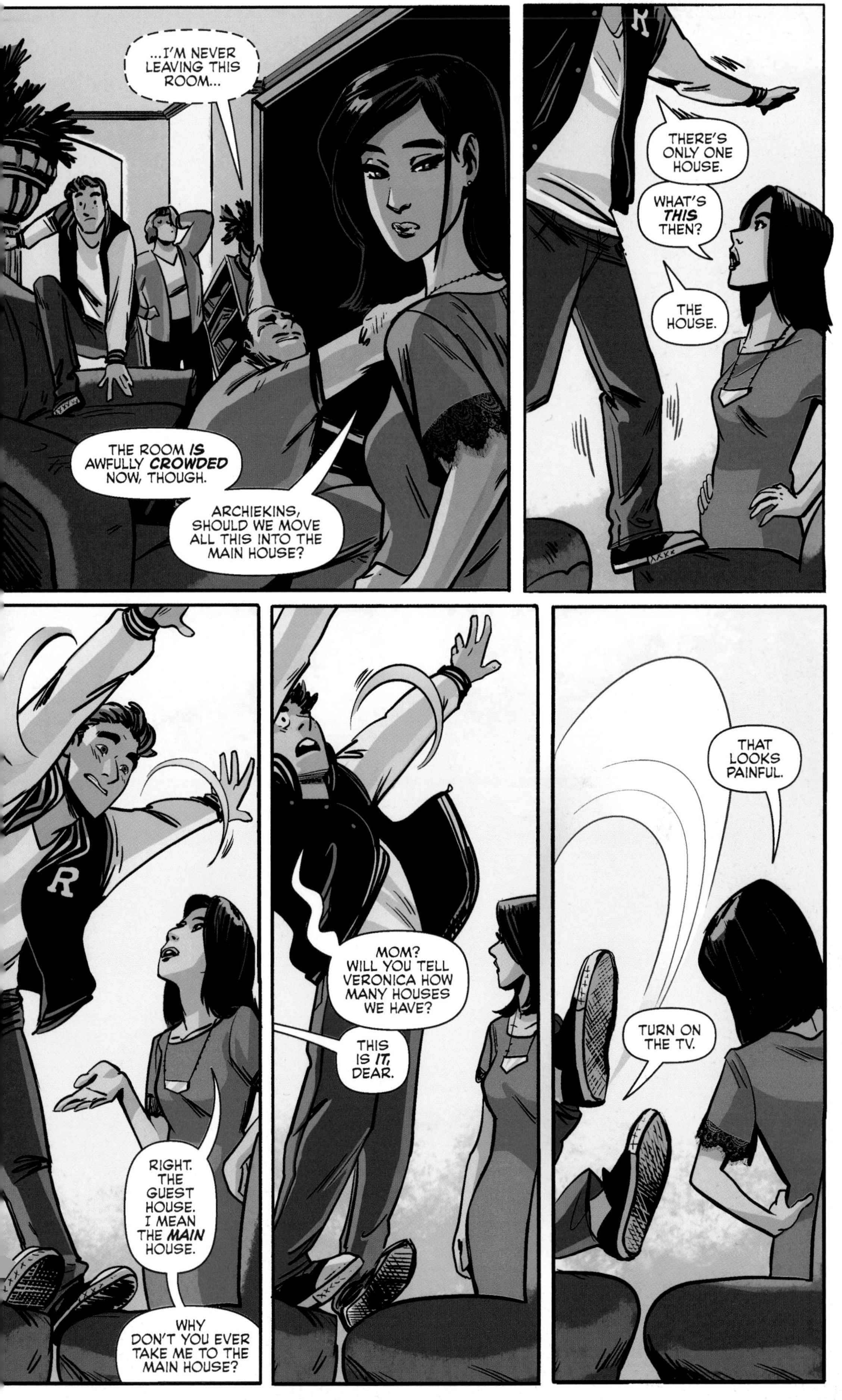
...I'M NEVER LEAVING THIS ROOM...
THE ROOM *IS* AWFULLY *CROWDED* NOW, THOUGH.
ARCHIEKINS, SHOULD WE MOVE ALL THIS INTO THE MAIN HOUSE?
THERE'S ONLY ONE HOUSE.
WHAT'S *THIS* THEN?
THE HOUSE.
RIGHT. THE GUEST HOUSE. I MEAN THE *MAIN* HOUSE.
WHY DON'T YOU EVER TAKE ME TO THE MAIN HOUSE?
MOM? WILL YOU TELL VERONICA HOW MANY HOUSES WE HAVE?
THIS IS *IT,* DEAR.
THAT LOOKS PAINFUL.
TURN ON THE TV.

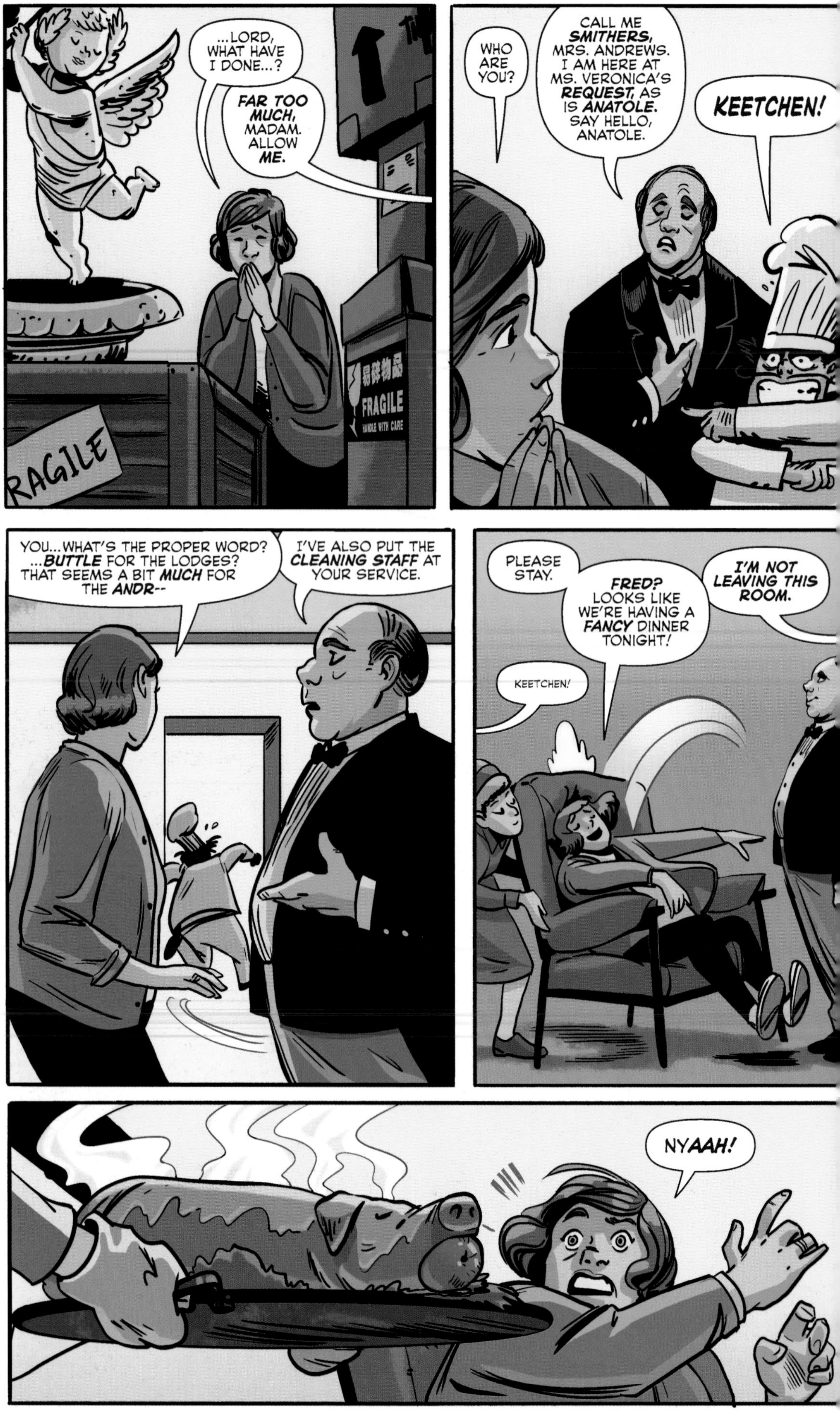
...LORD, WHAT HAVE I DONE...?
FAR TOO MUCH, MADAM. ALLOW ME.
FRAGILE
易碎物品 FRAGILE HANDLE WITH CARE
RAGILE
WHO ARE YOU?
CALL ME SMITHERS, MRS. ANDREWS. I AM HERE AT MS. VERONICA'S REQUEST, AS IS ANATOLE. SAY HELLO, ANATOLE.
KEETCHEN!
YOU...WHAT'S THE PROPER WORD? ...BUTTLE FOR THE LODGES? THAT SEEMS A BIT MUCH FOR THE ANDR--
I'VE ALSO PUT THE CLEANING STAFF AT YOUR SERVICE.
PLEASE STAY.
FRED? LOOKS LIKE WE'RE HAVING A FANCY DINNER TONIGHT!
I'M NOT LEAVING THIS ROOM.
KEETCHEN!
NYAAH!

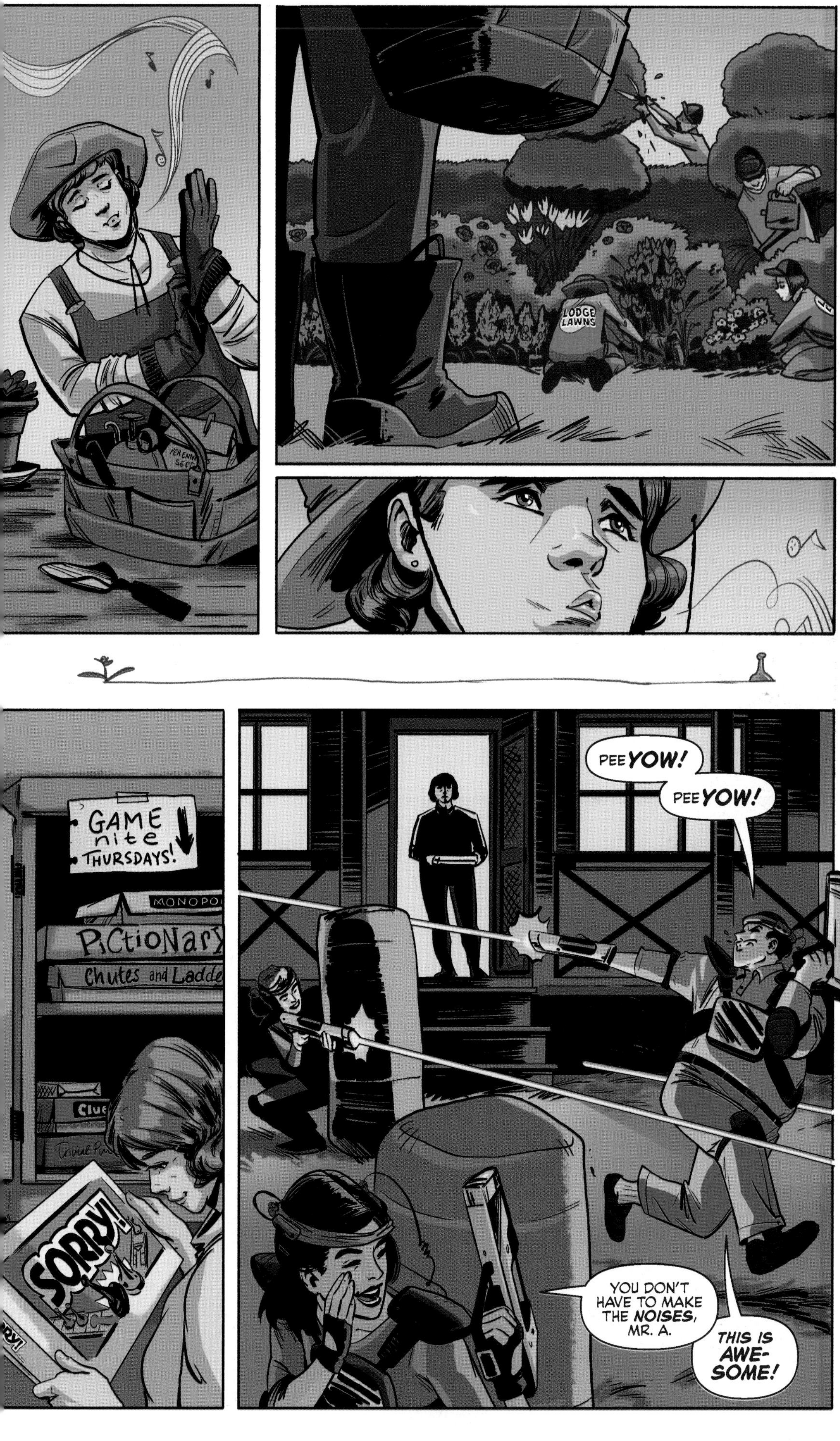
LODGE LAWNS
PERENNIAL SEEDS
GAME nite THURSDAYS!
MONOPO
PiCtioNary
Chutes and Ladde
Clue
SORRY!
PEE YOW!
PEE YOW!
YOU DON'T HAVE TO MAKE THE NOISES, MR. A.
THIS IS AWE-SOME!

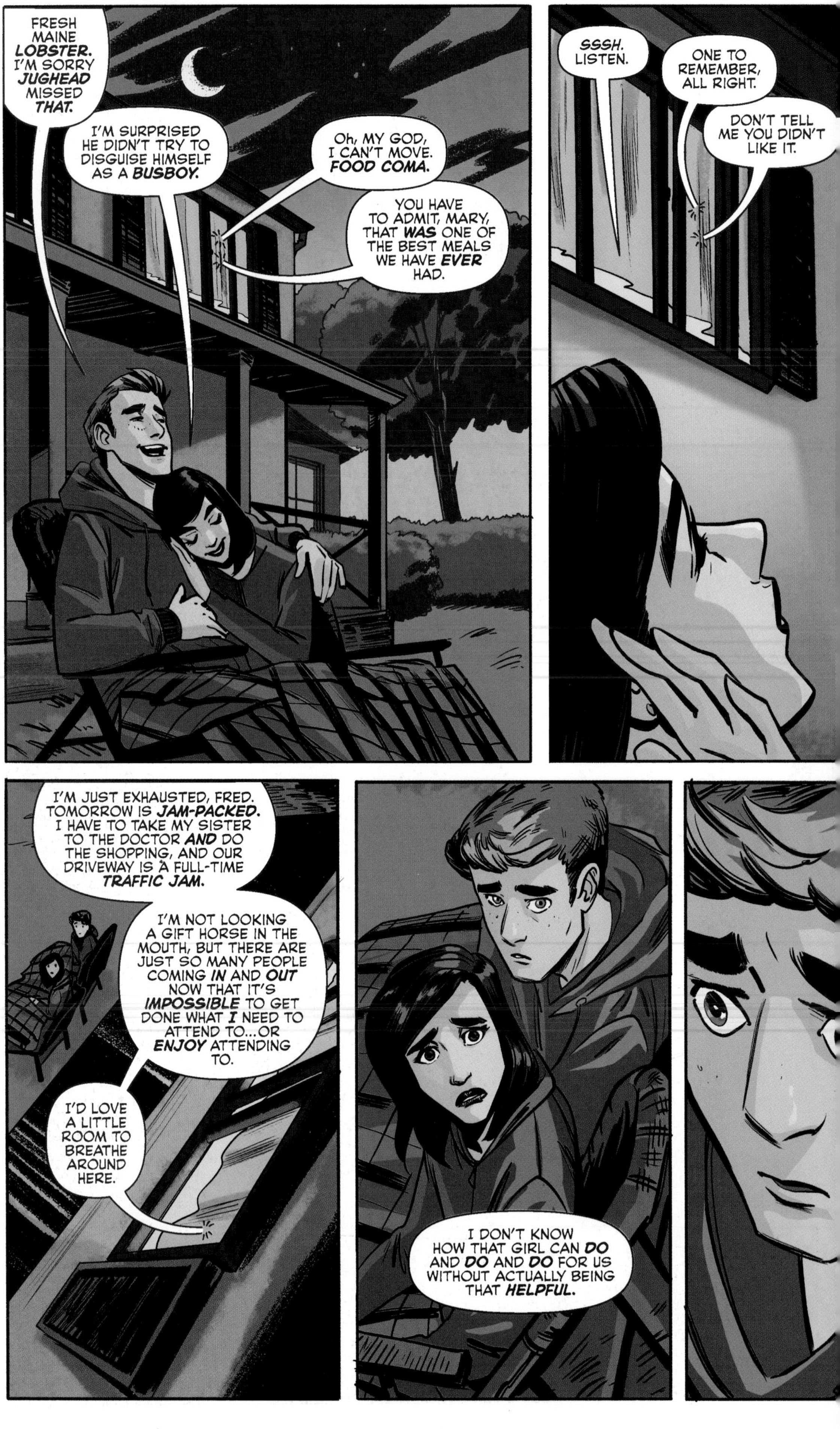
FRESH MAINE LOBSTER. I'M SORRY JUGHEAD MISSED THAT.
I'M SURPRISED HE DIDN'T TRY TO DISGUISE HIMSELF AS A BUSBOY.
Oh, MY GOD, I CAN'T MOVE. FOOD COMA.
YOU HAVE TO ADMIT, MARY, THAT WAS ONE OF THE BEST MEALS WE HAVE EVER HAD.
SSSH. LISTEN.
ONE TO REMEMBER, ALL RIGHT.
DON'T TELL ME YOU DIDN'T LIKE IT.
I'M JUST EXHAUSTED, FRED. TOMORROW IS JAM-PACKED. I HAVE TO TAKE MY SISTER TO THE DOCTOR AND DO THE SHOPPING, AND OUR DRIVEWAY IS A FULL-TIME TRAFFIC JAM.
I'M NOT LOOKING A GIFT HORSE IN THE MOUTH, BUT THERE ARE JUST SO MANY PEOPLE COMING IN AND OUT NOW THAT IT'S IMPOSSIBLE TO GET DONE WHAT I NEED TO ATTEND TO...OR ENJOY ATTENDING TO.
I'D LOVE A LITTLE ROOM TO BREATHE AROUND HERE.
I DON'T KNOW HOW THAT GIRL CAN DO AND DO AND DO FOR US WITHOUT ACTUALLY BEING THAT HELPFUL.

CHAPTER THREE: *Veg Oil*

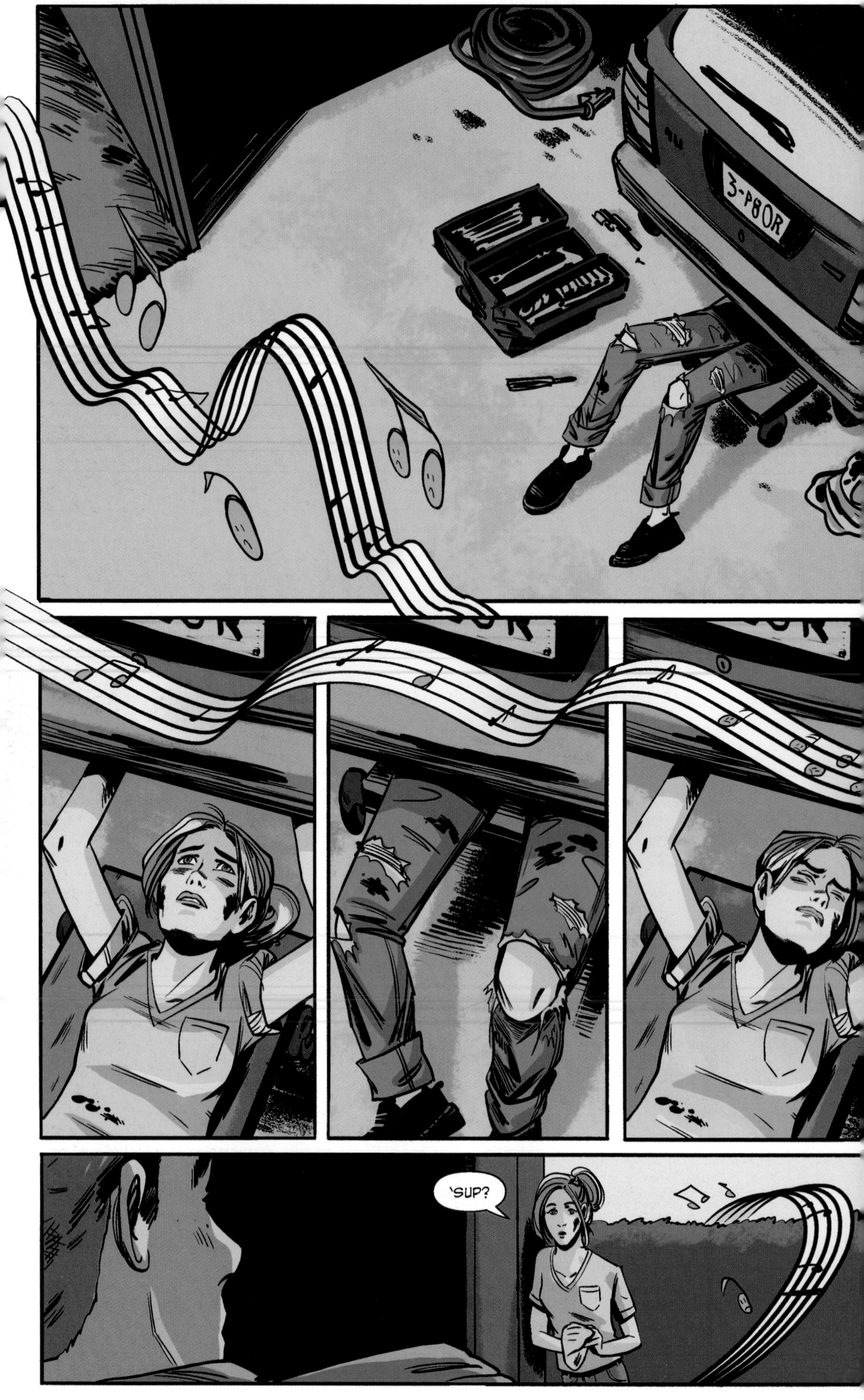
3-P8OR
'SUP?

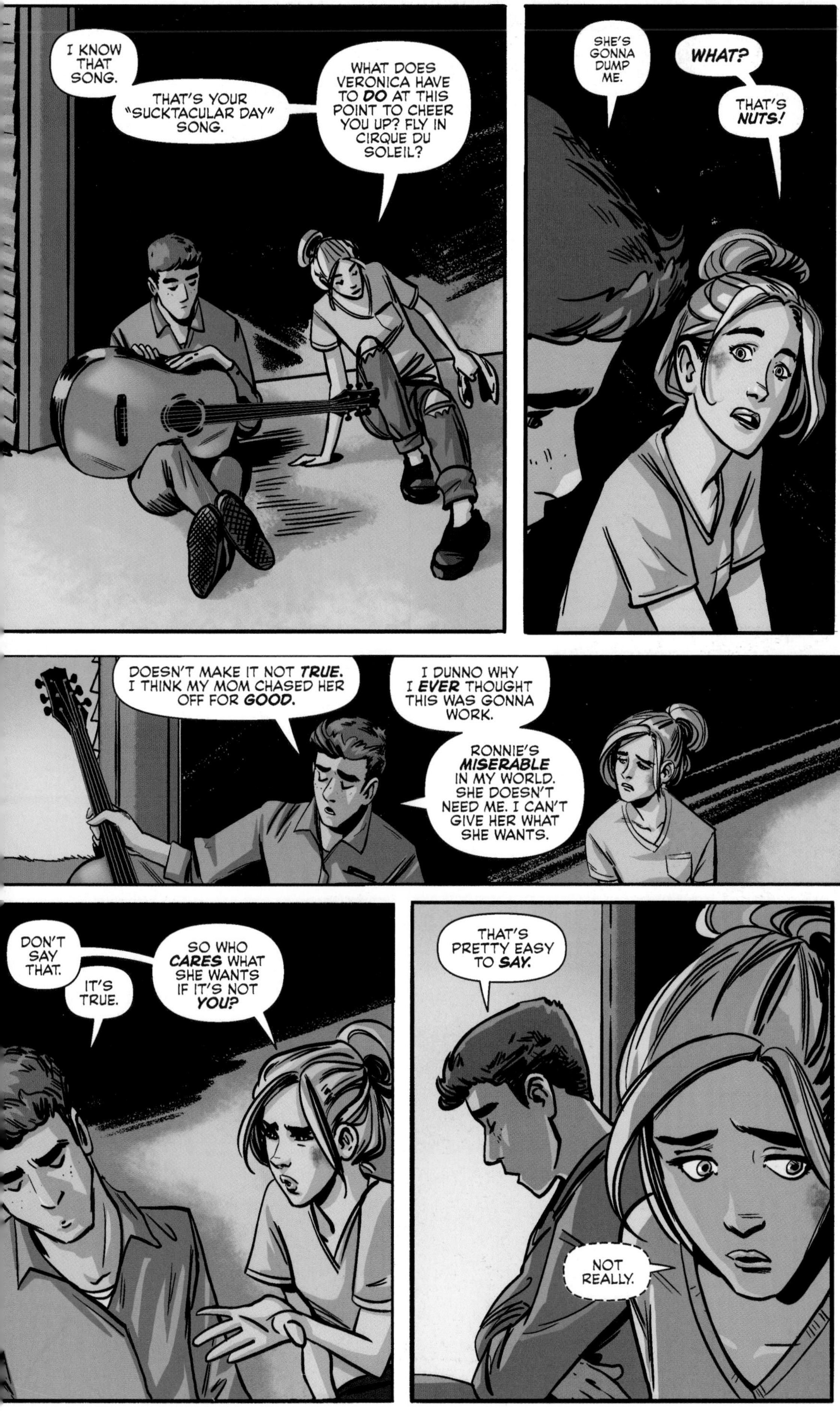
I KNOW THAT SONG.
THAT'S YOUR "SUCKTACULAR DAY" SONG.
WHAT DOES VERONICA HAVE TO *DO* AT THIS POINT TO CHEER YOU UP? FLY IN CIRQUE DU SOLEIL?
SHE'S GONNA DUMP ME.
WHAT?
THAT'S *NUTS!*
DOESN'T MAKE IT NOT *TRUE.* I THINK MY MOM CHASED HER OFF FOR *GOOD.*
I DUNNO WHY I *EVER* THOUGHT THIS WAS GONNA WORK.
RONNIE'S *MISERABLE* IN MY WORLD. SHE DOESN'T NEED ME. I CAN'T GIVE HER WHAT SHE WANTS.
DON'T SAY THAT.
IT'S TRUE.
SO WHO *CARES* WHAT SHE WANTS IF IT'S NOT *YOU?*
THAT'S PRETTY EASY TO *SAY.*
NOT REALLY.

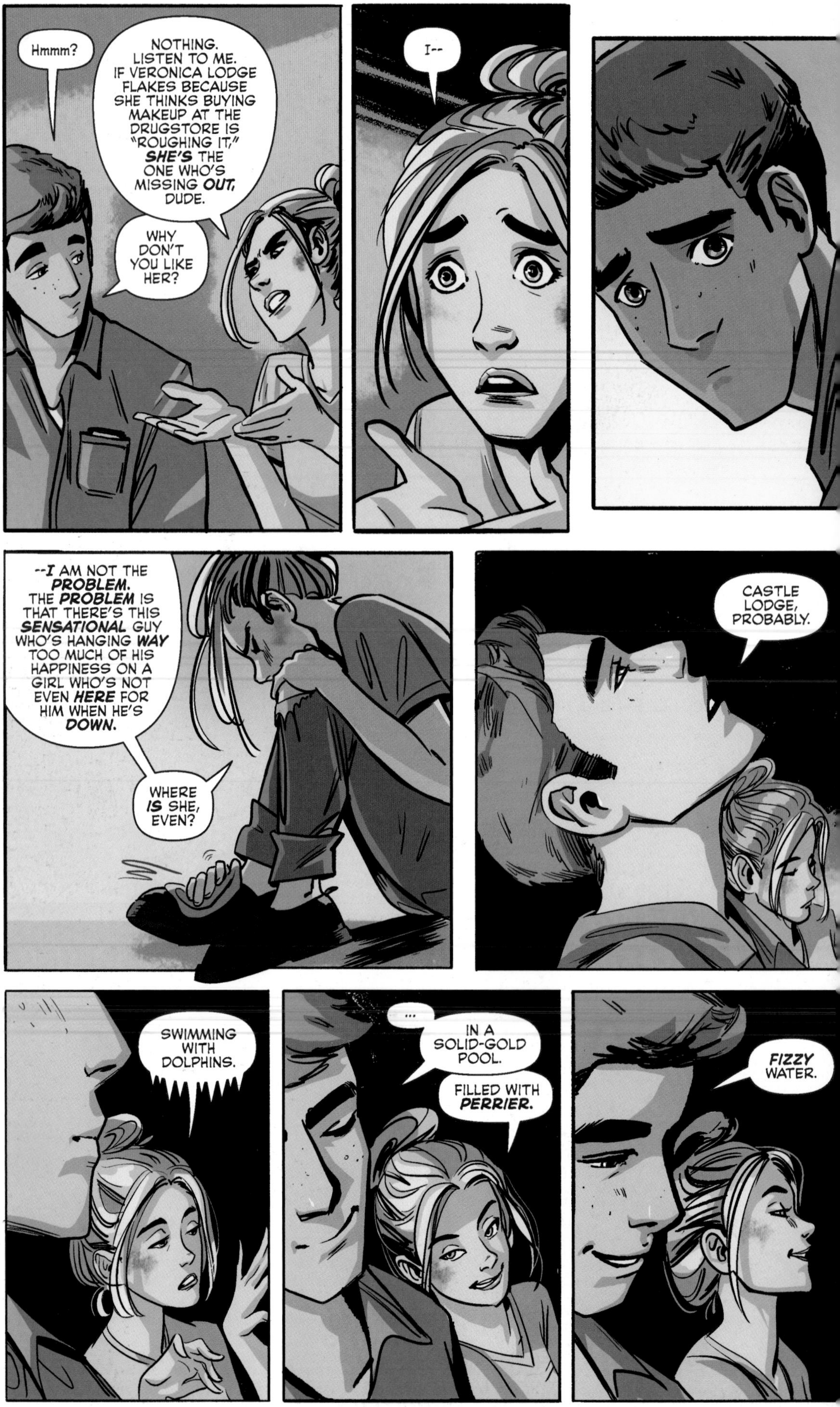
Hmmm?
NOTHING. LISTEN TO ME. IF VERONICA LODGE FLAKES BECAUSE SHE THINKS BUYING MAKEUP AT THE DRUGSTORE IS "ROUGHING IT," SHE'S THE ONE WHO'S MISSING OUT, DUDE.
WHY DON'T YOU LIKE HER?
I--
--I AM NOT THE PROBLEM. THE PROBLEM IS THAT THERE'S THIS SENSATIONAL GUY WHO'S HANGING WAY TOO MUCH OF HIS HAPPINESS ON A GIRL WHO'S NOT EVEN HERE FOR HIM WHEN HE'S DOWN.
WHERE IS SHE, EVEN?
CASTLE LODGE, PROBABLY.
SWIMMING WITH DOLPHINS.
...
IN A SOLID-GOLD POOL.
FILLED WITH PERRIER.
FIZZY WATER.

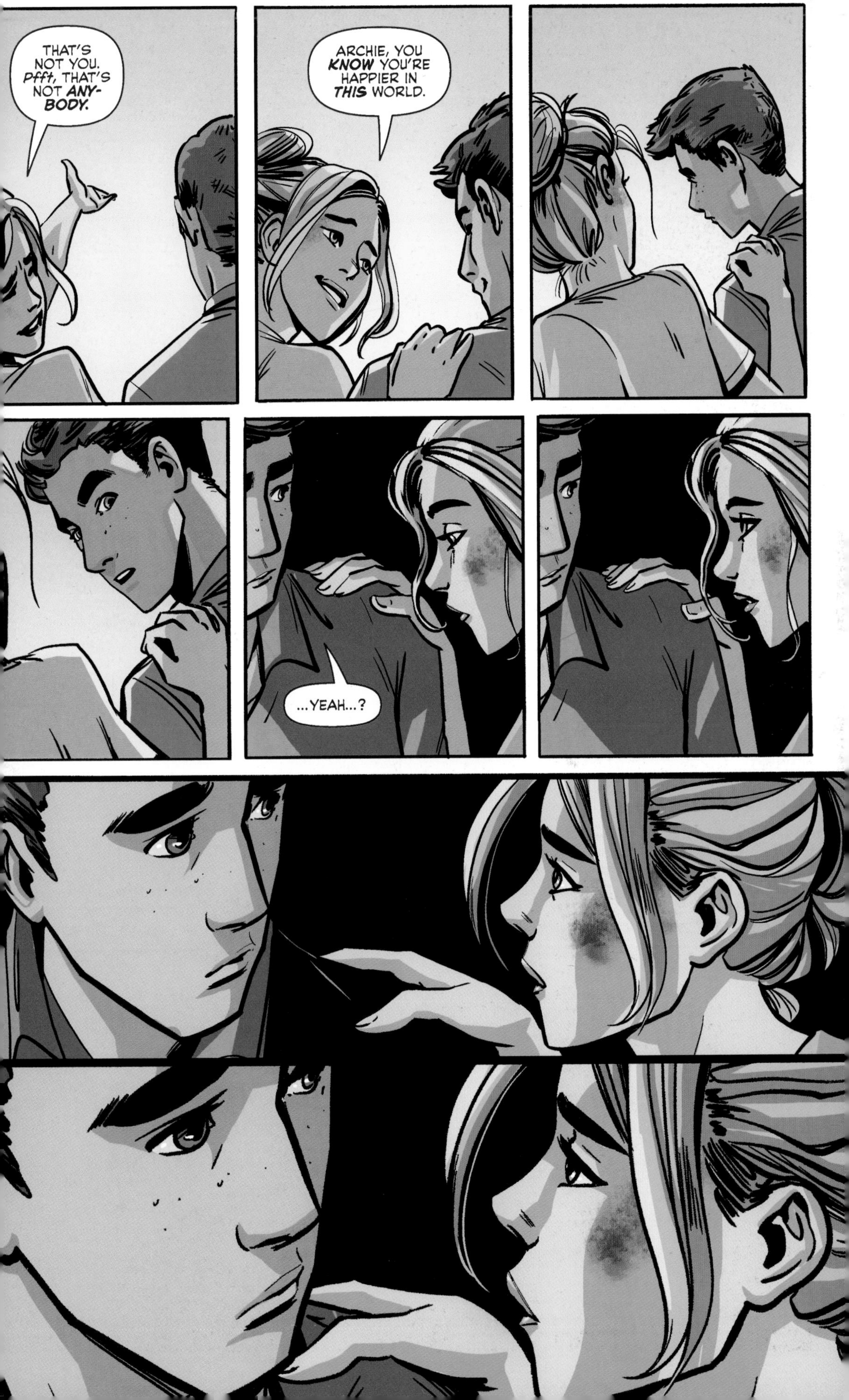
THAT'S NOT YOU. *Pfft,* THAT'S NOT **ANY-BODY.**
ARCHIE, YOU **KNOW** YOU'RE HAPPIER IN **THIS** WORLD.
...YEAH...?

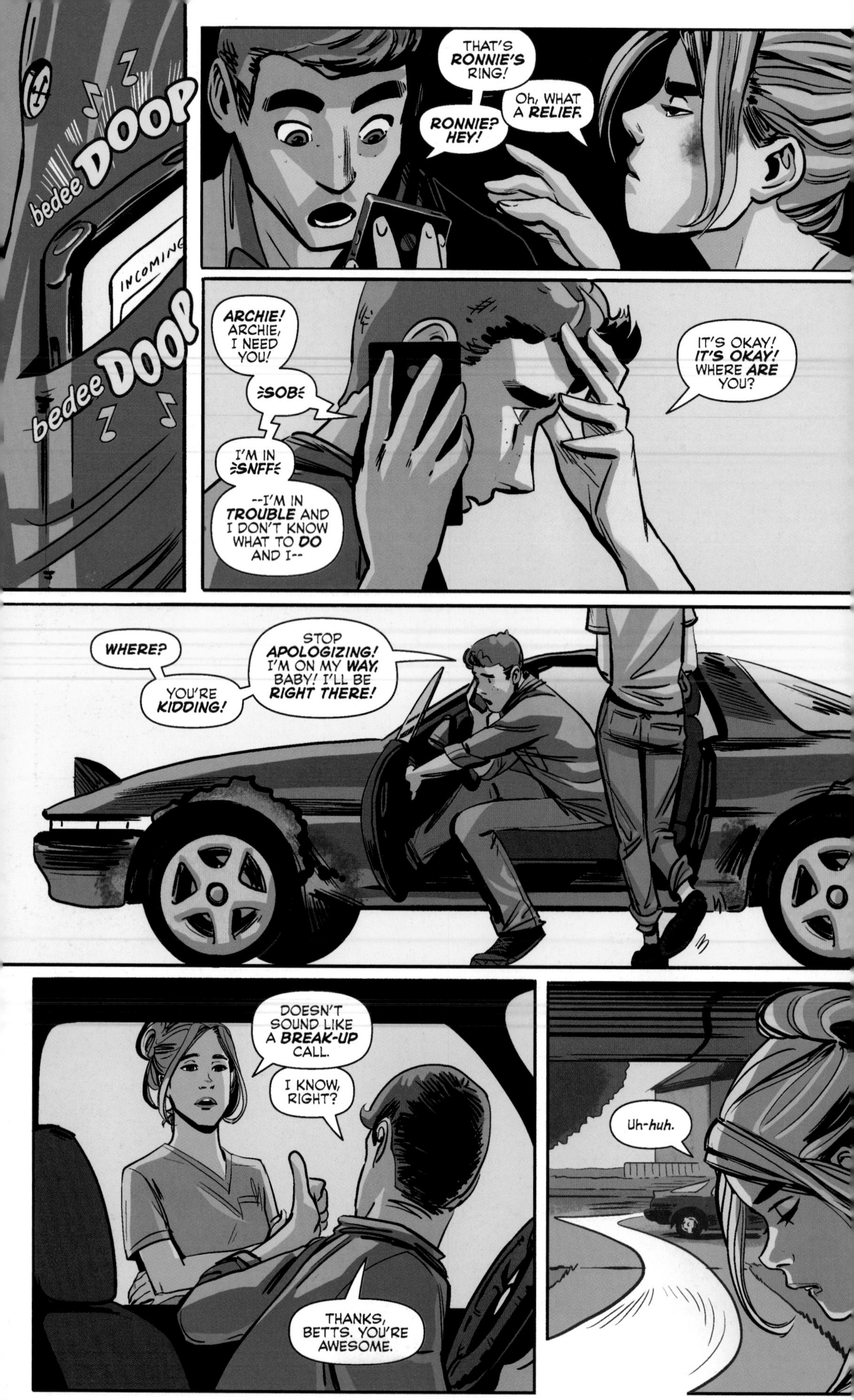
bedee DOOP
INCOMING
bedee DOOP
THAT'S RONNIE'S RING!
RONNIE? HEY!
Oh, WHAT A RELIEF.
ARCHIE! ARCHIE, I NEED YOU!
SOB
I'M IN SNFF
--I'M IN TROUBLE AND I DON'T KNOW WHAT TO DO AND I--
IT'S OKAY! IT'S OKAY! WHERE ARE YOU?
WHERE?
YOU'RE KIDDING!
STOP APOLOGIZING! I'M ON MY WAY, BABY! I'LL BE RIGHT THERE!
DOESN'T SOUND LIKE A BREAK-UP CALL.
I KNOW, RIGHT?
THANKS, BETTS. YOU'RE AWESOME.
Uh-huh.

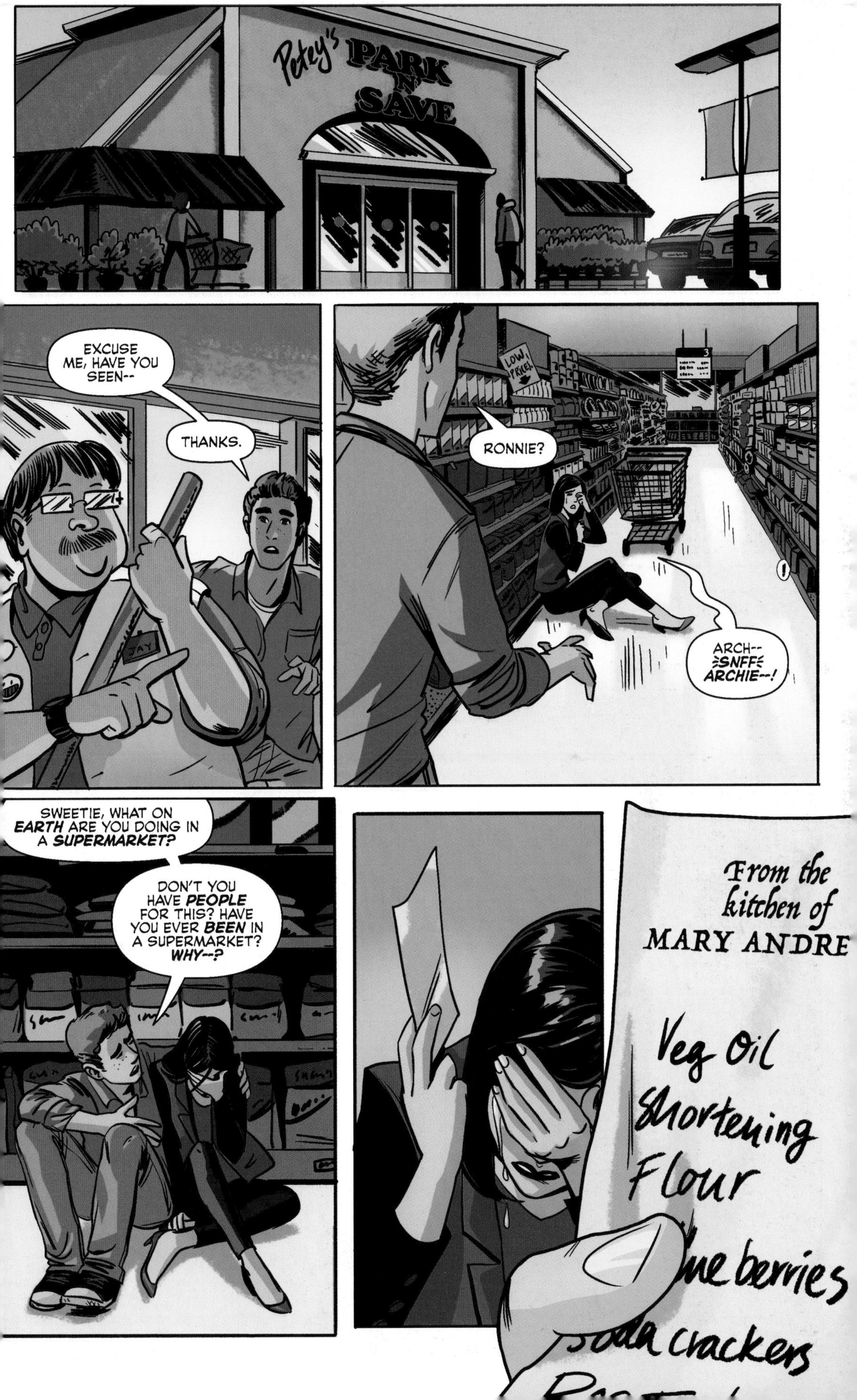
Petey's PARK N' SAVE
EXCUSE ME, HAVE YOU SEEN--
THANKS.
JAY
LOW PRICE!
RONNIE?
!
ARCH-- SNFF ARCHIE--!
SWEETIE, WHAT ON EARTH ARE YOU DOING IN A SUPERMARKET?
DON'T YOU HAVE PEOPLE FOR THIS? HAVE YOU EVER BEEN IN A SUPERMARKET? WHY--?
From the kitchen of MARY ANDRE
Veg Oil
Shortening
Flour
soda crackers

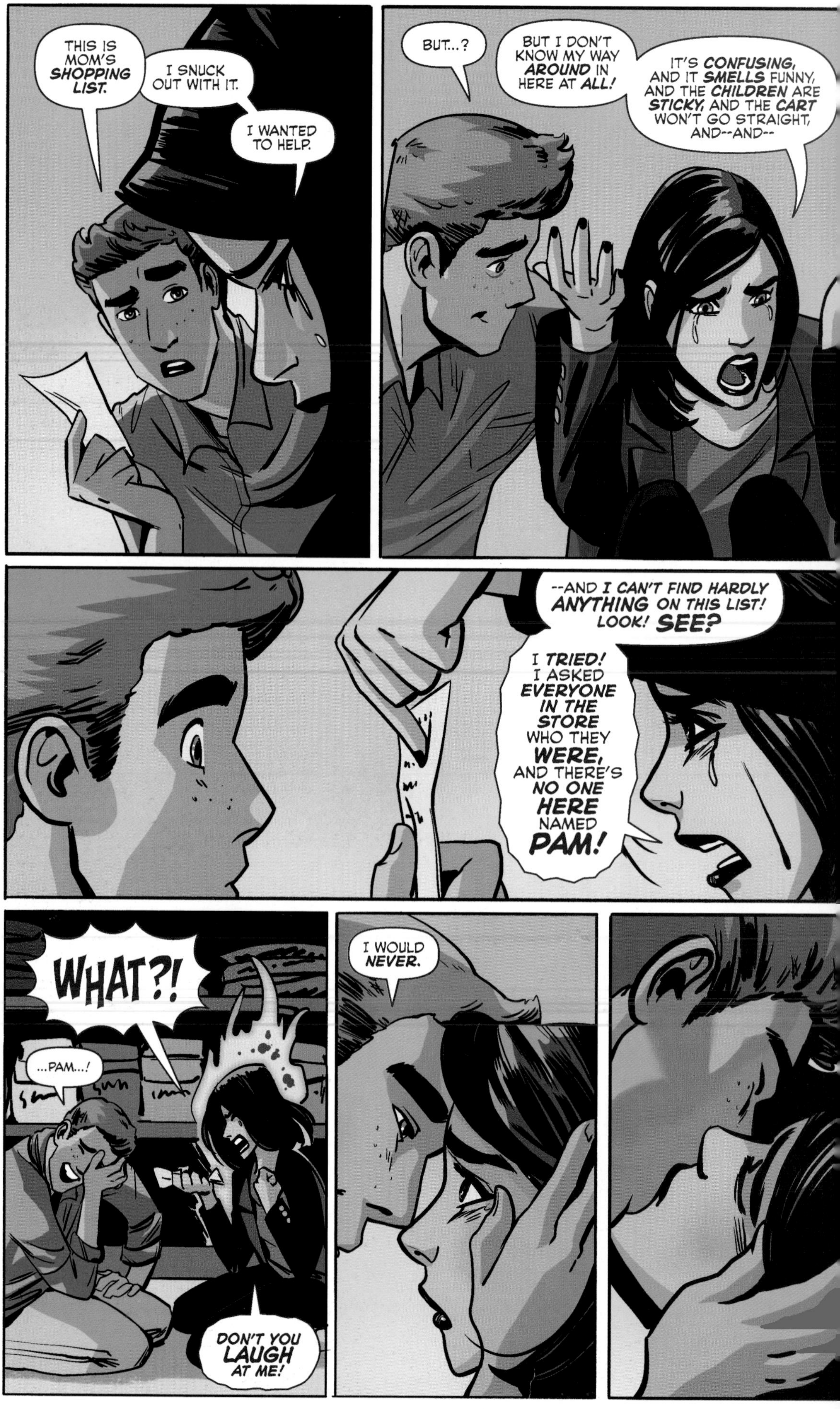

THIS IS MOM'S SHOPPING LIST.
I SNUCK OUT WITH IT.
I WANTED TO HELP.
BUT...?
BUT I DON'T KNOW MY WAY AROUND IN HERE AT ALL!
IT'S CONFUSING, AND IT SMELLS FUNNY, AND THE CHILDREN ARE STICKY, AND THE CART WON'T GO STRAIGHT, AND--AND--
--AND I CAN'T FIND HARDLY ANYTHING ON THIS LIST! LOOK! SEE?
I TRIED! I ASKED EVERYONE IN THE STORE WHO THEY WERE, AND THERE'S NO ONE HERE NAMED PAM!
WHAT?!
...PAM...!
DON'T YOU LAUGH AT ME!
I WOULD NEVER.

CHAPTER FOUR:

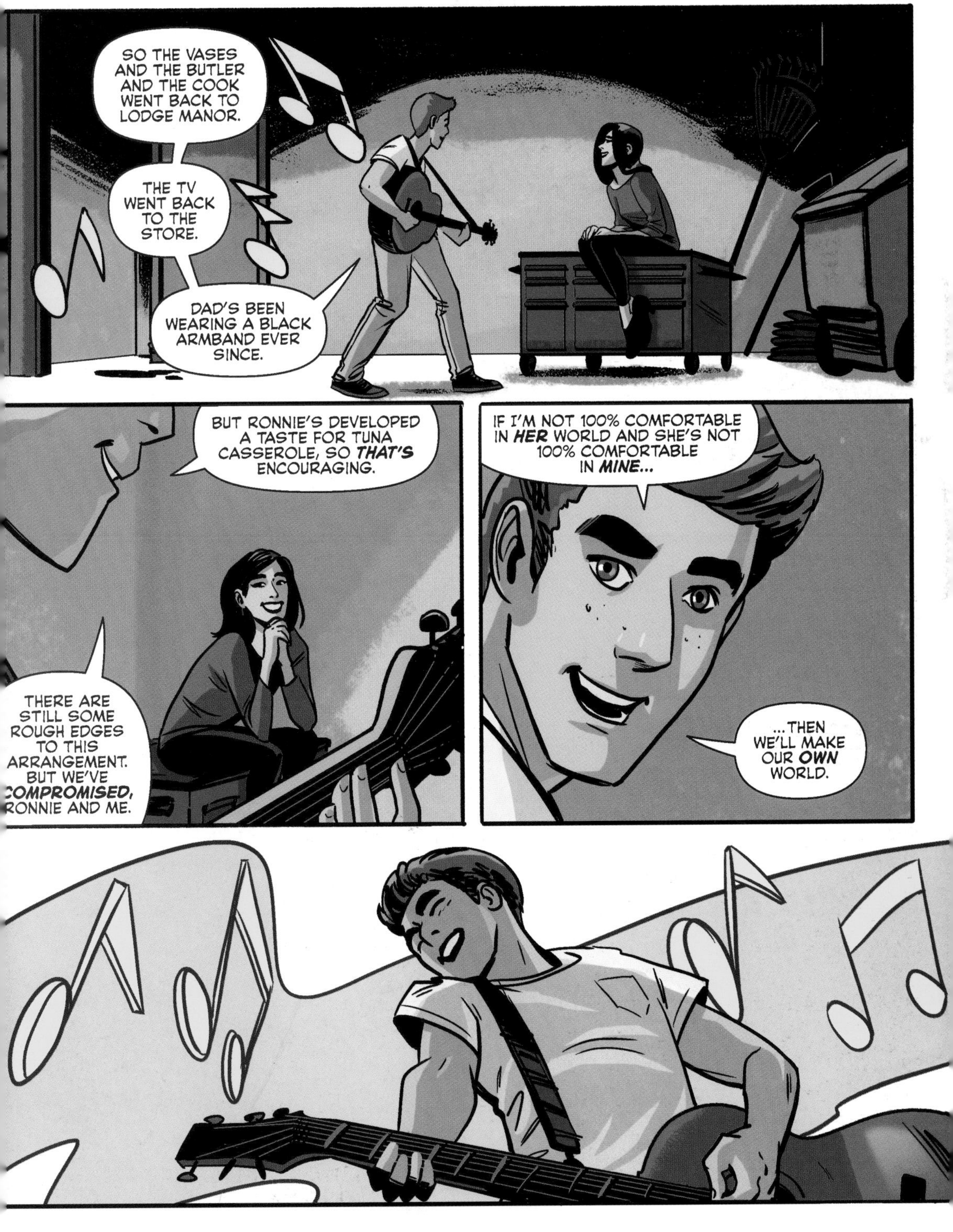
SO THE VASES AND THE BUTLER AND THE COOK WENT BACK TO LODGE MANOR.
THE TV WENT BACK TO THE STORE.
DAD'S BEEN WEARING A BLACK ARMBAND EVER SINCE.
BUT RONNIE'S DEVELOPED A TASTE FOR TUNA CASSEROLE, SO *THAT'S* ENCOURAGING.
THERE ARE STILL SOME ROUGH EDGES TO THIS ARRANGEMENT. BUT WE'VE *COMPROMISED,* RONNIE AND ME.
IF I'M NOT 100% COMFORTABLE IN *HER* WORLD AND SHE'S NOT 100% COMFORTABLE IN *MINE...*
...THEN WE'LL MAKE OUR *OWN* WORLD.

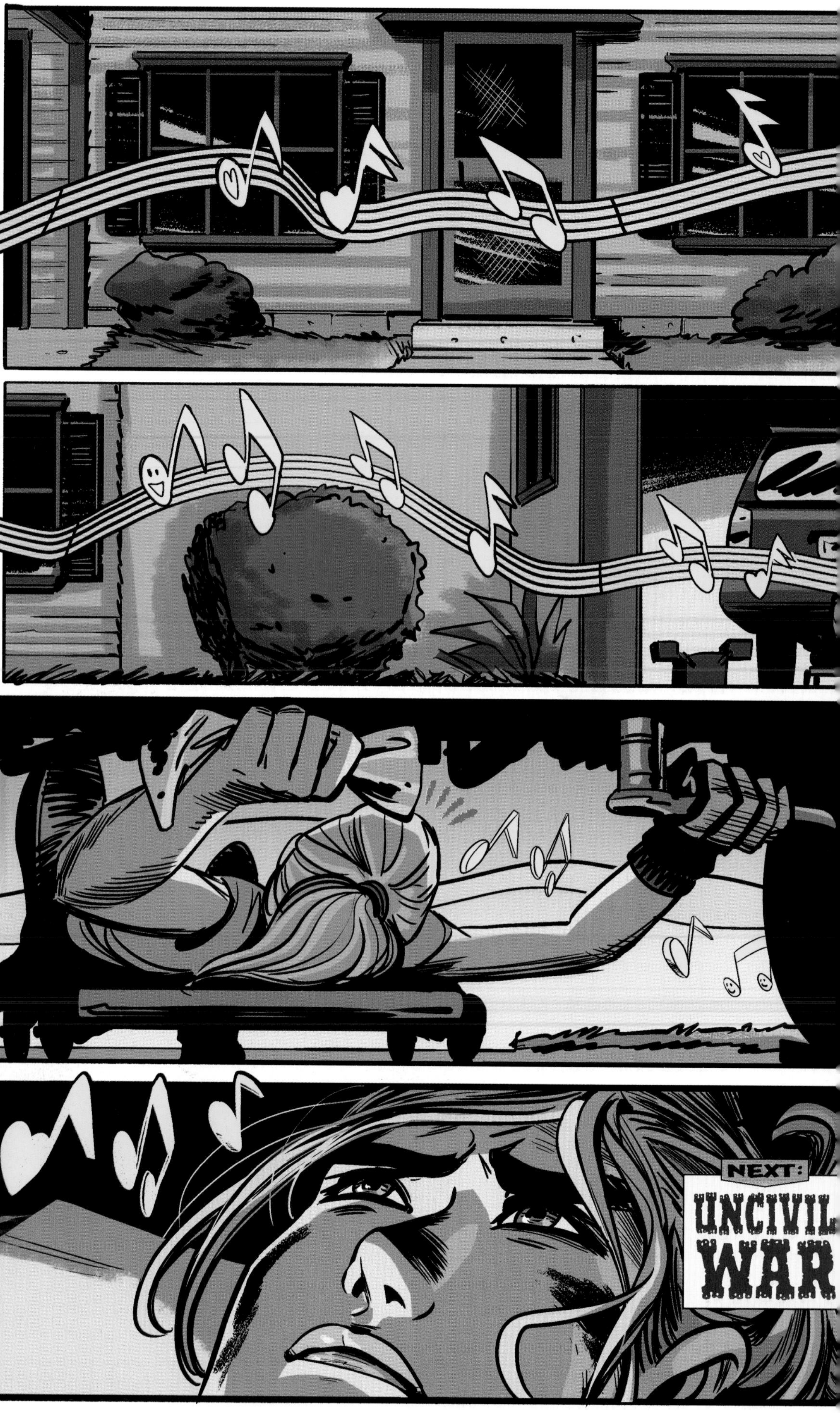
NEXT:
UNCIVIL WAR

TO BE CONTINUED...

ISSUE TEN

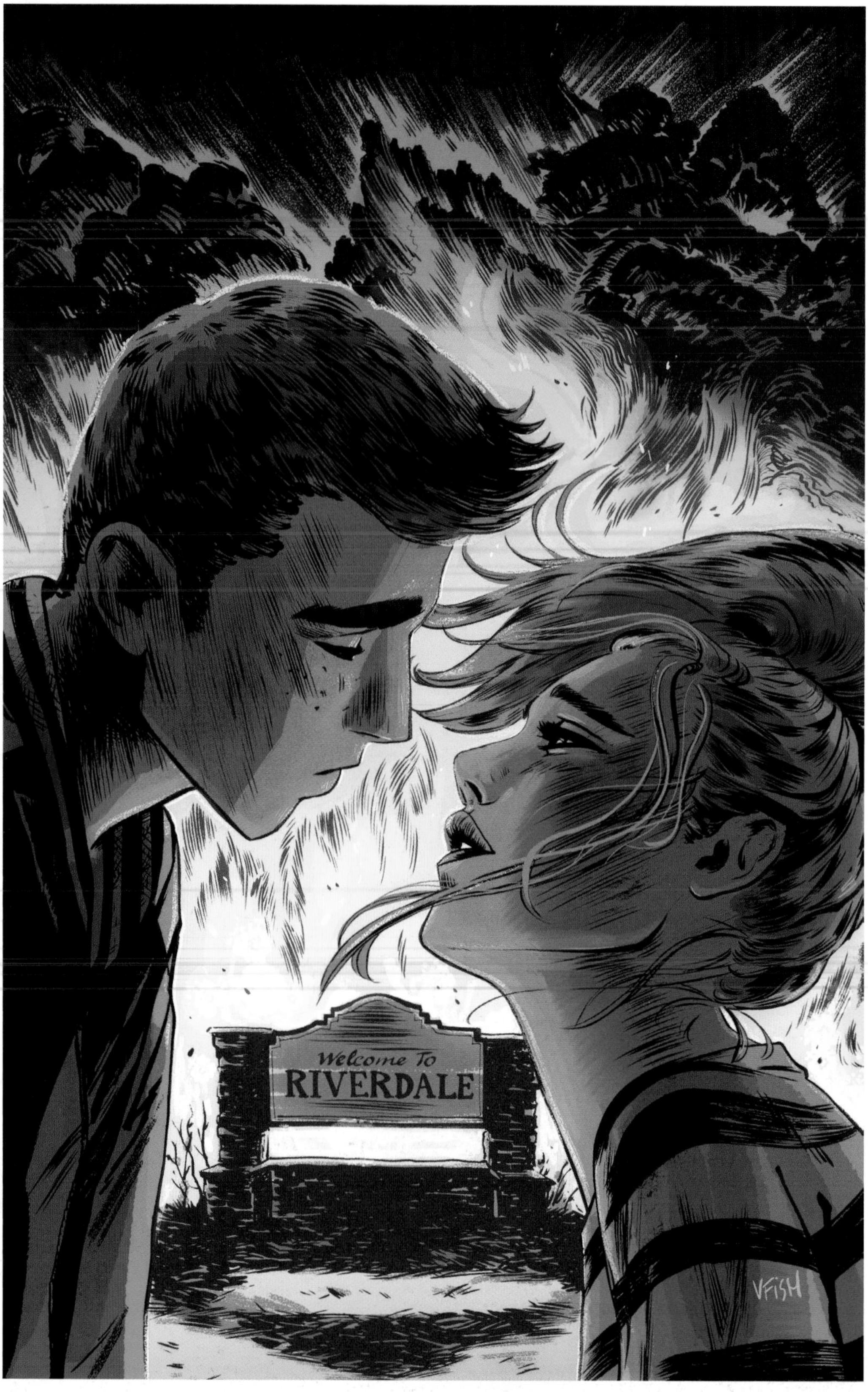
Welcome To
RIVERDALE
VFISH

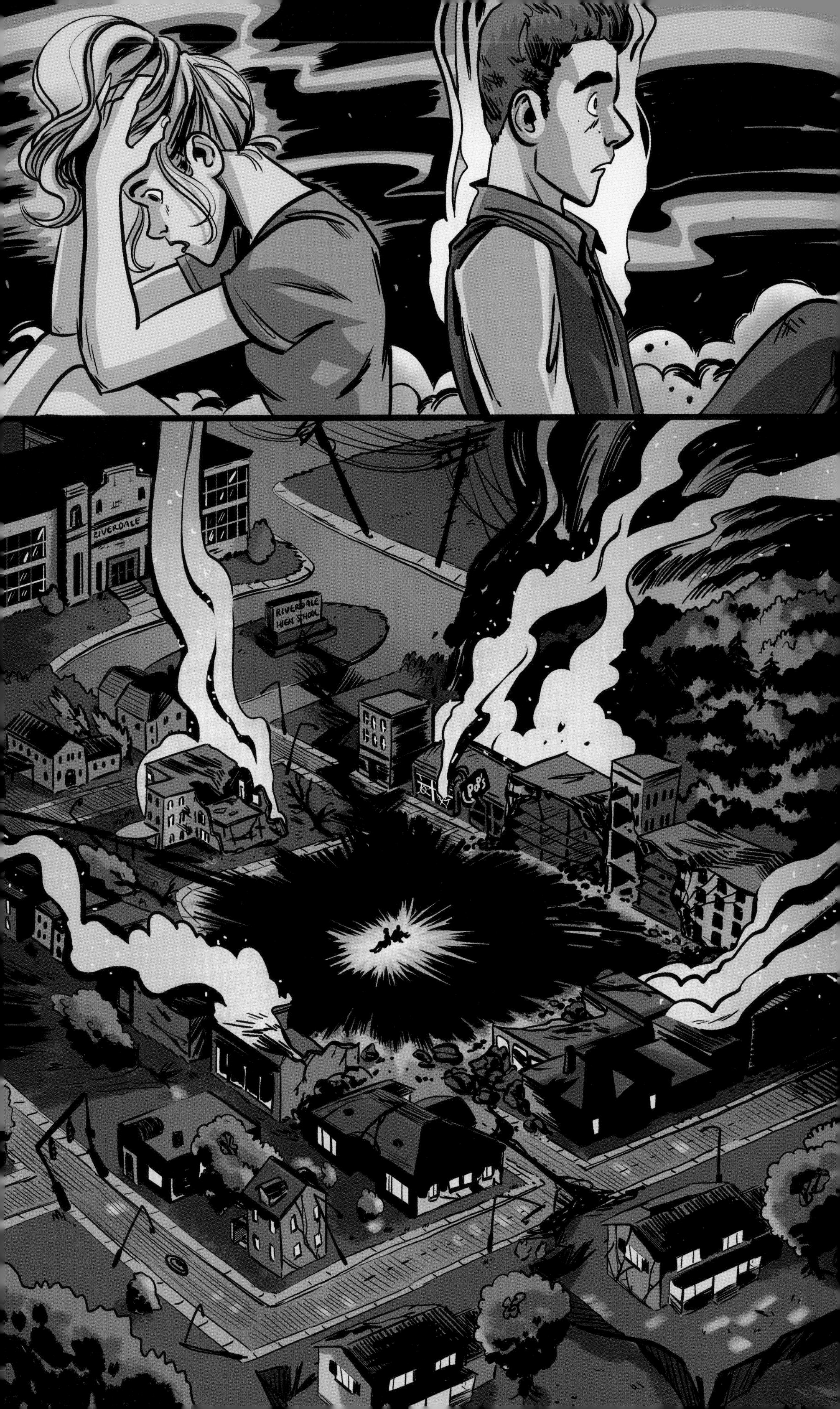
RIVERDALE
RIVERDALE HIGH SCHOOL
Pop's

CHAPTER ONE: I THOUGHT HE WAS A VALET

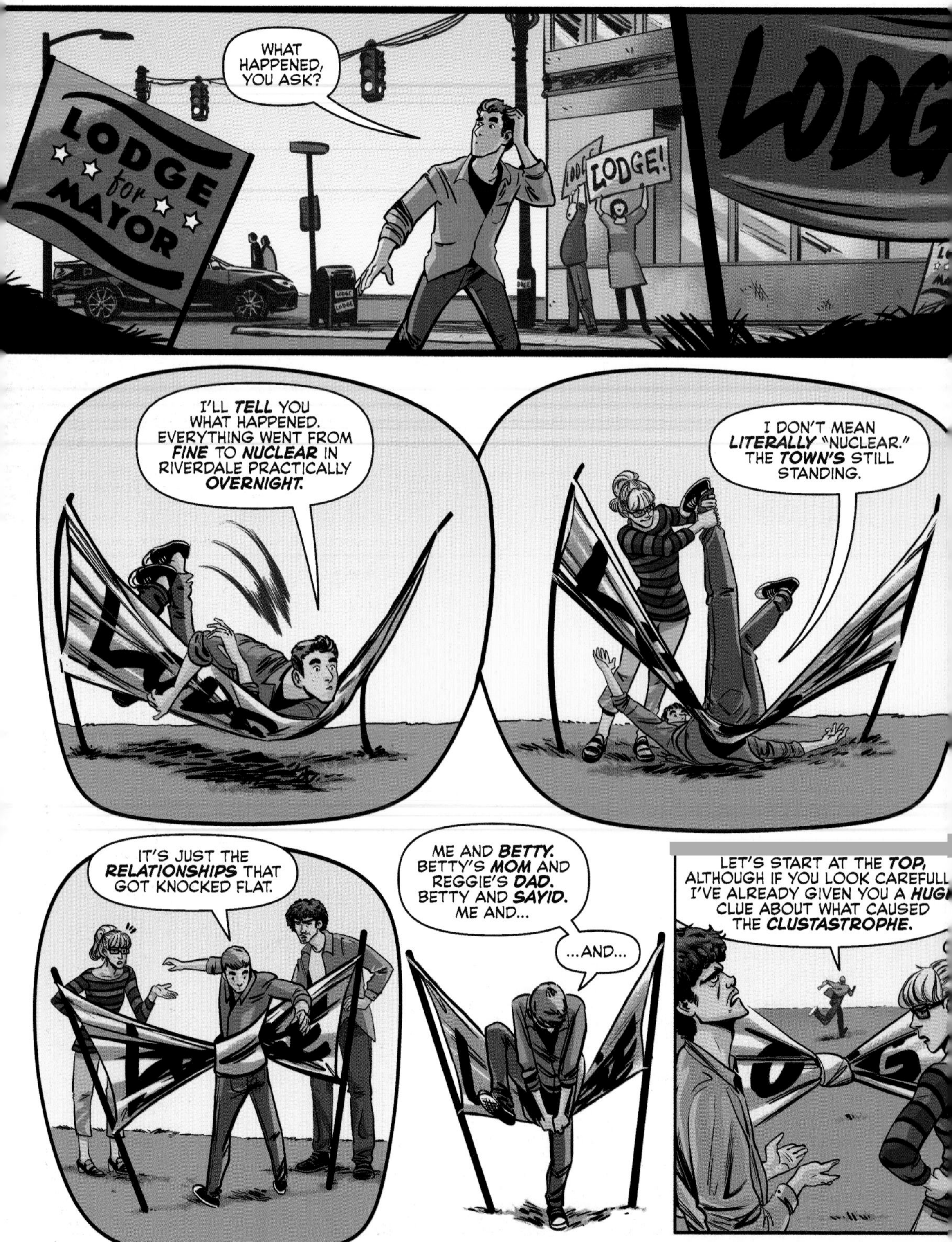
LODGE for MAYOR
WHAT HAPPENED, YOU ASK?
LODGE!
LODGE
I'LL TELL YOU WHAT HAPPENED. EVERYTHING WENT FROM FINE TO NUCLEAR IN RIVERDALE PRACTICALLY OVERNIGHT.
I DON'T MEAN LITERALLY "NUCLEAR." THE TOWN'S STILL STANDING.
IT'S JUST THE RELATIONSHIPS THAT GOT KNOCKED FLAT.
ME AND BETTY. BETTY'S MOM AND REGGIE'S DAD. BETTY AND SAYID. ME AND...
...AND...
LET'S START AT THE TOP, ALTHOUGH IF YOU LOOK CAREFULL I'VE ALREADY GIVEN YOU A HUG CLUE ABOUT WHAT CAUSED THE CLUSTASTROPHE.

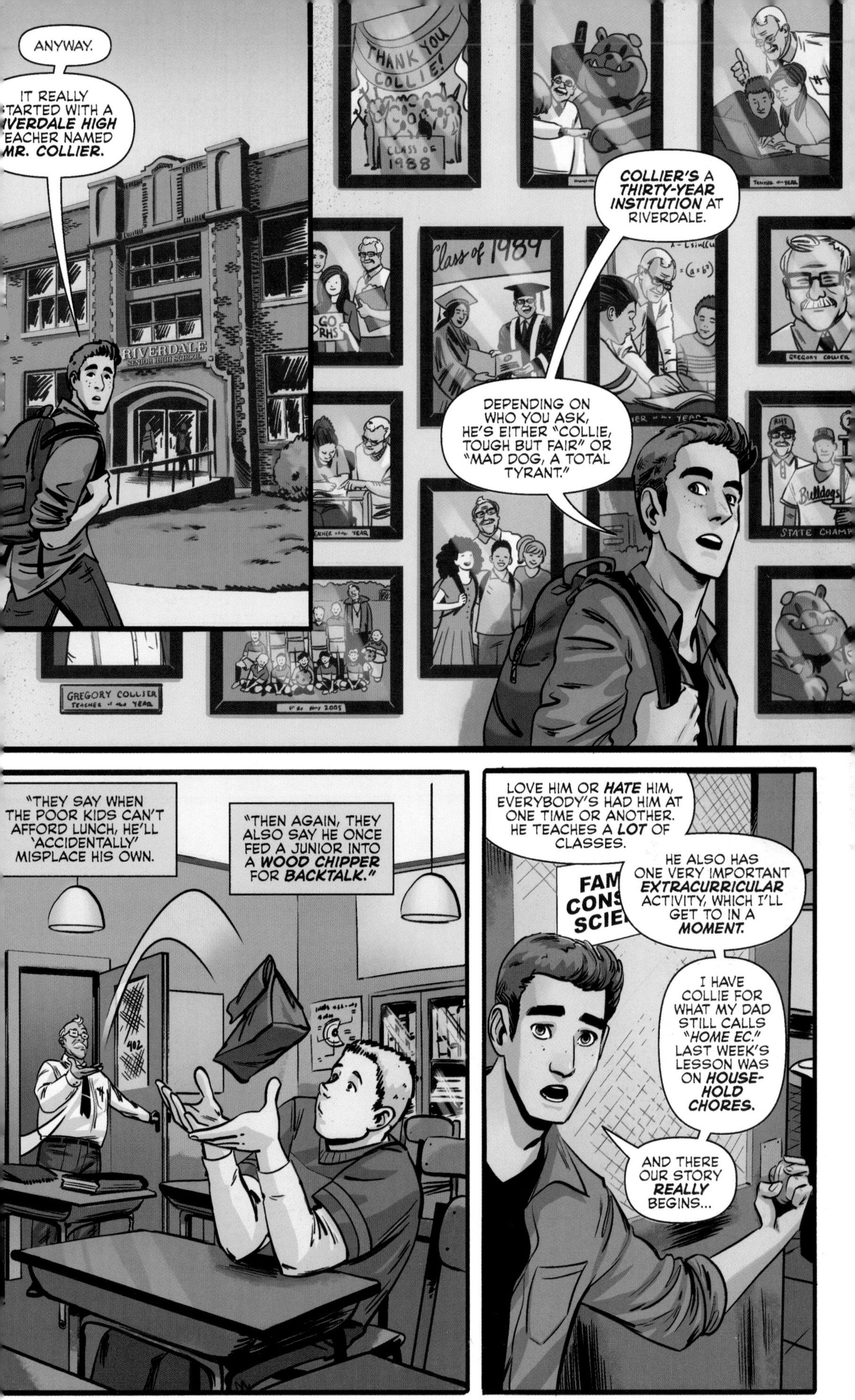

ANYWAY.
IT REALLY STARTED WITH A RIVERDALE HIGH TEACHER NAMED MR. COLLIER.
RIVERDALE SENIOR HIGH SCHOOL
THANK YOU COLLIE!
CLASS OF 1988
COLLIER'S A THIRTY-YEAR INSTITUTION AT RIVERDALE.
GO RHS
Class of 1989
GREGORY COLLIER
DEPENDING ON WHO YOU ASK, HE'S EITHER "COLLIE, TOUGH BUT FAIR" OR "MAD DOG, A TOTAL TYRANT."
STATE CHAMP
GREGORY COLLIER TEACHER of the YEAR
"THEY SAY WHEN THE POOR KIDS CAN'T AFFORD LUNCH, HE'LL 'ACCIDENTALLY' MISPLACE HIS OWN.
"THEN AGAIN, THEY ALSO SAY HE ONCE FED A JUNIOR INTO A WOOD CHIPPER FOR BACKTALK."
402
LOVE HIM OR HATE HIM, EVERYBODY'S HAD HIM AT ONE TIME OR ANOTHER. HE TEACHES A LOT OF CLASSES.
HE ALSO HAS ONE VERY IMPORTANT EXTRACURRICULAR ACTIVITY, WHICH I'LL GET TO IN A MOMENT.
I HAVE COLLIE FOR WHAT MY DAD STILL CALLS "HOME EC." LAST WEEK'S LESSON WAS ON HOUSE-HOLD CHORES.
AND THERE OUR STORY REALLY BEGINS...

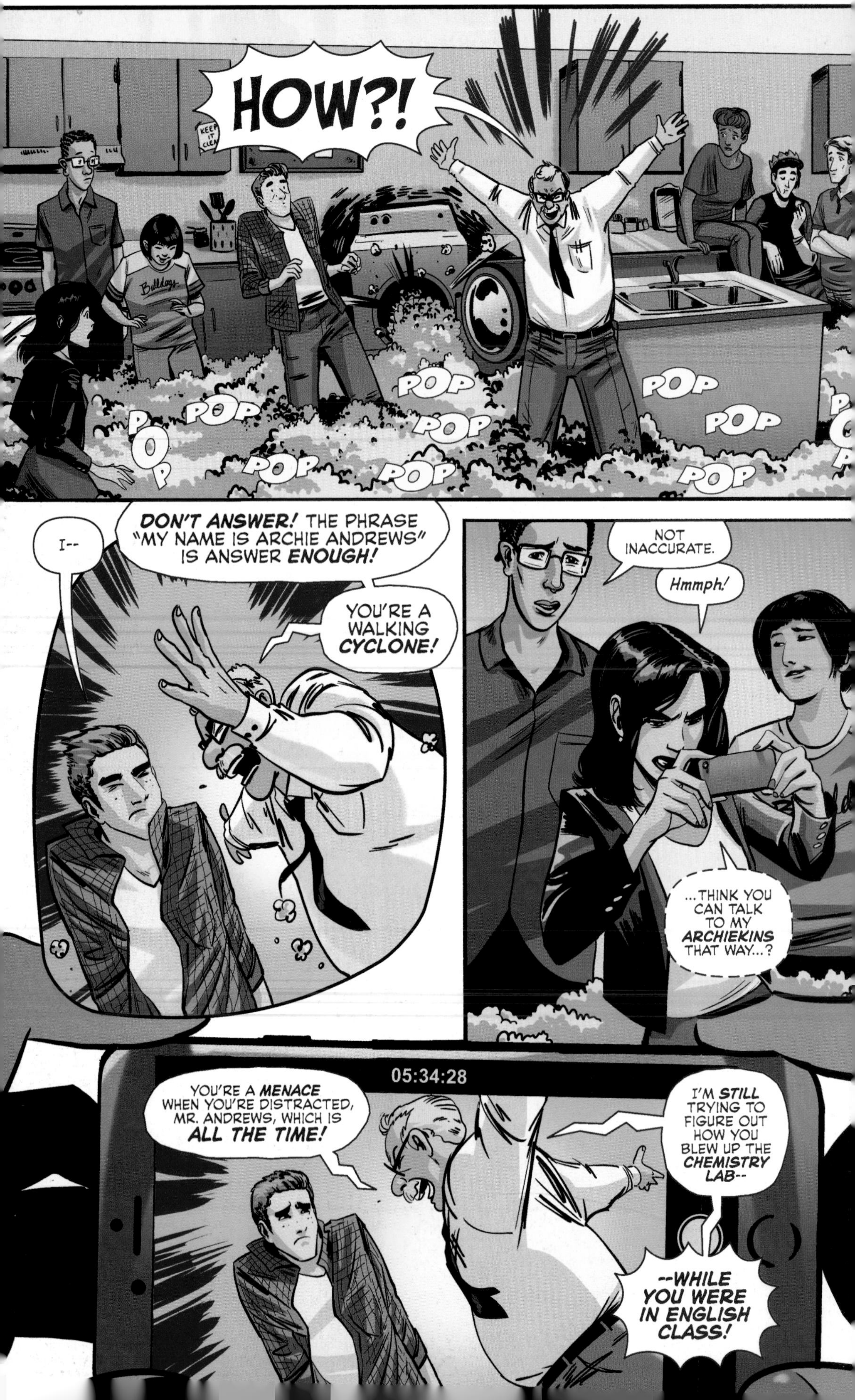
HOW?!
KEEP IT CLEA
Bulldogs
POP
POP
POP
POP
POP
POP
POP
POP
POP
I--
DON'T ANSWER! THE PHRASE "MY NAME IS ARCHIE ANDREWS" IS ANSWER ENOUGH!
YOU'RE A WALKING CYCLONE!
NOT INACCURATE.
Hmmph!
...THINK YOU CAN TALK TO MY ARCHIEKINS THAT WAY...?
05:34:28
YOU'RE A MENACE WHEN YOU'RE DISTRACTED, MR. ANDREWS, WHICH IS ALL THE TIME!
I'M STILL TRYING TO FIGURE OUT HOW YOU BLEW UP THE CHEMISTRY LAB--
--WHILE YOU WERE IN ENGLISH CLASS!

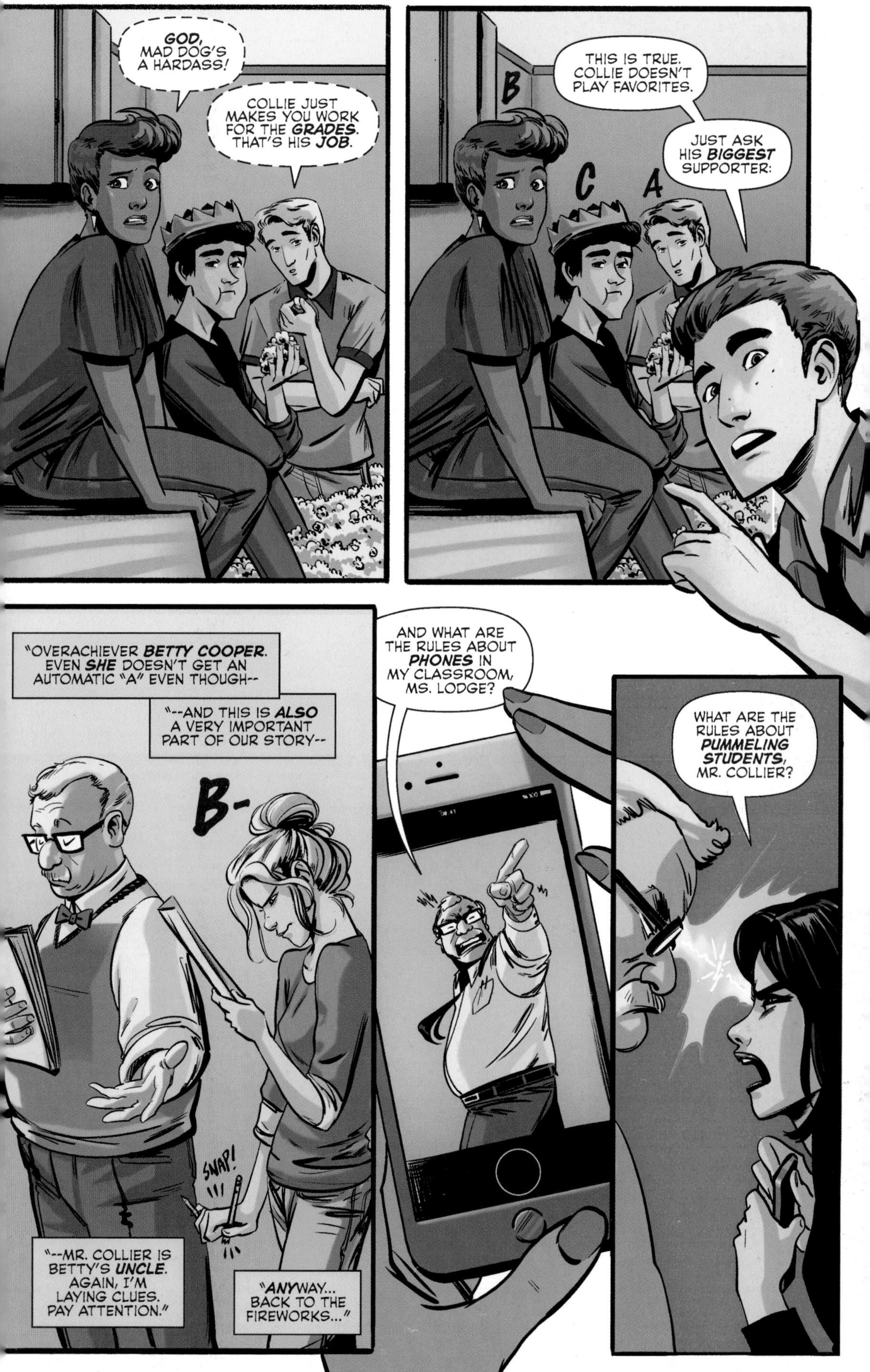
GOD, MAD DOG'S A HARDASS!
COLLIE JUST MAKES YOU WORK FOR THE GRADES. THAT'S HIS JOB.
THIS IS TRUE. COLLIE DOESN'T PLAY FAVORITES.
B
C
A
JUST ASK HIS BIGGEST SUPPORTER:
"OVERACHIEVER BETTY COOPER. EVEN SHE DOESN'T GET AN AUTOMATIC "A" EVEN THOUGH--
"--AND THIS IS ALSO A VERY IMPORTANT PART OF OUR STORY--
B-
SNAP!
"--MR. COLLIER IS BETTY'S UNCLE. AGAIN, I'M LAYING CLUES. PAY ATTENTION."
"ANYWAY... BACK TO THE FIREWORKS..."
AND WHAT ARE THE RULES ABOUT PHONES IN MY CLASSROOM, MS. LODGE?
WHAT ARE THE RULES ABOUT PUMMELING STUDENTS, MR. COLLIER?

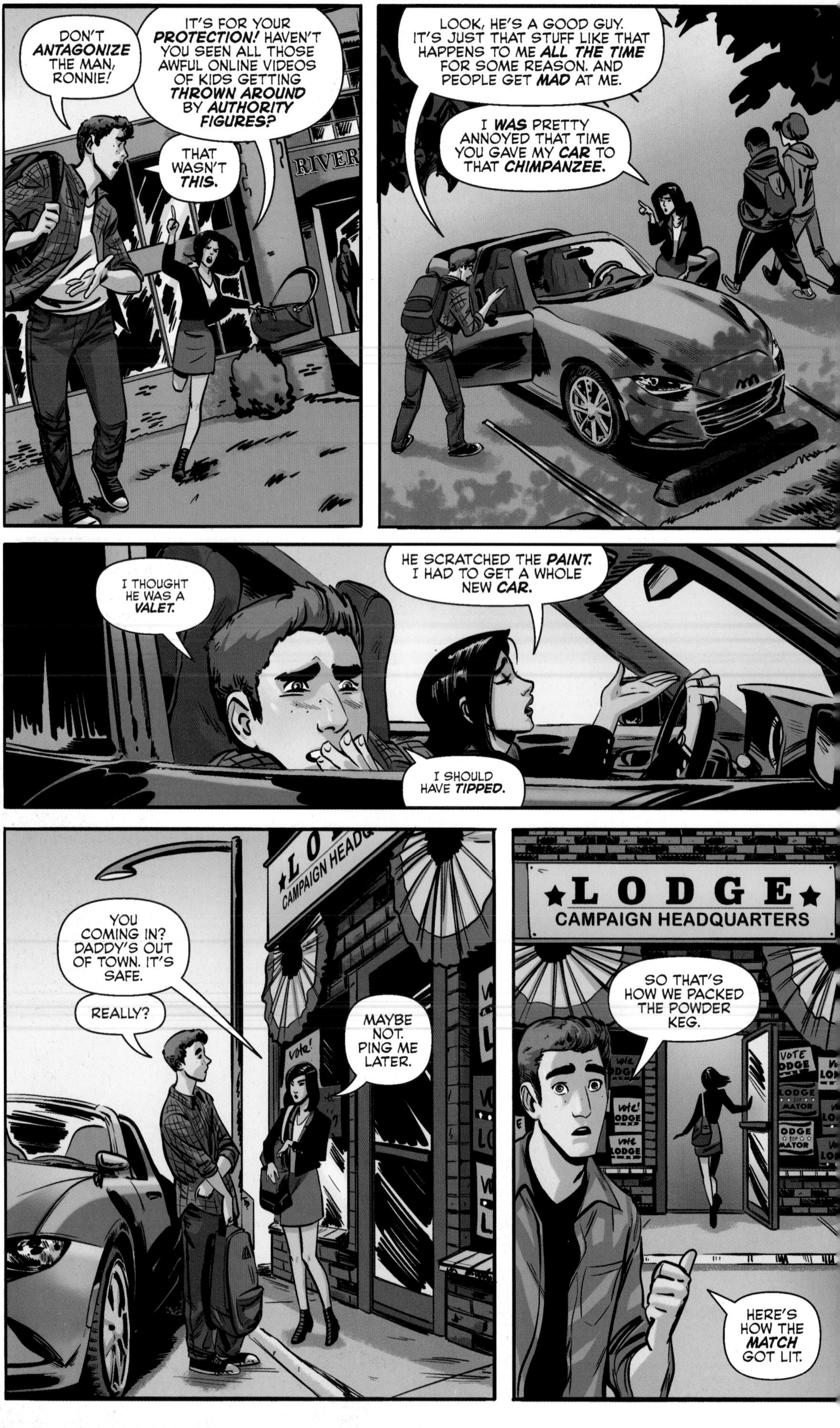

DON'T ANTAGONIZE THE MAN, RONNIE!
IT'S FOR YOUR PROTECTION! HAVEN'T YOU SEEN ALL THOSE AWFUL ONLINE VIDEOS OF KIDS GETTING THROWN AROUND BY AUTHORITY FIGURES?
THAT WASN'T THIS.
RIVER
LOOK, HE'S A GOOD GUY. IT'S JUST THAT STUFF LIKE THAT HAPPENS TO ME ALL THE TIME FOR SOME REASON. AND PEOPLE GET MAD AT ME.
I WAS PRETTY ANNOYED THAT TIME YOU GAVE MY CAR TO THAT CHIMPANZEE.
I THOUGHT HE WAS A VALET.
HE SCRATCHED THE PAINT. I HAD TO GET A WHOLE NEW CAR.
I SHOULD HAVE TIPPED.
YOU COMING IN? DADDY'S OUT OF TOWN. IT'S SAFE.
REALLY?
MAYBE NOT. PING ME LATER.
★LODGE★
CAMPAIGN HEADQUARTERS
SO THAT'S HOW WE PACKED THE POWDER KEG.
HERE'S HOW THE MATCH GOT LIT.

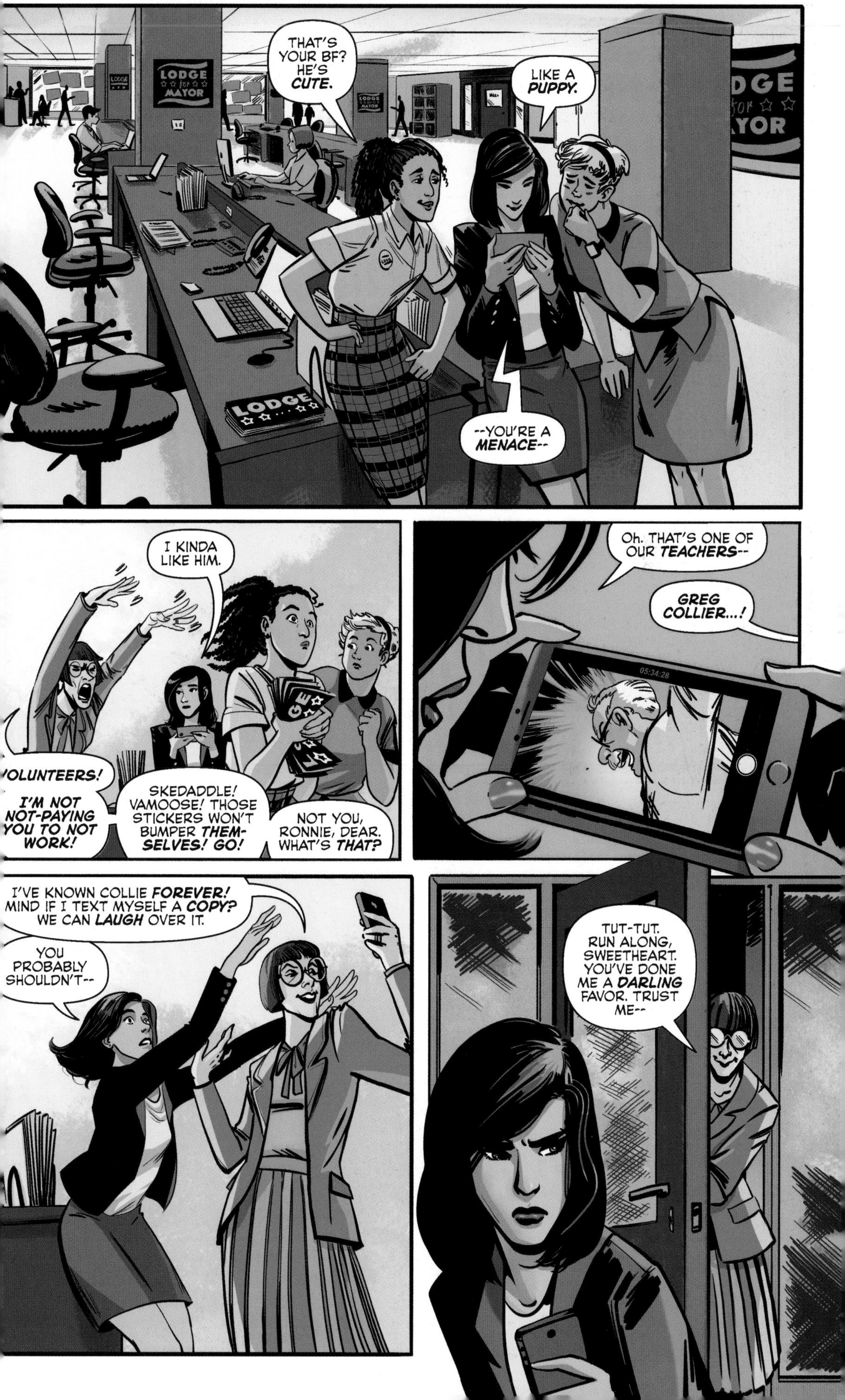
LODGE for MAYOR
THAT'S YOUR BF? HE'S *CUTE.*
LIKE A *PUPPY.*
--YOU'RE A *MENACE*--
LODGE
I KINDA LIKE HIM.
VOLUNTEERS!
I'M NOT NOT-PAYING YOU TO NOT WORK!
SKEDADDLE! VAMOOSE! THOSE STICKERS WON'T BUMPER *THEM-SELVES! GO!*
NOT YOU, RONNIE, DEAR. WHAT'S *THAT?*
Oh. THAT'S ONE OF OUR *TEACHERS*--
GREG COLLIER...!
05:34:28
I'VE KNOWN COLLIE *FOREVER!* MIND IF I TEXT MYSELF A *COPY?* WE CAN *LAUGH* OVER IT.
YOU PROBABLY SHOULDN'T--
TUT-TUT. RUN ALONG, SWEETHEART. YOU'VE DONE ME A *DARLING* FAVOR. TRUST ME--

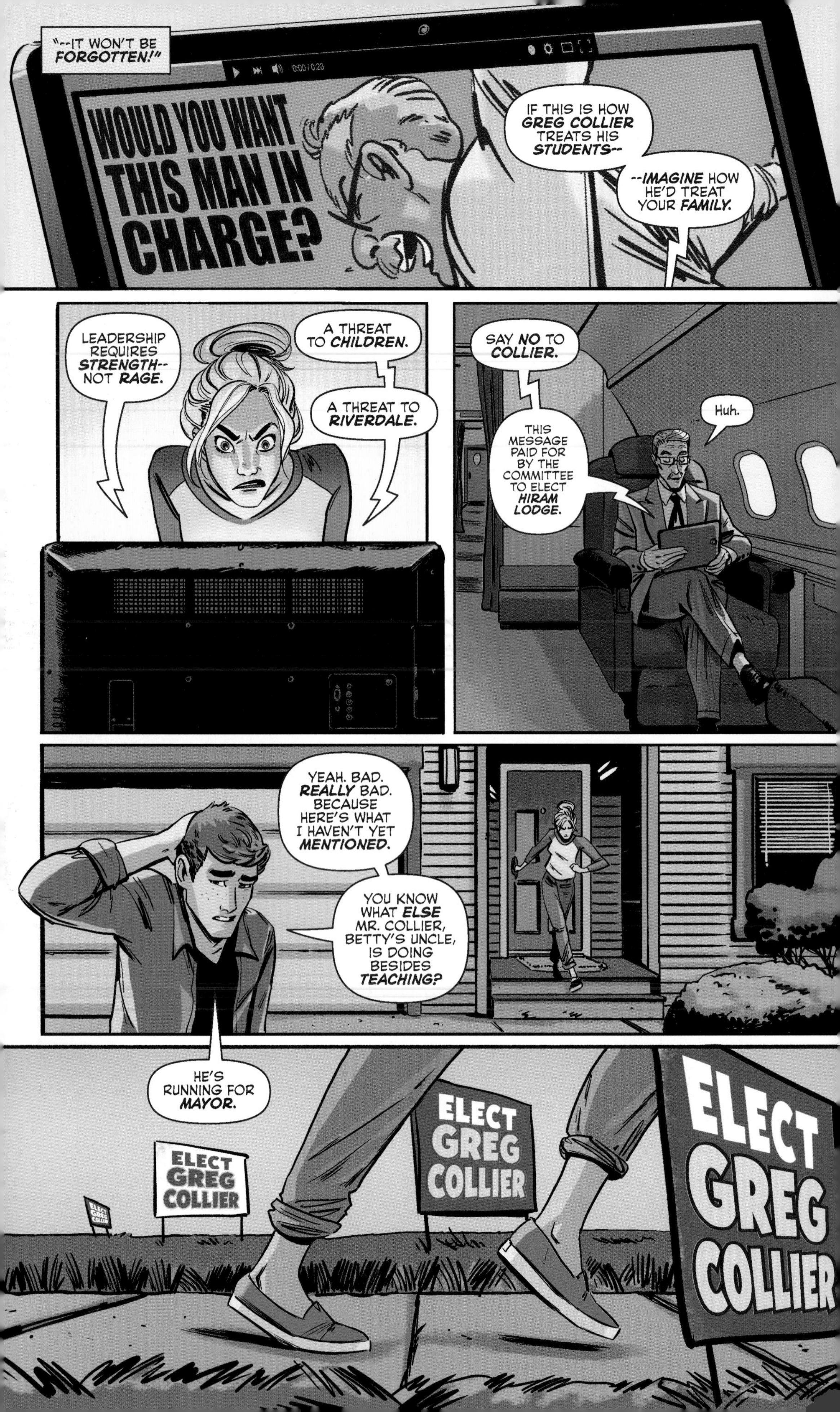
"--IT WON'T BE FORGOTTEN!"
0:00 / 0:23
WOULD YOU WANT THIS MAN IN CHARGE?
IF THIS IS HOW GREG COLLIER TREATS HIS STUDENTS--
--IMAGINE HOW HE'D TREAT YOUR FAMILY.
LEADERSHIP REQUIRES STRENGTH-- NOT RAGE.
A THREAT TO CHILDREN.
A THREAT TO RIVERDALE.
SAY NO TO COLLIER.
THIS MESSAGE PAID FOR BY THE COMMITTEE TO ELECT HIRAM LODGE.
Huh.
YEAH. BAD. REALLY BAD. BECAUSE HERE'S WHAT I HAVEN'T YET MENTIONED.
YOU KNOW WHAT ELSE MR. COLLIER, BETTY'S UNCLE, IS DOING BESIDES TEACHING?
HE'S RUNNING FOR MAYOR.
ELECT GREG COLLIER
ELECT GREG COLLIER
ELECT GREG COLLIER
ELECT GREG COLLIER

CHAPTER TWO: I'M FINE

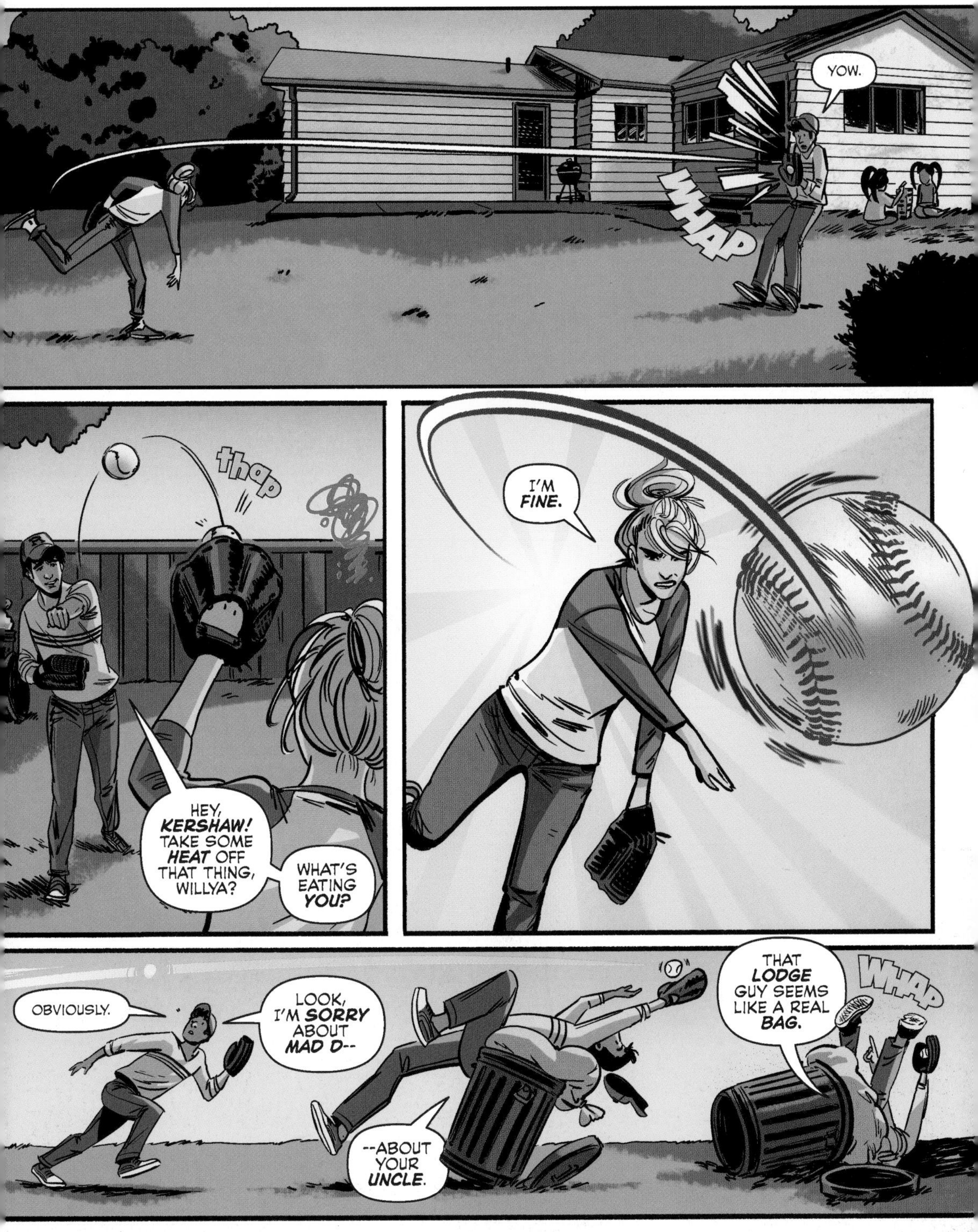

WHAP
YOW.
thap
HEY, KERSHAW! TAKE SOME HEAT OFF THAT THING, WILLYA?
WHAT'S EATING YOU?
I'M FINE.
OBVIOUSLY.
LOOK, I'M SORRY ABOUT MAD D--
--ABOUT YOUR UNCLE.
THAT LODGE GUY SEEMS LIKE A REAL BAG.
WHAP

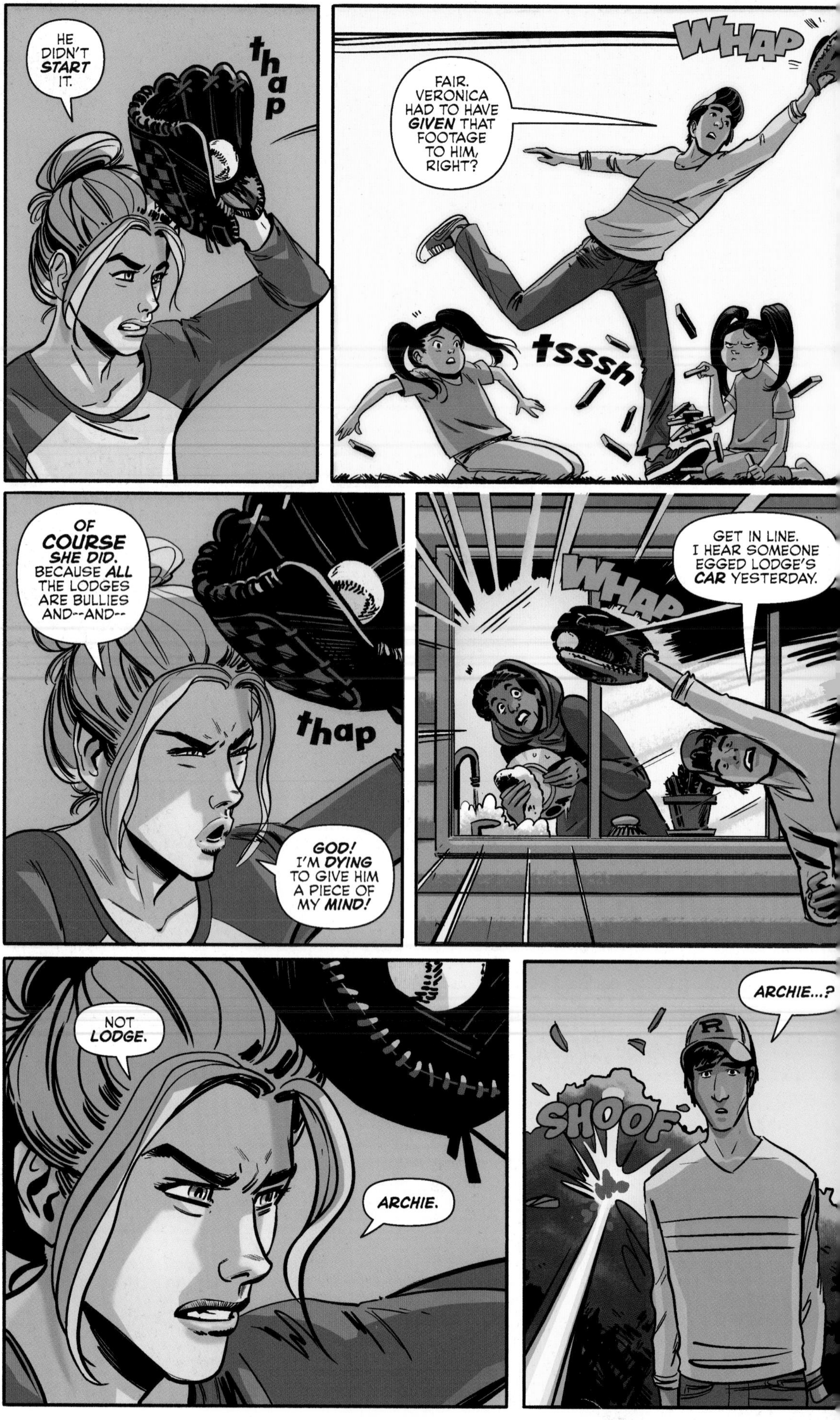
HE DIDN'T START IT.
thap
WHAP
FAIR. VERONICA HAD TO HAVE GIVEN THAT FOOTAGE TO HIM, RIGHT?
tsssh
OF COURSE SHE DID. BECAUSE ALL THE LODGES ARE BULLIES AND--AND--
thap
GOD! I'M DYING TO GIVE HIM A PIECE OF MY MIND!
WHAP
GET IN LINE. I HEAR SOMEONE EGGED LODGE'S CAR YESTERDAY.
NOT LODGE.
ARCHIE.
ARCHIE...?
SHOOF

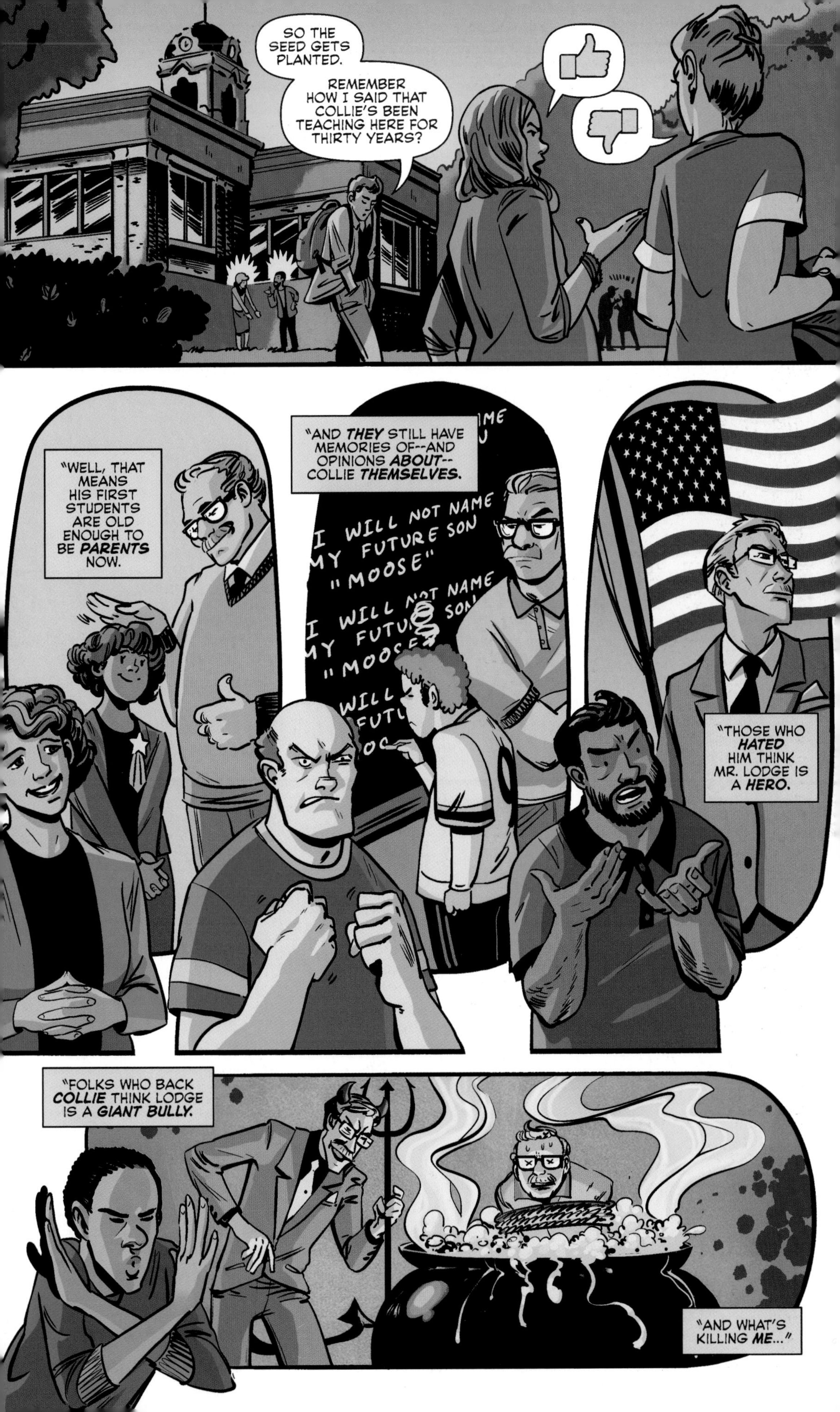
SO THE SEED GETS PLANTED.
REMEMBER HOW I SAID THAT COLLIE'S BEEN TEACHING HERE FOR THIRTY YEARS?
"WELL, THAT MEANS HIS FIRST STUDENTS ARE OLD ENOUGH TO BE PARENTS NOW.
"AND THEY STILL HAVE MEMORIES OF--AND OPINIONS ABOUT--COLLIE THEMSELVES.
I WILL NOT NAME MY FUTURE SON "MOOSE"
I WILL NOT NAME MY FUTURE SON "MOOSE"
"THOSE WHO HATED HIM THINK MR. LODGE IS A HERO.
"FOLKS WHO BACK COLLIE THINK LODGE IS A GIANT BULLY.
"AND WHAT'S KILLING ME..."

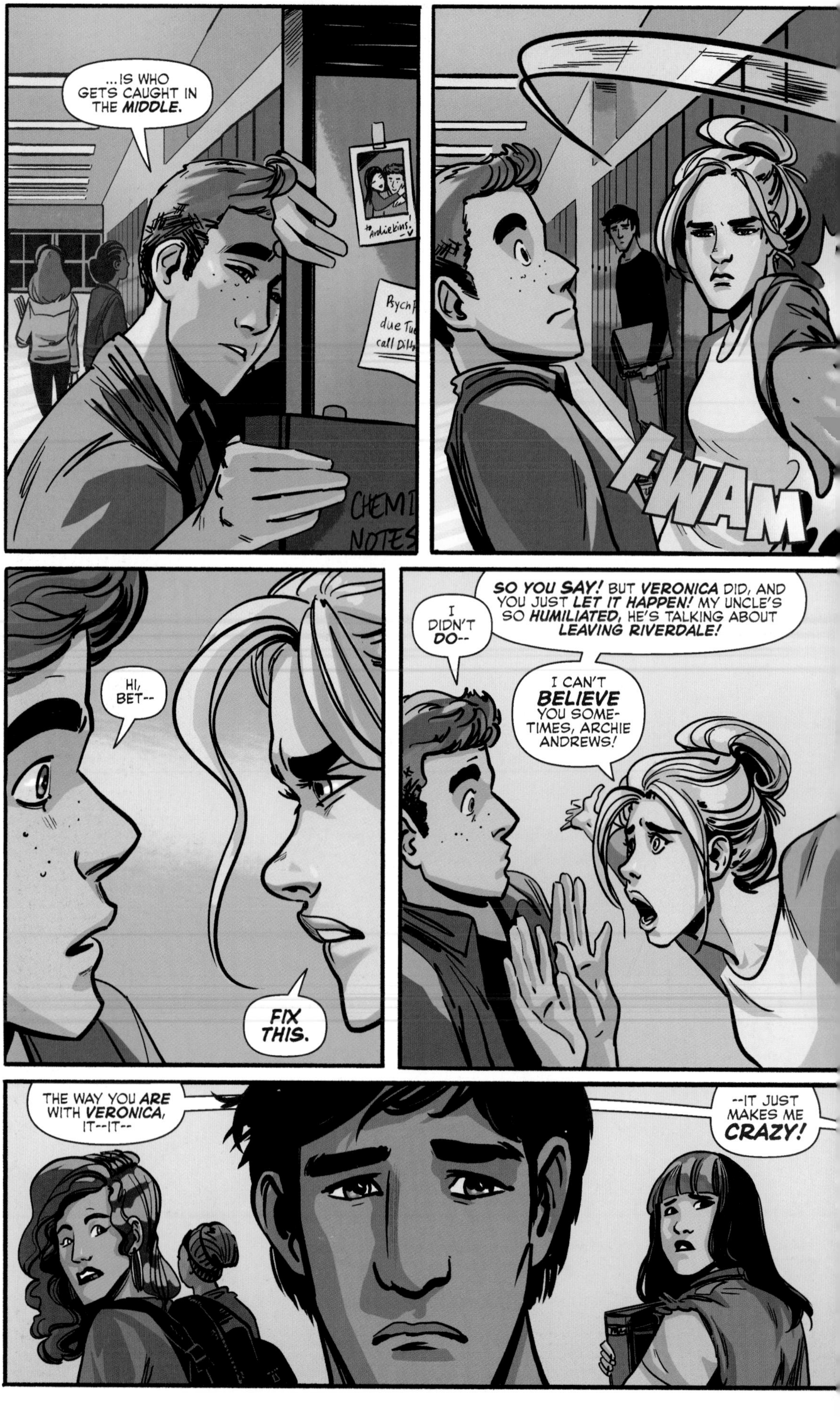
...IS WHO GETS CAUGHT IN THE MIDDLE.
FWAM
HI, BET--
FIX THIS.
I DIDN'T DO--
SO YOU SAY! BUT VERONICA DID, AND YOU JUST LET IT HAPPEN! MY UNCLE'S SO HUMILIATED, HE'S TALKING ABOUT LEAVING RIVERDALE!
I CAN'T BELIEVE YOU SOME-TIMES, ARCHIE ANDREWS!
THE WAY YOU ARE WITH VERONICA, IT--IT--
--IT JUST MAKES ME CRAZY!

...

I'LL FIX IT.

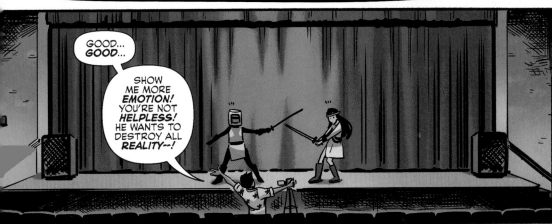

GOOD... GOOD...

SHOW ME MORE EMOTION! YOU'RE NOT HELPLESS! HE WANTS TO DESTROY ALL REALITY--!

RAJ. COME.

EEP.

WHAT ARE WE DOING?

JUST STAY DOWN AND KEEP FILMING.

CHAPTER THREE: HEY, DOGCATCHER

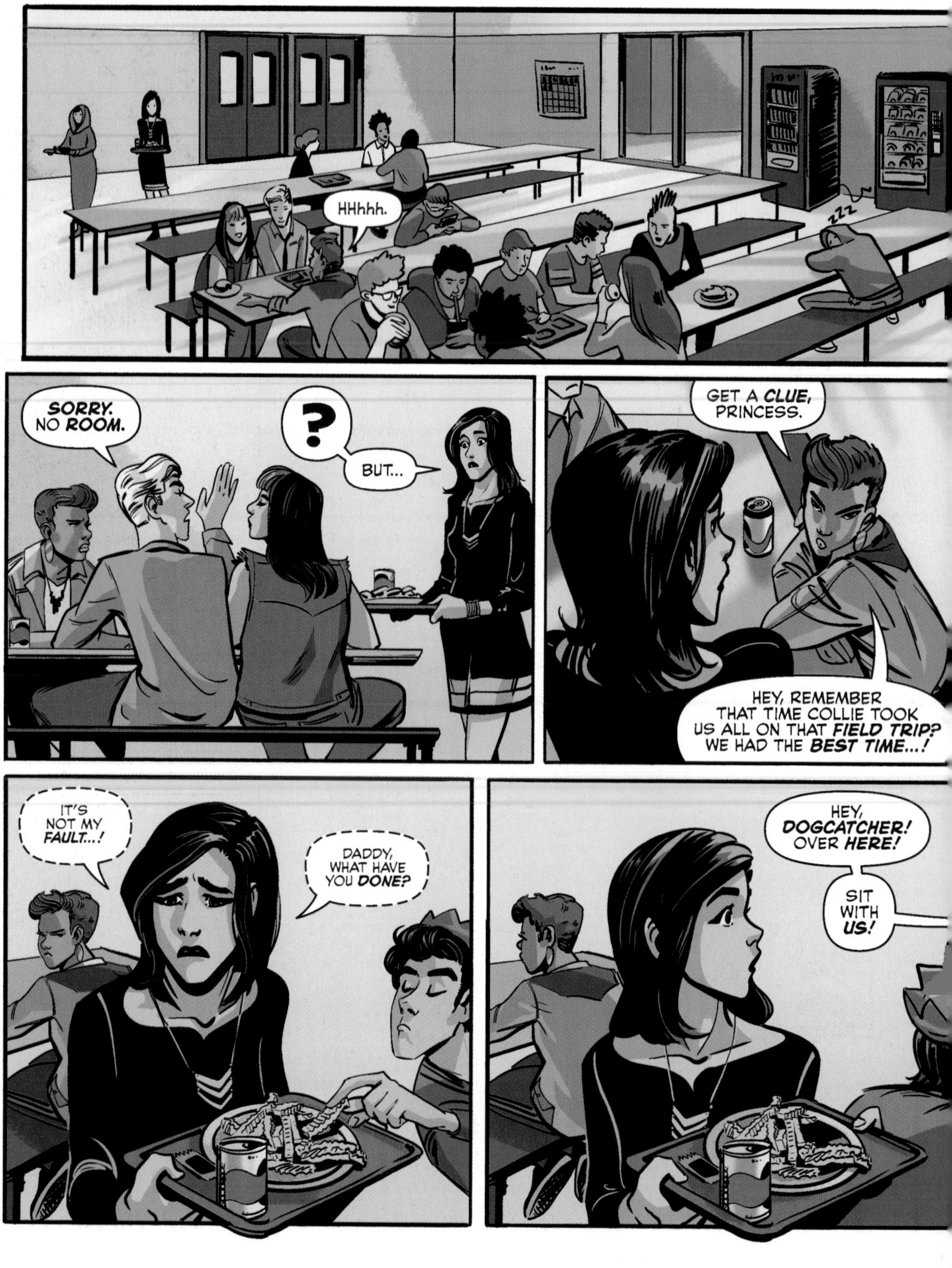

HHhhh.
SORRY. NO ROOM.
?
BUT...
GET A CLUE, PRINCESS.
HEY, REMEMBER THAT TIME COLLIE TOOK US ALL ON THAT FIELD TRIP? WE HAD THE BEST TIME...!
IT'S NOT MY FAULT...!
DADDY, WHAT HAVE YOU DONE?
HEY, DOGCATCHER! OVER HERE!
SIT WITH US!

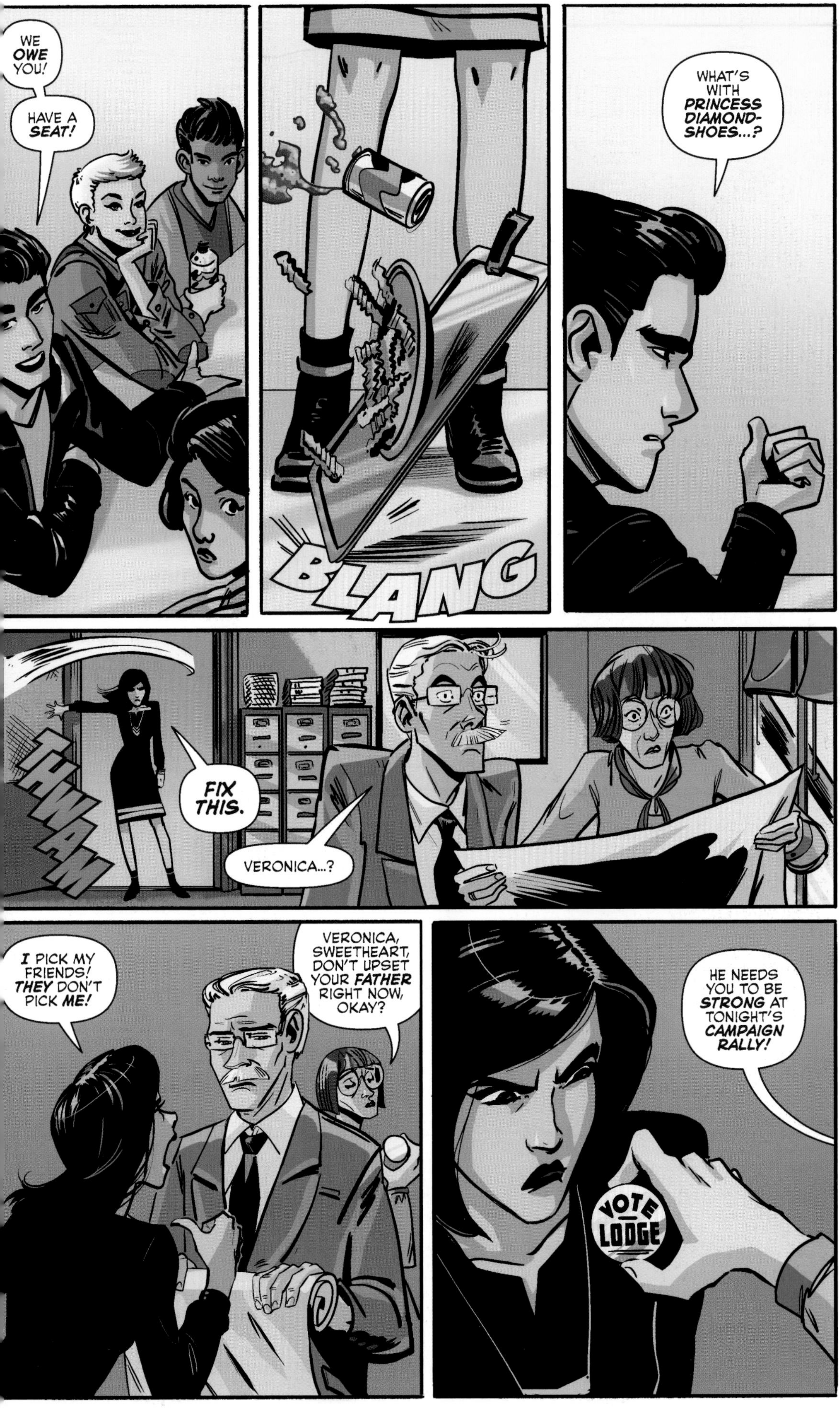
WE OWE YOU!
HAVE A SEAT!
BLANG
WHAT'S WITH PRINCESS DIAMOND-SHOES...?
THWAM
FIX THIS.
VERONICA...?
I PICK MY FRIENDS! THEY DON'T PICK ME!
VERONICA, SWEETHEART, DON'T UPSET YOUR FATHER RIGHT NOW, OKAY?
HE NEEDS YOU TO BE STRONG AT TONIGHT'S CAMPAIGN RALLY!
VOTE LODGE

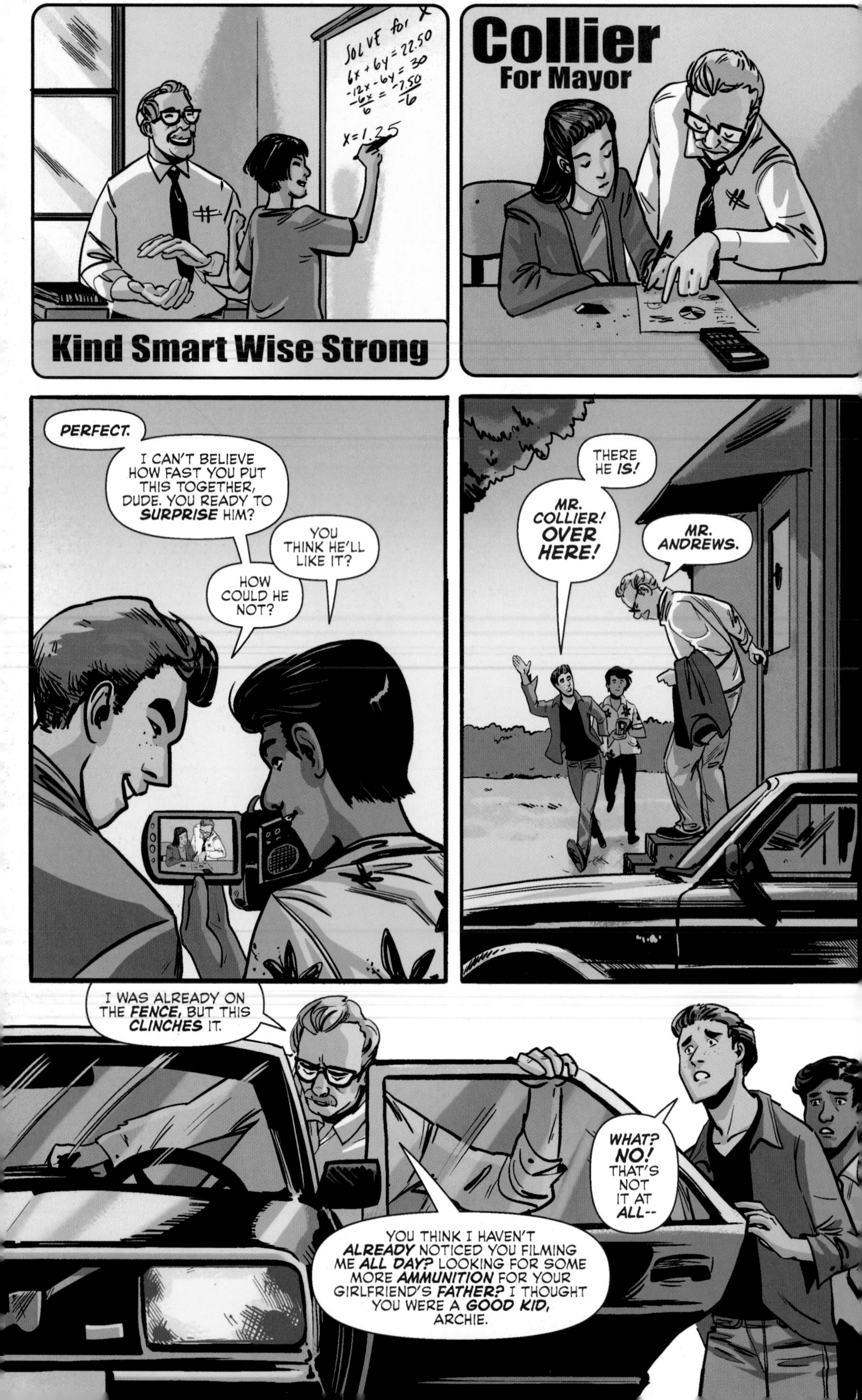
SOLVE for X
6x + 6y = 22.50
-12x - 6y = -30
-6x = -7.50
x = 1.25
Kind Smart Wise Strong
Collier For Mayor
PERFECT.
I CAN'T BELIEVE HOW FAST YOU PUT THIS TOGETHER, DUDE. YOU READY TO SURPRISE HIM?
YOU THINK HE'LL LIKE IT?
HOW COULD HE NOT?
THERE HE IS!
MR. COLLIER! OVER HERE!
MR. ANDREWS.
I WAS ALREADY ON THE FENCE, BUT THIS CLINCHES IT.
WHAT? NO! THAT'S NOT IT AT ALL--
YOU THINK I HAVEN'T ALREADY NOTICED YOU FILMING ME ALL DAY? LOOKING FOR SOME MORE AMMUNITION FOR YOUR GIRLFRIEND'S FATHER? I THOUGHT YOU WERE A GOOD KID, ARCHIE.

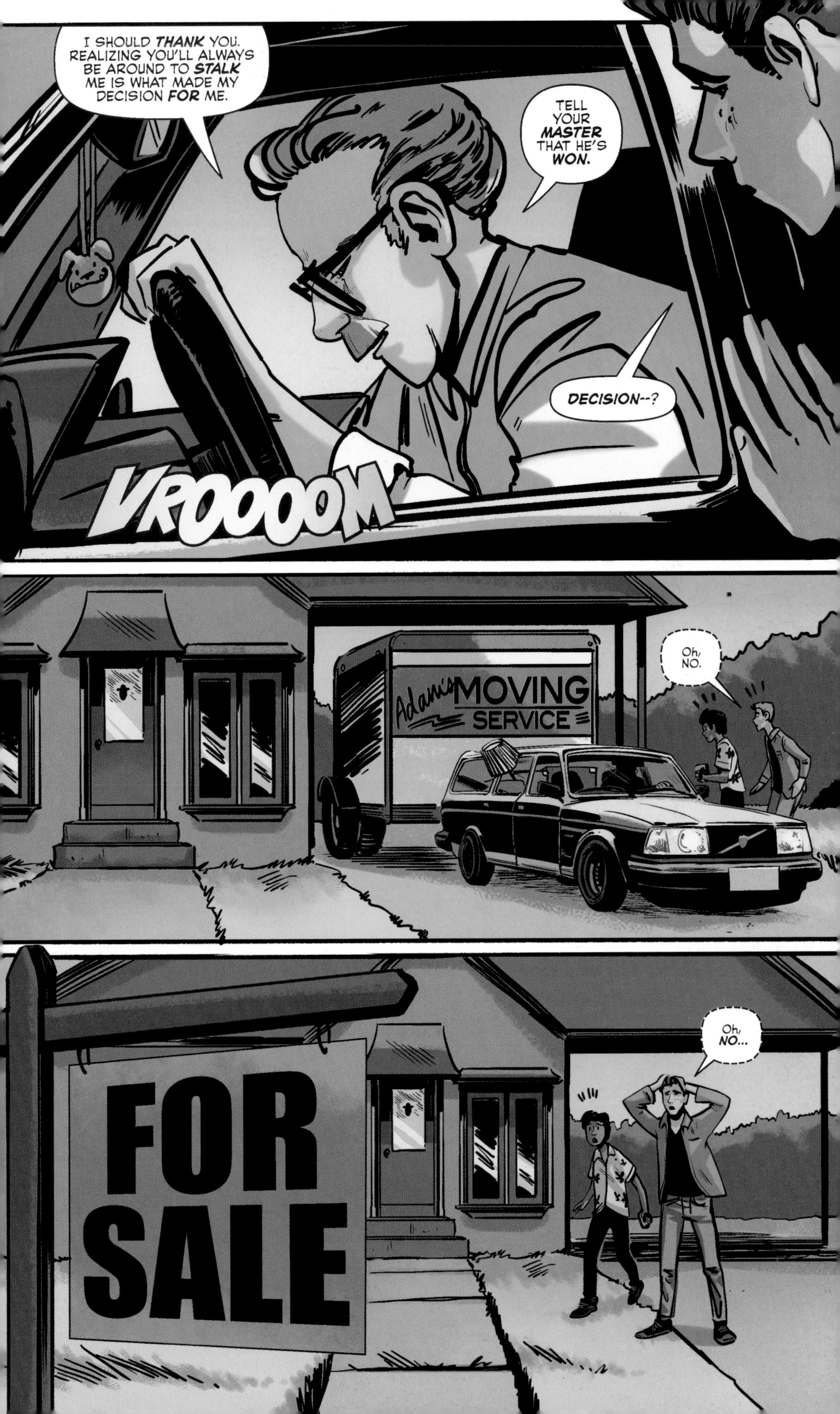
I SHOULD THANK YOU. REALIZING YOU'LL ALWAYS BE AROUND TO STALK ME IS WHAT MADE MY DECISION FOR ME.
TELL YOUR MASTER THAT HE'S WON.
DECISION--?
VROOOOM
Adam's MOVING SERVICE
Oh, NO.
Oh, NO...
FOR SALE

CHAPTER FOUR: PIGS DON'T FLY

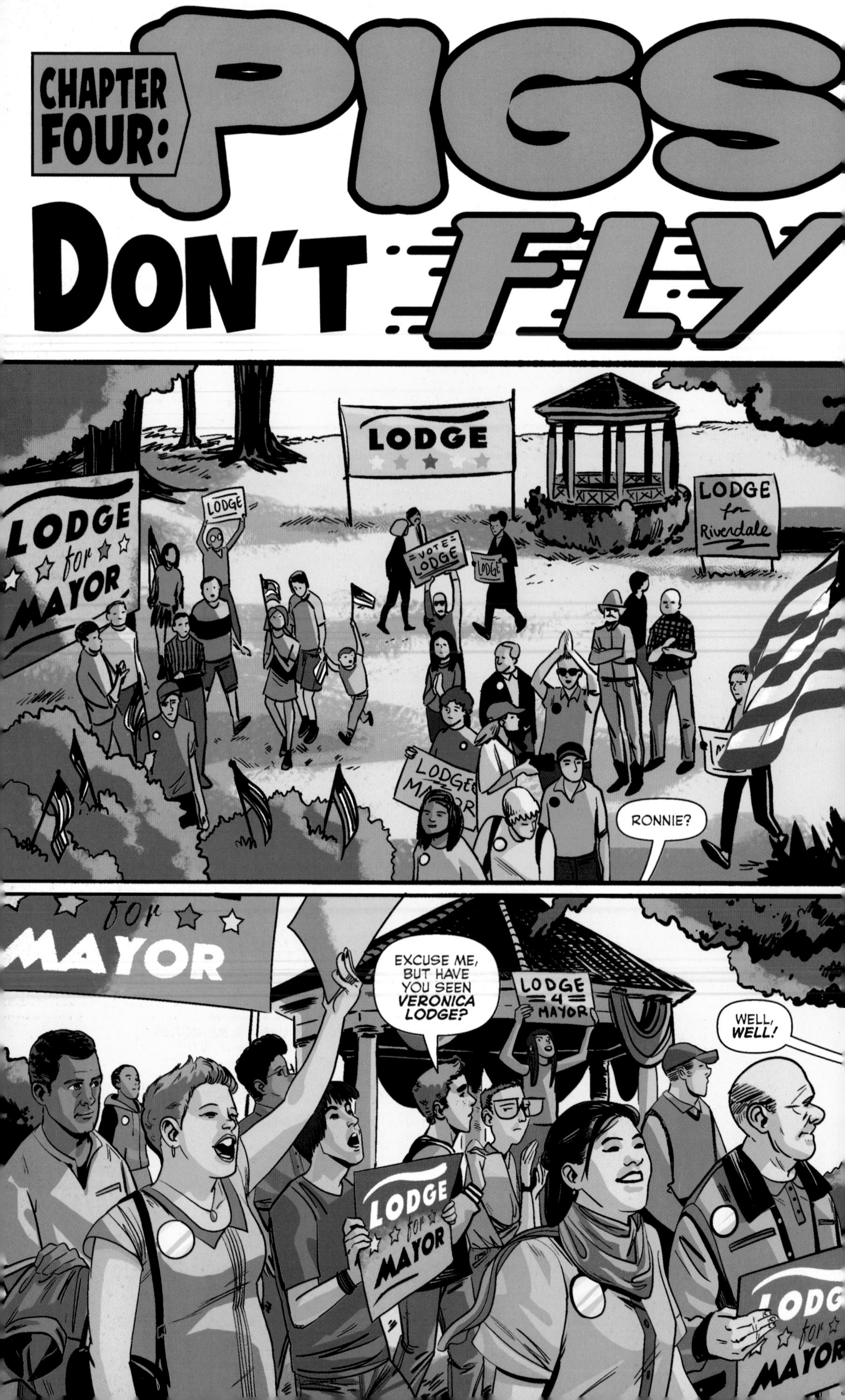
LODGE
LODGE for MAYOR
LODGE
VOTE LODGE
LODGE
LODGE for Riverdale
RONNIE?
for MAYOR
EXCUSE ME, BUT HAVE YOU SEEN *VERONICA LODGE?*
LODGE 4 MAYOR
WELL, **WELL!**
LODGE for MAYOR

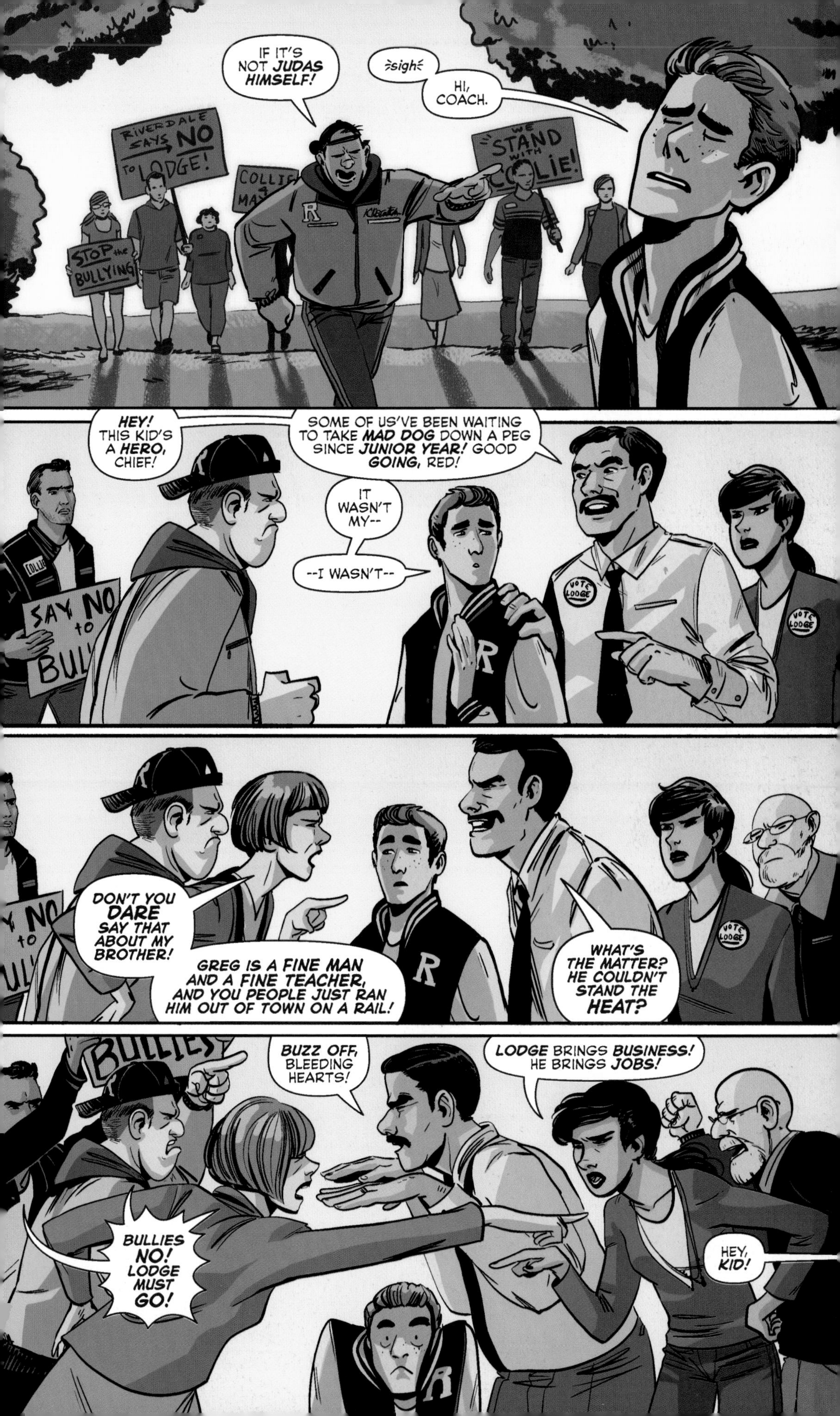
RIVERDALE SAYS NO TO LODGE!
STOP the BULLYING
WE STAND with COLLIE!
IF IT'S NOT JUDAS HIMSELF!
sigh
HI, COACH.
HEY! THIS KID'S A HERO, CHIEF!
SOME OF US'VE BEEN WAITING TO TAKE MAD DOG DOWN A PEG SINCE JUNIOR YEAR! GOOD GOING, RED!
IT WASN'T MY--
--I WASN'T--
VOTE LODGE
DON'T YOU DARE SAY THAT ABOUT MY BROTHER!
GREG IS A FINE MAN AND A FINE TEACHER, AND YOU PEOPLE JUST RAN HIM OUT OF TOWN ON A RAIL!
WHAT'S THE MATTER? HE COULDN'T STAND THE HEAT?
BUZZ OFF, BLEEDING HEARTS!
LODGE BRINGS BUSINESS! HE BRINGS JOBS!
BULLIES NO! LODGE MUST GO!
HEY, KID!

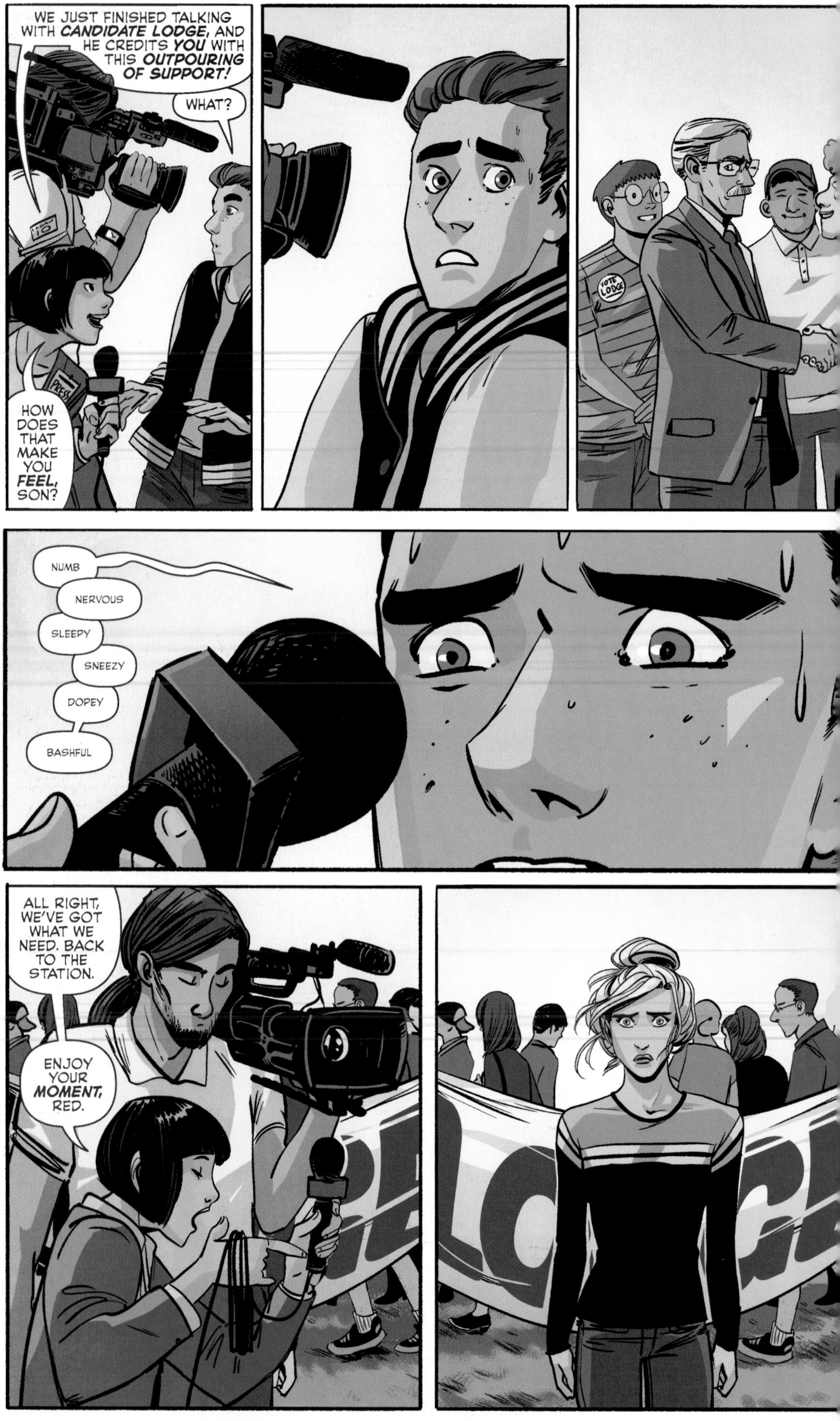
WE JUST FINISHED TALKING WITH CANDIDATE LODGE, AND HE CREDITS YOU WITH THIS OUTPOURING OF SUPPORT!
WHAT?
HOW DOES THAT MAKE YOU FEEL, SON?
VOTE LODGE
NUMB
NERVOUS
SLEEPY
SNEEZY
DOPEY
BASHFUL
ALL RIGHT, WE'VE GOT WHAT WE NEED. BACK TO THE STATION.
ENJOY YOUR MOMENT, RED.

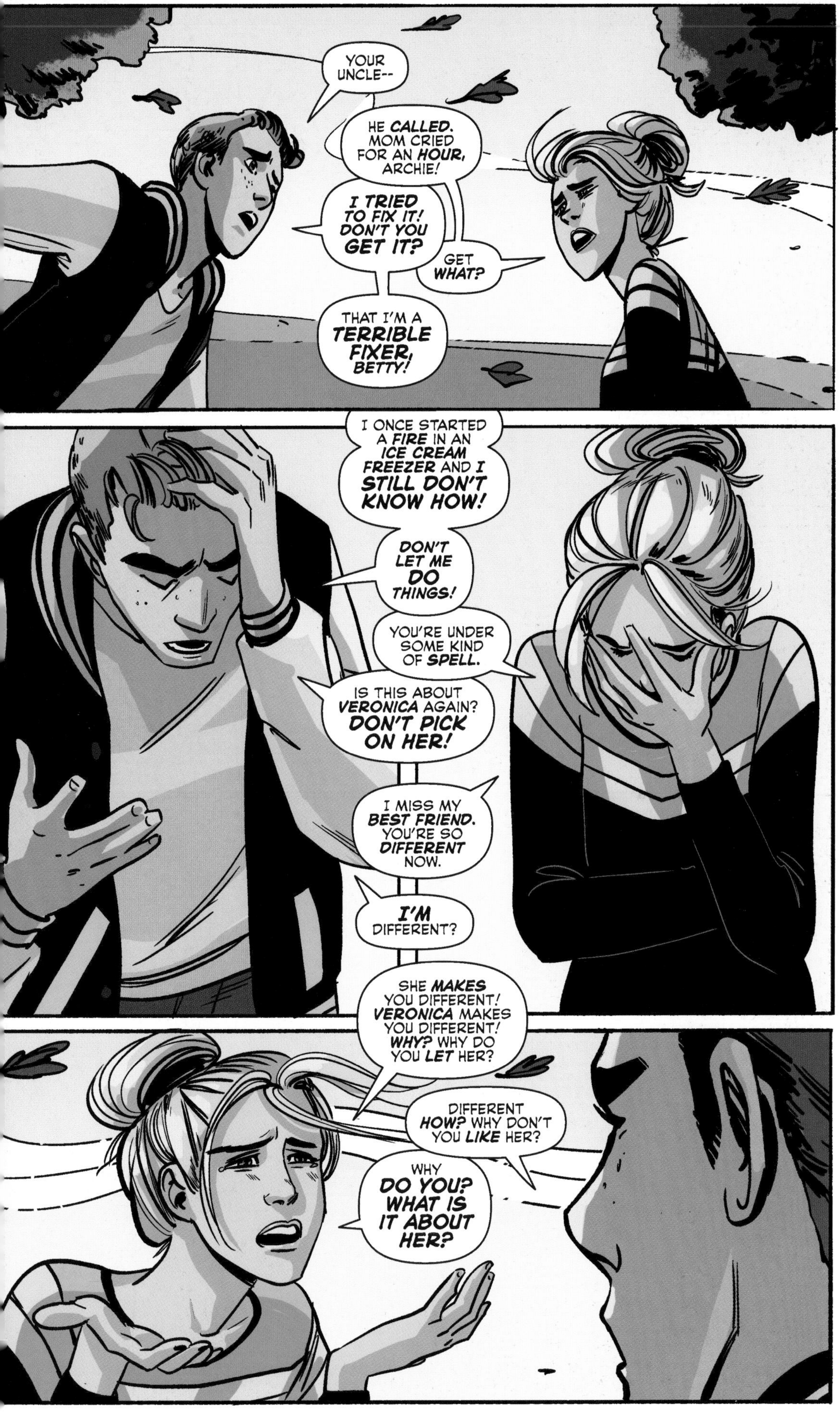

YOUR UNCLE--
HE CALLED. MOM CRIED FOR AN HOUR, ARCHIE!
I TRIED TO FIX IT! DON'T YOU GET IT?
GET WHAT?
THAT I'M A TERRIBLE FIXER, BETTY!
I ONCE STARTED A FIRE IN AN ICE CREAM FREEZER AND I STILL DON'T KNOW HOW!
DON'T LET ME DO THINGS!
YOU'RE UNDER SOME KIND OF SPELL.
IS THIS ABOUT VERONICA AGAIN? DON'T PICK ON HER!
I MISS MY BEST FRIEND. YOU'RE SO DIFFERENT NOW.
I'M DIFFERENT?
SHE MAKES YOU DIFFERENT! VERONICA MAKES YOU DIFFERENT! WHY? WHY DO YOU LET HER?
DIFFERENT HOW? WHY DON'T YOU LIKE HER?
WHY DO YOU? WHAT IS IT ABOUT HER?

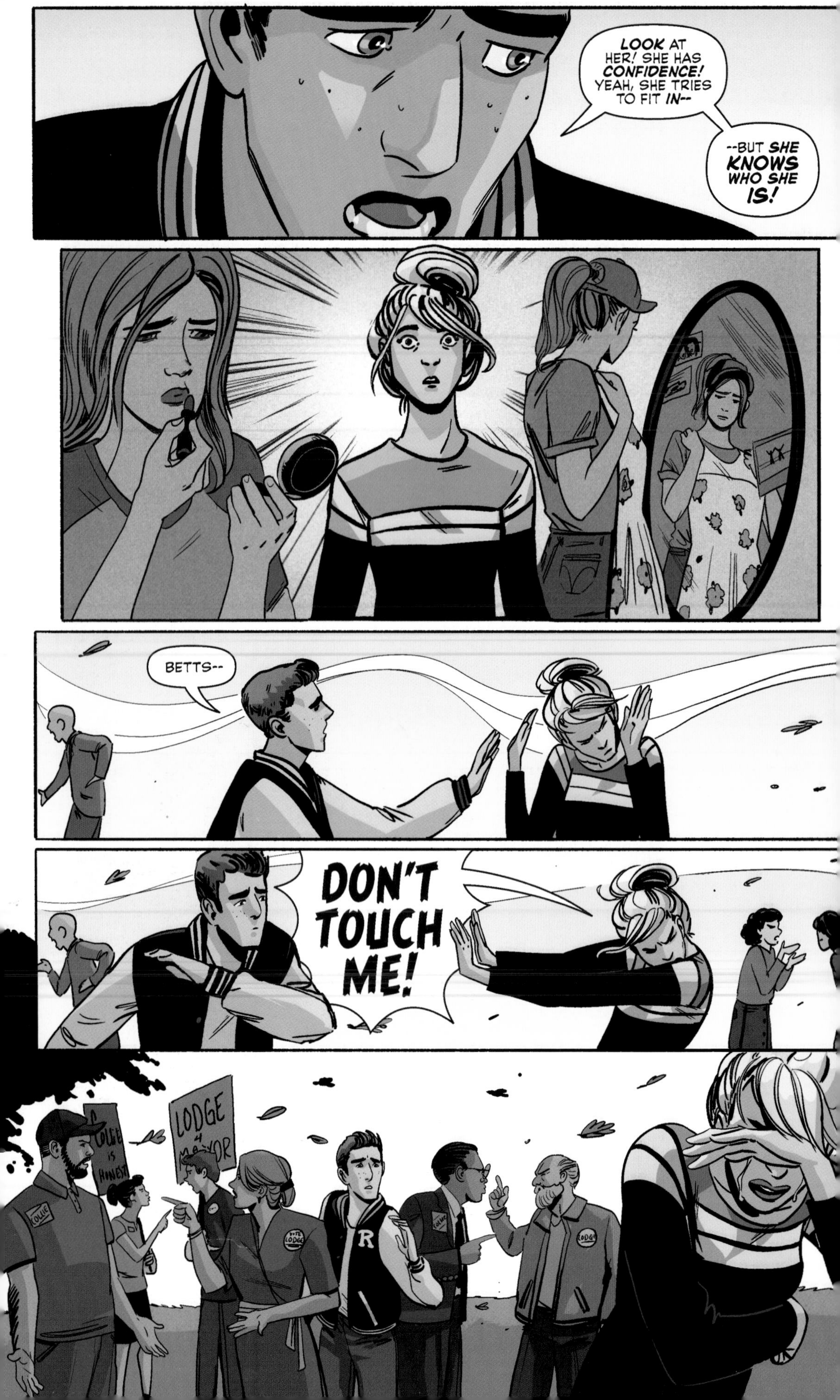
LOOK AT HER! SHE HAS CONFIDENCE! YEAH, SHE TRIES TO FIT IN--
--BUT SHE KNOWS WHO SHE IS!
BETTS--
DON'T TOUCH ME!
LODGE 4 MAYOR

TO BE CONTINUED...

ISSUE ELEVEN

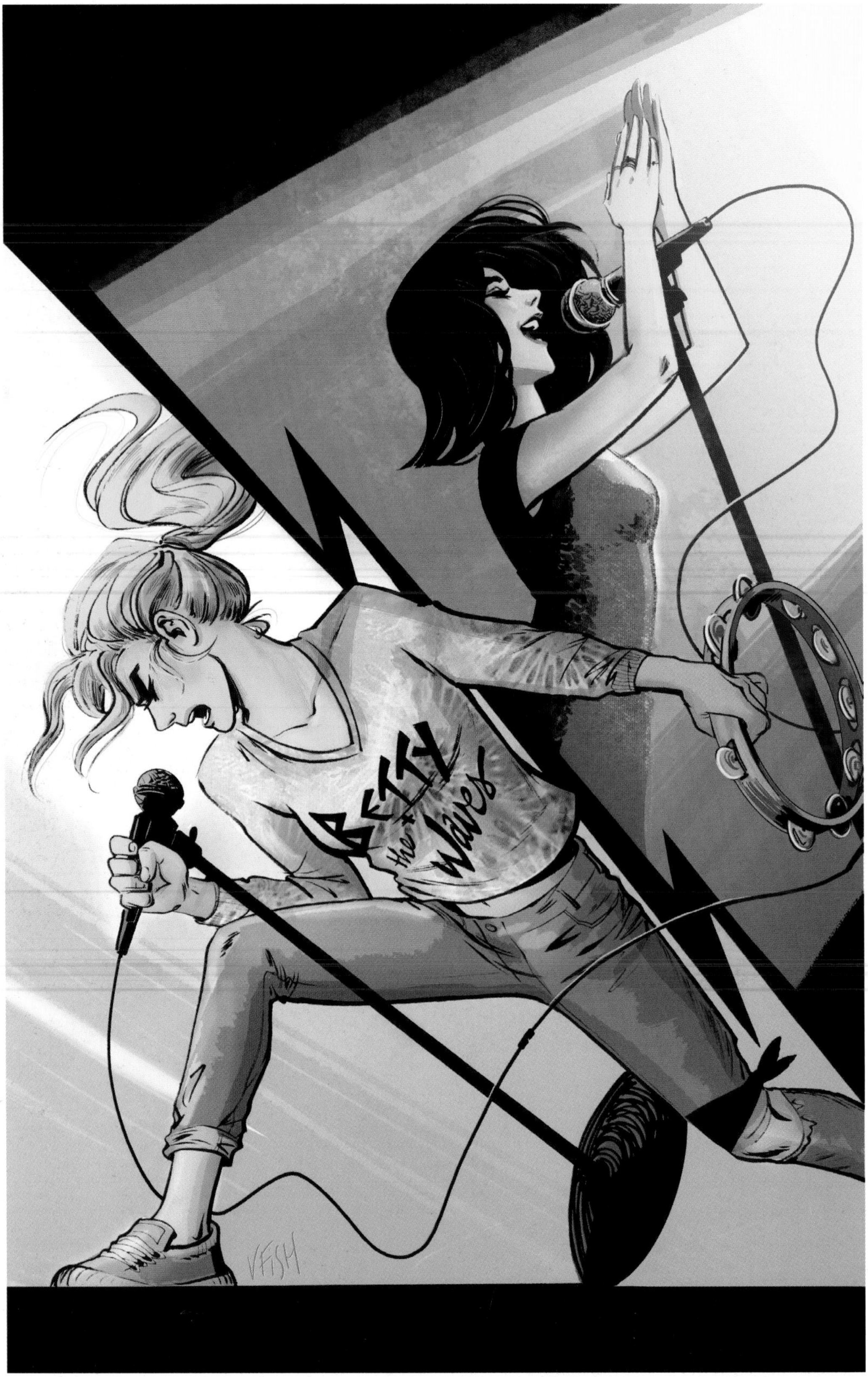
BETTY
the +
Waves
VFISH

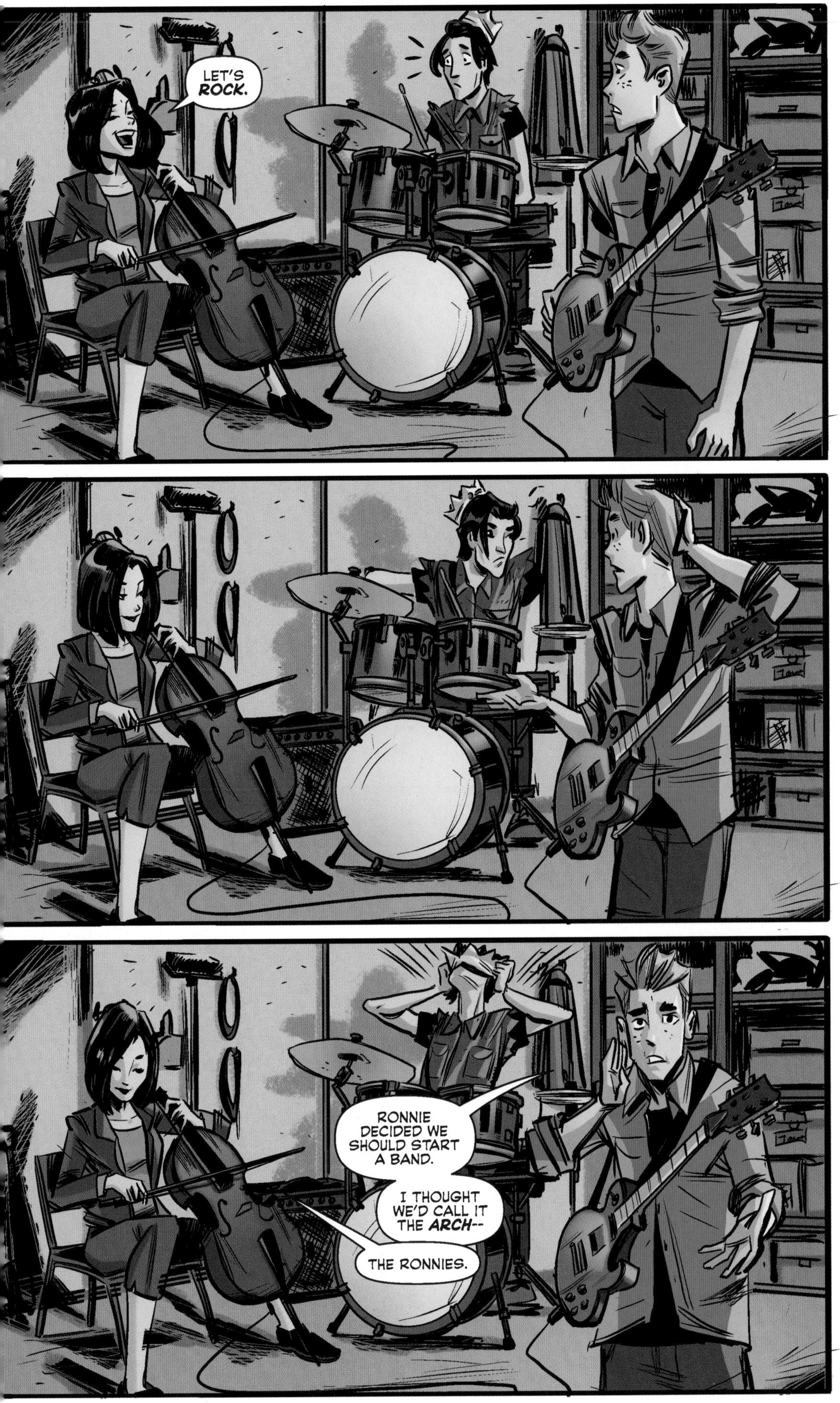
LET'S ROCK.
RONNIE DECIDED WE SHOULD START A BAND.
I THOUGHT WE'D CALL IT THE ARCH--
THE RONNIES.

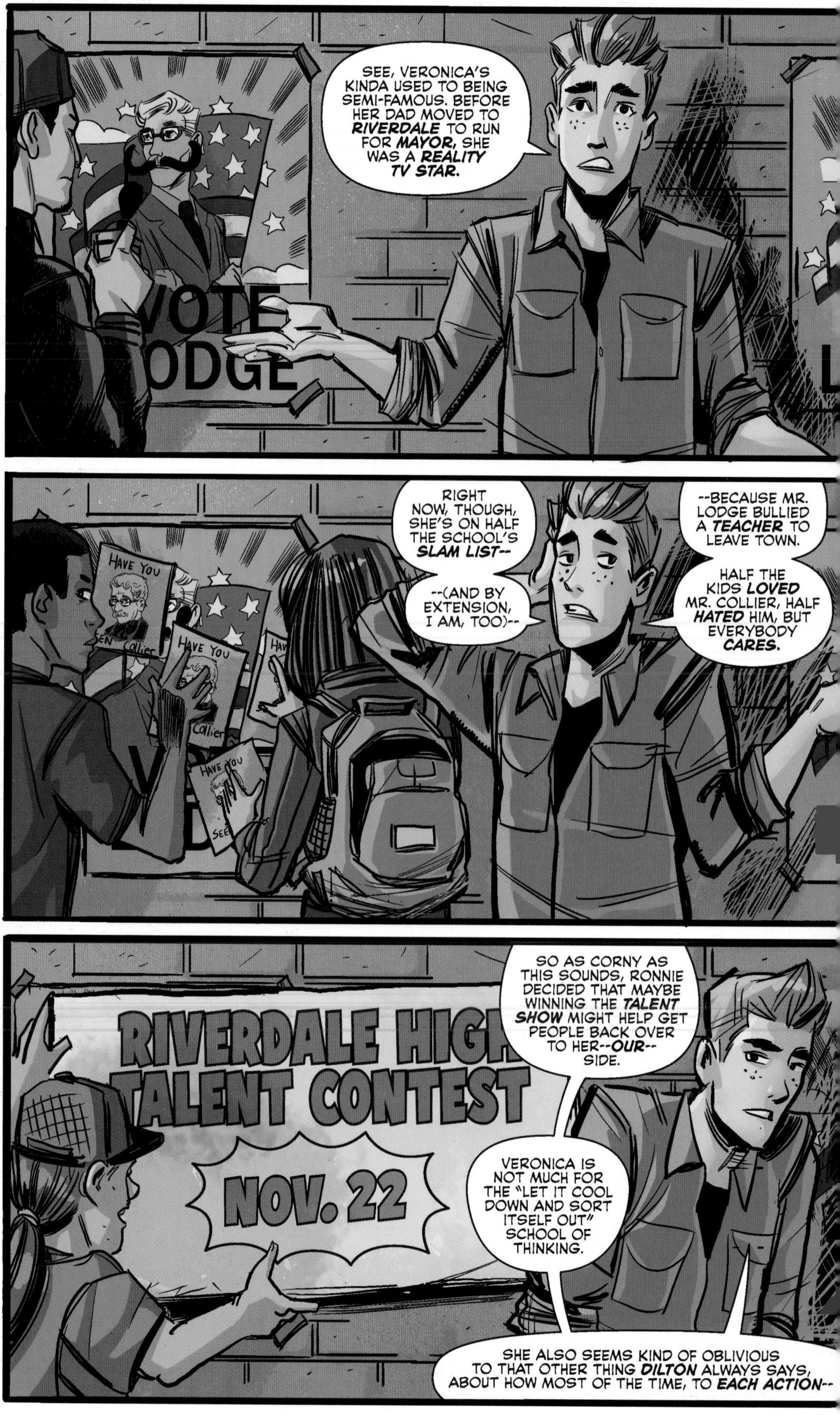
VOTE
ODGE
SEE, VERONICA'S KINDA USED TO BEING SEMI-FAMOUS. BEFORE HER DAD MOVED TO **RIVERDALE** TO RUN FOR **MAYOR,** SHE WAS A **REALITY TV STAR.**
HAVE YOU
SEEN Collier
RIGHT NOW, THOUGH, SHE'S ON HALF THE SCHOOL'S **SLAM LIST--**
--(AND BY EXTENSION, I AM, TOO)--
--BECAUSE MR. LODGE BULLIED A **TEACHER** TO LEAVE TOWN.
HALF THE KIDS **LOVED** MR. COLLIER, HALF **HATED** HIM, BUT EVERYBODY **CARES.**
RIVERDALE HIGH
TALENT CONTEST
NOV. 22
SO AS CORNY AS THIS SOUNDS, RONNIE DECIDED THAT MAYBE WINNING THE **TALENT SHOW** MIGHT HELP GET PEOPLE BACK OVER TO HER--**OUR**--SIDE.
VERONICA IS NOT MUCH FOR THE "LET IT COOL DOWN AND SORT ITSELF OUT" SCHOOL OF THINKING.
SHE ALSO SEEMS KIND OF OBLIVIOUS TO THAT OTHER THING **DILTON** ALWAYS SAYS, ABOUT HOW MOST OF THE TIME, TO **EACH ACTION--**

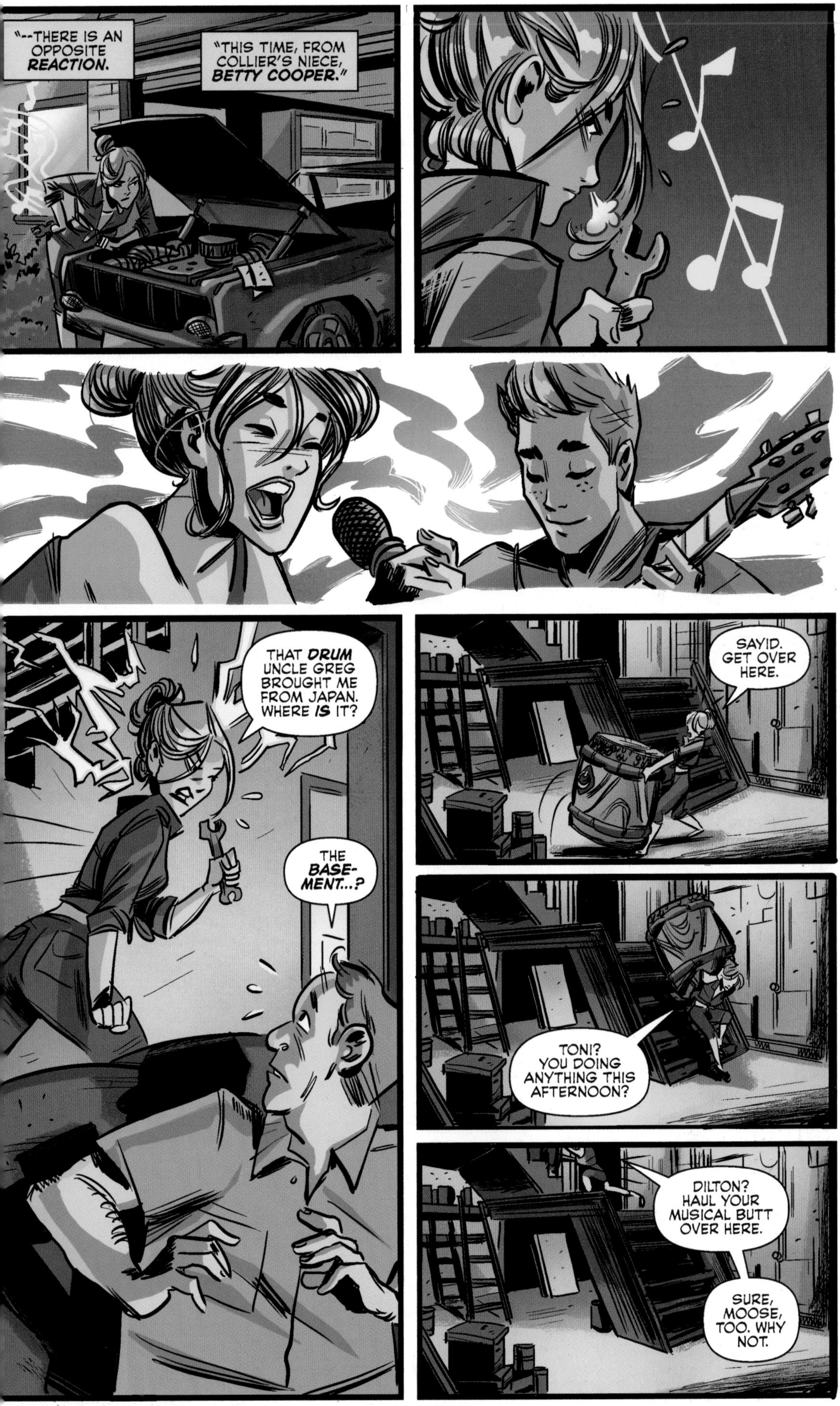
"--THERE IS AN OPPOSITE REACTION.
"THIS TIME, FROM COLLIER'S NIECE, BETTY COOPER."
THAT DRUM UNCLE GREG BROUGHT ME FROM JAPAN. WHERE IS IT?
THE BASE-MENT...?
SAYID. GET OVER HERE.
TONI? YOU DOING ANYTHING THIS AFTERNOON?
DILTON? HAUL YOUR MUSICAL BUTT OVER HERE.
SURE, MOOSE, TOO. WHY NOT.

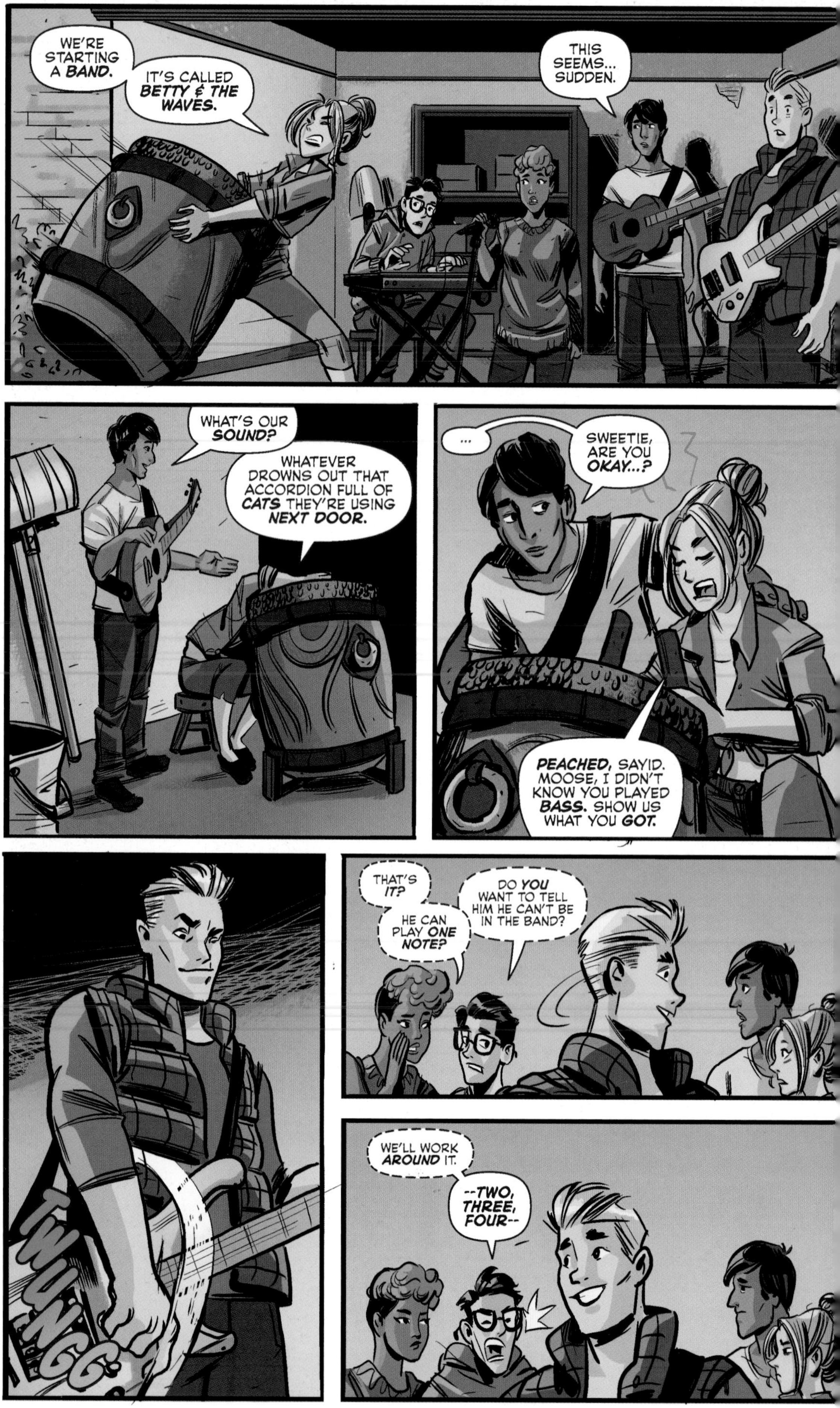

WE'RE STARTING A **BAND.**
IT'S CALLED **BETTY & THE WAVES.**
THIS SEEMS... SUDDEN.
WHAT'S OUR **SOUND?**
WHATEVER DROWNS OUT THAT ACCORDION FULL OF **CATS** THEY'RE USING **NEXT DOOR.**
...
SWEETIE, ARE YOU **OKAY...?**
PEACHED, SAYID. MOOSE, I DIDN'T KNOW YOU PLAYED **BASS.** SHOW US WHAT YOU **GOT.**
TWUNGG
THAT'S **IT?**
HE CAN PLAY **ONE NOTE?**
DO **YOU** WANT TO TELL HIM HE CAN'T BE IN THE BAND?
WE'LL WORK **AROUND** IT.
--TWO, THREE, FOUR--

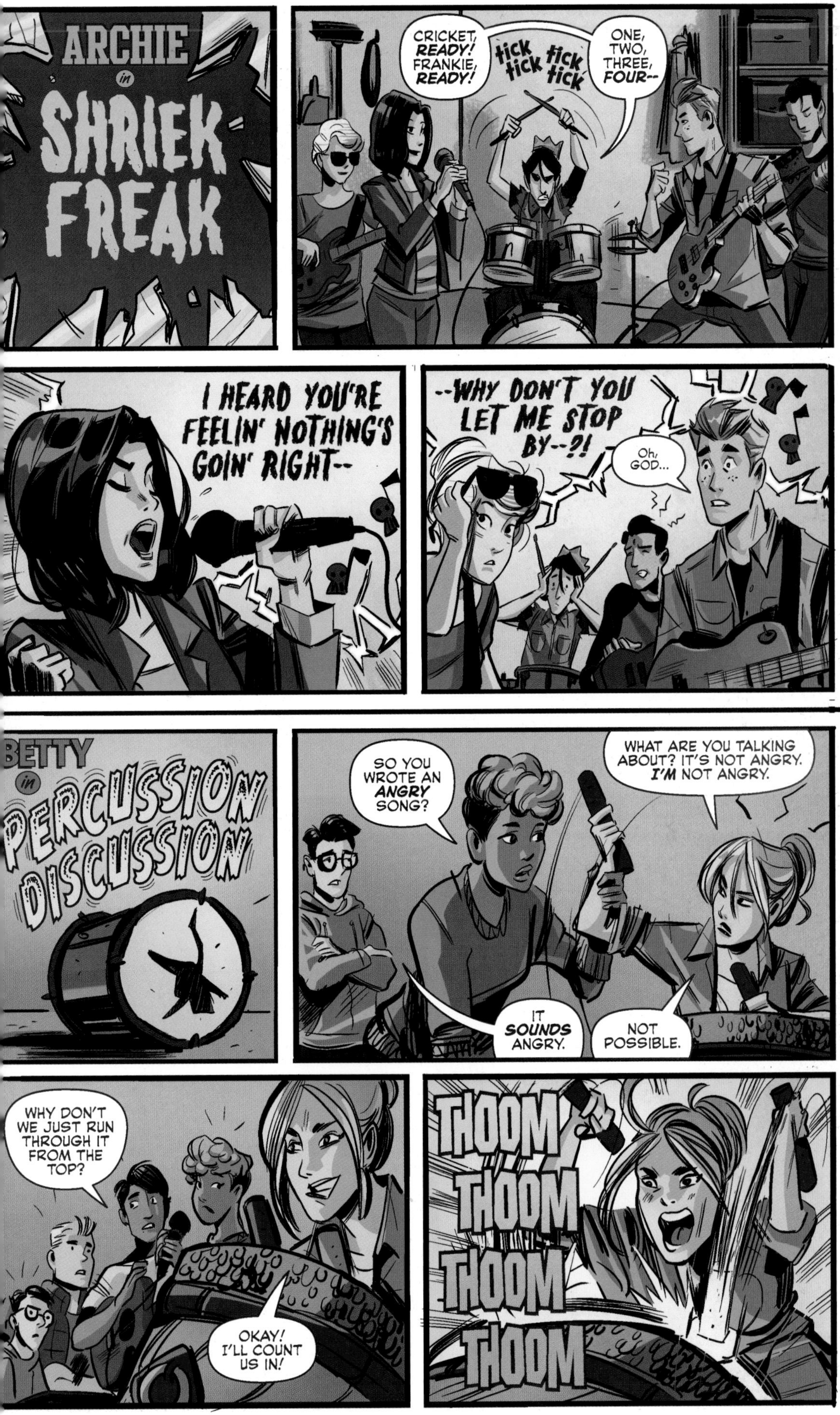
ARCHIE in
SHRIEK FREAK
CRICKET, READY! FRANKIE, READY!
tick tick tick tick
ONE, TWO, THREE, FOUR--
I HEARD YOU'RE FEELIN' NOTHING'S GOIN' RIGHT--
--WHY DON'T YOU LET ME STOP BY--?!
Oh, GOD...
BETTY in
PERCUSSION DISCUSSION
SO YOU WROTE AN ANGRY SONG?
WHAT ARE YOU TALKING ABOUT? IT'S NOT ANGRY. I'M NOT ANGRY.
IT SOUNDS ANGRY.
NOT POSSIBLE.
WHY DON'T WE JUST RUN THROUGH IT FROM THE TOP?
OKAY! I'LL COUNT US IN!
THOOM THOOM THOOM THOOM

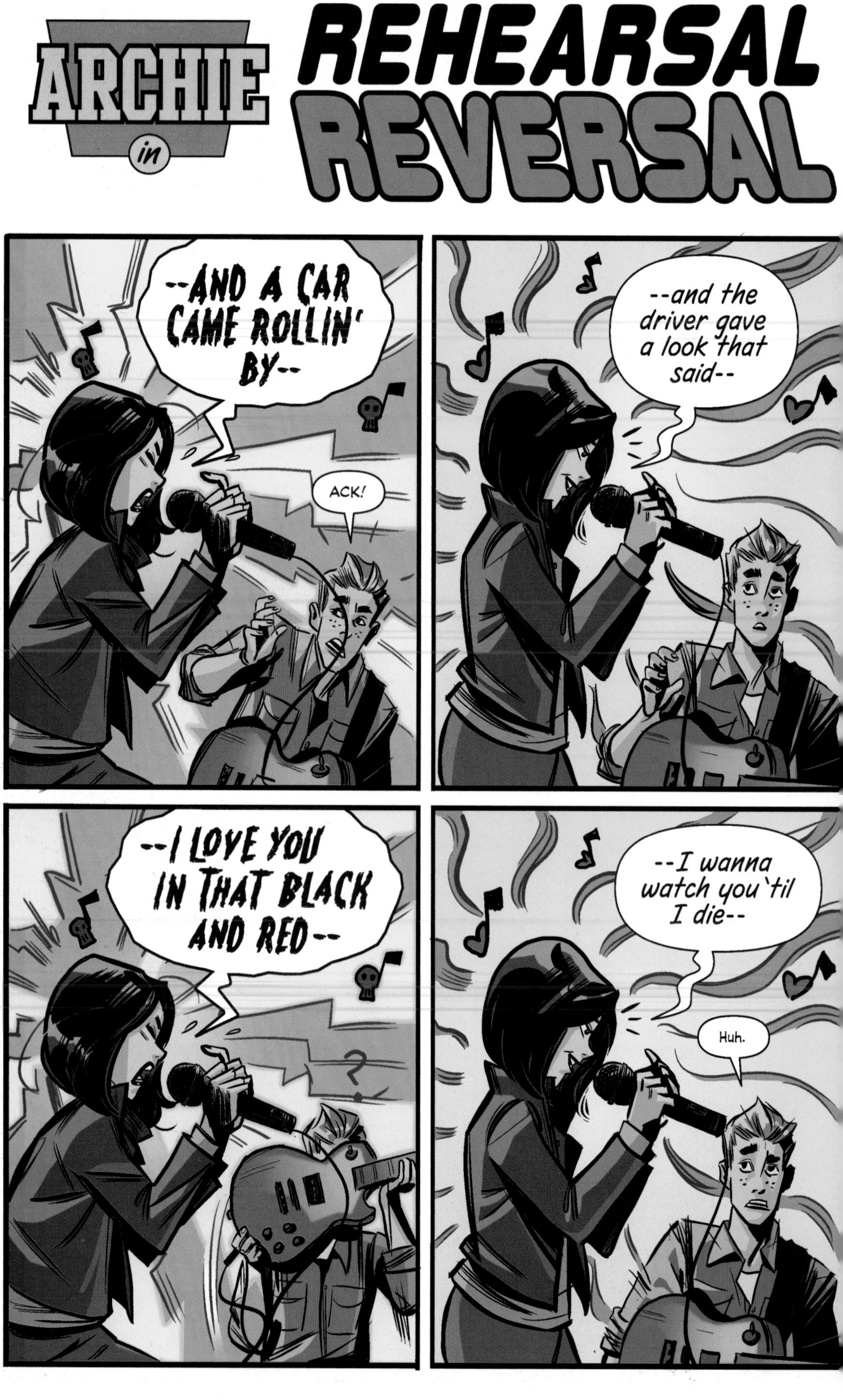
ARCHIE in
REHEARSAL REVERSAL
--AND A CAR CAME ROLLIN' BY--
ACK!
--and the driver gave a look that said--
--I LOVE YOU IN THAT BLACK AND RED--
?
--I wanna watch you 'til I die--
Huh.

TONI TOPAZ in SWEAT FRET

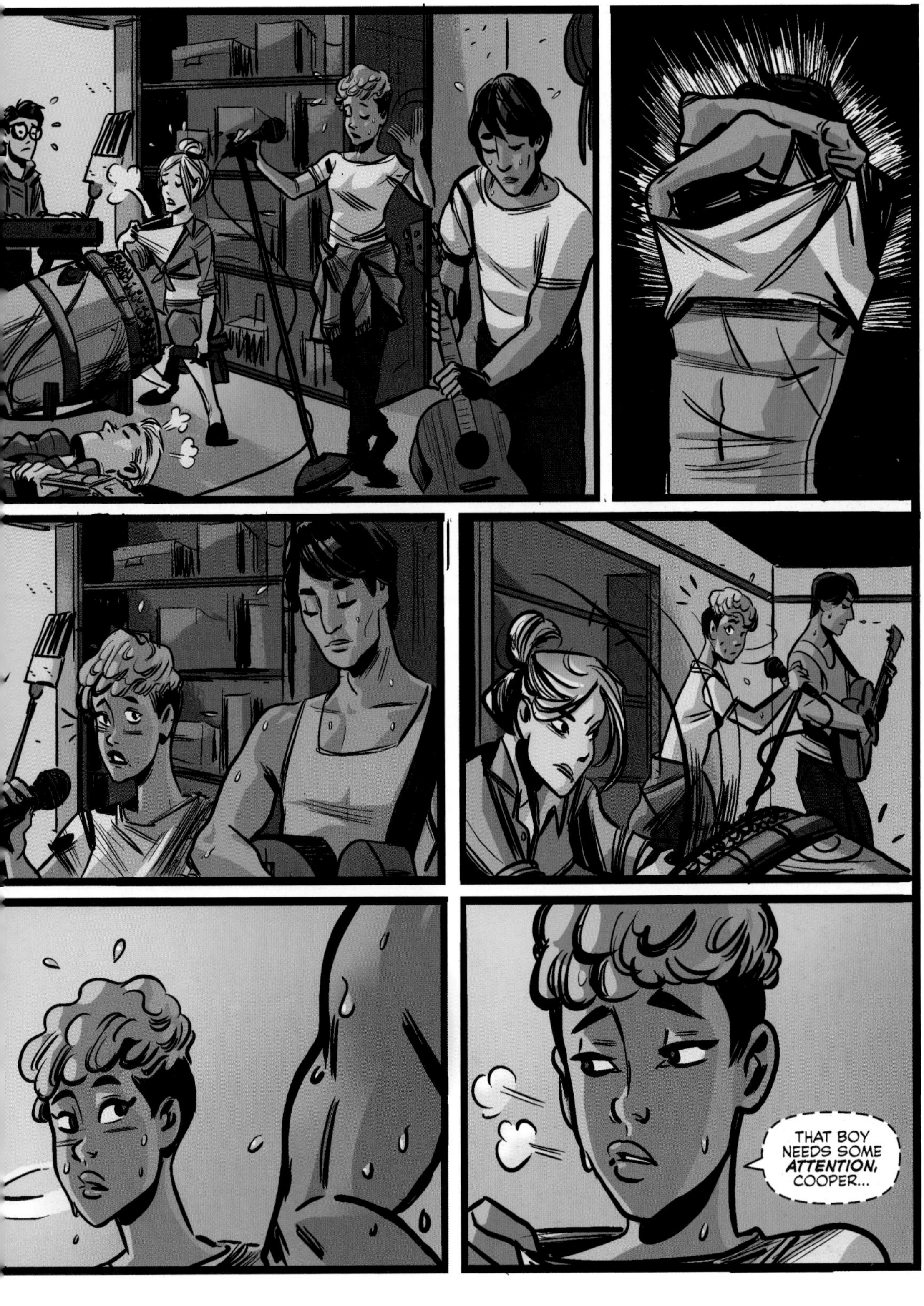
THAT BOY NEEDS SOME *ATTENTION,* COOPER...

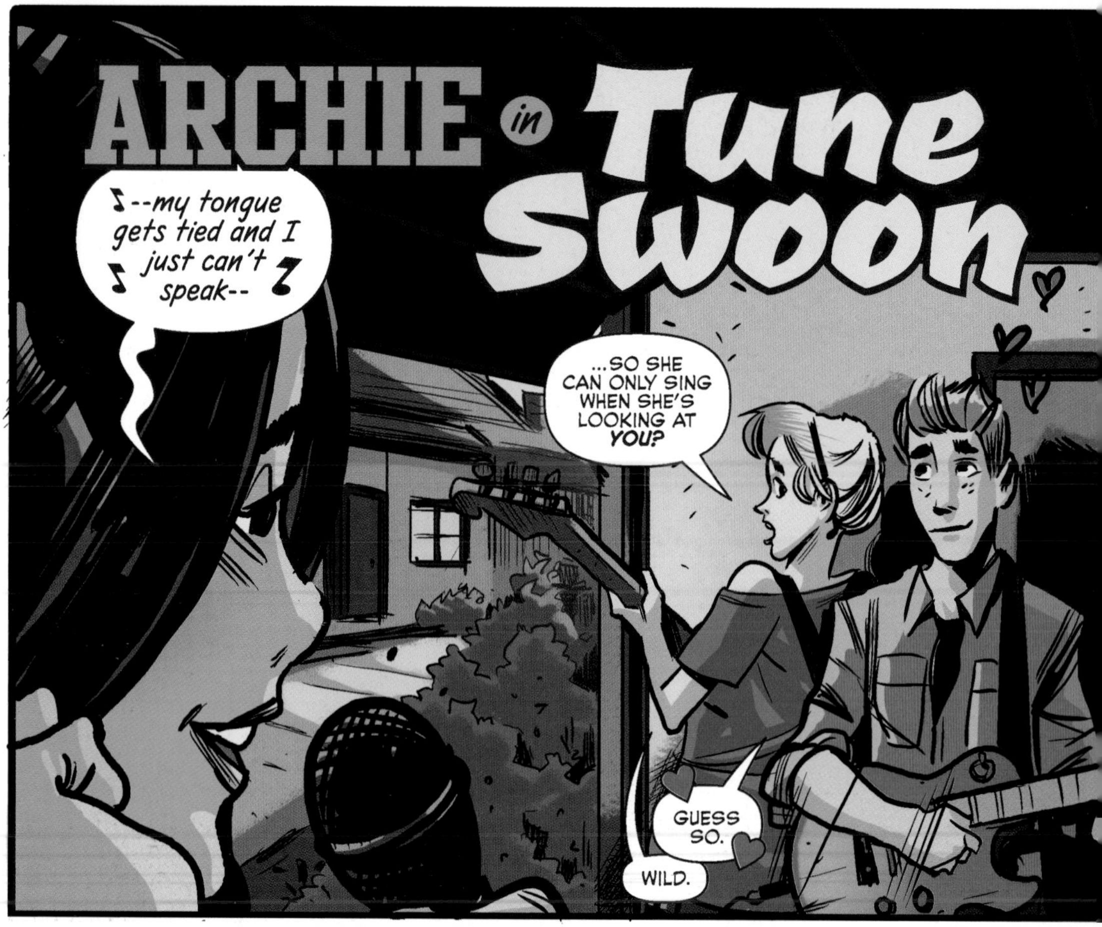
ARCHIE in Tune Swoon
--my tongue gets tied and I just can't speak--
...SO SHE CAN ONLY SING WHEN SHE'S LOOKING AT YOU?
GUESS SO.
WILD.

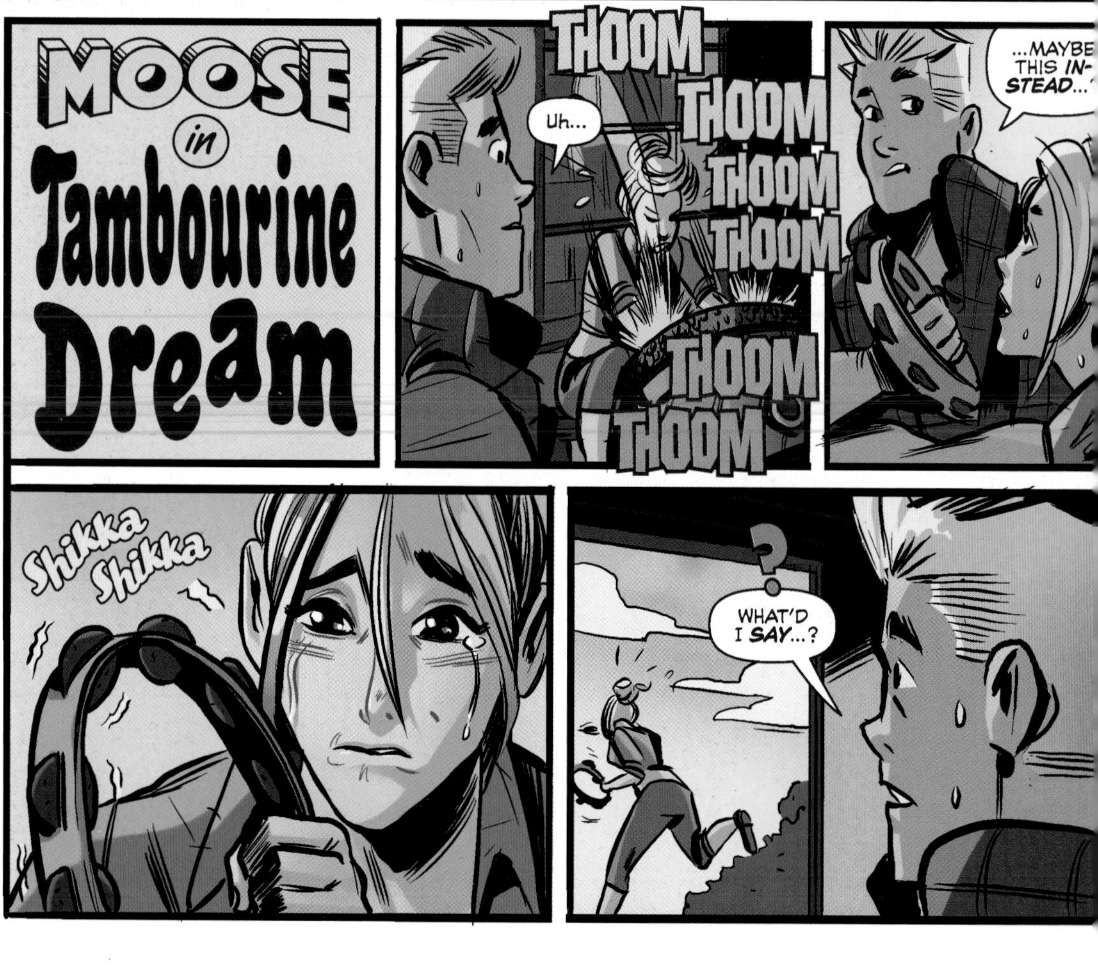
MOOSE in Tambourine Dream
Uh...
THOOM
THOOM
THOOM
THOOM
THOOM
THOOM
...MAYBE THIS IN-STEAD...
Shikka Shikka
WHAT'D I SAY...?

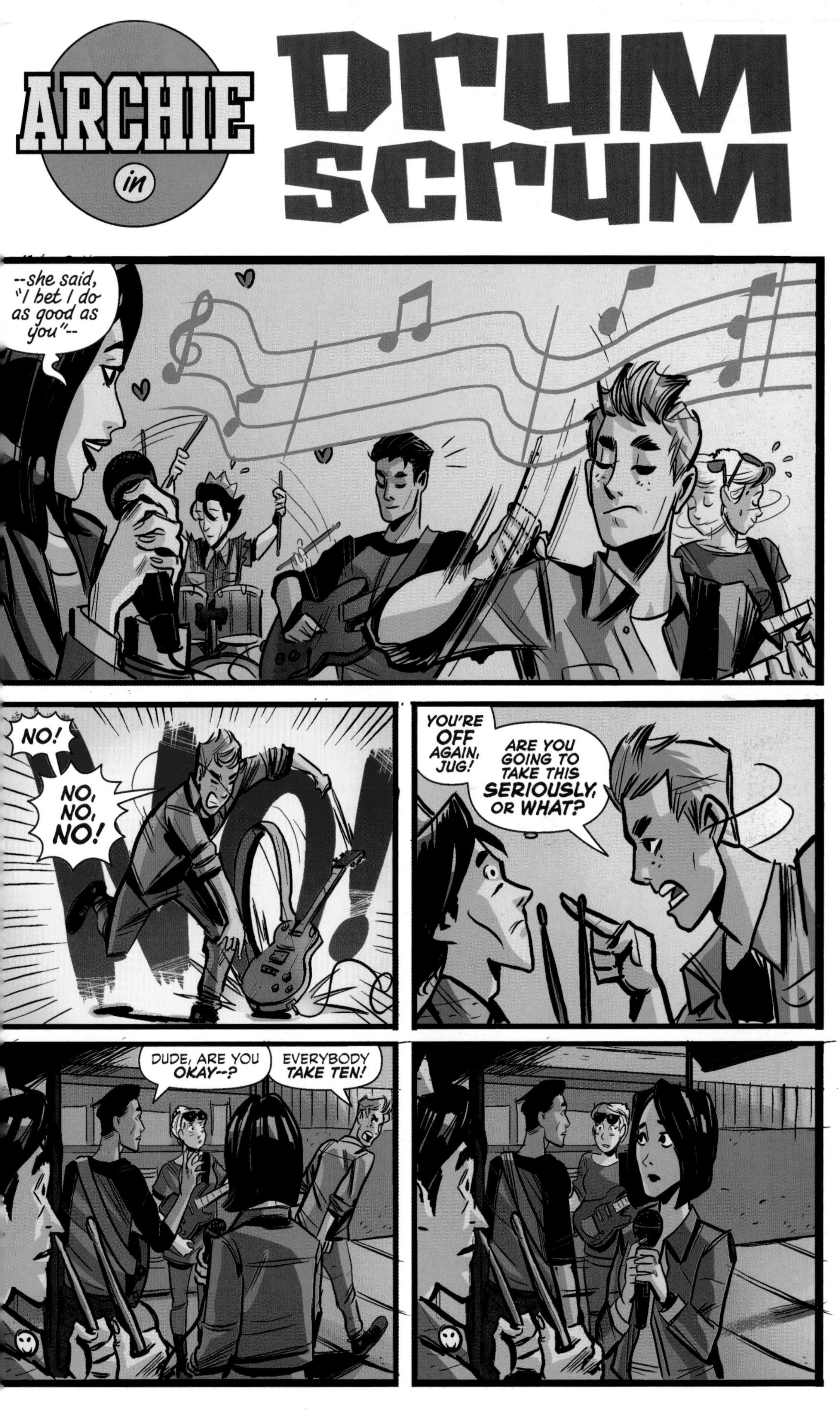
ARCHIE
in
DRUM SCRUM
--she said, "I bet I do as good as you"--
NO!
NO, NO, NO!
YOU'RE OFF AGAIN, JUG!
ARE YOU GOING TO TAKE THIS SERIOUSLY, OR WHAT?
DUDE, ARE YOU OKAY--?
EVERYBODY TAKE TEN!

Jughead in Pals 'n' Gals

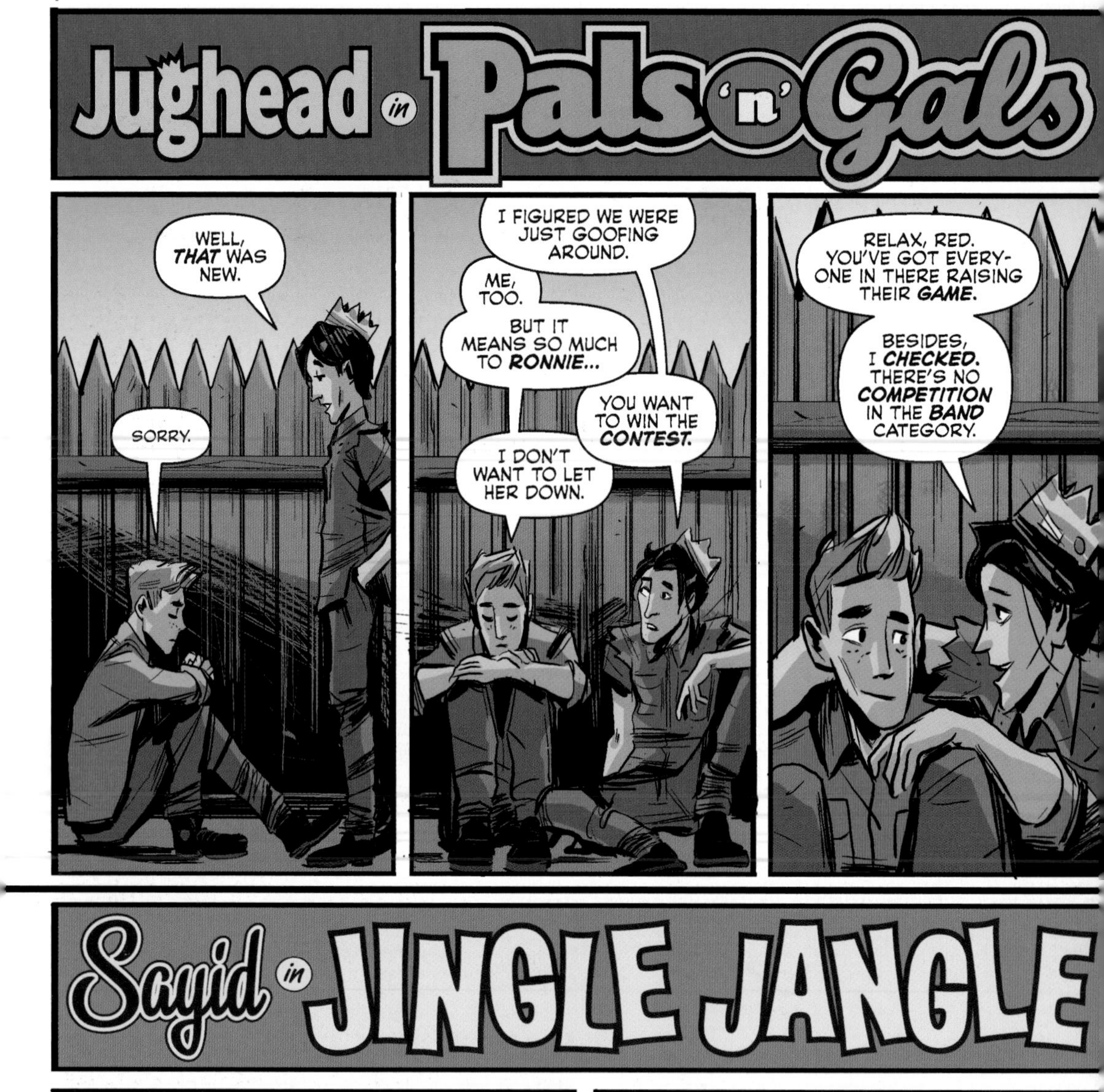
WELL, *THAT* WAS NEW.
SORRY.
I FIGURED WE WERE JUST GOOFING AROUND.
ME, TOO.
BUT IT MEANS SO MUCH TO *RONNIE*...
YOU WANT TO WIN THE *CONTEST.*
I DON'T WANT TO LET HER DOWN.
RELAX, RED. YOU'VE GOT EVERY-ONE IN THERE RAISING THEIR *GAME.*
BESIDES, I *CHECKED.* THERE'S NO *COMPETITION* IN THE *BAND* CATEGORY.

Sayid in JINGLE JANGLE

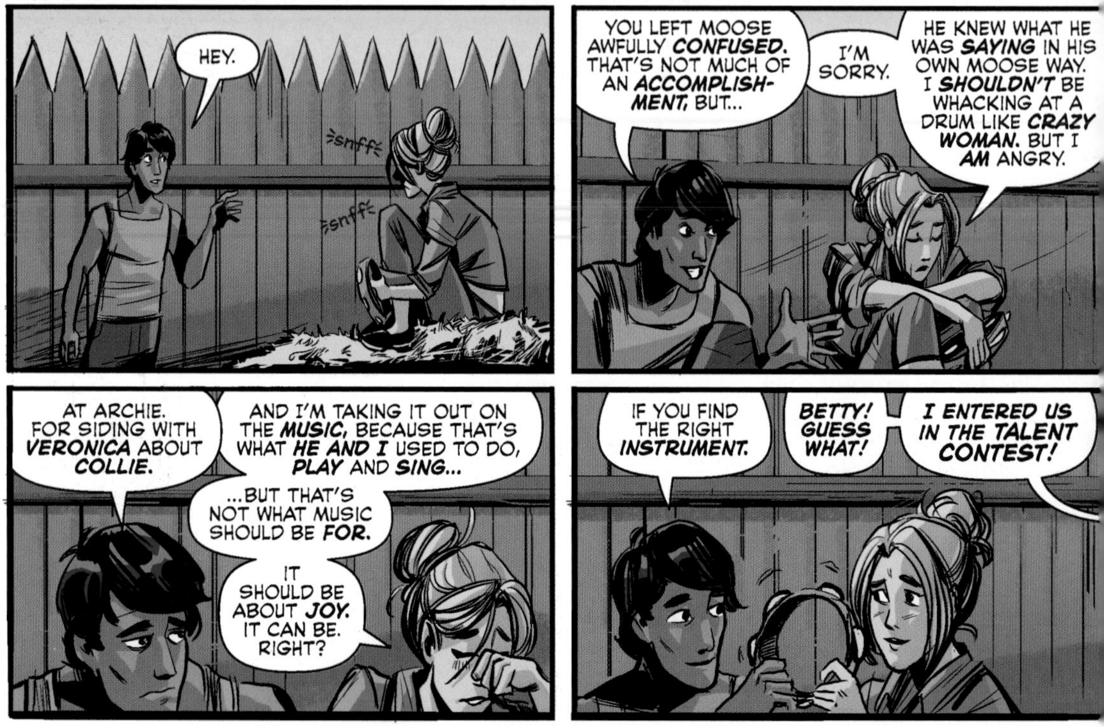
HEY.
SNFF
SNFF
YOU LEFT MOOSE AWFULLY *CONFUSED.* THAT'S NOT MUCH OF AN *ACCOMPLISH-MENT,* BUT...
I'M SORRY.
HE KNEW WHAT HE WAS *SAYING* IN HIS OWN MOOSE WAY. I *SHOULDN'T* BE WHACKING AT A DRUM LIKE *CRAZY WOMAN.* BUT I *AM* ANGRY.
AT ARCHIE. FOR SIDING WITH *VERONICA* ABOUT *COLLIE.*
AND I'M TAKING IT OUT ON THE *MUSIC,* BECAUSE THAT'S WHAT *HE AND I* USED TO DO, *PLAY* AND *SING*...
...BUT THAT'S NOT WHAT MUSIC SHOULD BE *FOR.*
IT SHOULD BE ABOUT *JOY.* IT CAN BE. RIGHT?
IF YOU FIND THE RIGHT *INSTRUMENT.*
BETTY! GUESS WHAT!
I ENTERED US IN THE TALENT CONTEST!

CHAPTER TWO: TWINGG

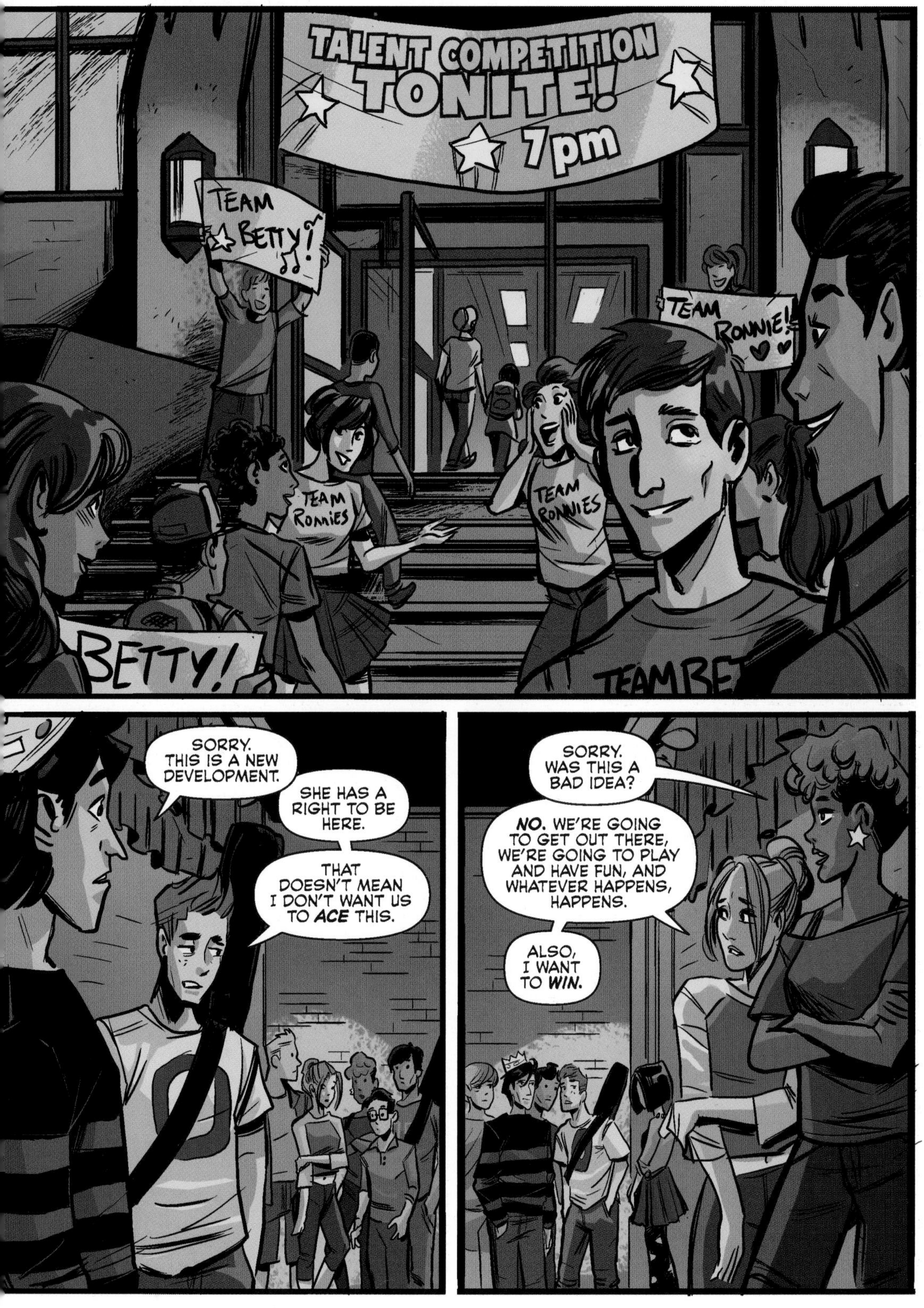
TALENT COMPETITION TONITE! 7pm
TEAM BETTY!
TEAM RONNIE!
TEAM RONNIES
TEAM RONNIES
BETTY!
TEAM BE
SORRY. THIS IS A NEW DEVELOPMENT.
SHE HAS A RIGHT TO BE HERE.
THAT DOESN'T MEAN I DON'T WANT US TO *ACE* THIS.
SORRY. WAS THIS A BAD IDEA?
NO. WE'RE GOING TO GET OUT THERE, WE'RE GOING TO PLAY AND HAVE FUN, AND WHATEVER HAPPENS, HAPPENS.
ALSO, I WANT TO *WIN.*

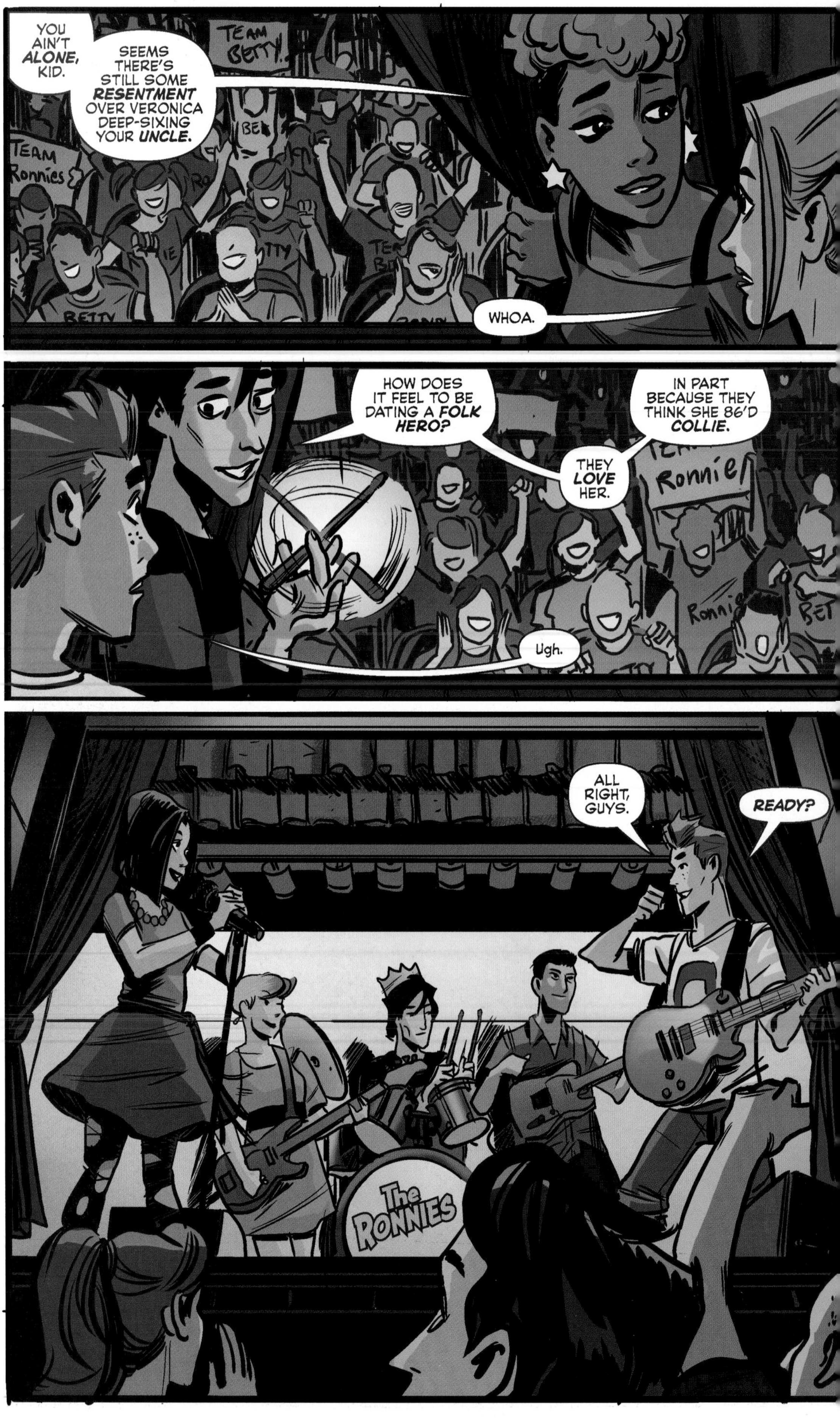
TEAM BETTY!
TEAM Ronnie
YOU AIN'T ALONE, KID.
SEEMS THERE'S STILL SOME RESENTMENT OVER VERONICA DEEP-SIXING YOUR UNCLE.
WHOA.
HOW DOES IT FEEL TO BE DATING A FOLK HERO?
THEY LOVE HER.
IN PART BECAUSE THEY THINK SHE 86'D COLLIE.
Ronnie
Ugh.
ALL RIGHT, GUYS.
READY?
The RONNIES

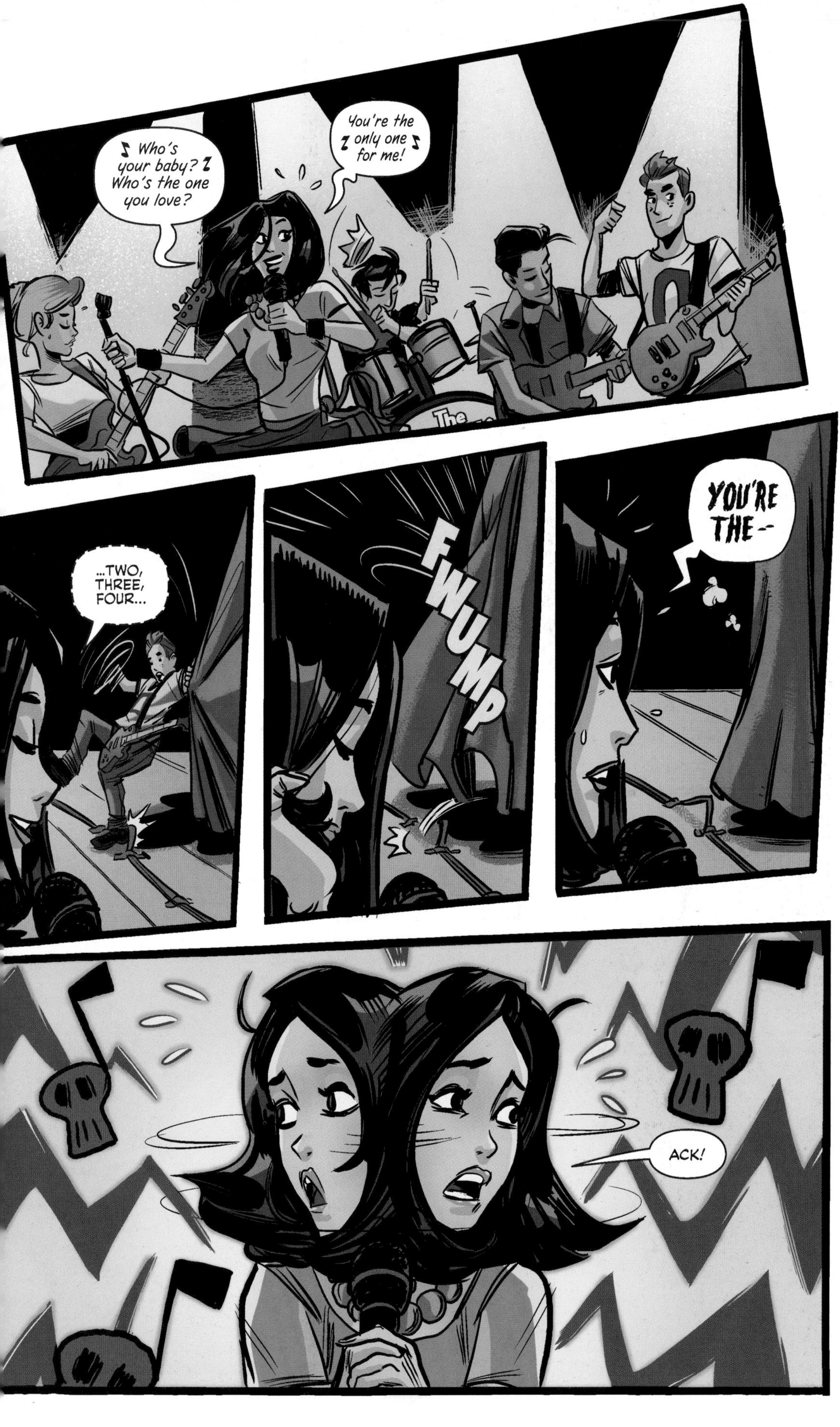
Who's your baby? Who's the one you love?
You're the only one for me!
The
...TWO, THREE, FOUR...
FWUMP
YOU'RE THE--
ACK!

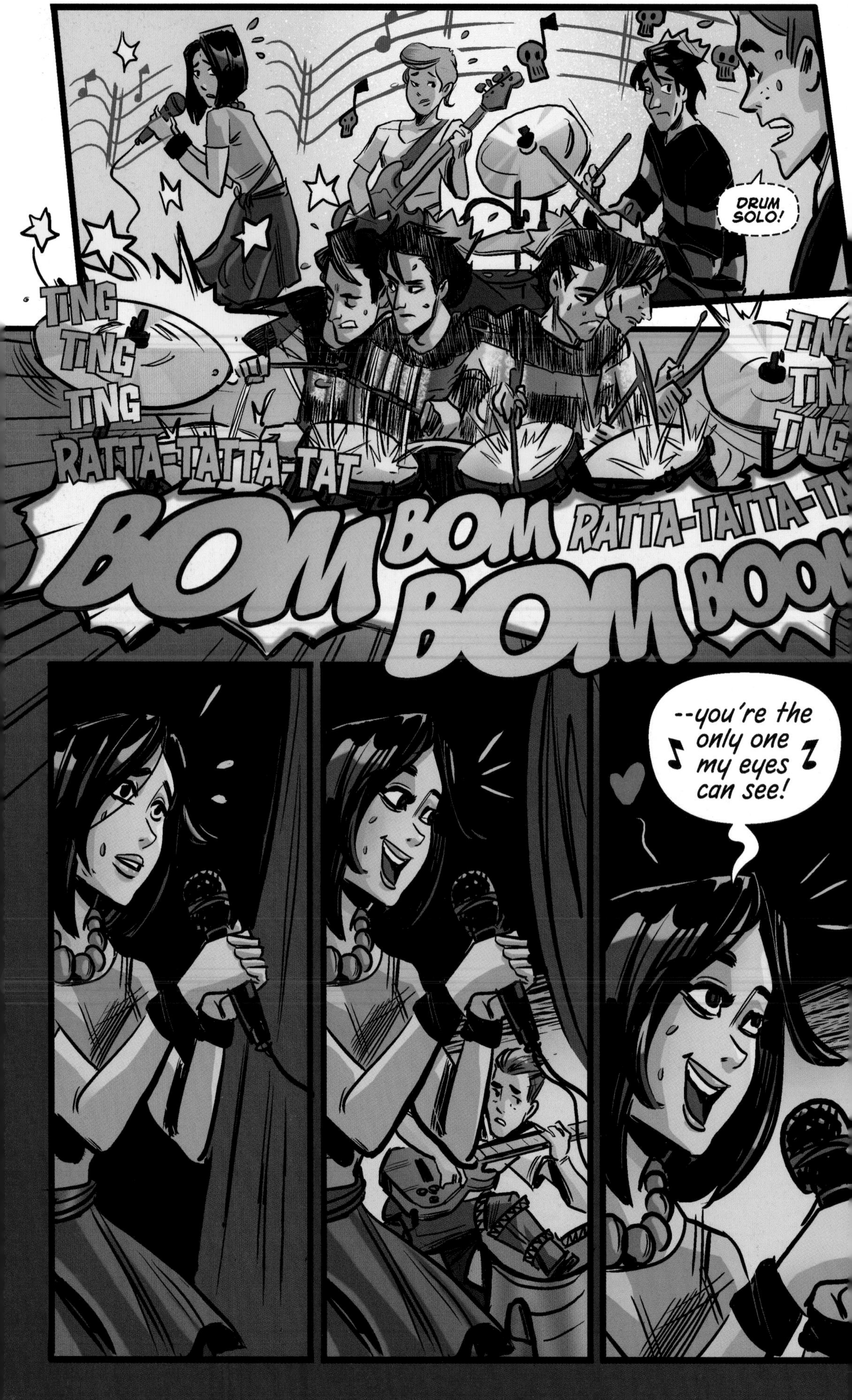
DRUM SOLO!
TING
TING
TING
RATTA-TATTA-TAT
TING
TING
TING
BOM BOM RATTA-TATTA-TA
BOM BOO
--you're the only one my eyes can see!

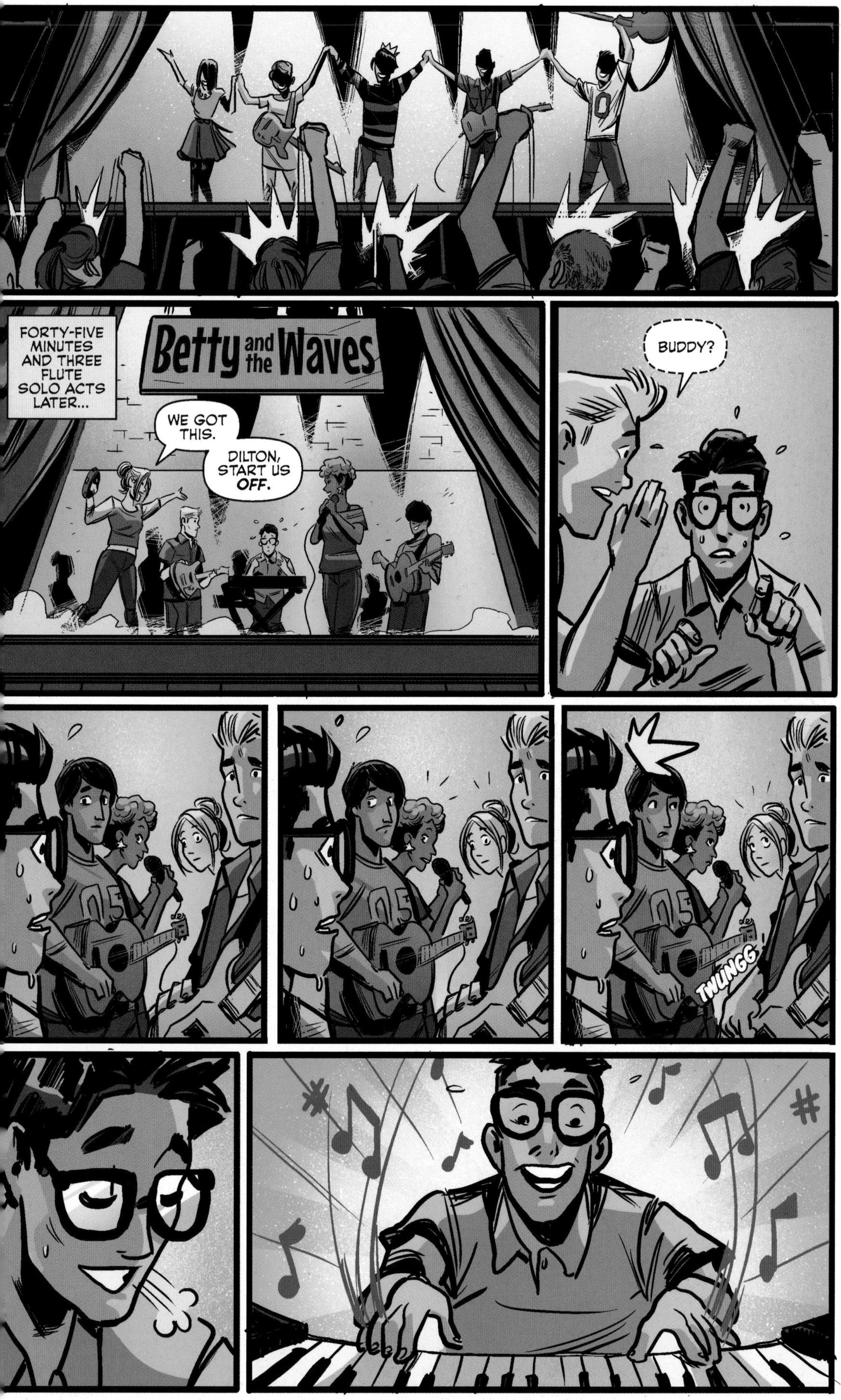
FORTY-FIVE MINUTES AND THREE FLUTE SOLO ACTS LATER...
Betty and the Waves
WE GOT THIS.
DILTON, START US OFF.
BUDDY?
TWUNGG

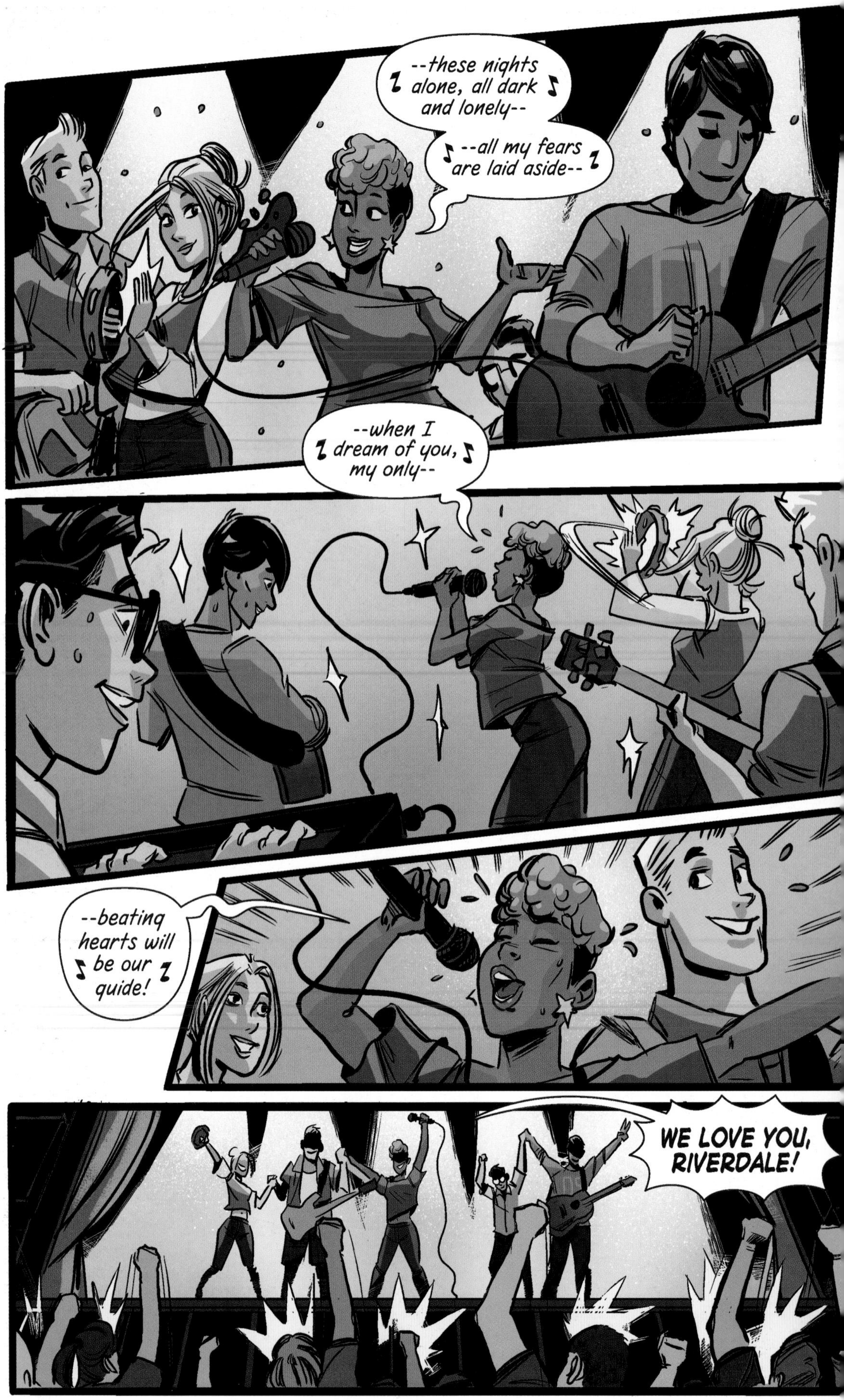
--these nights alone, all dark and lonely--
--all my fears are laid aside--
--when I dream of you, my only--
--beating hearts will be our guide!
WE LOVE YOU, RIVERDALE!

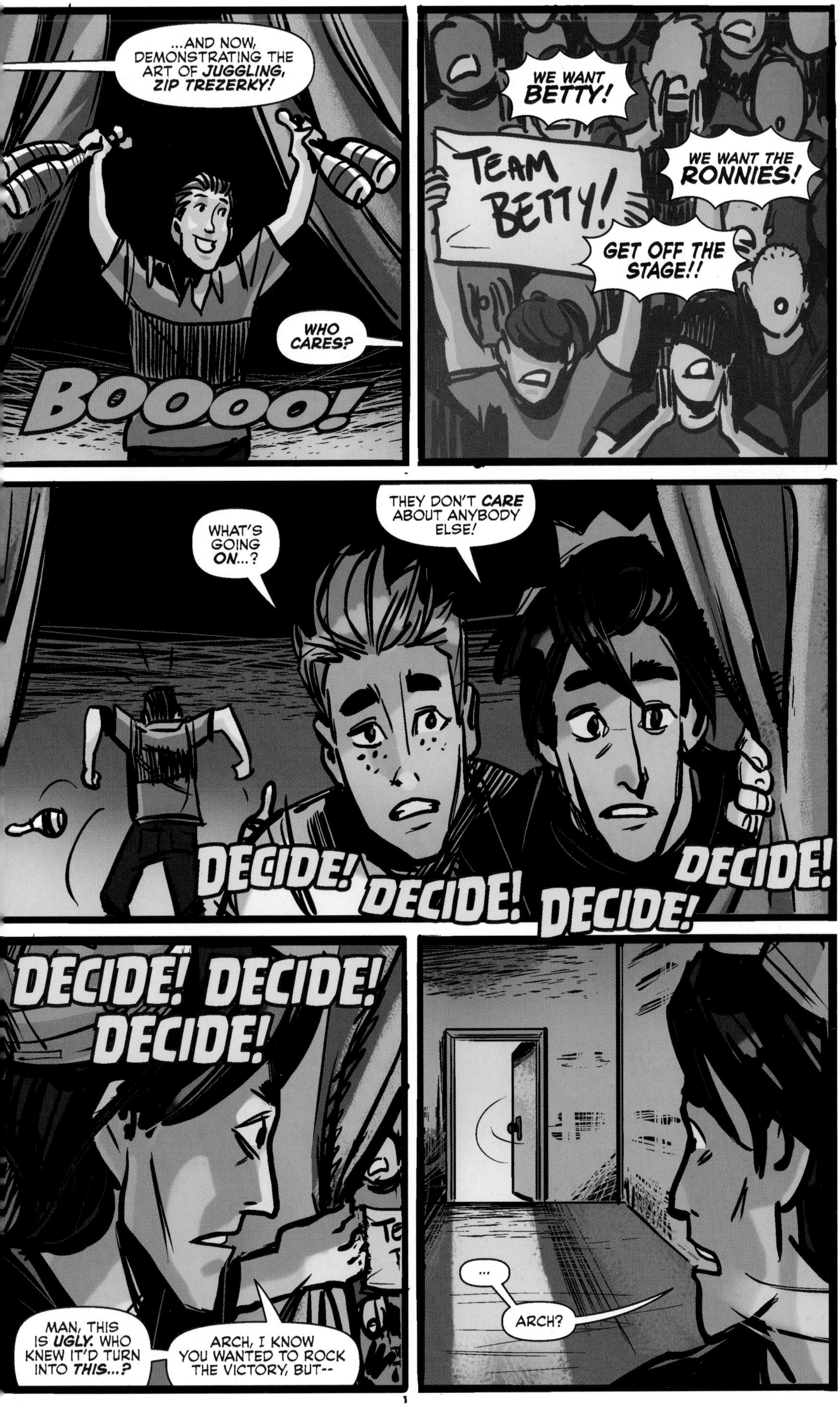

...AND NOW, DEMONSTRATING THE ART OF JUGGLING, ZIP TREZERKY!
WHO CARES?
BOOOOO!
WE WANT BETTY!
TEAM BETTY!
WE WANT THE RONNIES!
GET OFF THE STAGE!!
WHAT'S GOING ON...?
THEY DON'T CARE ABOUT ANYBODY ELSE!
DECIDE! DECIDE! DECIDE! DECIDE!
DECIDE! DECIDE! DECIDE!
MAN, THIS IS UGLY. WHO KNEW IT'D TURN INTO THIS...?
ARCH, I KNOW YOU WANTED TO ROCK THE VICTORY, BUT--
...
ARCH?

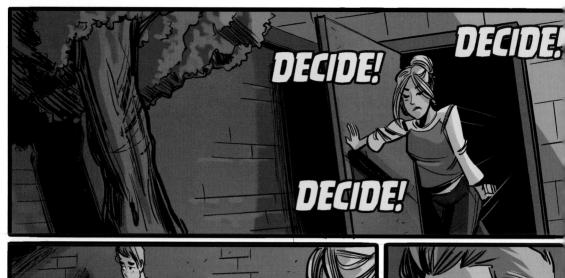

DECIDE! DECIDE! DECIDE!

I'M SORRY.

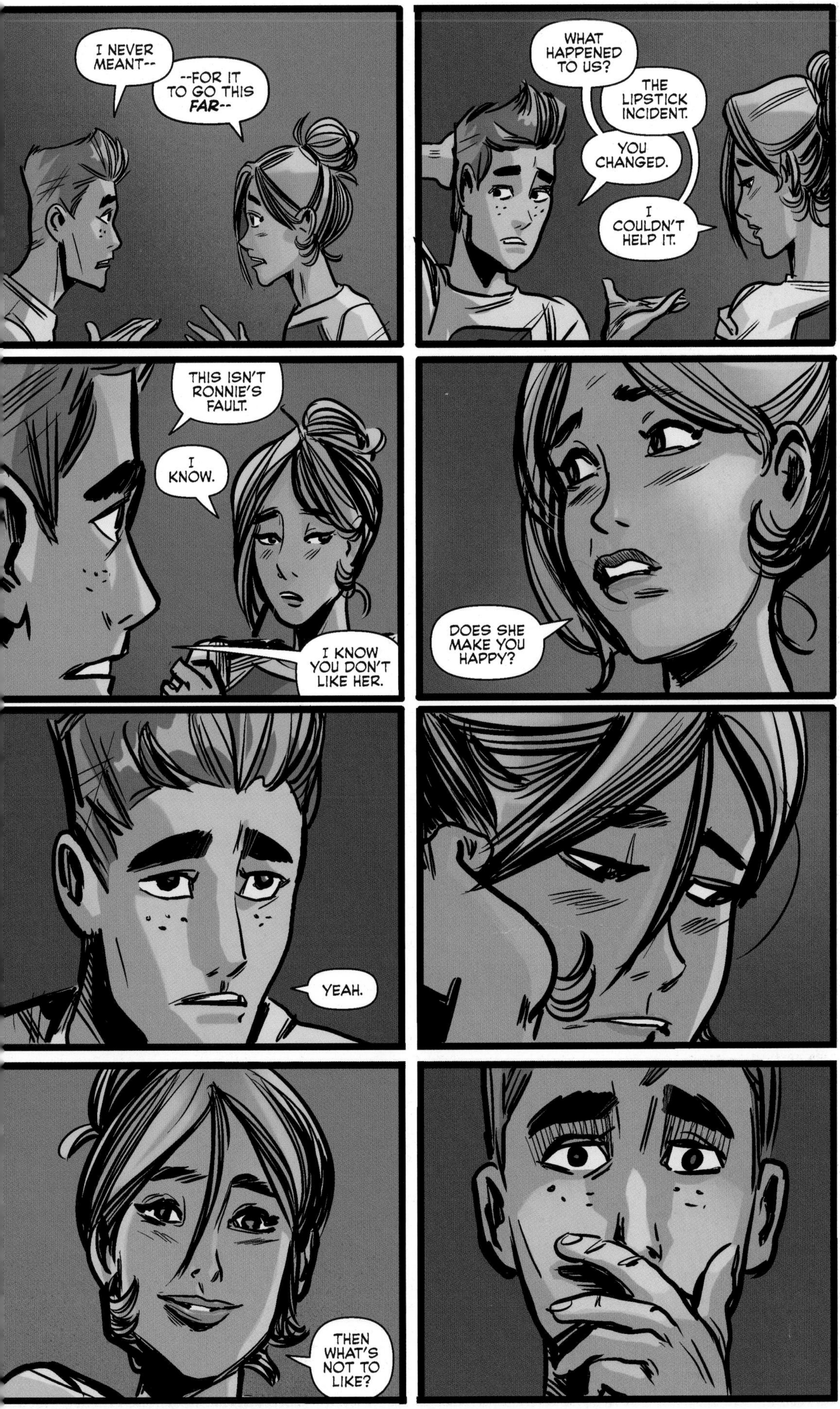
I NEVER MEANT--
--FOR IT TO GO THIS **FAR**--
WHAT HAPPENED TO US?
THE LIPSTICK INCIDENT.
YOU CHANGED.
I COULDN'T HELP IT.
THIS ISN'T RONNIE'S FAULT.
I KNOW.
I KNOW YOU DON'T LIKE HER.
DOES SHE MAKE YOU HAPPY?
YEAH.
THEN WHAT'S NOT TO LIKE?

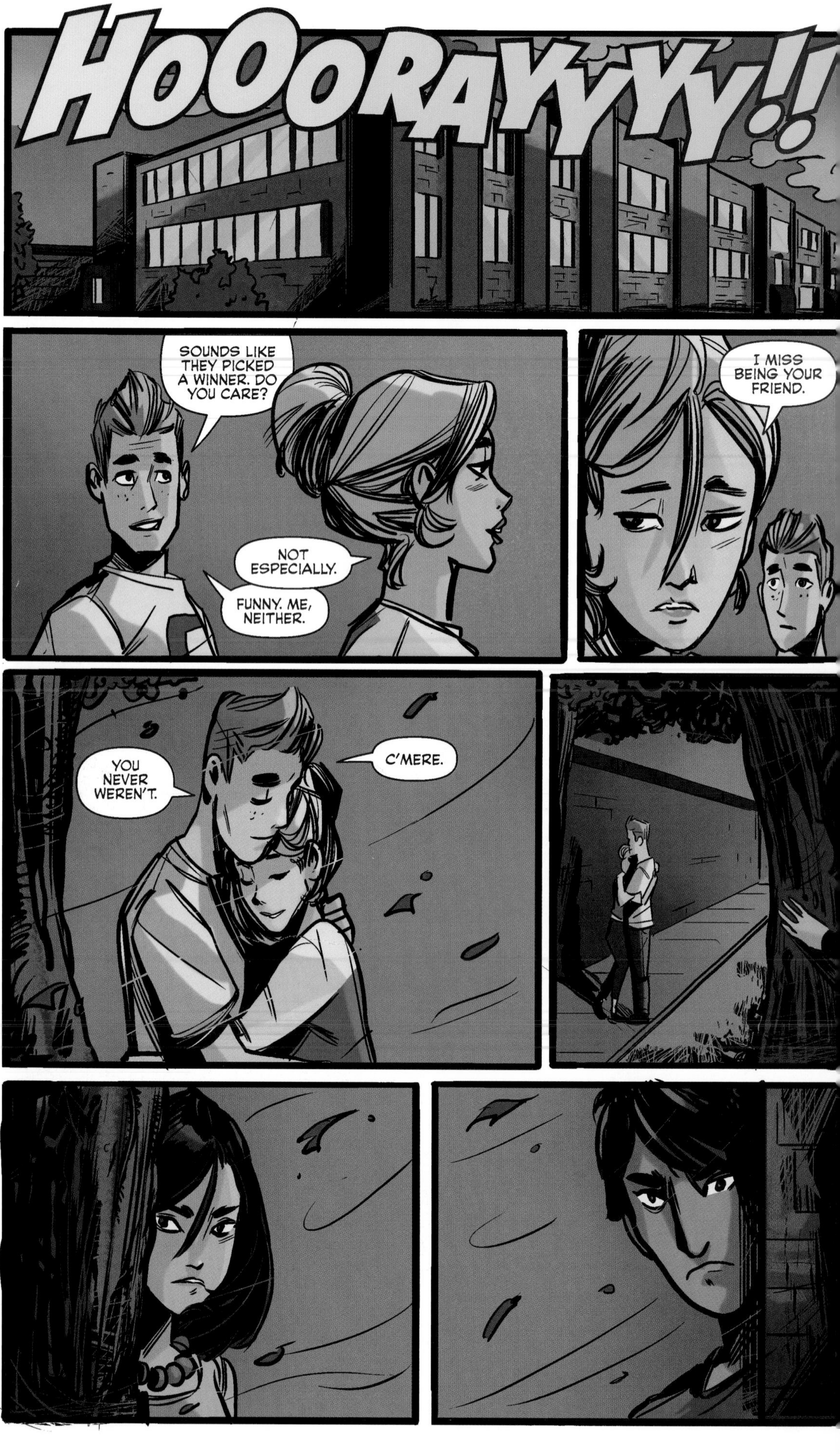
HOOORAYYYY!!
SOUNDS LIKE THEY PICKED A WINNER. DO YOU CARE?
NOT ESPECIALLY.
FUNNY. ME, NEITHER.
I MISS BEING YOUR FRIEND.
YOU NEVER WEREN'T.
C'MERE.

TO BE CONTINUED...

ISSUE TWELVE

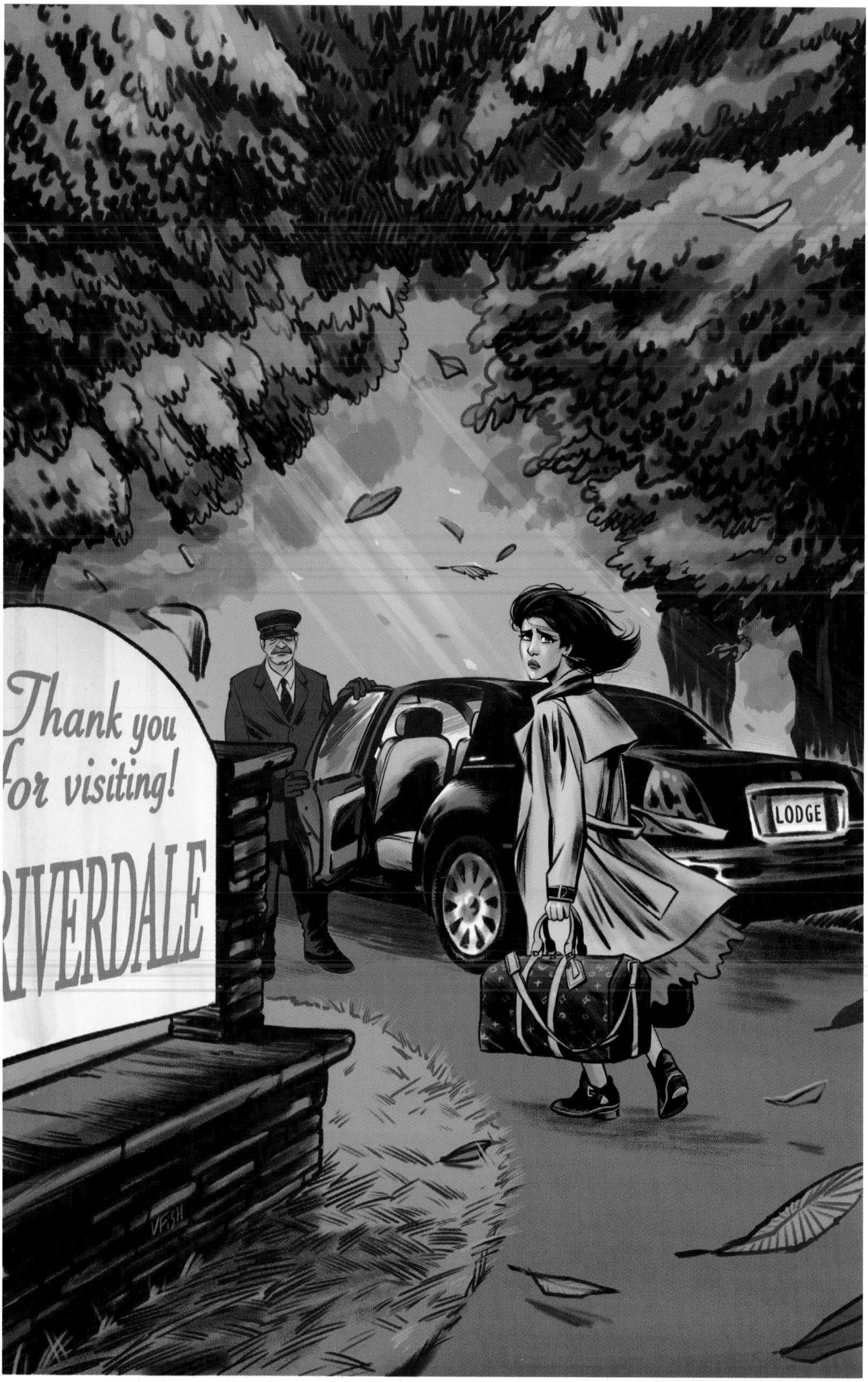
Thank you
for visiting!
RIVERDALE
LODGE
VFISH

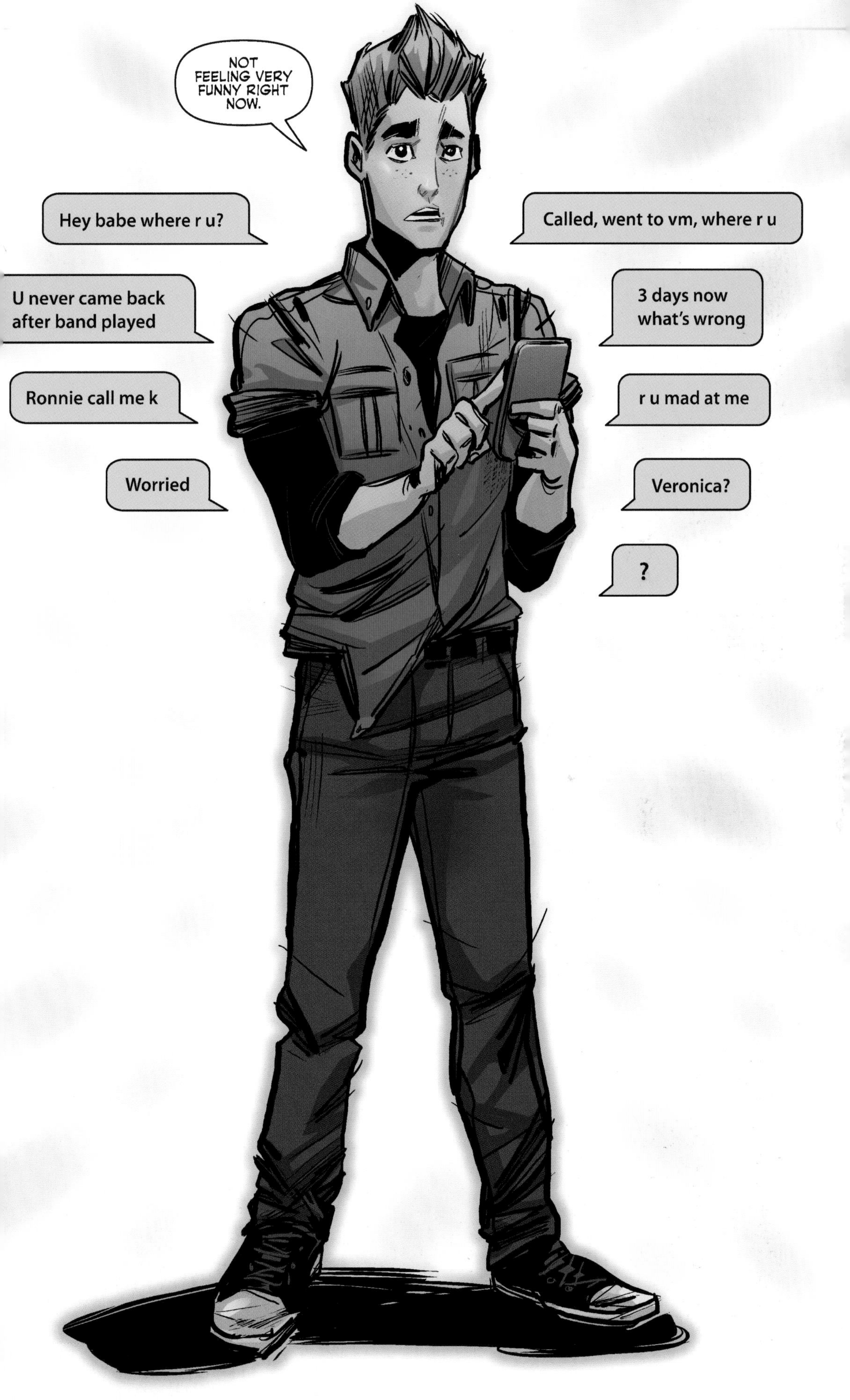
NOT FEELING VERY FUNNY RIGHT NOW.
Hey babe where r u?
Called, went to vm, where r u
U never came back after band played
3 days now what's wrong
Ronnie call me k
r u mad at me
Worried
Veronica?
?

CHAPTER ONE: ...NOW YOU DON'T.

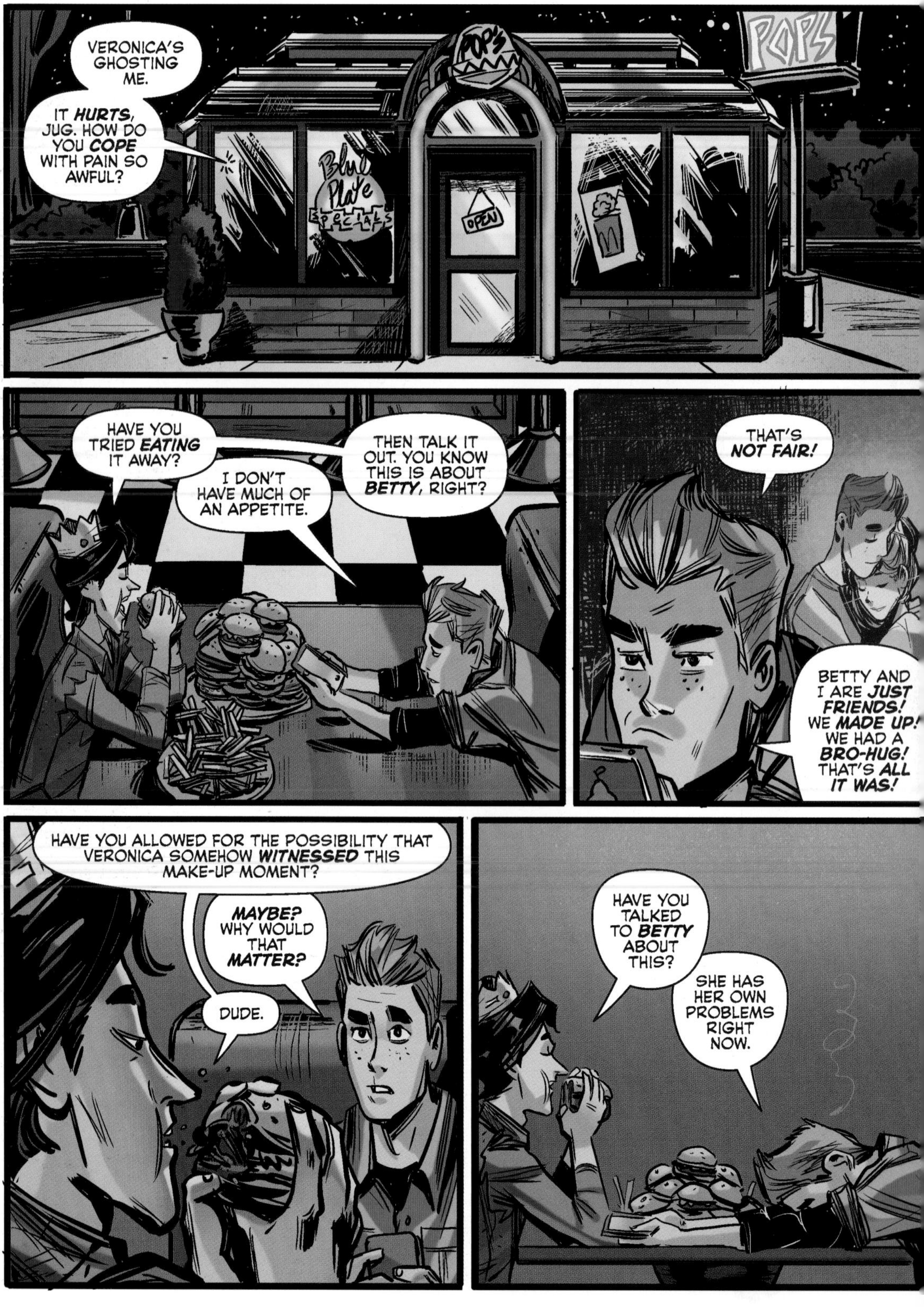

POP'S
VERONICA'S GHOSTING ME.
IT HURTS, JUG. HOW DO YOU COPE WITH PAIN SO AWFUL?
OPEN
HAVE YOU TRIED EATING IT AWAY?
I DON'T HAVE MUCH OF AN APPETITE.
THEN TALK IT OUT. YOU KNOW THIS IS ABOUT BETTY, RIGHT?
THAT'S NOT FAIR!
BETTY AND I ARE JUST FRIENDS! WE MADE UP! WE HAD A BRO-HUG! THAT'S ALL IT WAS!
HAVE YOU ALLOWED FOR THE POSSIBILITY THAT VERONICA SOMEHOW WITNESSED THIS MAKE-UP MOMENT?
MAYBE? WHY WOULD THAT MATTER?
DUDE.
HAVE YOU TALKED TO BETTY ABOUT THIS?
SHE HAS HER OWN PROBLEMS RIGHT NOW.

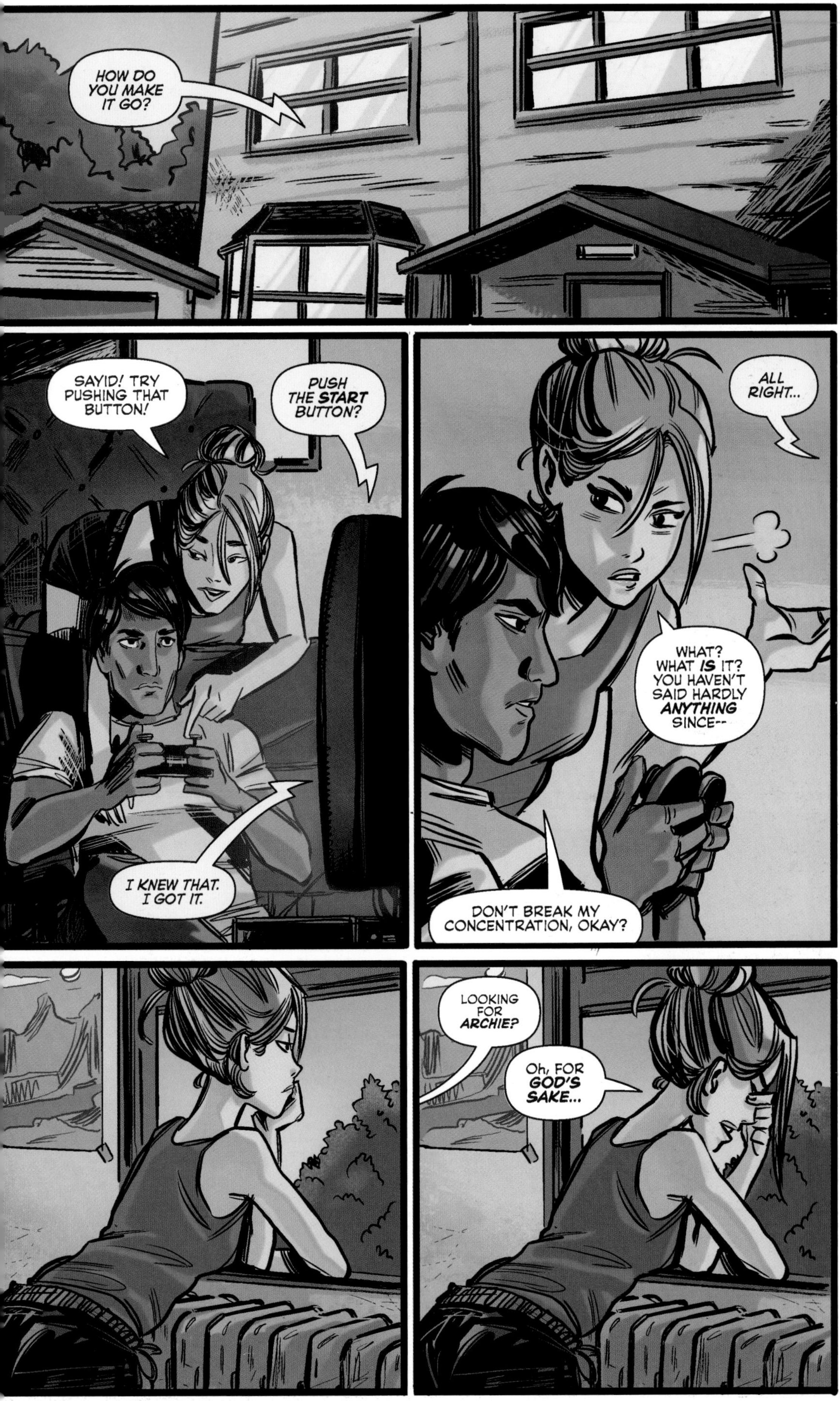
HOW DO YOU MAKE IT GO?
SAYID! TRY PUSHING THAT BUTTON!
PUSH THE START BUTTON?
I KNEW THAT. I GOT IT.
ALL RIGHT...
WHAT? WHAT IS IT? YOU HAVEN'T SAID HARDLY ANYTHING SINCE--
DON'T BREAK MY CONCENTRATION, OKAY?
LOOKING FOR ARCHIE?
Oh, FOR GOD'S SAKE...

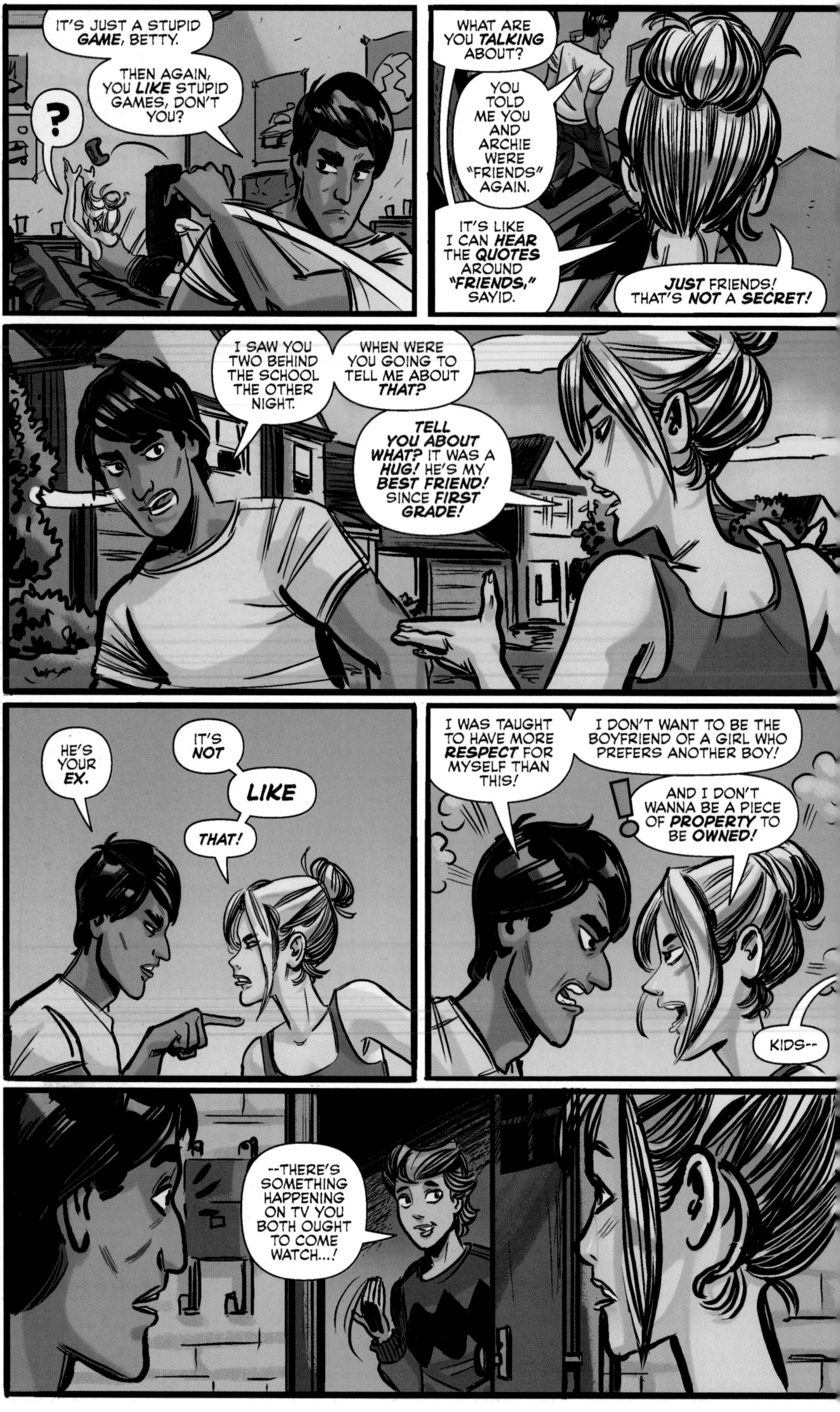
IT'S JUST A STUPID GAME, BETTY.
THEN AGAIN, YOU LIKE STUPID GAMES, DON'T YOU?
?
WHAT ARE YOU TALKING ABOUT?
YOU TOLD ME YOU AND ARCHIE WERE "FRIENDS" AGAIN.
IT'S LIKE I CAN HEAR THE QUOTES AROUND "FRIENDS," SAYID.
JUST FRIENDS! THAT'S NOT A SECRET!
I SAW YOU TWO BEHIND THE SCHOOL THE OTHER NIGHT.
WHEN WERE YOU GOING TO TELL ME ABOUT THAT?
TELL YOU ABOUT WHAT? IT WAS A HUG! HE'S MY BEST FRIEND! SINCE FIRST GRADE!
HE'S YOUR EX.
IT'S NOT
LIKE
THAT!
I WAS TAUGHT TO HAVE MORE RESPECT FOR MYSELF THAN THIS!
I DON'T WANT TO BE THE BOYFRIEND OF A GIRL WHO PREFERS ANOTHER BOY!
!
AND I DON'T WANNA BE A PIECE OF PROPERTY TO BE OWNED!
KIDS--
--THERE'S SOMETHING HAPPENING ON TV YOU BOTH OUGHT TO COME WATCH...!

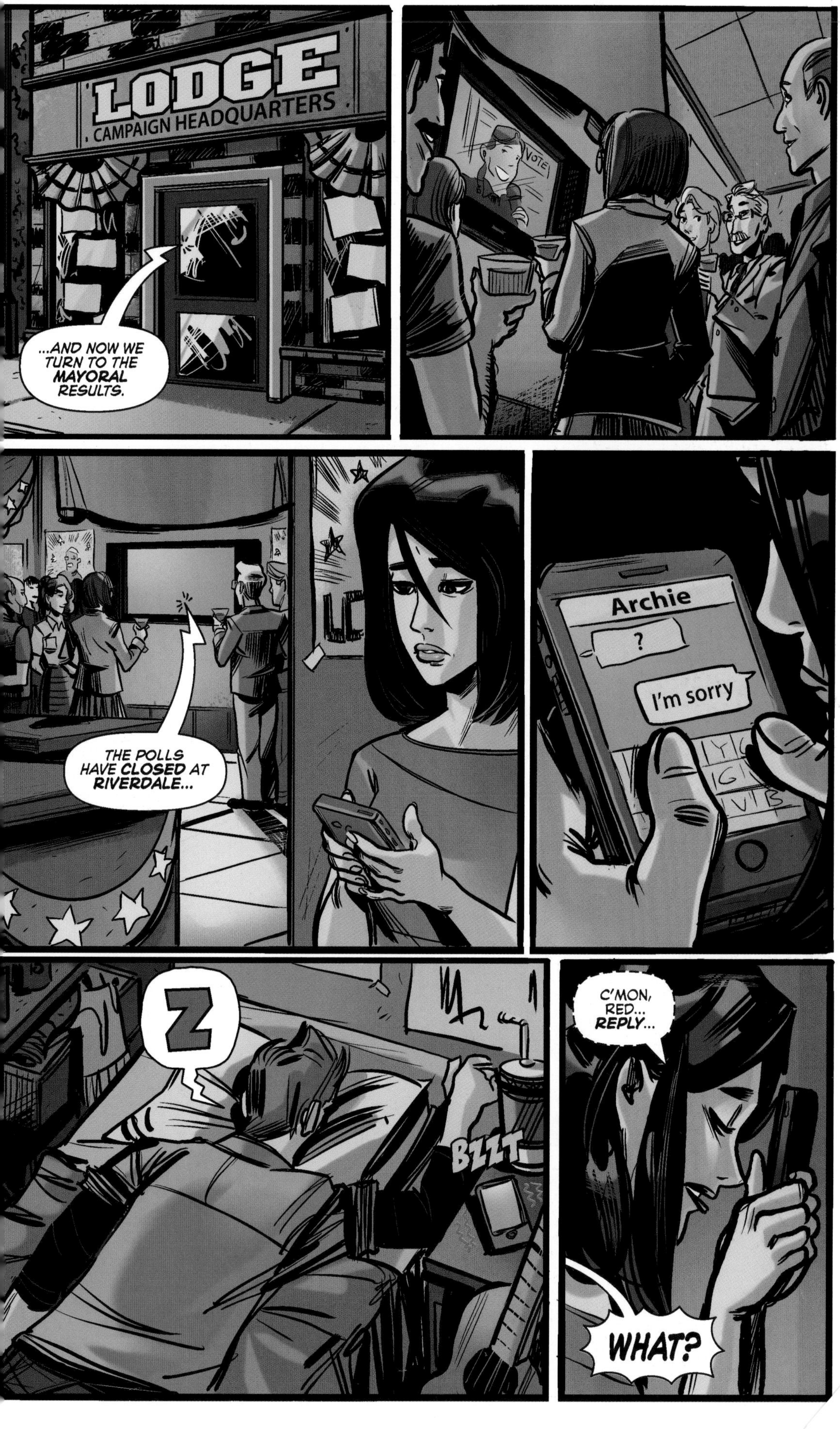
LODGE
CAMPAIGN HEADQUARTERS
...AND NOW WE TURN TO THE MAYORAL RESULTS.
VOTE
THE POLLS HAVE CLOSED AT RIVERDALE...
Archie
?
I'm sorry
Z
BZZZT
C'MON, RED... REPLY...
WHAT?

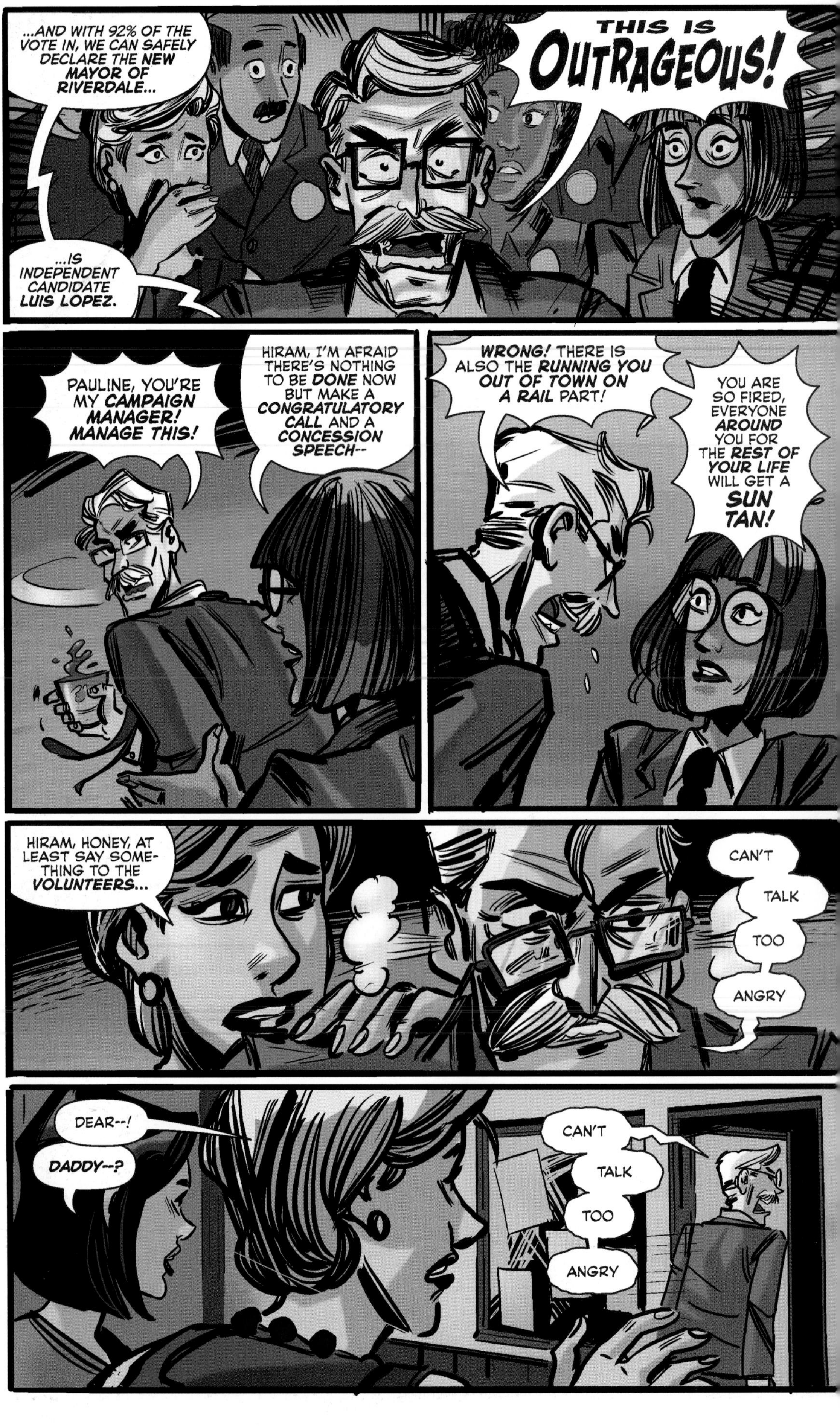
...AND WITH 92% OF THE VOTE IN, WE CAN SAFELY DECLARE THE NEW MAYOR OF RIVERDALE...
...IS INDEPENDENT CANDIDATE LUIS LOPEZ.
THIS IS OUTRAGEOUS!
PAULINE, YOU'RE MY CAMPAIGN MANAGER! MANAGE THIS!
HIRAM, I'M AFRAID THERE'S NOTHING TO BE DONE NOW BUT MAKE A CONGRATULATORY CALL AND A CONCESSION SPEECH--
WRONG! THERE IS ALSO THE RUNNING YOU OUT OF TOWN ON A RAIL PART!
YOU ARE SO FIRED, EVERYONE AROUND YOU FOR THE REST OF YOUR LIFE WILL GET A SUN TAN!
HIRAM, HONEY, AT LEAST SAY SOME-THING TO THE VOLUNTEERS...
CAN'T
TALK
TOO
ANGRY
DEAR--!
DADDY--?
CAN'T
TALK
TOO
ANGRY

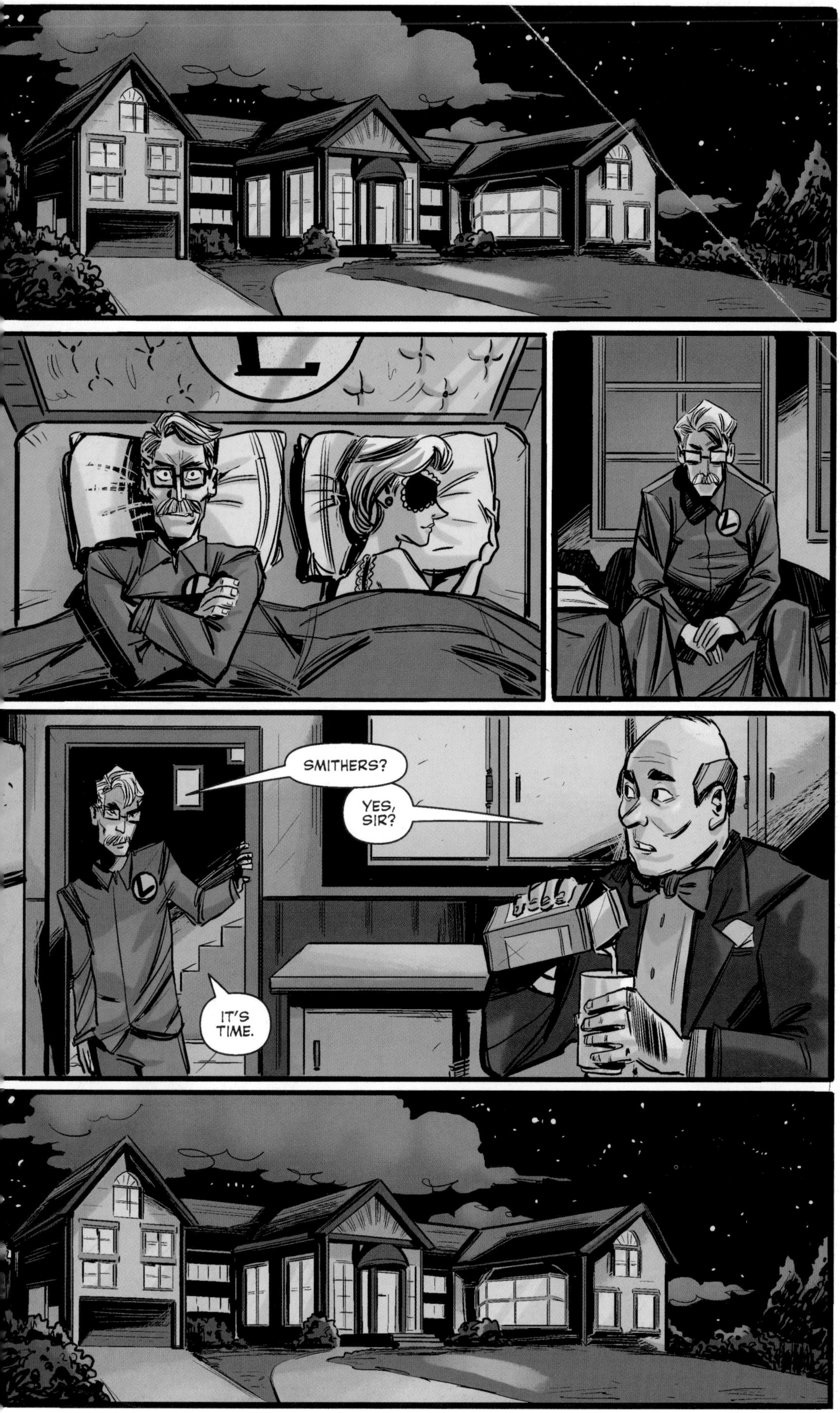
SMITHERS?
YES, SIR?
IT'S TIME.

CHAPTER TWO: MORNING IN RIVERDALE

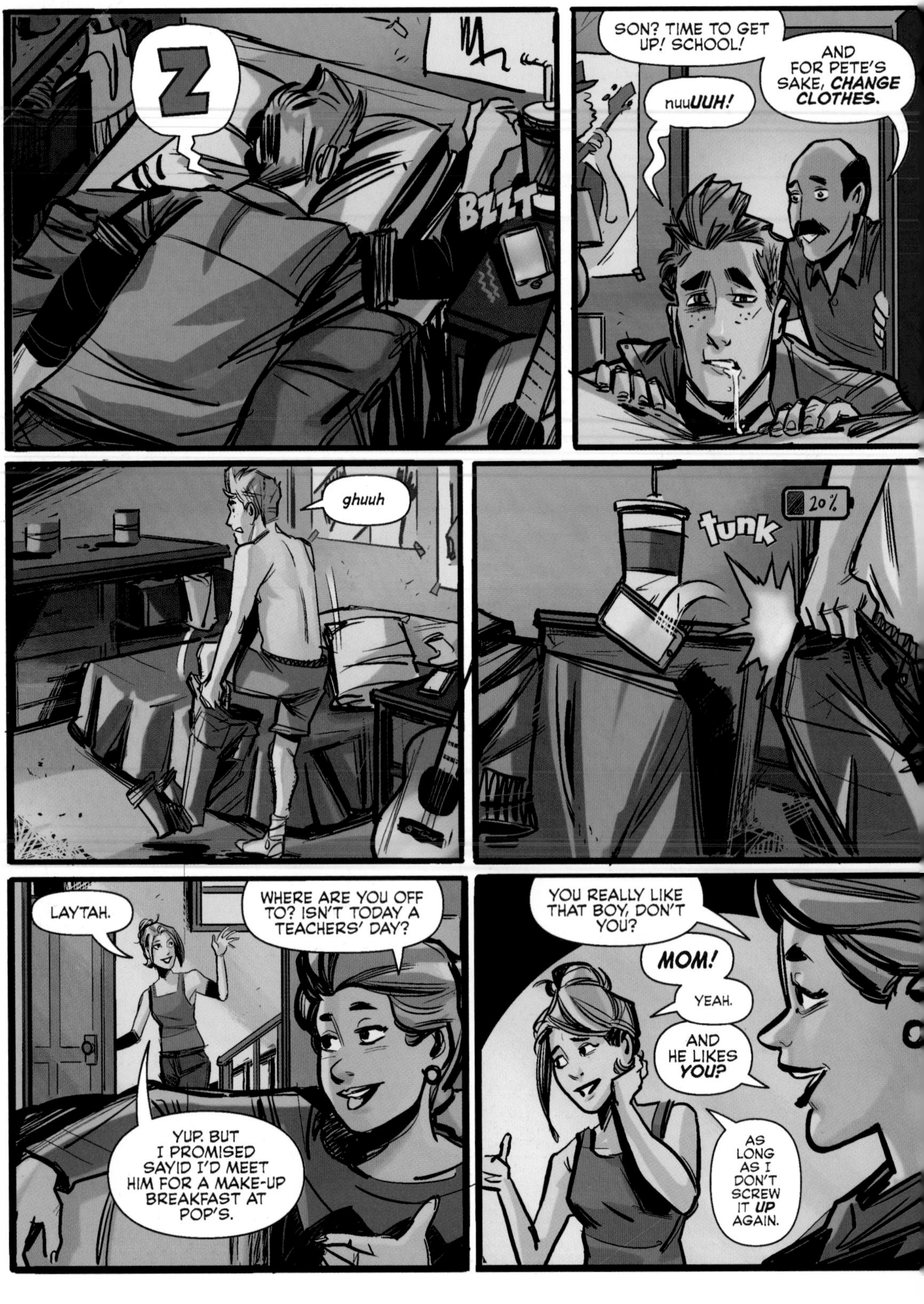
Z
BZZT
SON? TIME TO GET UP! SCHOOL!
nuuUUH!
AND FOR PETE'S SAKE, **CHANGE CLOTHES.**
ghuuh
20%
tunk
LAYTAH.
WHERE ARE YOU OFF TO? ISN'T TODAY A TEACHERS' DAY?
YUP. BUT I PROMISED SAYID I'D MEET HIM FOR A MAKE-UP BREAKFAST AT POP'S.
YOU REALLY LIKE THAT BOY, DON'T YOU?
MOM!
YEAH.
AND HE LIKES ***YOU?***
AS LONG AS I DON'T SCREW IT ***UP*** AGAIN.

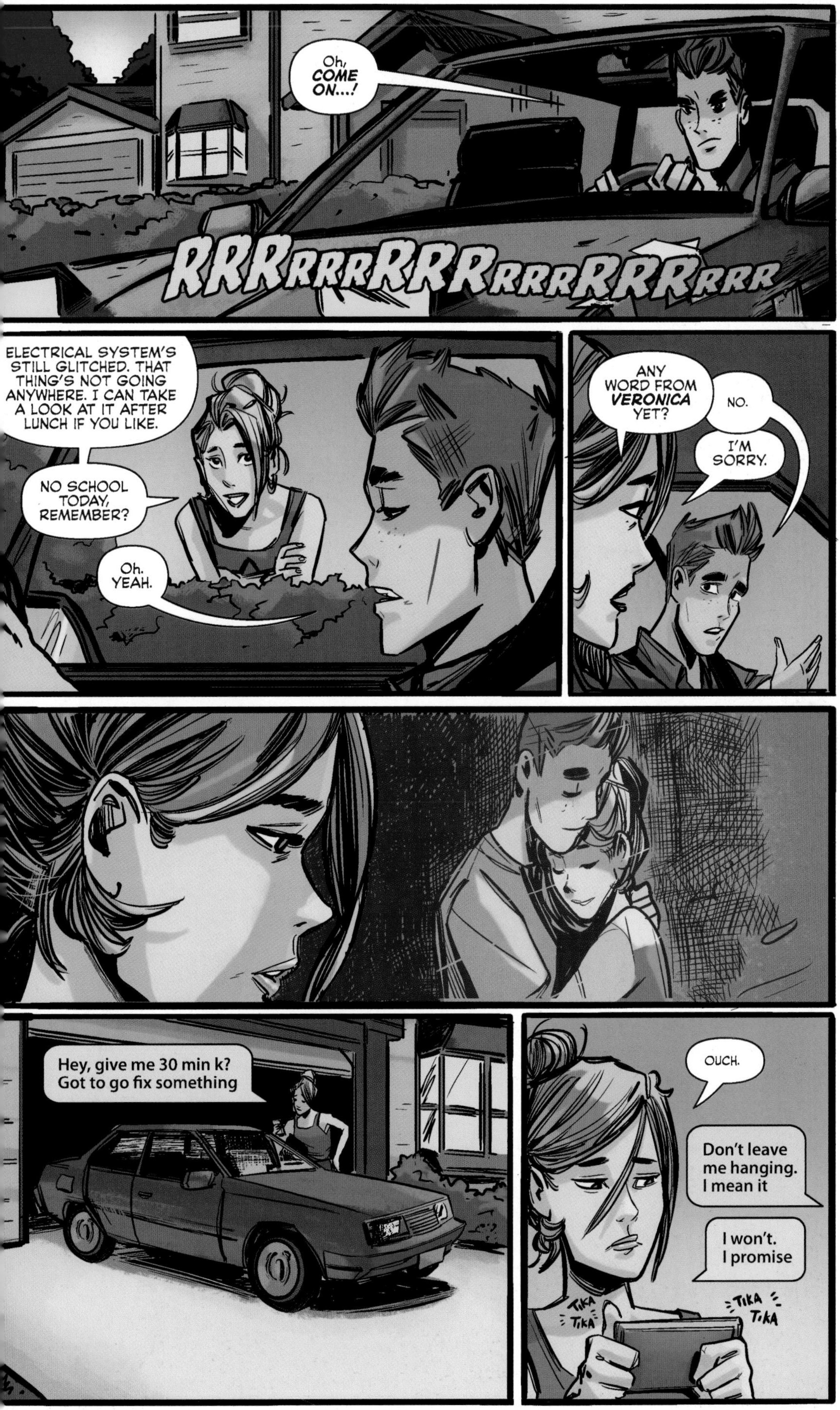

Oh, COME ON...!
RRRrrrRRRrrrRRRrrr
ELECTRICAL SYSTEM'S STILL GLITCHED. THAT THING'S NOT GOING ANYWHERE. I CAN TAKE A LOOK AT IT AFTER LUNCH IF YOU LIKE.
NO SCHOOL TODAY, REMEMBER?
Oh. YEAH.
ANY WORD FROM VERONICA YET?
NO.
I'M SORRY.
Hey, give me 30 min k? Got to go fix something
OUCH.
Don't leave me hanging. I mean it
I won't. I promise
TIKA TIKA
TIKA TIKA

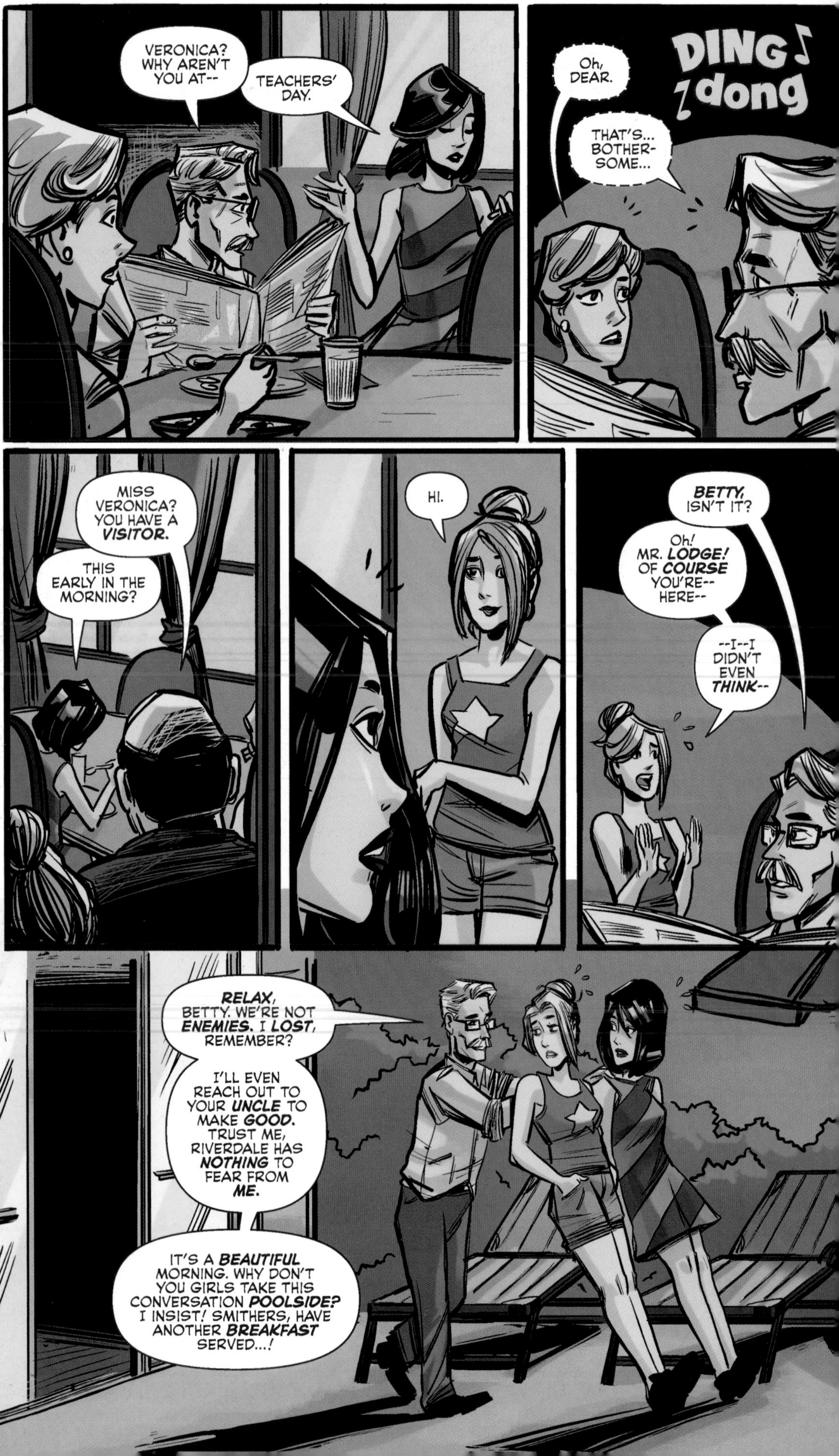
VERONICA? WHY AREN'T YOU AT--
TEACHERS' DAY.
Oh, DEAR.
THAT'S... BOTHER-SOME...
DING dong
MISS VERONICA? YOU HAVE A VISITOR.
THIS EARLY IN THE MORNING?
HI.
BETTY, ISN'T IT?
Oh! MR. LODGE! OF COURSE YOU'RE-- HERE--
--I--I DIDN'T EVEN THINK--
RELAX, BETTY. WE'RE NOT ENEMIES. I LOST, REMEMBER?
I'LL EVEN REACH OUT TO YOUR UNCLE TO MAKE GOOD. TRUST ME, RIVERDALE HAS NOTHING TO FEAR FROM ME.
IT'S A BEAUTIFUL MORNING. WHY DON'T YOU GIRLS TAKE THIS CONVERSATION POOLSIDE? I INSIST! SMITHERS, HAVE ANOTHER BREAKFAST SERVED...!

CHAPTER THREE: RRRrrrRRRrrr

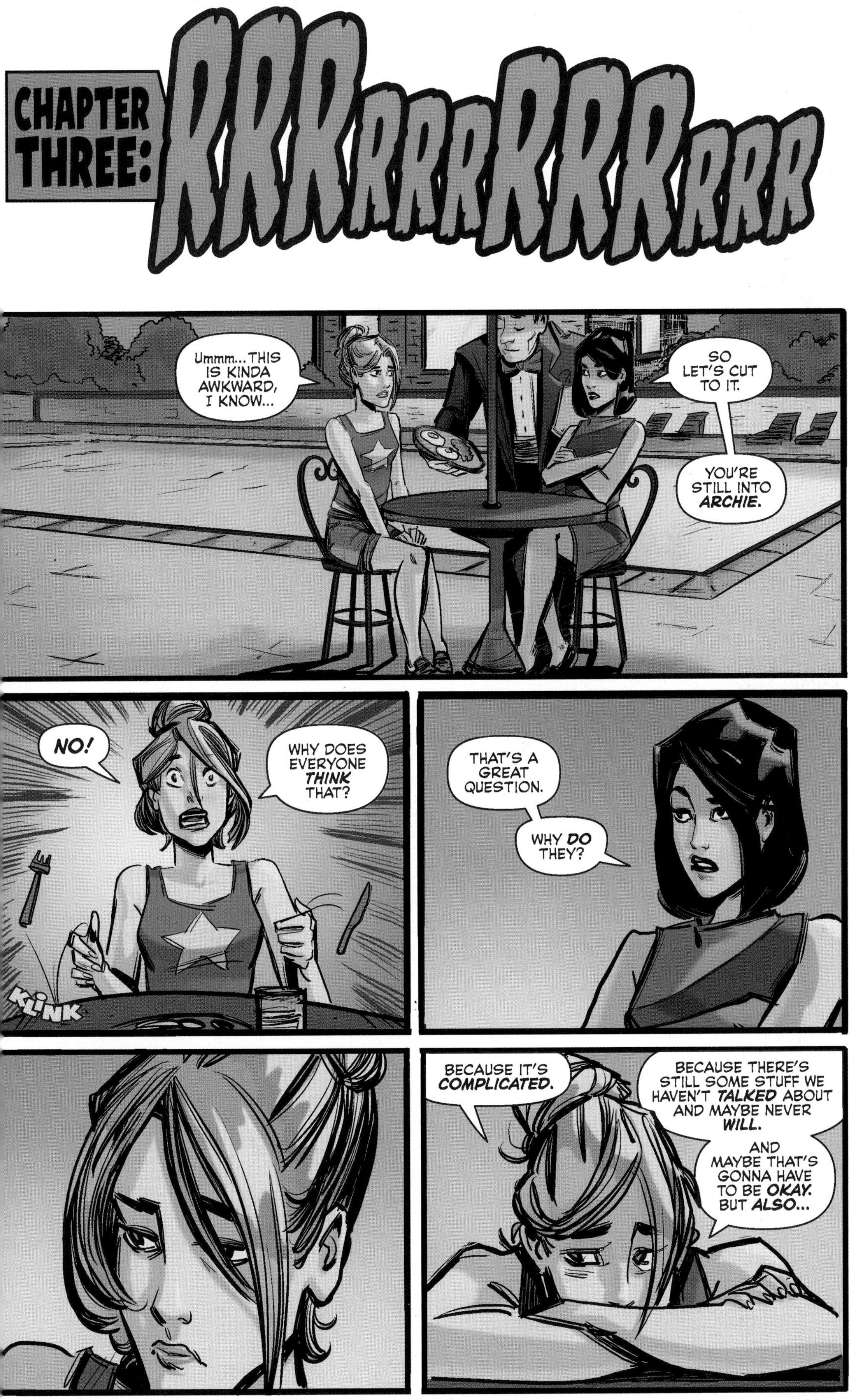

Ummm...THIS IS KINDA AWKWARD, I KNOW...
SO LET'S CUT TO IT.
YOU'RE STILL INTO ARCHIE.
NO!
WHY DOES EVERYONE THINK THAT?
KLINK
THAT'S A GREAT QUESTION.
WHY DO THEY?
BECAUSE IT'S COMPLICATED.
BECAUSE THERE'S STILL SOME STUFF WE HAVEN'T TALKED ABOUT AND MAYBE NEVER WILL.
AND MAYBE THAT'S GONNA HAVE TO BE OKAY. BUT ALSO...

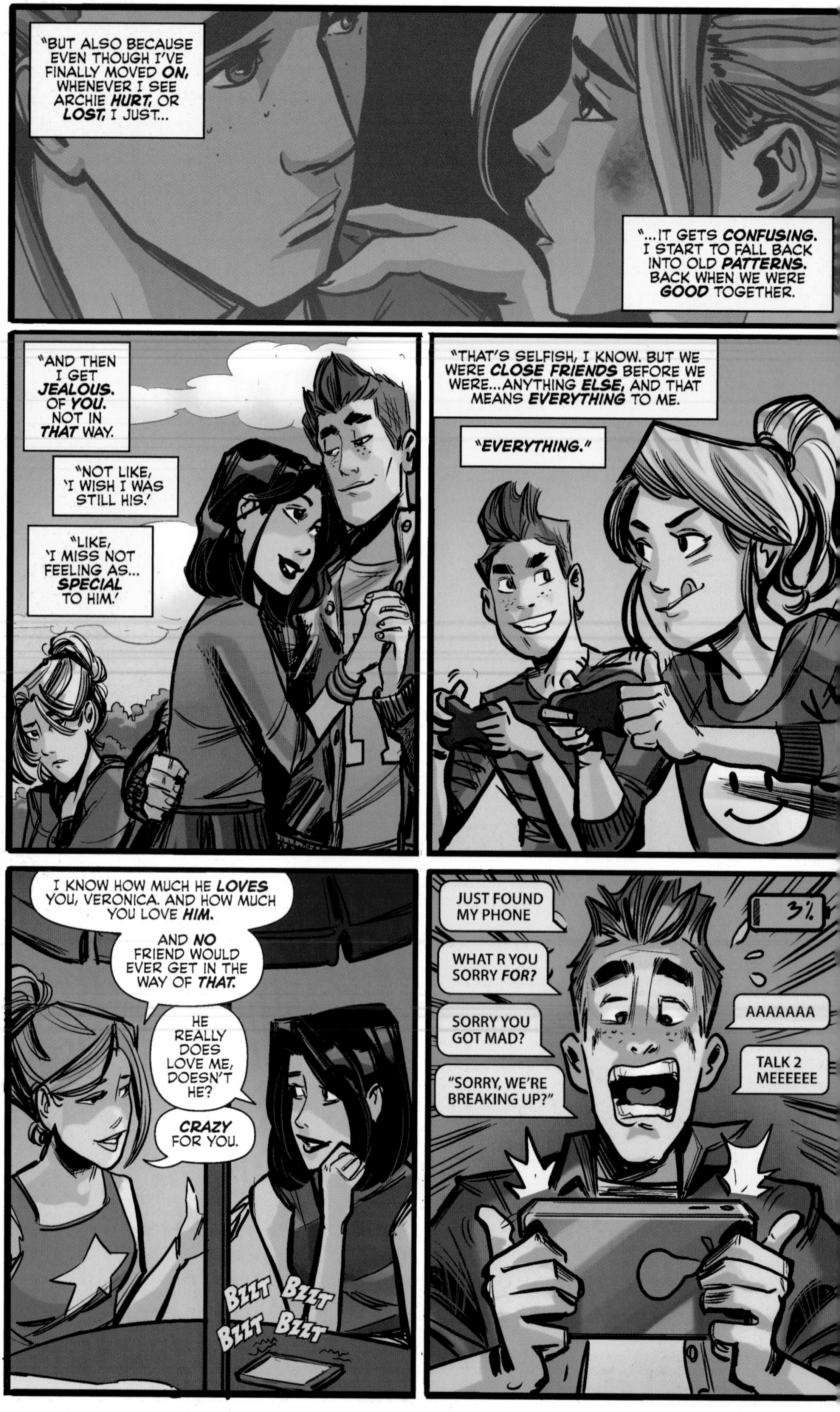

"BUT ALSO BECAUSE EVEN THOUGH I'VE FINALLY MOVED **ON,** WHENEVER I SEE ARCHIE **HURT,** OR **LOST,** I JUST...
"...IT GETS **CONFUSING.** I START TO FALL BACK INTO OLD **PATTERNS.** BACK WHEN WE WERE **GOOD** TOGETHER.
"AND THEN I GET **JEALOUS.** OF **YOU.** NOT IN **THAT** WAY.
"NOT LIKE, 'I WISH I WAS STILL HIS.'
"LIKE, 'I MISS NOT FEELING AS... **SPECIAL** TO HIM.'
"THAT'S SELFISH, I KNOW. BUT WE WERE **CLOSE FRIENDS** BEFORE WE WERE...ANYTHING **ELSE,** AND THAT MEANS **EVERYTHING** TO ME.
"**EVERYTHING.**"
I KNOW HOW MUCH HE **LOVES** YOU, VERONICA. AND HOW MUCH YOU LOVE **HIM.**
AND **NO** FRIEND WOULD EVER GET IN THE WAY OF **THAT.**
HE REALLY DOES LOVE ME, DOESN'T HE?
CRAZY FOR YOU.
BZZT BZZT BZZT BZZT
JUST FOUND MY PHONE
WHAT R YOU SORRY **FOR?**
SORRY YOU GOT MAD?
"SORRY, WE'RE BREAKING UP?"
3%
AAAAAAA
TALK 2 MEEEEEE

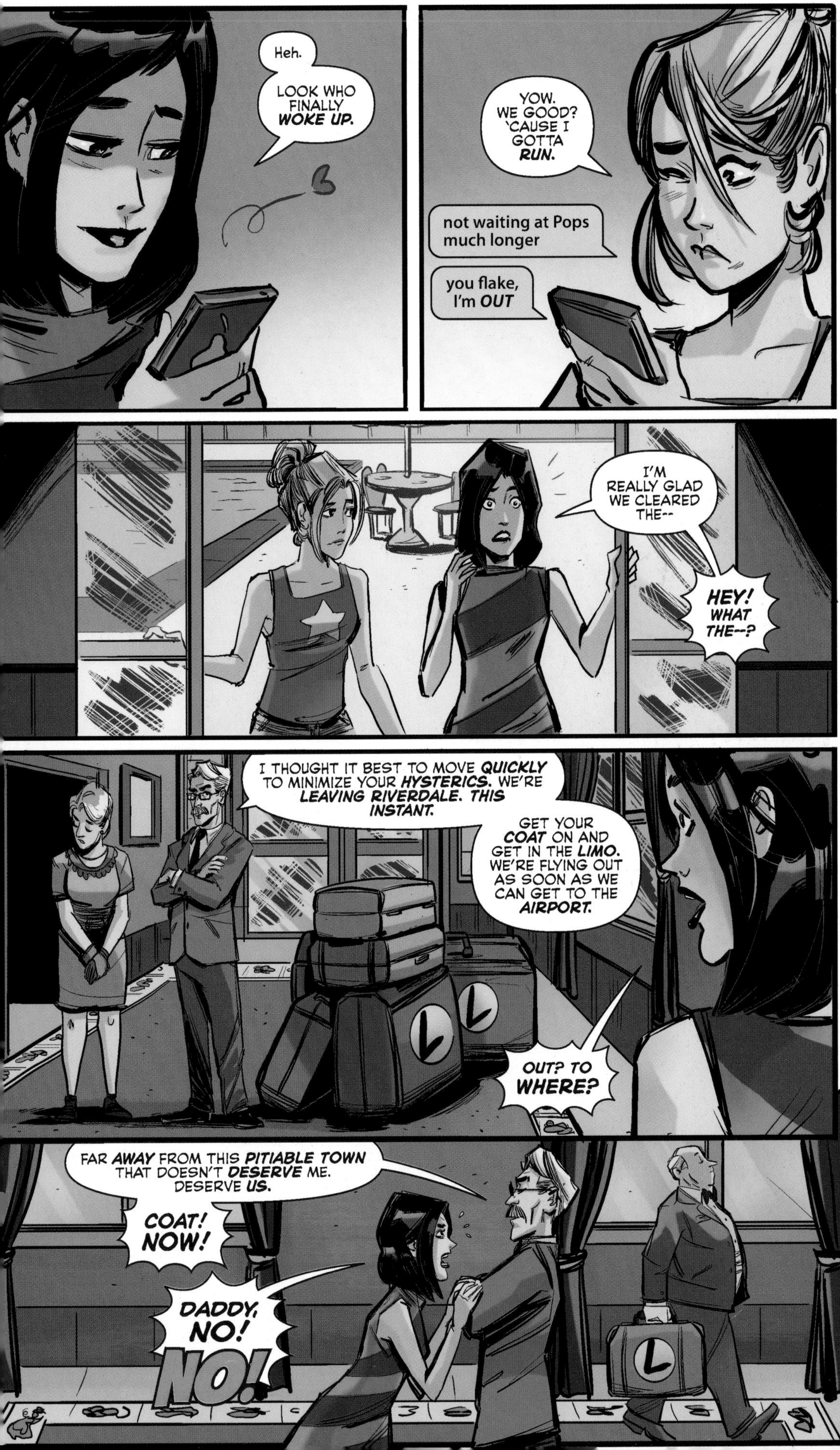
Heh.
LOOK WHO FINALLY WOKE UP.
YOW. WE GOOD? 'CAUSE I GOTTA RUN.
not waiting at Pops much longer
you flake, I'm OUT
I'M REALLY GLAD WE CLEARED THE--
HEY! WHAT THE--?
I THOUGHT IT BEST TO MOVE QUICKLY TO MINIMIZE YOUR HYSTERICS. WE'RE LEAVING RIVERDALE. THIS INSTANT.
GET YOUR COAT ON AND GET IN THE LIMO. WE'RE FLYING OUT AS SOON AS WE CAN GET TO THE AIRPORT.
OUT? TO WHERE?
FAR AWAY FROM THIS PITIABLE TOWN THAT DOESN'T DESERVE ME. DESERVE US.
COAT! NOW!
DADDY, NO!
NO!

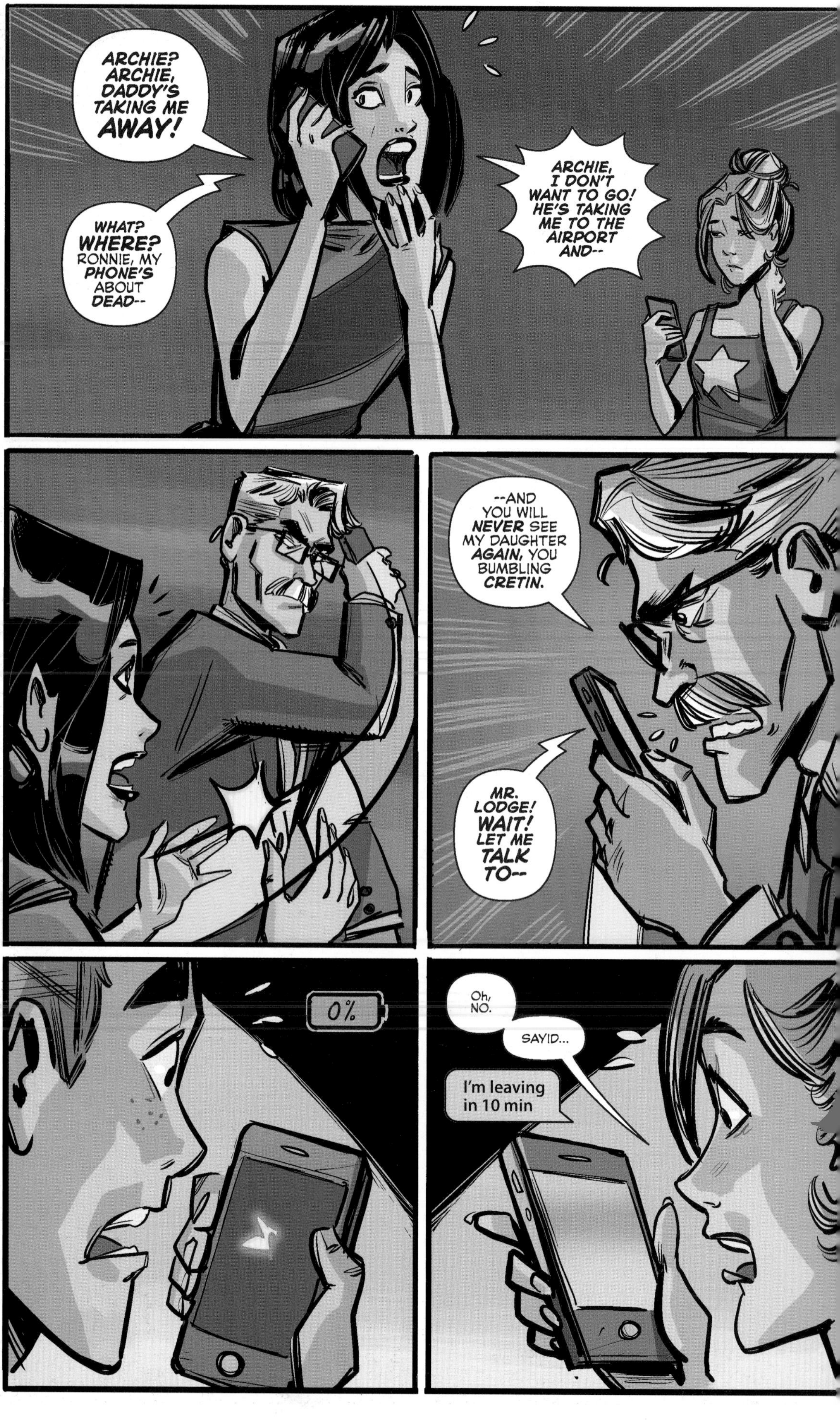
ARCHIE? ARCHIE, DADDY'S TAKING ME AWAY!
WHAT? WHERE? RONNIE, MY PHONE'S ABOUT DEAD--
ARCHIE, I DON'T WANT TO GO! HE'S TAKING ME TO THE AIRPORT AND--
--AND YOU WILL NEVER SEE MY DAUGHTER AGAIN, YOU BUMBLING CRETIN.
MR. LODGE! WAIT! LET ME TALK TO--
0%
Oh, NO.
SAYID...
I'm leaving in 10 min

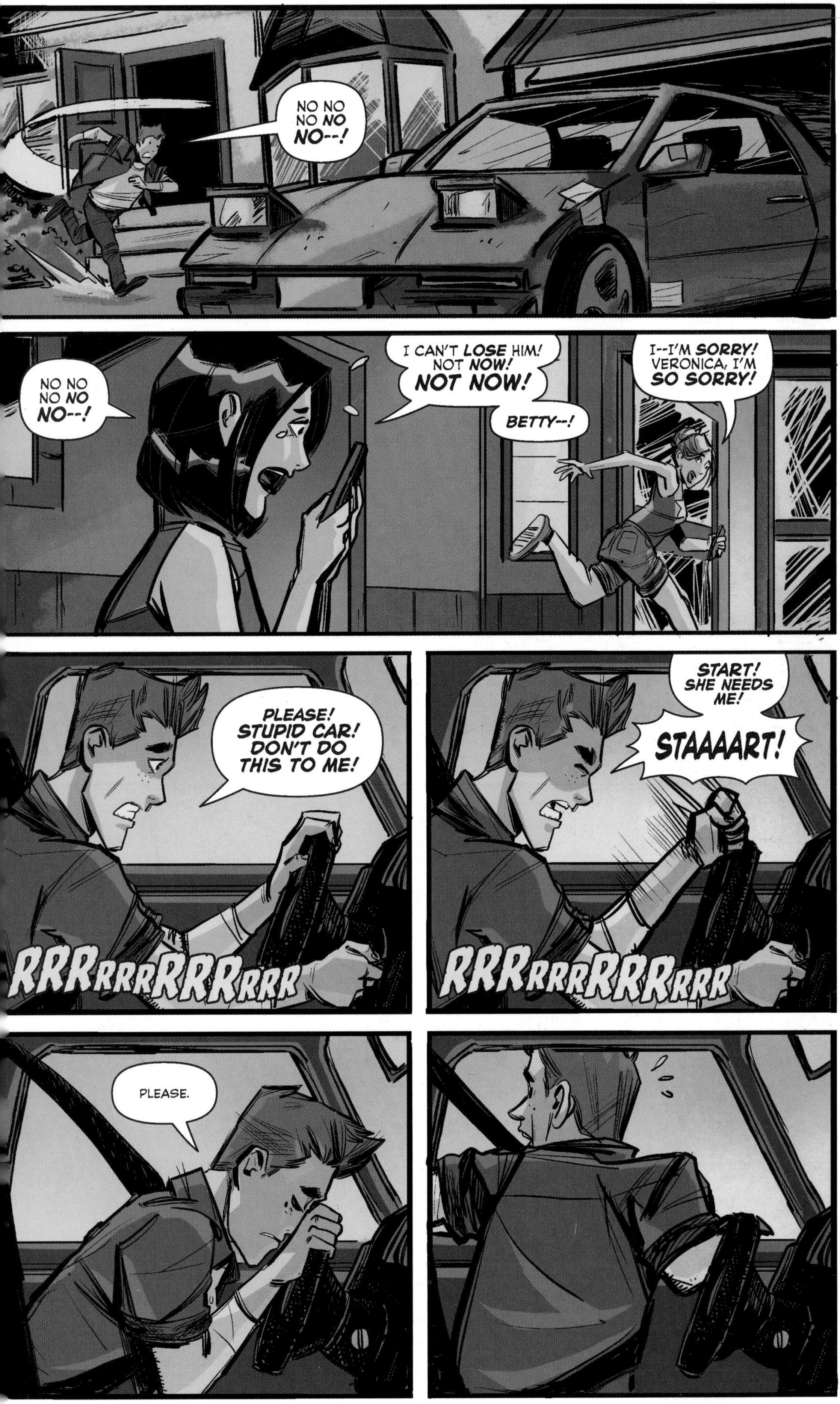

NO NO NO NO NO--!
NO NO NO NO NO--!
I CAN'T LOSE HIM! NOT NOW! NOT NOW!
BETTY--!
I--I'M SORRY! VERONICA, I'M SO SORRY!
PLEASE! STUPID CAR! DON'T DO THIS TO ME!
RRRrrrRRRrrr
START! SHE NEEDS ME!
STAAAART!
RRRrrrRRRrrr
PLEASE.

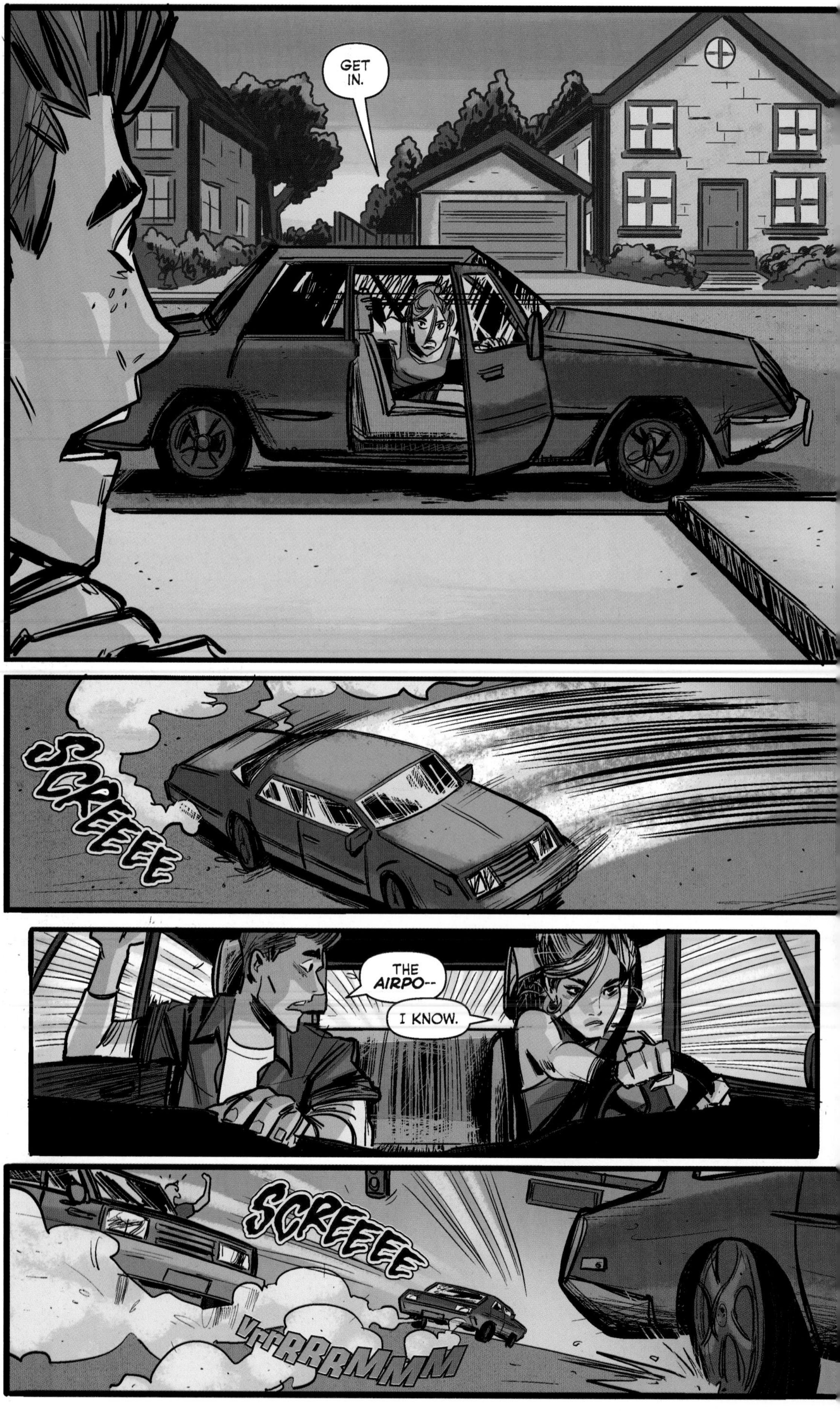
GET IN.
SCREEEE
THE AIRPO--
I KNOW.
SCREEEE
VRRRRRMMMM

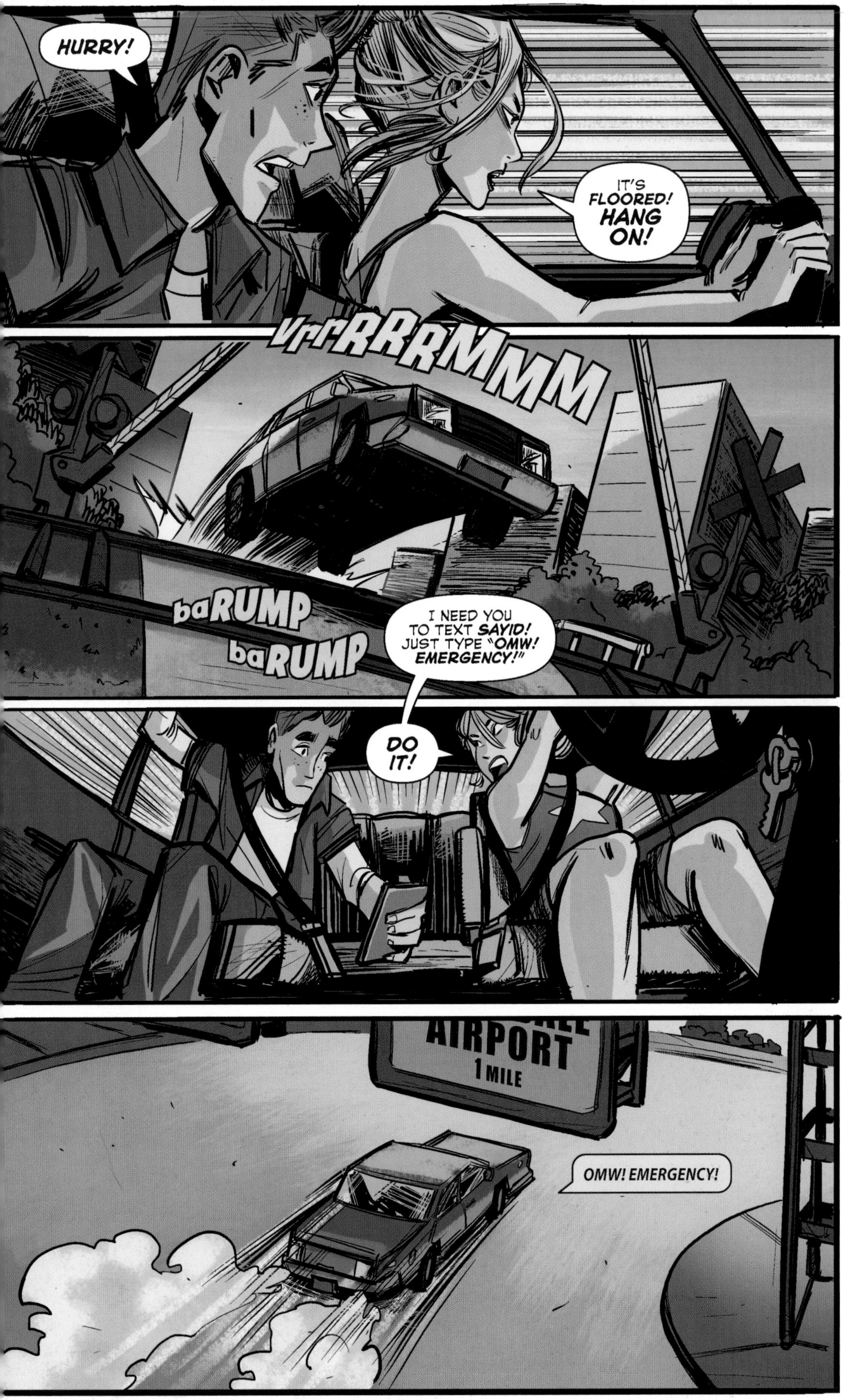
HURRY!
IT'S FLOORED! HANG ON!
VrrrRRRRMMMM
baRUMP
baRUMP
I NEED YOU TO TEXT SAYID! JUST TYPE "OMW! EMERGENCY!"
DO IT!
AIRPORT
1 MILE
OMW! EMERGENCY!

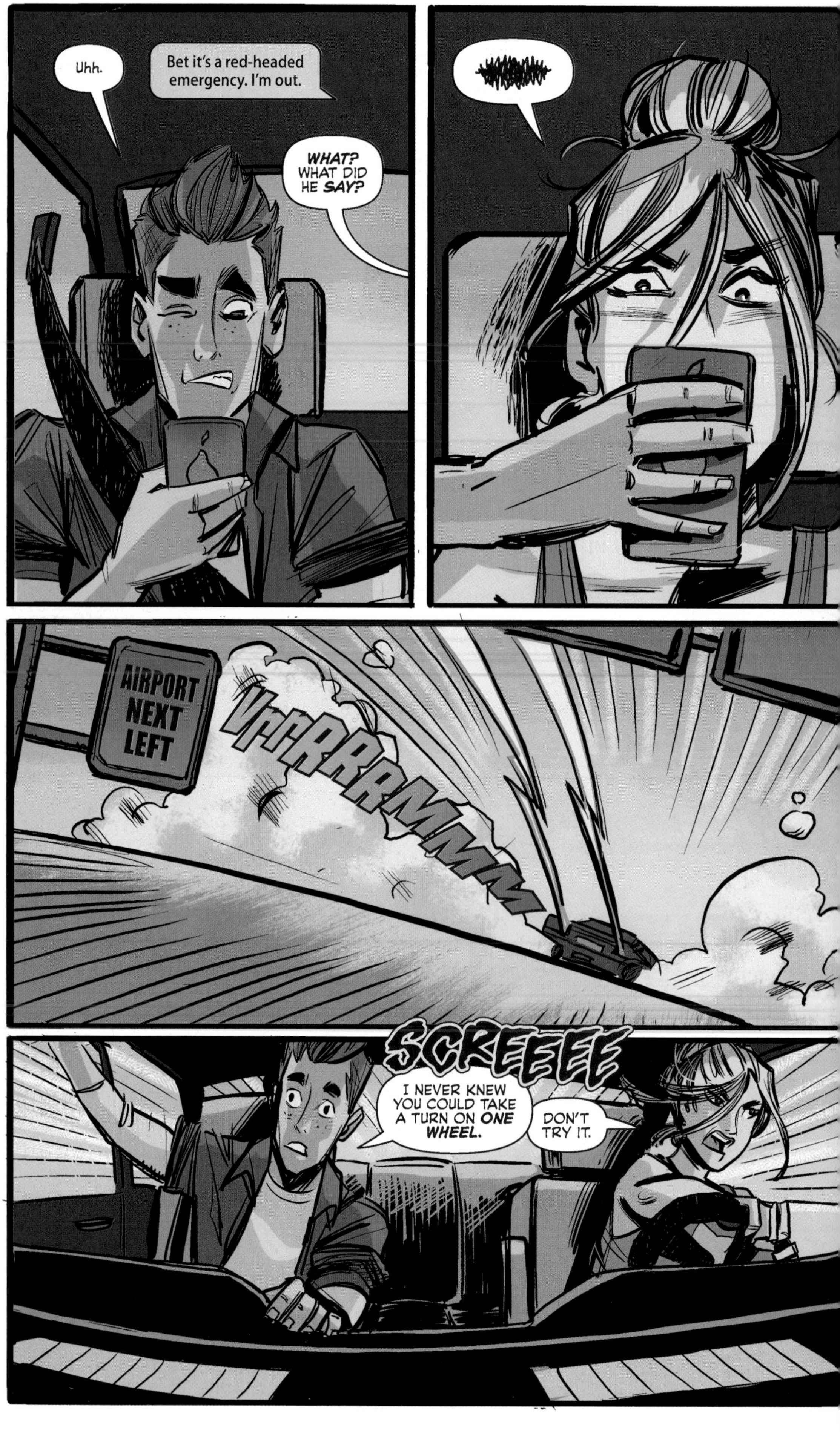
Uhh.
Bet it's a red-headed emergency. I'm out.
WHAT? WHAT DID HE SAY?
AIRPORT NEXT LEFT
VrrRRRRMMMM
SCREEEE
I NEVER KNEW YOU COULD TAKE A TURN ON ONE WHEEL.
DON'T TRY IT.

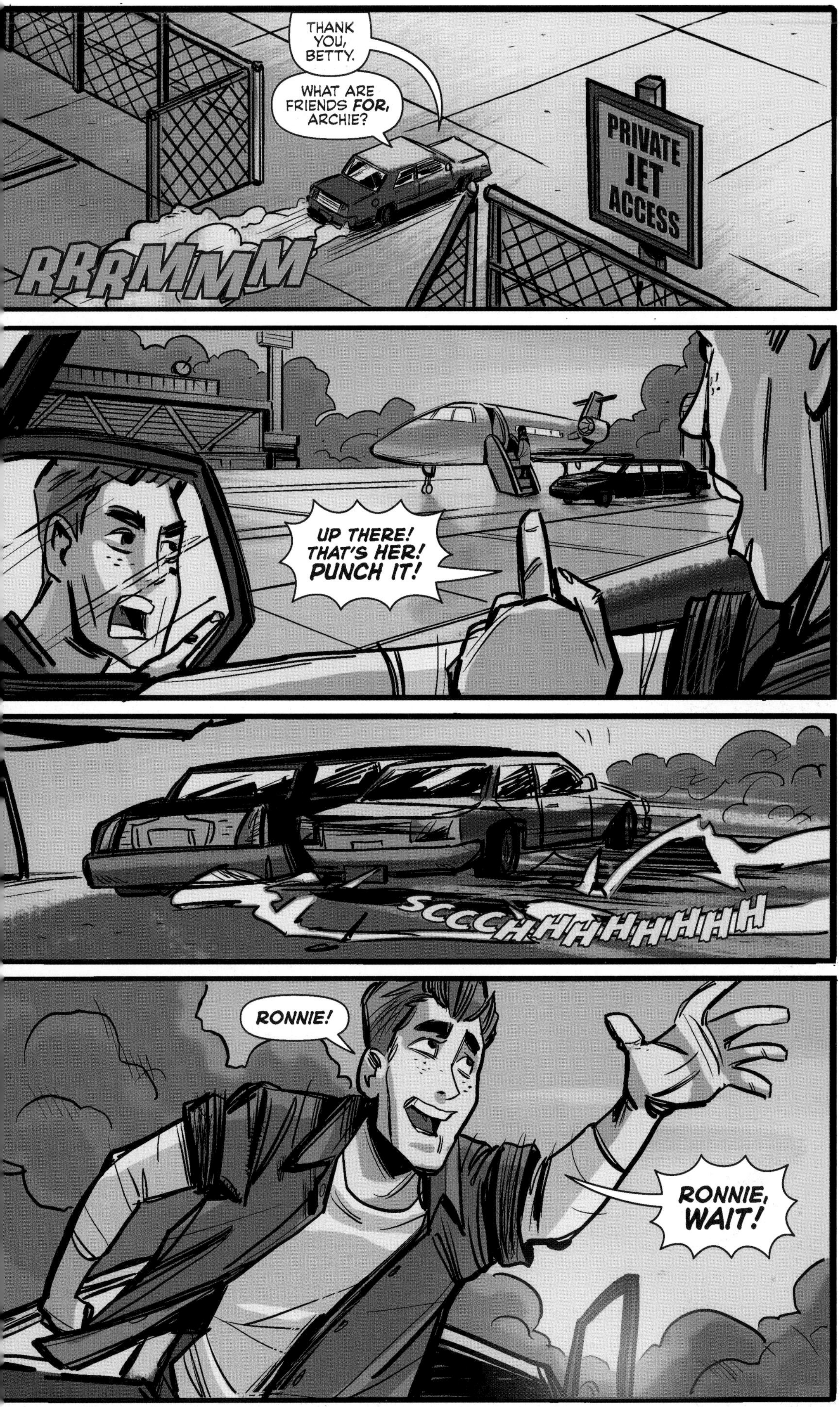
THANK YOU, BETTY.
WHAT ARE FRIENDS FOR, ARCHIE?
PRIVATE JET ACCESS
RRRMMMM
UP THERE! THAT'S HER! PUNCH IT!
SCCCHHHHHHHHHH
RONNIE!
RONNIE, WAIT!

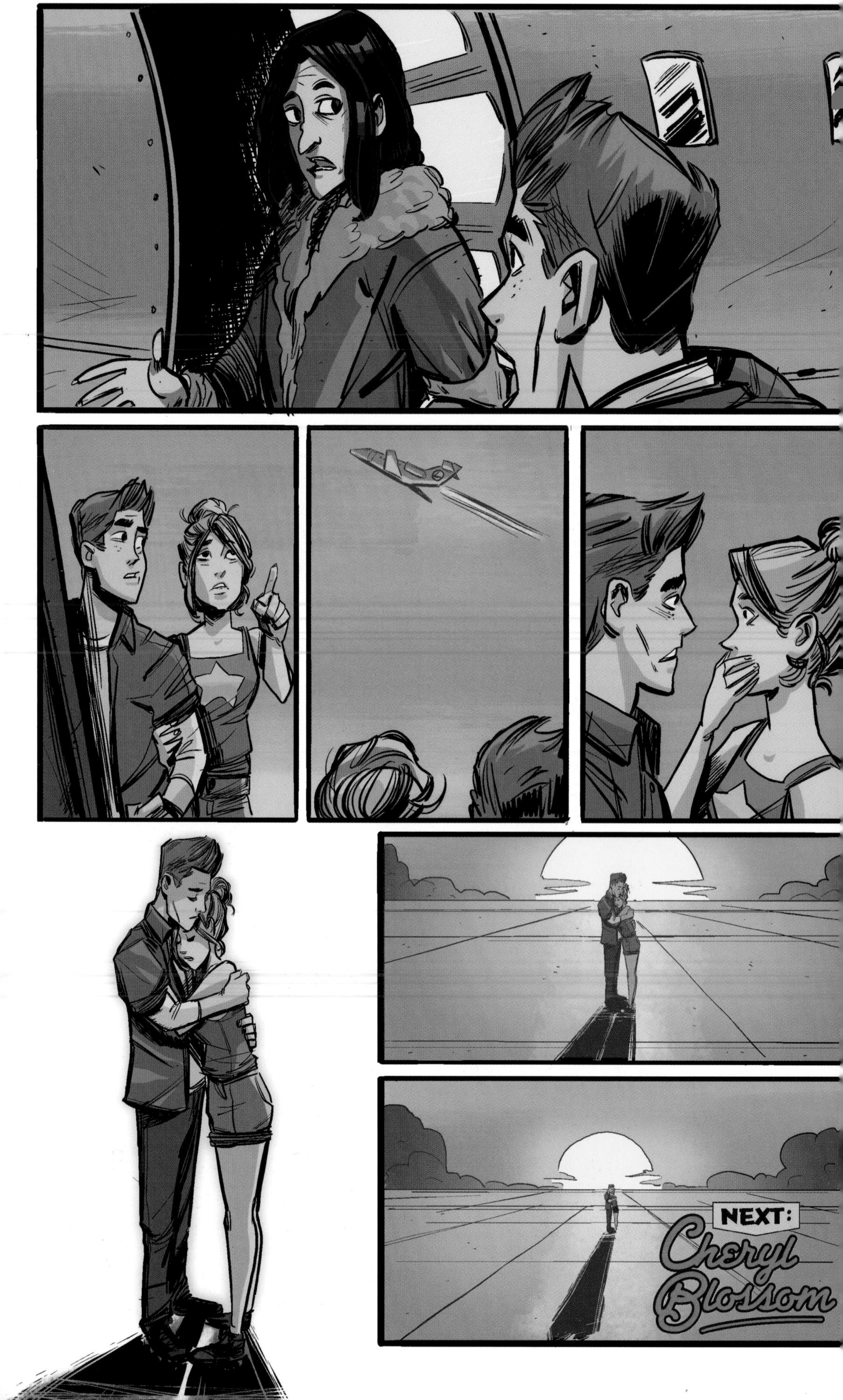
NEXT:
Cheryl Blossom

ARCHIE®

SPECIAL FEATURES

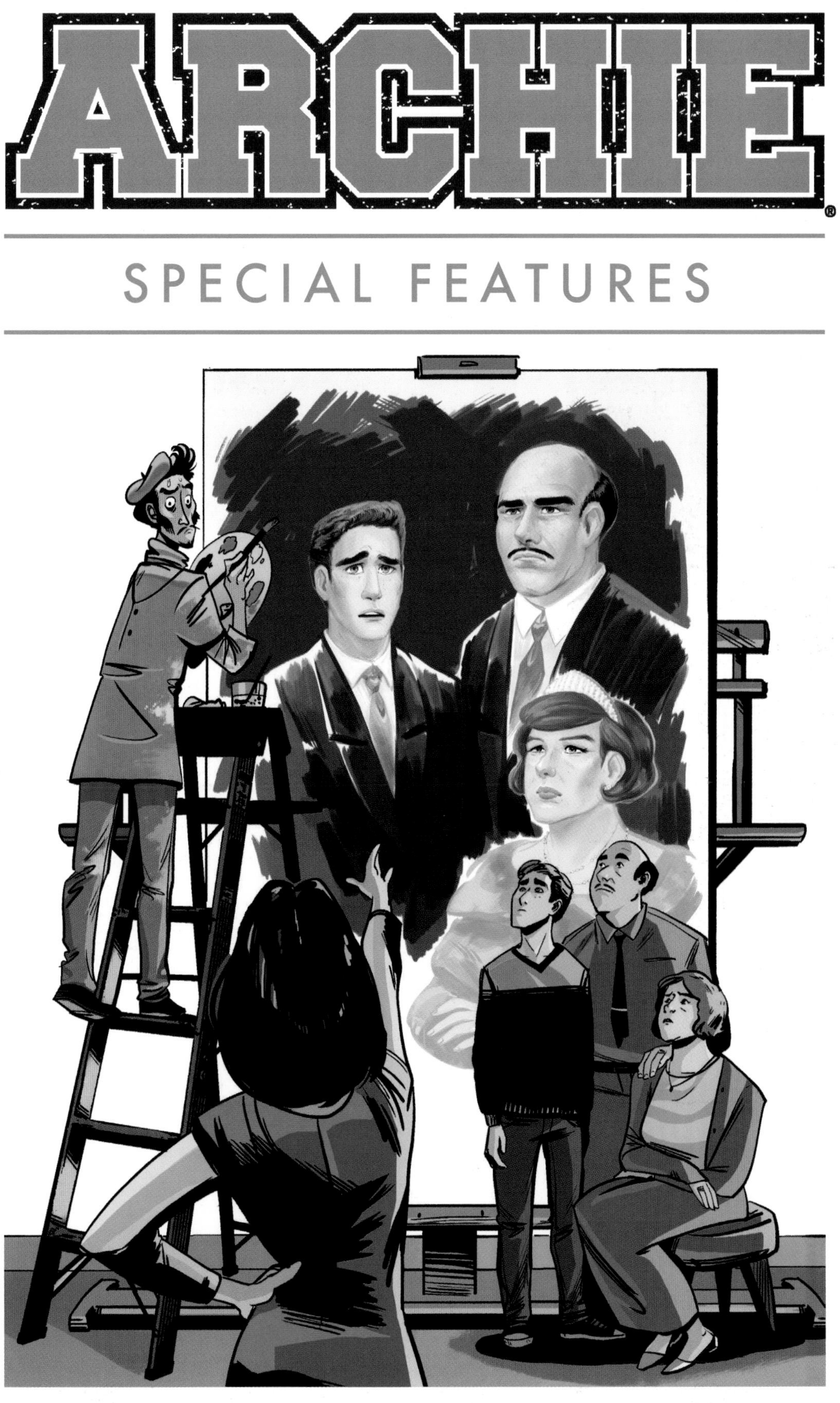

COVER GALLERY

In addition to the amazing main covers we have for each issue, we also receive gorgeous artwork from an array of talented artists for our direct market exclusive covers. Here are all of the main and variant covers for each of the six issues in Archie Volume Two.

ISSUE SEVEN

VERONICA FISH   DJIBRIL MORISSETTE-PHAN   MARGUERITE SAUVAGE

ISSUE EIGHT

VERONICA FISH   ANTON EMDIN   FAITH ERIN HICKS

ISSUE NINE

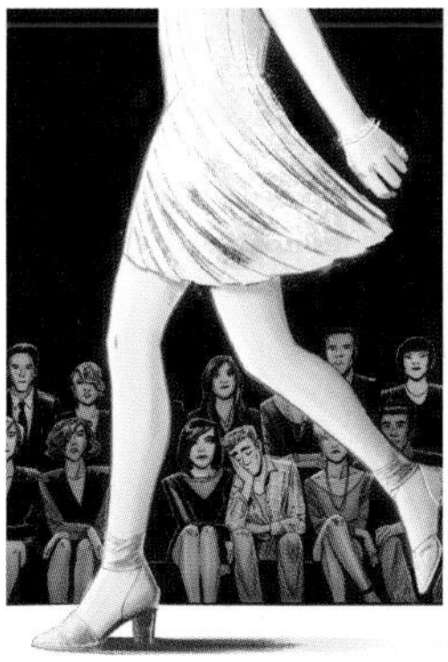

VERONICA FISH

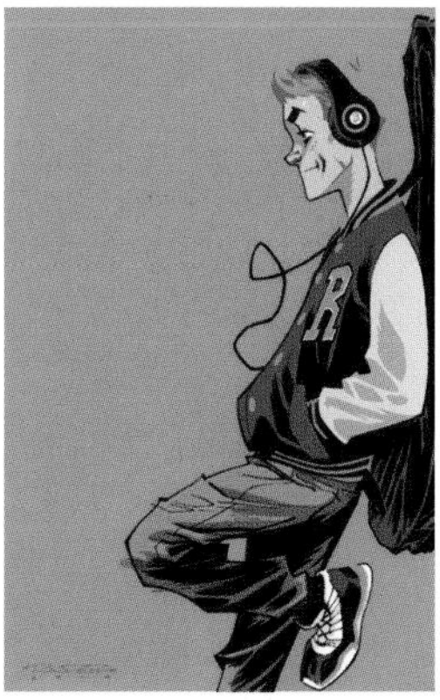

KHARY RANDOLPH

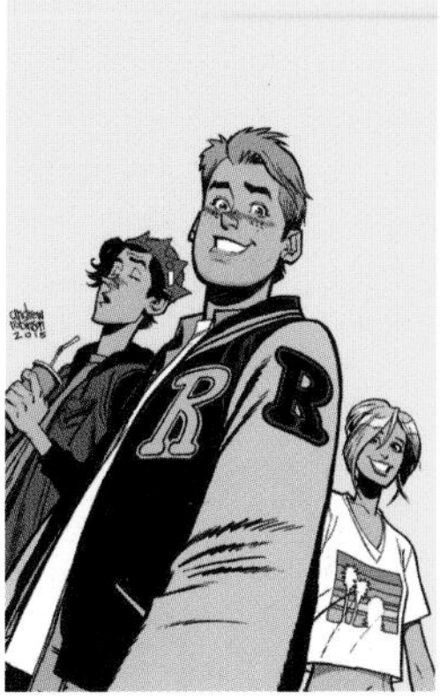

ANDREW ROBINSON

ISSUE TEN

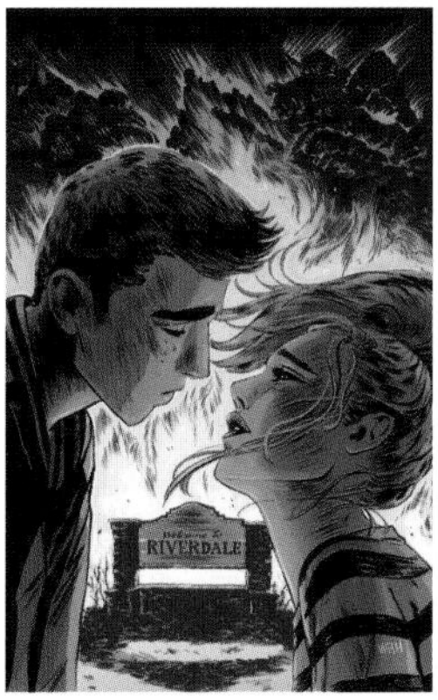
RIVERDALE

VERONICA FISH

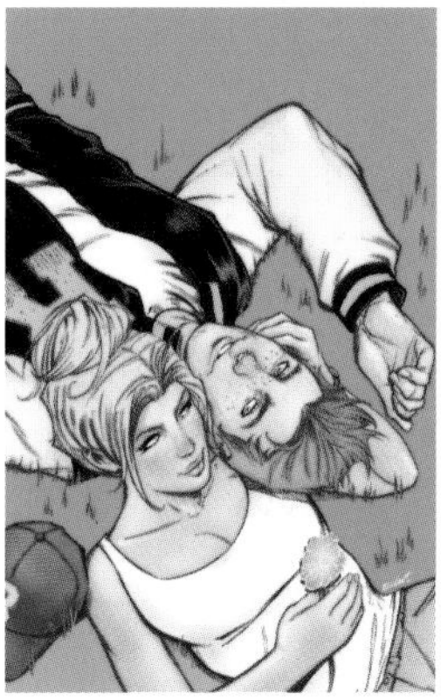

ELLIOT FERNANDEZ

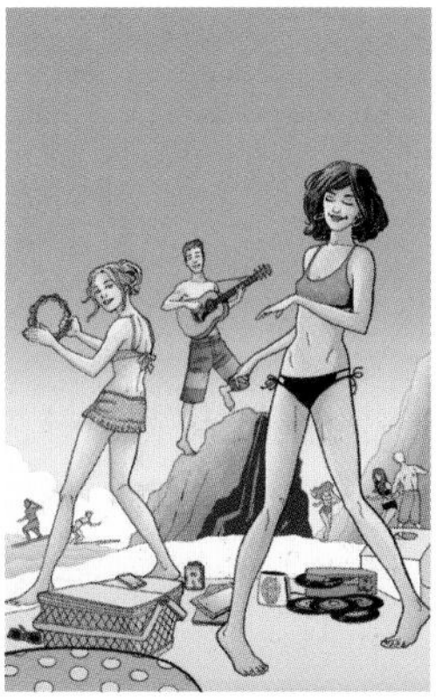

SANDY JARRELL

ISSUE LEVEN

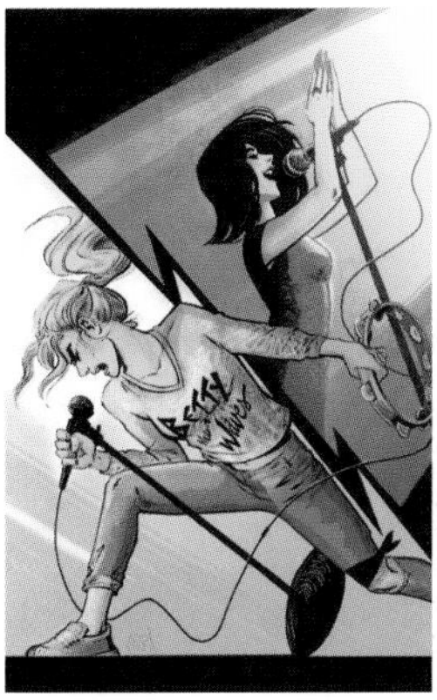

VERONICA FISH

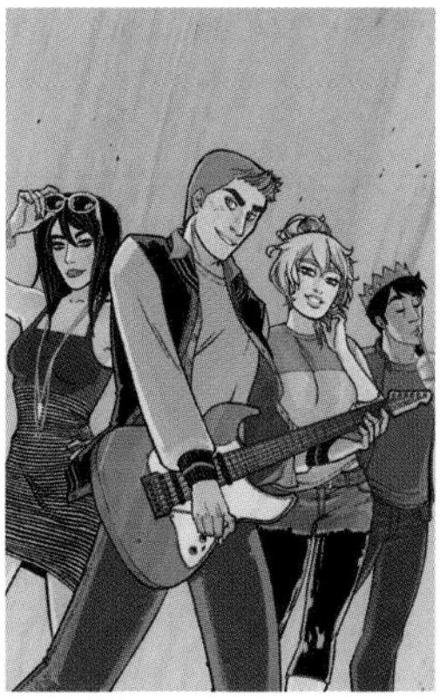

SANYA ANWAR

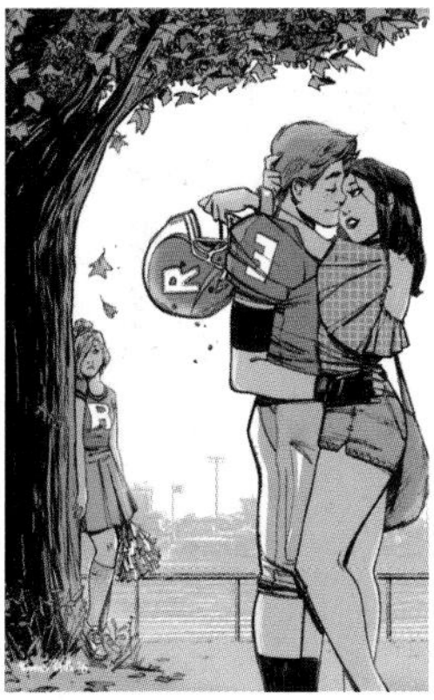

THOMAS PITILLI

ISSUE WELVE

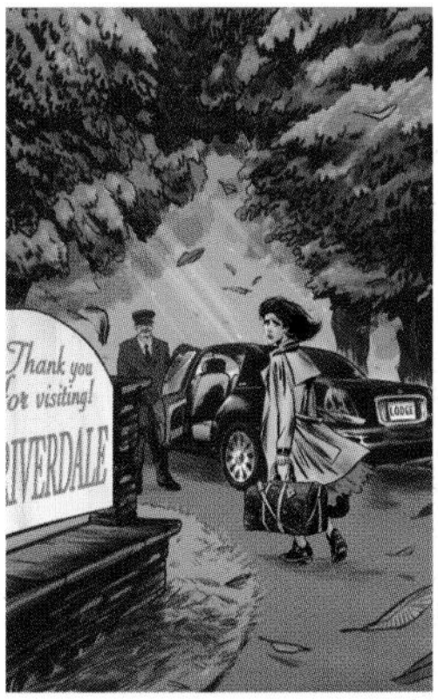
Thank you
or visiting!
IVERDALE
LODGE

VERONICA FISH

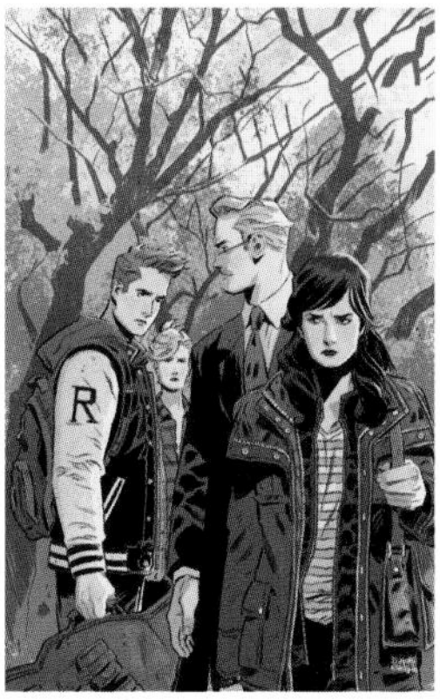

BILQUIS EVELY

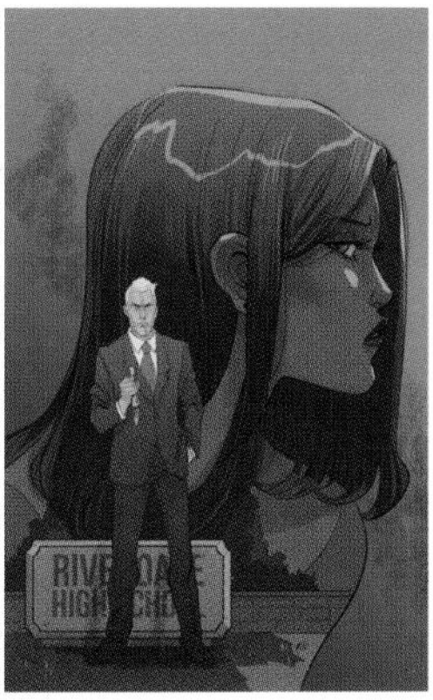

MARGUERITE SAUVAGE

COVER SKETCHES

Before each issue goes through the solicitation process, our esteemed writer MARK WAID gives us a synopsis of what will occur in each upcoming issue, and from that our talented interior artist will come up with some main cover ideas and send in rough drafts of how they would like the cover to look. Here are a few of VERONICA FISH's brilliant cover sketches along with how they appeared in the final versions.

ISSUE EIGHT **SKETCH**

ISSUE EIGHT **FINAL**

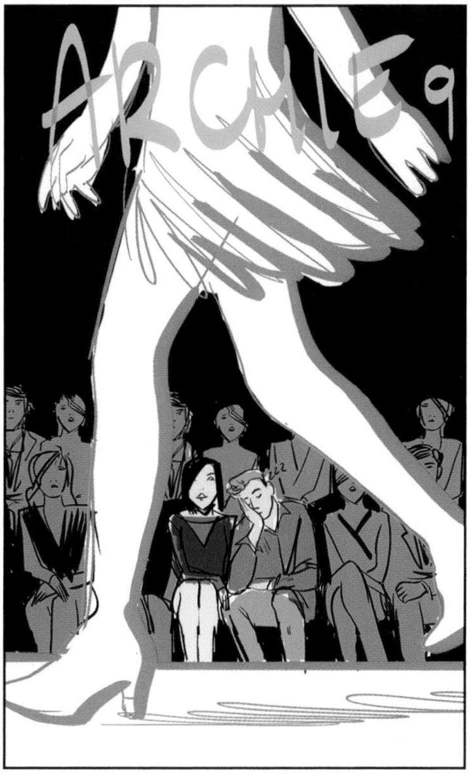
ARCHIE 9

ISSUE NINE **SKETCH**

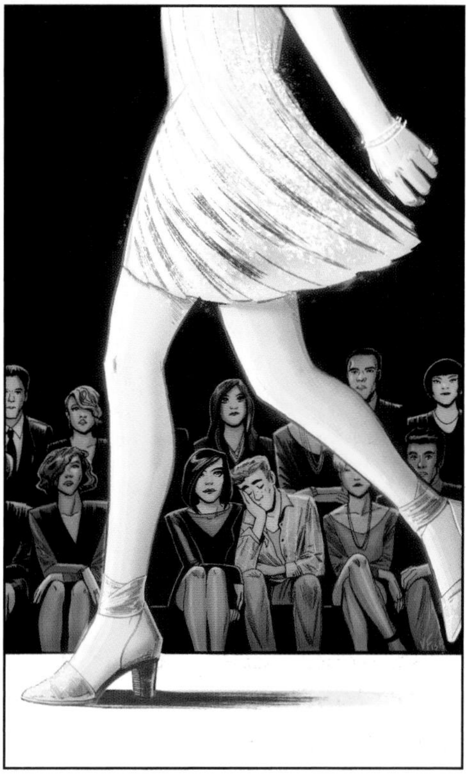

ISSUE NINE **FINAL**

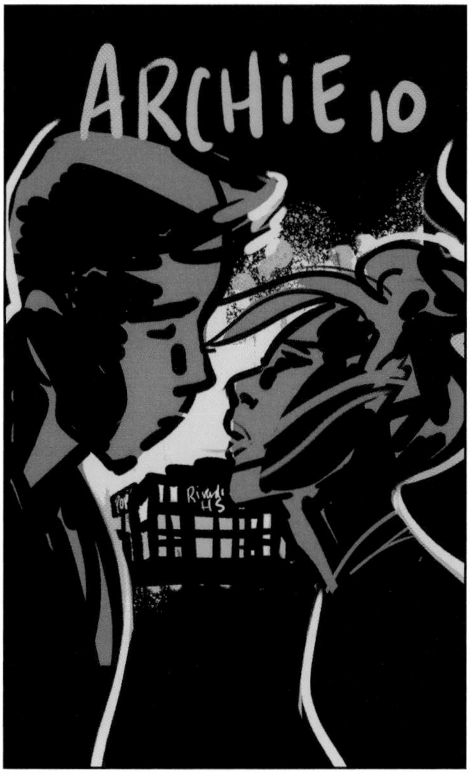
ARCHIE 10

ISSUE TEN **SKETCH**

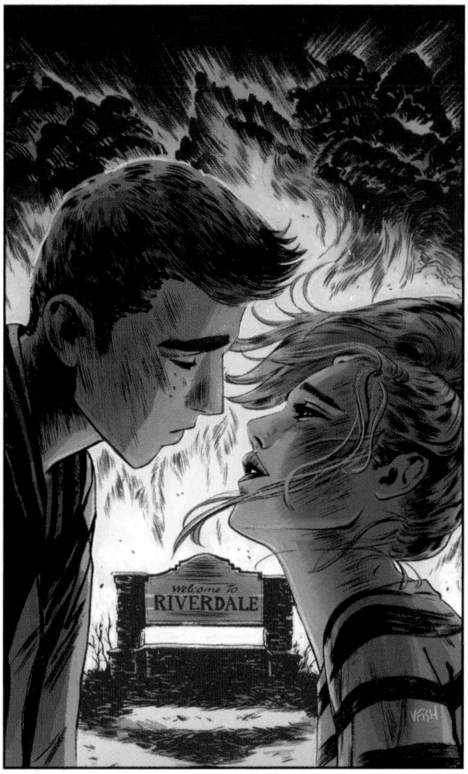
Welcome To
RIVERDALE

ISSUE TEN **FINAL**

ISSUE 11-12 PROCESS

For issues 11 and 12 of Archie, we handled things a bit differently from the normal process. Here's an behind-the-scenes peek at how it was done!

BREAKDOWNS

After recieving the script from MARK WAID, Archie Action artist RYAN JAMPOLE handled the pencil breakdowns, creating layouts and loose pencils for each page of the script.

FINISHES

Illustrator THOMAS PITILLI then finalized the breakdowns and brought his own style to the pages with his inks.

INKS

THOMAS PITILLI would then send in the inked pages to the team at Archie for internal proofing as well as for feedback from writer MARK WAID.

LETTERING

Once the inked pages are approved, letterer extraordinaire JACK MORELLI would then add the lettering and word balloons before sending off to our excellent colorist ANDRE SZYMANOWICZ.

It was a team effort that resulted in some really awesome pages!

LET'S ROCK.
RONNIE DECIDED WE SHOULD START A BAND.
I THOUGHT WE'D CALL IT THE ARCH--
THE RONNIES.

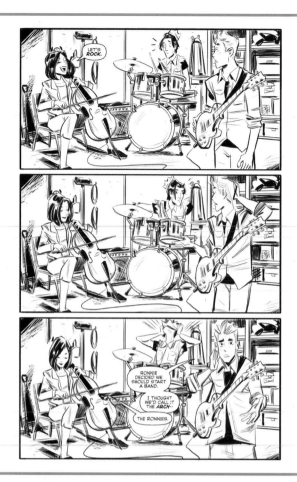

FINAL

SCRIPT BY
MARK WAID

BREAKDOWNS BY
RYAN JAMPOLE

FINISHES BY
THOMAS PITILLI

LETTERING BY
JACK MORELLI

COLORS BY
ANDRE SZYMANOWICZ

LET'S ROCK.
RONNIE DECIDED WE SHOULD START A BAND.
I THOUGHT WE'D CALL IT THE ARCH--
THE RONNIES.

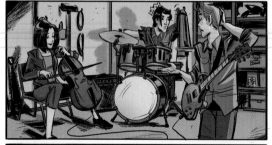

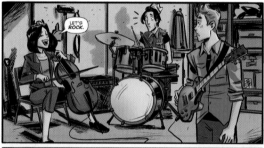

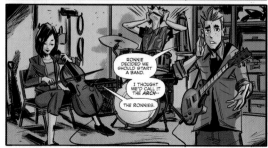

SPECIAL PREVIEW

FROM COMICS LEGEND **ADAM HUGHES**
WITH **JOSÉ VILLARRUBIA**

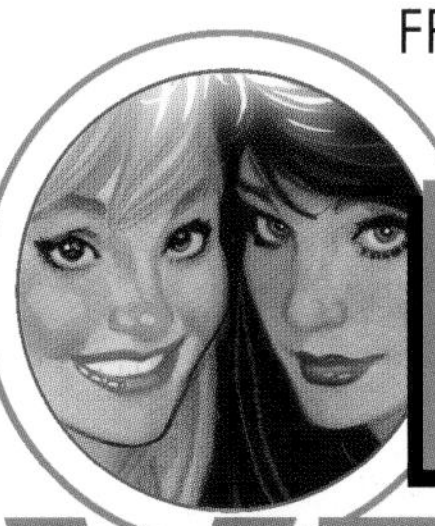

BETTY & VERONICA®

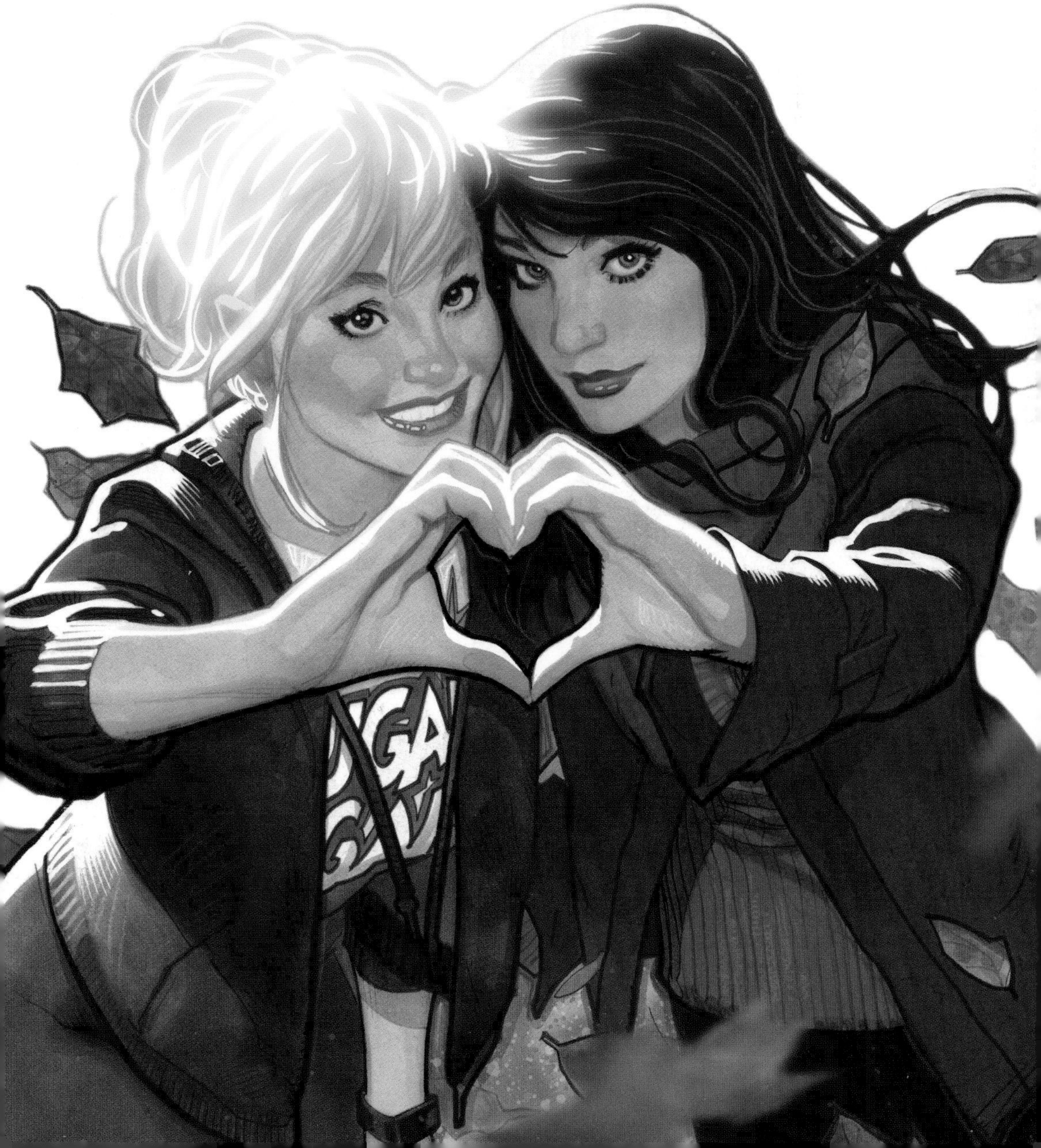

ISSUE ONE

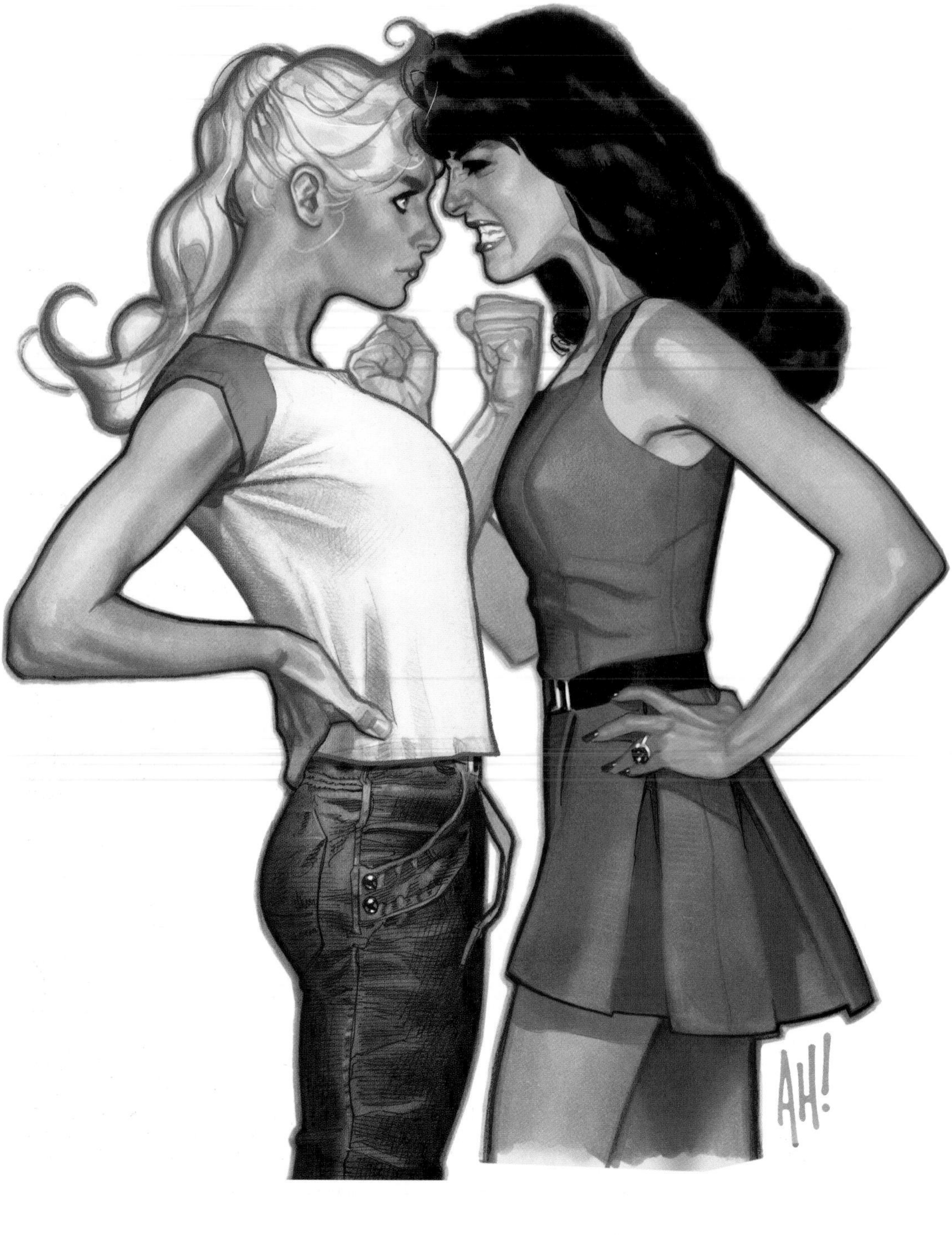
AH!

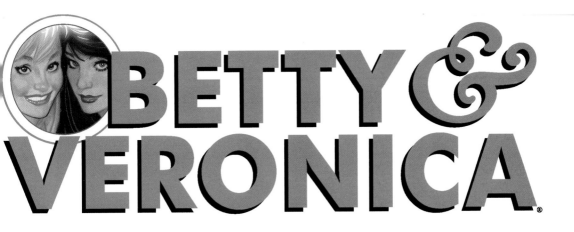

BETTY & VERONICA®

Friendship isn't easy.

Even the best gal pals hit rough patches, even in idyllic Riverdale.

And let's face it—you can't have a New Riverdale without its two most important girls: Betty and Veronica. This is the first of what will surely be many stories featuring everyone's favorite best friends in new, beautifully-rendered adventures. But as most diehard Archie Comics fans know, B&V have been fast frenemies for over 75 years.

And, once again, welcome to the New Riverdale—it's as smart, alluring, funny and entertaining as ever before. We hope you'll enjoy your time here!

— Jon Goldwater,
Publisher/Co-CEO, Archie Comics

#TEAMBETT
AH!

VERONICA
AH!

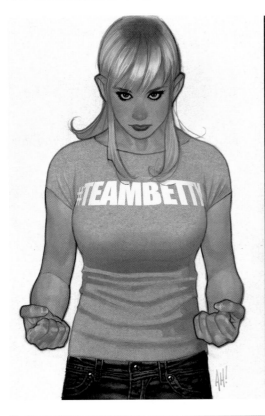

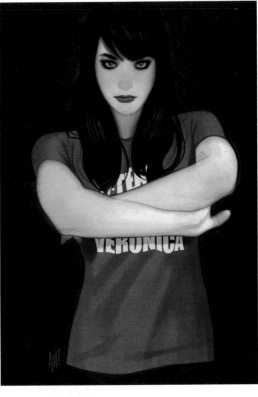

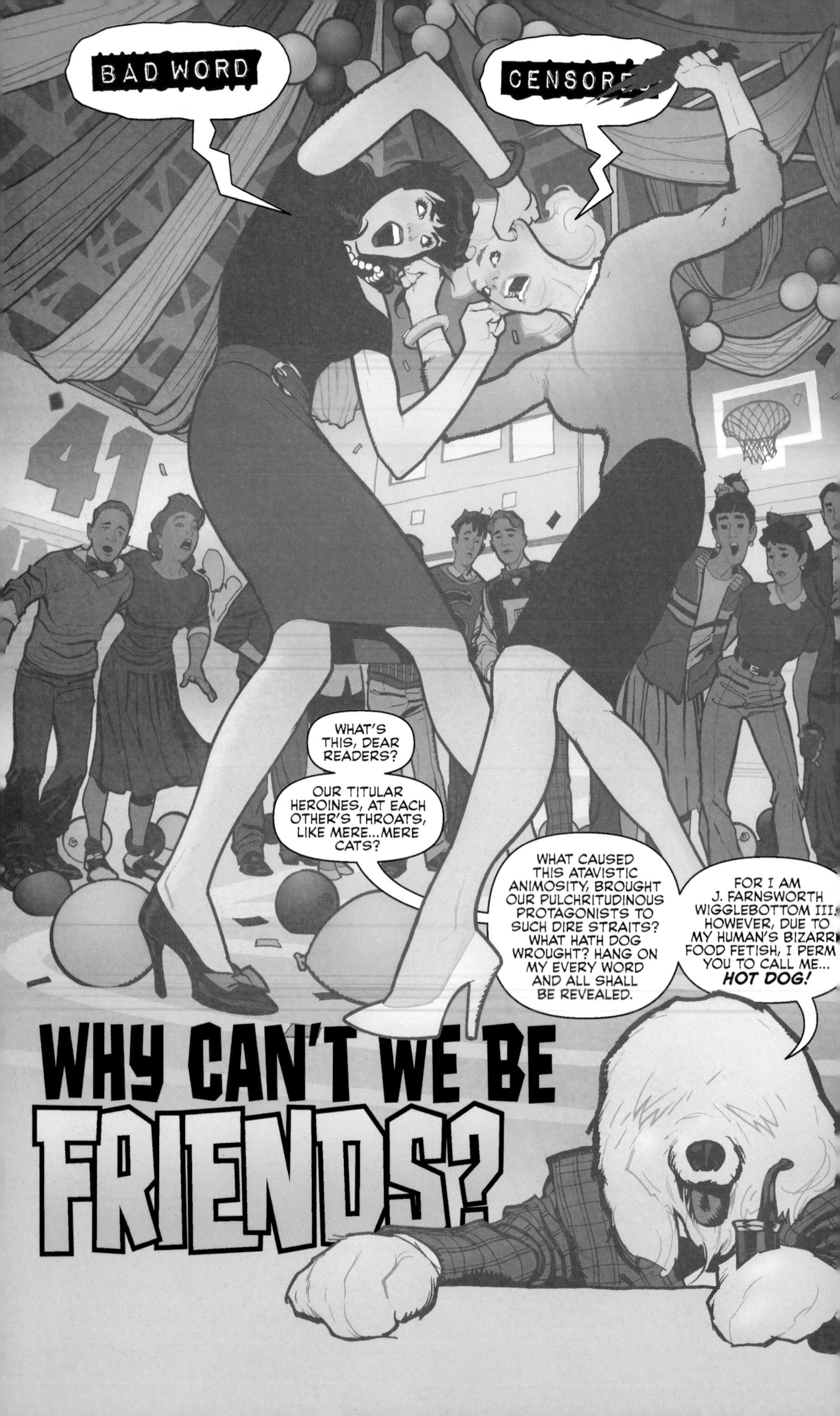
BAD WORD
CENSORE
WHAT'S THIS, DEAR READERS?
OUR TITULAR HEROINES, AT EACH OTHER'S THROATS, LIKE MERE...MERE CATS?
WHAT CAUSED THIS ATAVISTIC ANIMOSITY, BROUGHT OUR PULCHRITUDINOUS PROTAGONISTS TO SUCH DIRE STRAITS? WHAT HATH DOG WROUGHT? HANG ON MY EVERY WORD AND ALL SHALL BE REVEALED.
FOR I AM J. FARNSWORTH WIGGLEBOTTOM III. HOWEVER, DUE TO MY HUMAN'S BIZARR FOOD FETISH, I PERM YOU TO CALL ME... HOT DOG!
WHY CAN'T WE BE FRIENDS?

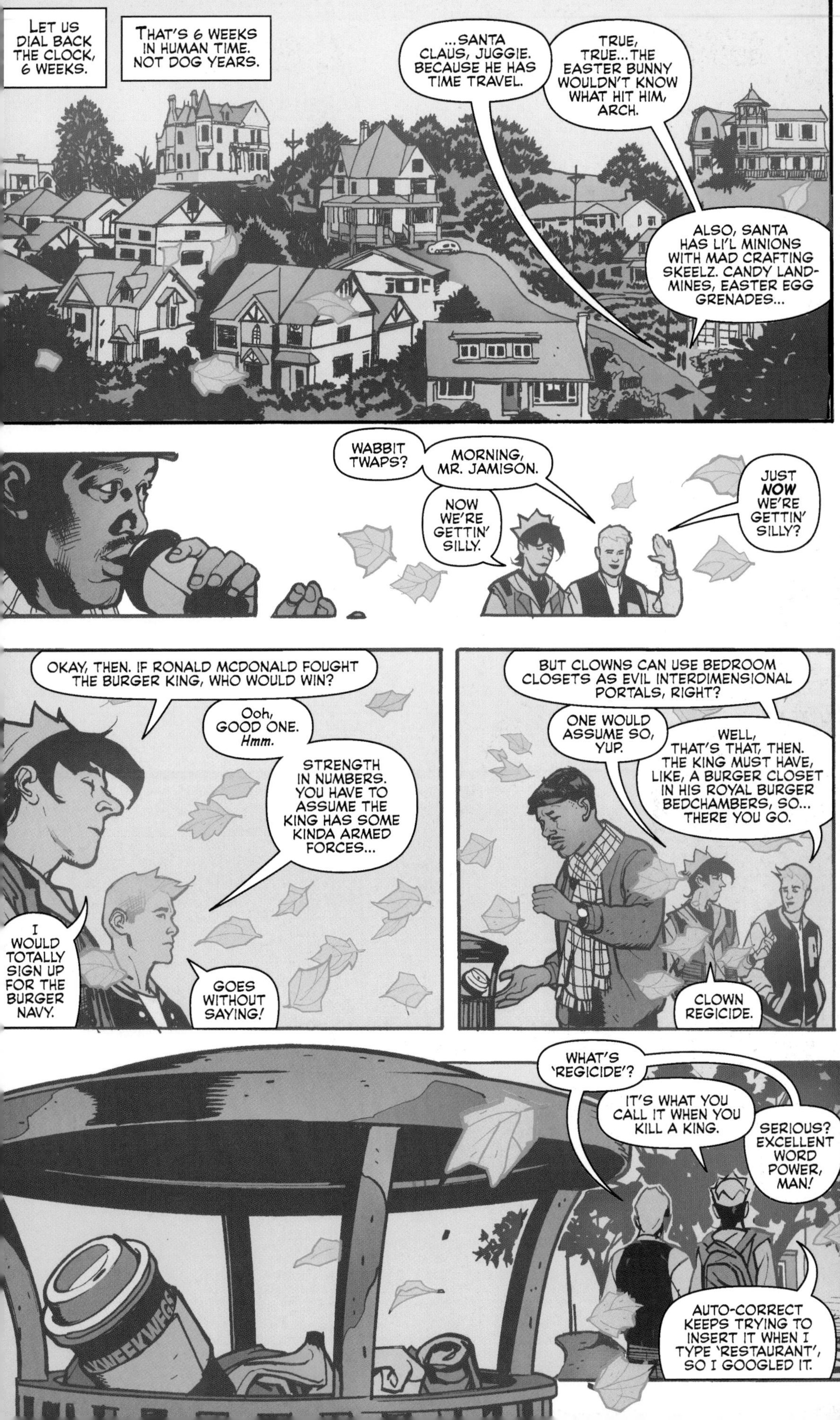
LET US DIAL BACK THE CLOCK, 6 WEEKS.
THAT'S 6 WEEKS IN HUMAN TIME. NOT DOG YEARS.
...SANTA CLAUS, JUGGIE. BECAUSE HE HAS TIME TRAVEL.
TRUE, TRUE...THE EASTER BUNNY WOULDN'T KNOW WHAT HIT HIM, ARCH.
ALSO, SANTA HAS LI'L MINIONS WITH MAD CRAFTING SKEELZ. CANDY LAND-MINES, EASTER EGG GRENADES...
WABBIT TWAPS?
MORNING, MR. JAMISON.
NOW WE'RE GETTIN' SILLY.
JUST *NOW* WE'RE GETTIN' SILLY?
OKAY, THEN. IF RONALD MCDONALD FOUGHT THE BURGER KING, WHO WOULD WIN?
Ooh, GOOD ONE. *Hmm.*
STRENGTH IN NUMBERS. YOU HAVE TO ASSUME THE KING HAS SOME KINDA ARMED FORCES...
I WOULD TOTALLY SIGN UP FOR THE BURGER NAVY.
GOES WITHOUT SAYING!
BUT CLOWNS CAN USE BEDROOM CLOSETS AS EVIL INTERDIMENSIONAL PORTALS, RIGHT?
ONE WOULD ASSUME SO, YUP.
WELL, THAT'S THAT, THEN. THE KING MUST HAVE, LIKE, A BURGER CLOSET IN HIS ROYAL BURGER BEDCHAMBERS, SO... THERE YOU GO.
CLOWN REGICIDE.
WHAT'S 'REGICIDE'?
IT'S WHAT YOU CALL IT WHEN YOU KILL A KING.
SERIOUS? EXCELLENT WORD POWER, MAN!
AUTO-CORRECT KEEPS TRYING TO INSERT IT WHEN I TYPE 'RESTAURANT', SO I GOOGLED IT.

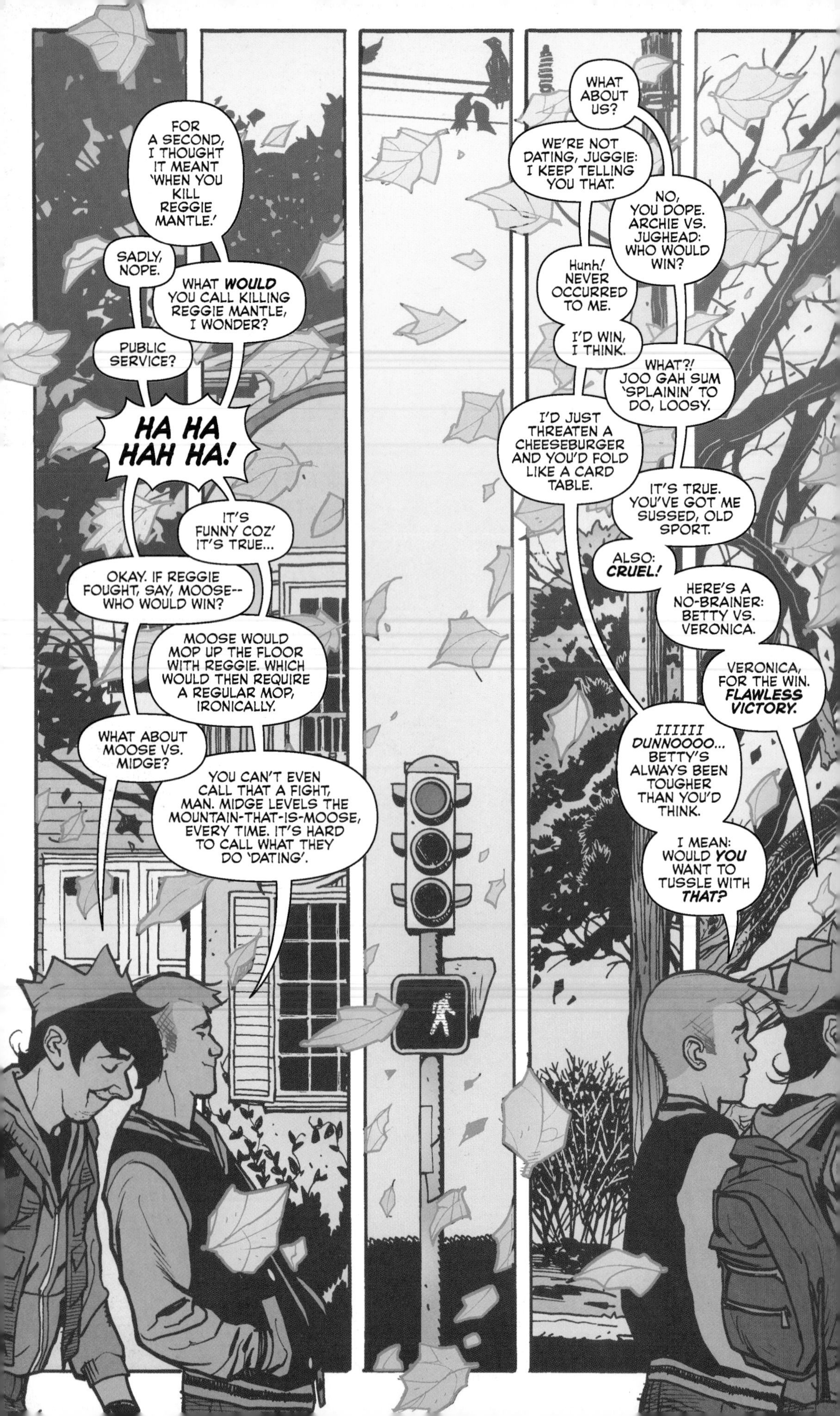
FOR A SECOND, I THOUGHT IT MEANT 'WHEN YOU KILL REGGIE MANTLE.'
SADLY, NOPE.
WHAT **WOULD** YOU CALL KILLING REGGIE MANTLE, I WONDER?
PUBLIC SERVICE?
HA HA HAH HA!
IT'S FUNNY COZ' IT'S TRUE...
OKAY. IF REGGIE FOUGHT, SAY, MOOSE-- WHO WOULD WIN?
MOOSE WOULD MOP UP THE FLOOR WITH REGGIE. WHICH WOULD THEN REQUIRE A REGULAR MOP, IRONICALLY.
WHAT ABOUT MOOSE VS. MIDGE?
YOU CAN'T EVEN CALL THAT A FIGHT, MAN. MIDGE LEVELS THE MOUNTAIN-THAT-IS-MOOSE, EVERY TIME. IT'S HARD TO CALL WHAT THEY DO 'DATING'.
WHAT ABOUT US?
WE'RE NOT DATING, JUGGIE: I KEEP TELLING YOU THAT.
NO, YOU DOPE. ARCHIE VS. JUGHEAD: WHO WOULD WIN?
Hunh! NEVER OCCURRED TO ME.
I'D WIN, I THINK.
WHAT?! JOO GAH SUM 'SPLAININ' TO DO, LOOSY.
I'D JUST THREATEN A CHEESEBURGER AND YOU'D FOLD LIKE A CARD TABLE.
IT'S TRUE. YOU'VE GOT ME SUSSED, OLD SPORT.
ALSO: ***CRUEL!***
HERE'S A NO-BRAINER: BETTY VS. VERONICA.
VERONICA, FOR THE WIN. ***FLAWLESS VICTORY.***
IIIIII DUNNOOOO... BETTY'S ALWAYS BEEN TOUGHER THAN YOU'D THINK.
I MEAN: WOULD **YOU** WANT TO TUSSLE WITH **THAT?**

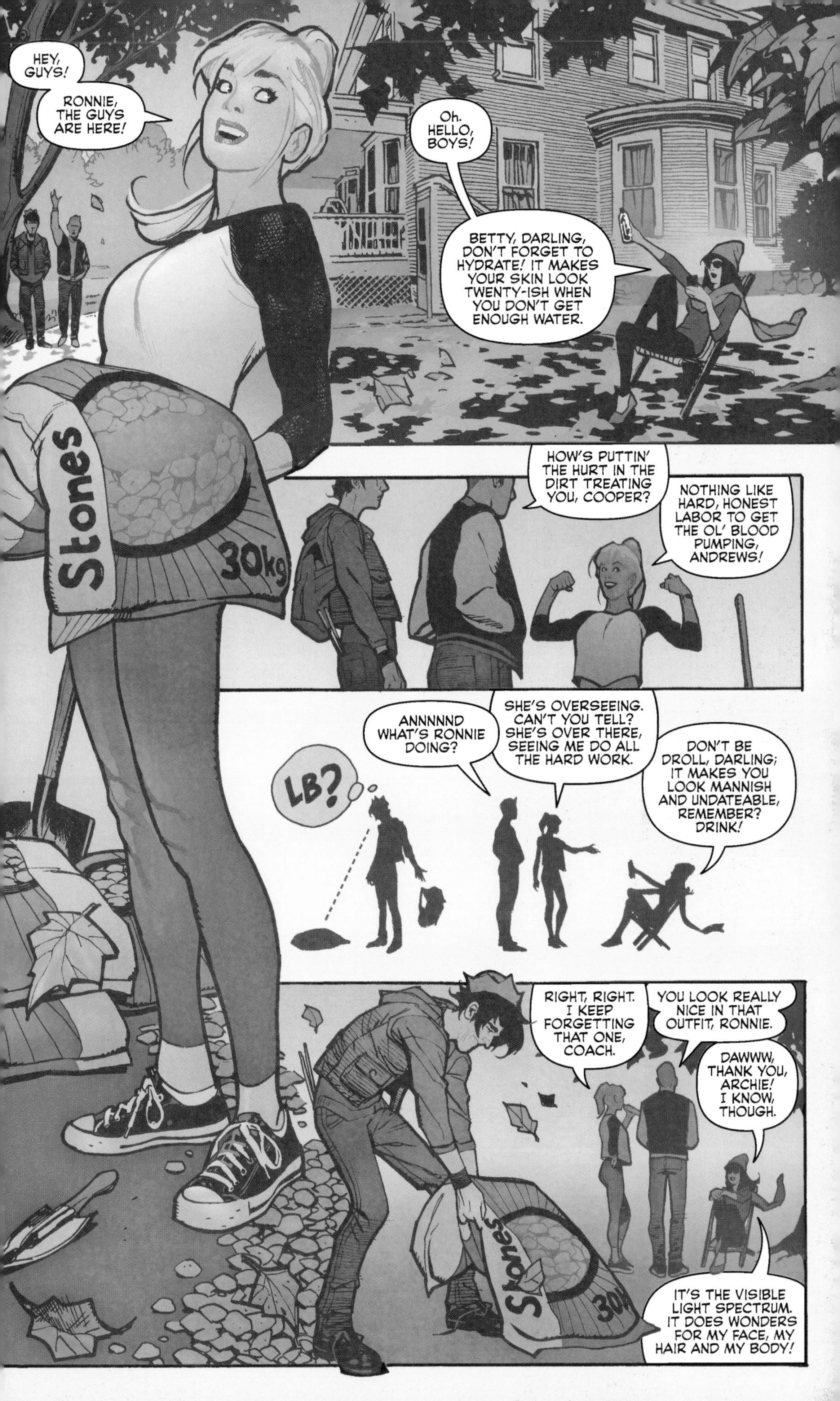
HEY, GUYS!
RONNIE, THE GUYS ARE HERE!
Oh. HELLO, BOYS!
BETTY, DARLING, DON'T FORGET TO HYDRATE! IT MAKES YOUR SKIN LOOK TWENTY-ISH WHEN YOU DON'T GET ENOUGH WATER.
Stones
30kg
HOW'S PUTTIN' THE HURT IN THE DIRT TREATING YOU, COOPER?
NOTHING LIKE HARD, HONEST LABOR TO GET THE OL' BLOOD PUMPING, ANDREWS!
ANNNNND WHAT'S RONNIE DOING?
SHE'S OVERSEEING. CAN'T YOU TELL? SHE'S OVER THERE, SEEING ME DO ALL THE HARD WORK.
LB?
DON'T BE DROLL, DARLING; IT MAKES YOU LOOK MANNISH AND UNDATEABLE, REMEMBER? DRINK!
RIGHT, RIGHT. I KEEP FORGETTING THAT ONE, COACH.
YOU LOOK REALLY NICE IN THAT OUTFIT, RONNIE.
DAWWW, THANK YOU, ARCHIE! I KNOW, THOUGH.
IT'S THE VISIBLE LIGHT SPECTRUM. IT DOES WONDERS FOR MY FACE, MY HAIR AND MY BODY!
Stones

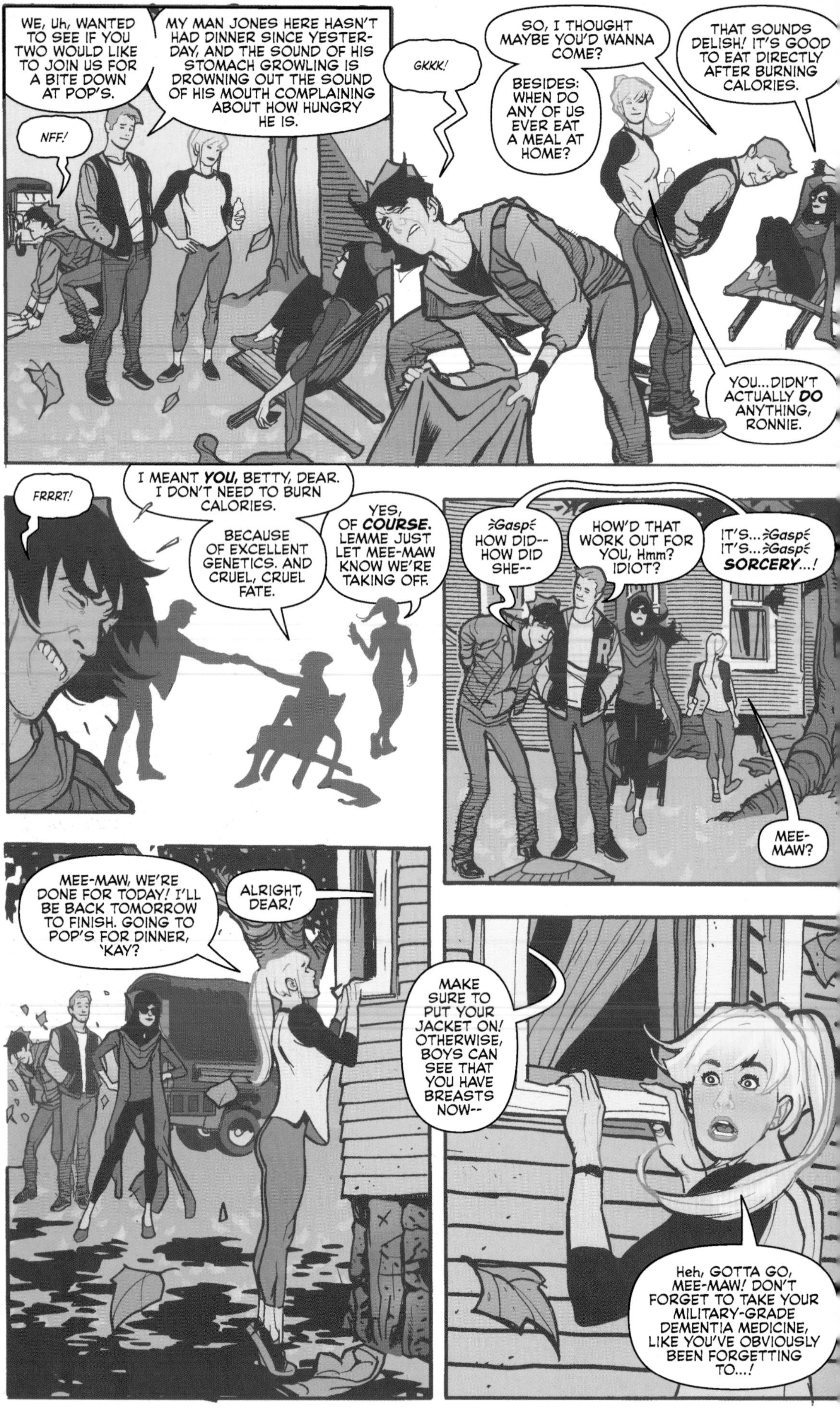

WE, Uh, WANTED TO SEE IF YOU TWO WOULD LIKE TO JOIN US FOR A BITE DOWN AT POP'S.
MY MAN JONES HERE HASN'T HAD DINNER SINCE YESTER-DAY, AND THE SOUND OF HIS STOMACH GROWLING IS DROWNING OUT THE SOUND OF HIS MOUTH COMPLAINING ABOUT HOW HUNGRY HE IS.
NFF!
GKKK!
SO, I THOUGHT MAYBE YOU'D WANNA COME?
BESIDES: WHEN DO ANY OF US EVER EAT A MEAL AT HOME?
THAT SOUNDS DELISH! IT'S GOOD TO EAT DIRECTLY AFTER BURNING CALORIES.
YOU...DIDN'T ACTUALLY DO ANYTHING, RONNIE.
FRRRT!
I MEANT YOU, BETTY, DEAR. I DON'T NEED TO BURN CALORIES.
BECAUSE OF EXCELLENT GENETICS. AND CRUEL, CRUEL FATE.
YES, OF COURSE. LEMME JUST LET MEE-MAW KNOW WE'RE TAKING OFF.
Gasp HOW DID-- HOW DID SHE--
HOW'D THAT WORK OUT FOR YOU, Hmm? IDIOT?
IT'S...Gasp IT'S...Gasp SORCERY...!
MEE-MAW?
MEE-MAW, WE'RE DONE FOR TODAY! I'LL BE BACK TOMORROW TO FINISH. GOING TO POP'S FOR DINNER, 'KAY?
ALRIGHT, DEAR!
MAKE SURE TO PUT YOUR JACKET ON! OTHERWISE, BOYS CAN SEE THAT YOU HAVE BREASTS NOW--
Heh, GOTTA GO, MEE-MAW! DON'T FORGET TO TAKE YOUR MILITARY-GRADE DEMENTIA MEDICINE, LIKE YOU'VE OBVIOUSLY BEEN FORGETTING TO...!

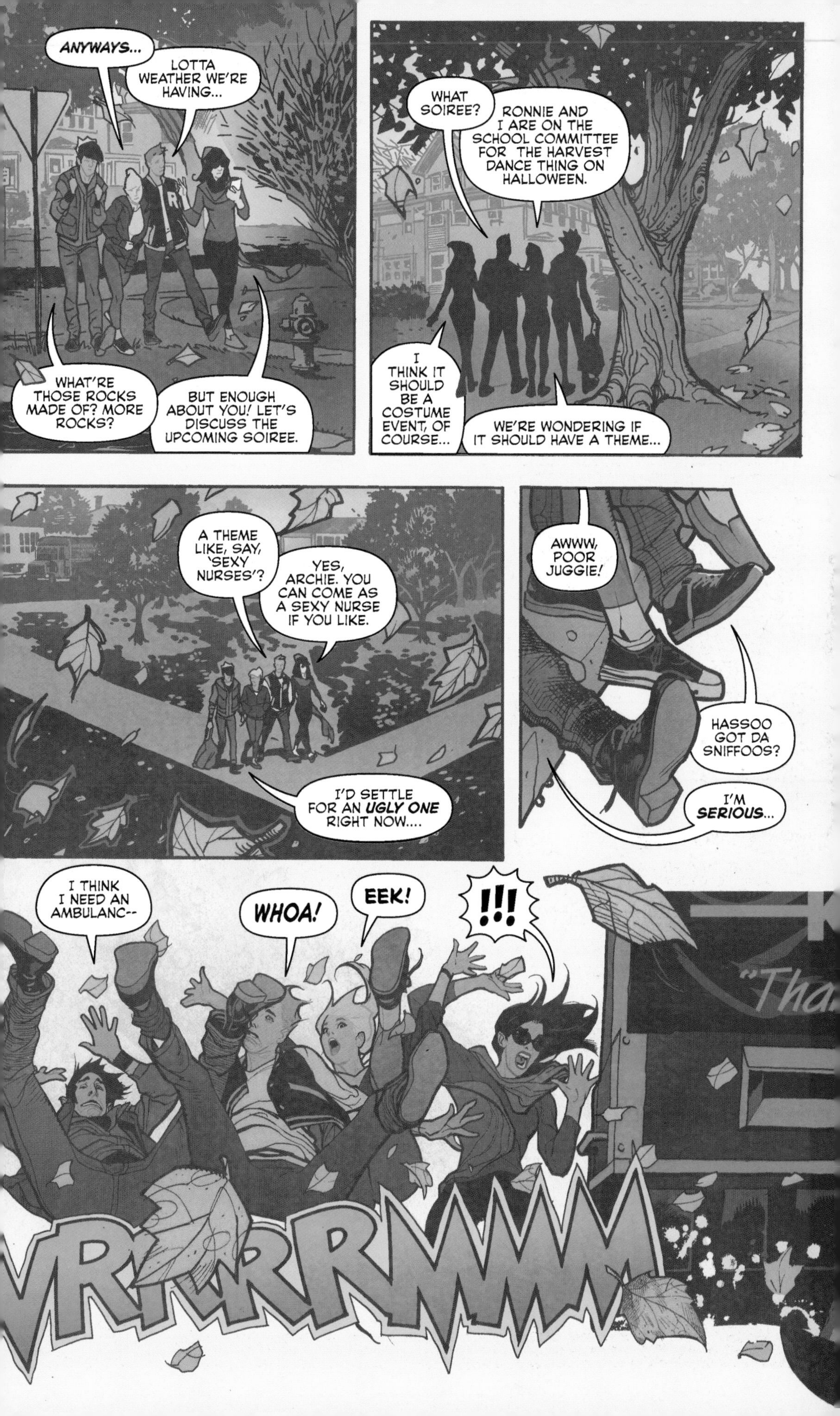
ANYWAYS...
LOTTA WEATHER WE'RE HAVING...
WHAT'RE THOSE ROCKS MADE OF? MORE ROCKS?
BUT ENOUGH ABOUT YOU! LET'S DISCUSS THE UPCOMING SOIREE.
WHAT SOIREE?
RONNIE AND I ARE ON THE SCHOOL COMMITTEE FOR THE HARVEST DANCE THING ON HALLOWEEN.
I THINK IT SHOULD BE A COSTUME EVENT, OF COURSE...
WE'RE WONDERING IF IT SHOULD HAVE A THEME...
A THEME LIKE, SAY, 'SEXY NURSES'?
YES, ARCHIE. YOU CAN COME AS A SEXY NURSE IF YOU LIKE.
I'D SETTLE FOR AN UGLY ONE RIGHT NOW....
AWWW, POOR JUGGIE!
HASSOO GOT DA SNIFFOOS?
I'M SERIOUS...
I THINK I NEED AN AMBULANC--
WHOA!
EEK!
!!!
VRRRRMMM

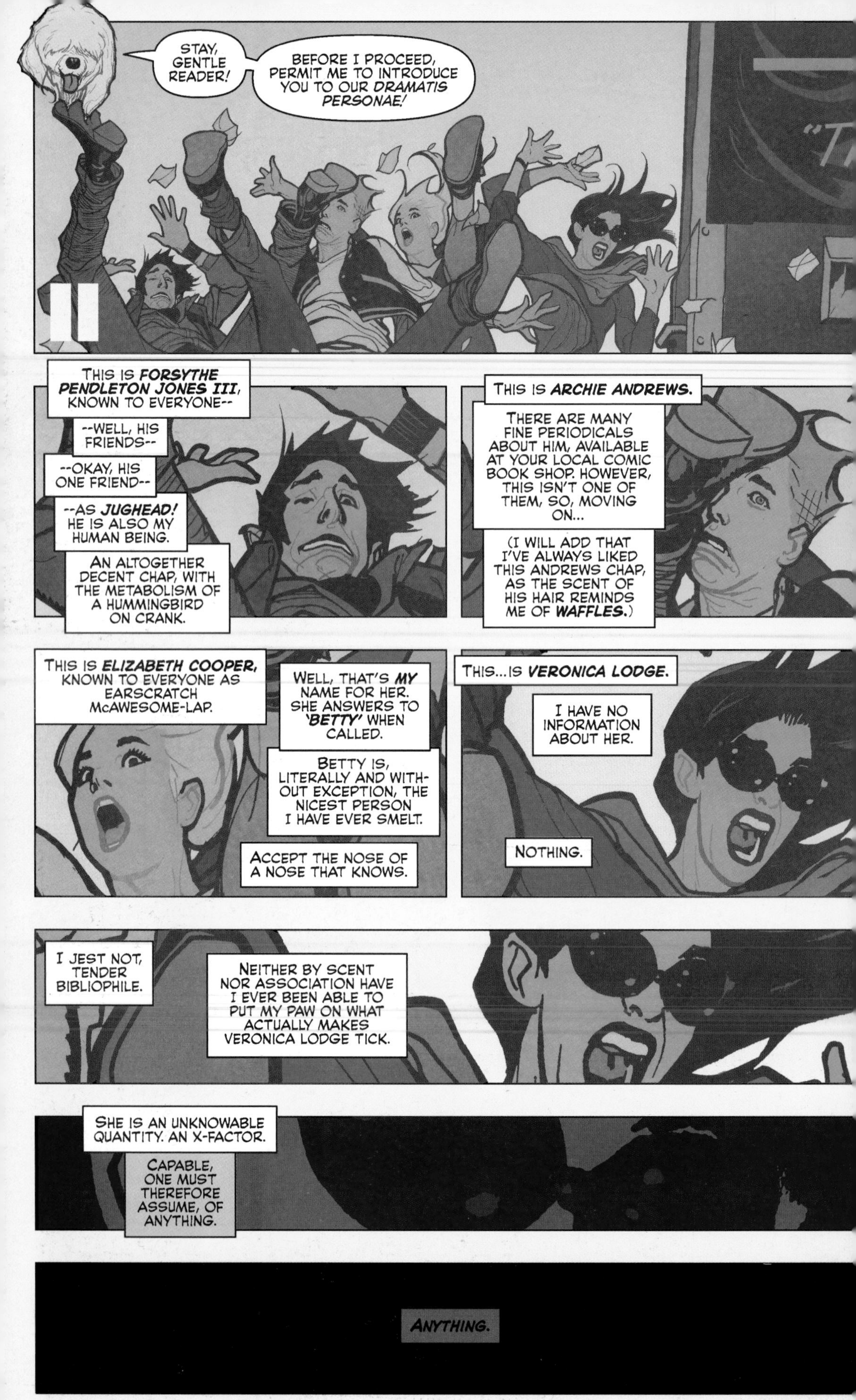
STAY, GENTLE READER!
BEFORE I PROCEED, PERMIT ME TO INTRODUCE YOU TO OUR DRAMATIS PERSONAE!
THIS IS FORSYTHE PENDLETON JONES III, KNOWN TO EVERYONE--
--WELL, HIS FRIENDS--
--OKAY, HIS ONE FRIEND--
--AS JUGHEAD! HE IS ALSO MY HUMAN BEING.
AN ALTOGETHER DECENT CHAP, WITH THE METABOLISM OF A HUMMINGBIRD ON CRANK.
THIS IS ARCHIE ANDREWS.
THERE ARE MANY FINE PERIODICALS ABOUT HIM, AVAILABLE AT YOUR LOCAL COMIC BOOK SHOP. HOWEVER, THIS ISN'T ONE OF THEM, SO, MOVING ON...
(I WILL ADD THAT I'VE ALWAYS LIKED THIS ANDREWS CHAP, AS THE SCENT OF HIS HAIR REMINDS ME OF WAFFLES.)
THIS IS ELIZABETH COOPER, KNOWN TO EVERYONE AS EARSCRATCH McAWESOME-LAP.
WELL, THAT'S MY NAME FOR HER. SHE ANSWERS TO 'BETTY' WHEN CALLED.
BETTY IS, LITERALLY AND WITH-OUT EXCEPTION, THE NICEST PERSON I HAVE EVER SMELT.
ACCEPT THE NOSE OF A NOSE THAT KNOWS.
THIS...IS VERONICA LODGE.
I HAVE NO INFORMATION ABOUT HER.
NOTHING.
I JEST NOT, TENDER BIBLIOPHILE.
NEITHER BY SCENT NOR ASSOCIATION HAVE I EVER BEEN ABLE TO PUT MY PAW ON WHAT ACTUALLY MAKES VERONICA LODGE TICK.
SHE IS AN UNKNOWABLE QUANTITY. AN X-FACTOR.
CAPABLE, ONE MUST THEREFORE ASSUME, OF ANYTHING.
ANYTHING.

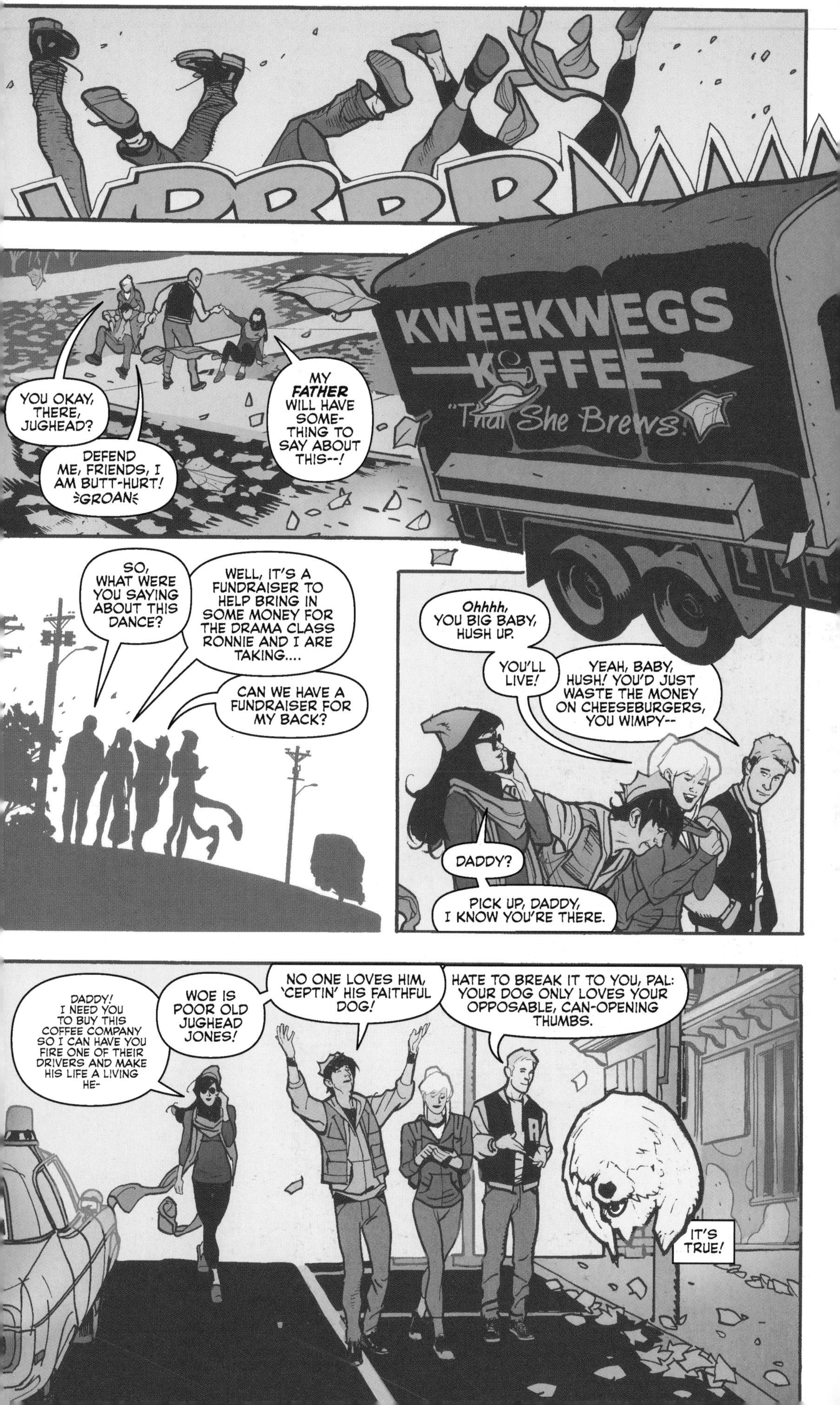

VRRRRAAAAAA
KWEEKWEGS KOFFEE "Thar She Brews!"
YOU OKAY, THERE, JUGHEAD?
DEFEND ME, FRIENDS, I AM BUTT-HURT! GROAN
MY FATHER WILL HAVE SOME-THING TO SAY ABOUT THIS--!
SO, WHAT WERE YOU SAYING ABOUT THIS DANCE?
WELL, IT'S A FUNDRAISER TO HELP BRING IN SOME MONEY FOR THE DRAMA CLASS RONNIE AND I ARE TAKING....
CAN WE HAVE A FUNDRAISER FOR MY BACK?
Ohhhh, YOU BIG BABY, HUSH UP.
YOU'LL LIVE!
YEAH, BABY, HUSH! YOU'D JUST WASTE THE MONEY ON CHEESEBURGERS, YOU WIMPY--
DADDY?
PICK UP, DADDY, I KNOW YOU'RE THERE.
DADDY! I NEED YOU TO BUY THIS COFFEE COMPANY SO I CAN HAVE YOU FIRE ONE OF THEIR DRIVERS AND MAKE HIS LIFE A LIVING HE-
WOE IS POOR OLD JUGHEAD JONES!
NO ONE LOVES HIM, 'CEPTIN' HIS FAITHFUL DOG!
HATE TO BREAK IT TO YOU, PAL: YOUR DOG ONLY LOVES YOUR OPPOSABLE, CAN-OPENING THUMBS.
IT'S TRUE!

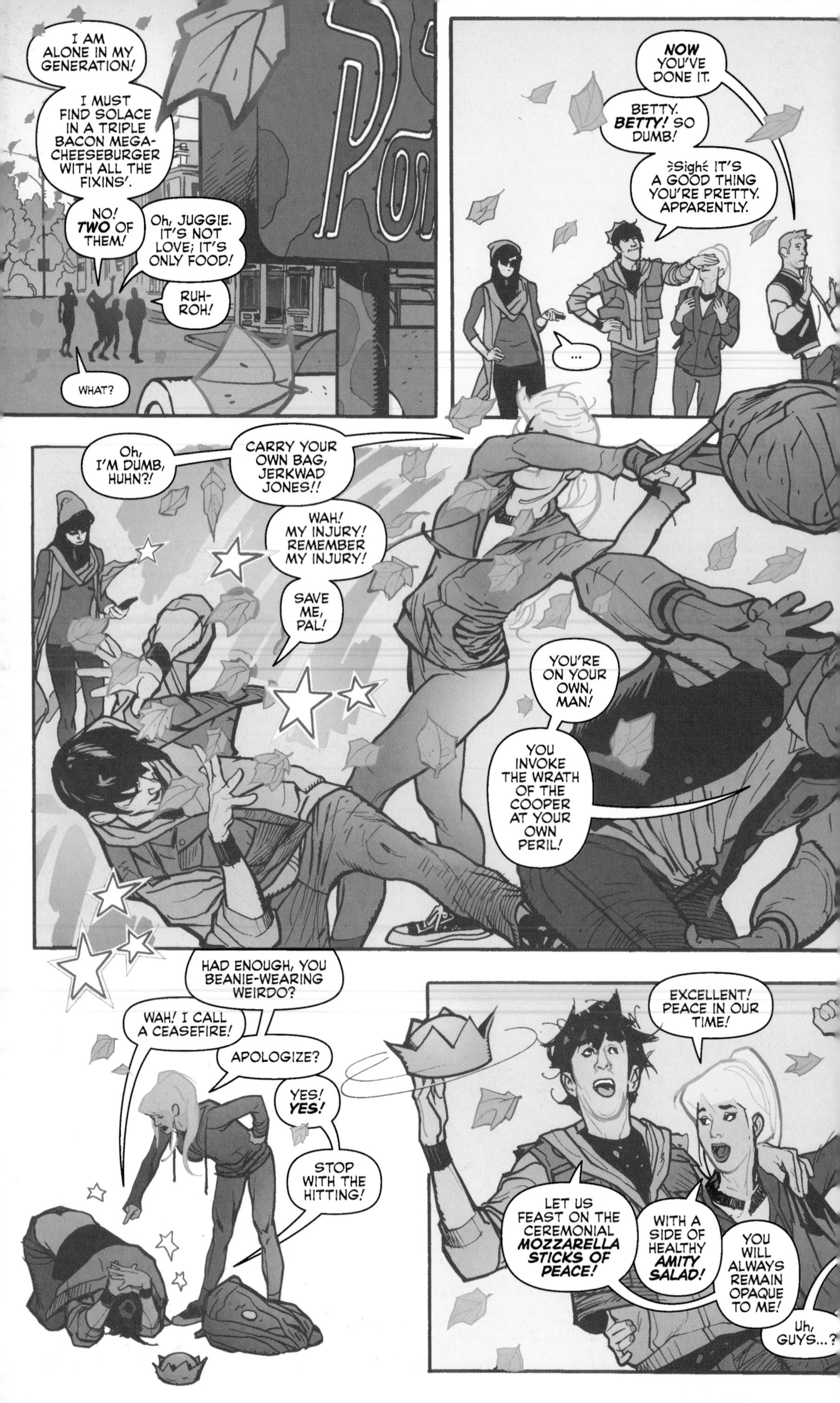

I AM ALONE IN MY GENERATION!
I MUST FIND SOLACE IN A TRIPLE BACON MEGA-CHEESEBURGER WITH ALL THE FIXINS'.
NO! **TWO** OF THEM!
Oh, JUGGIE. IT'S NOT LOVE; IT'S ONLY FOOD!
RUH-ROH!
WHAT?
NOW YOU'VE DONE IT.
BETTY. **BETTY!** SO DUMB!
⪾Sigh⪽ IT'S A GOOD THING YOU'RE PRETTY. APPARENTLY.
...
CARRY YOUR OWN BAG, JERKWAD JONES!!
Oh, I'M DUMB, HUHN?!
WAH! MY INJURY! REMEMBER MY INJURY!
SAVE ME, PAL!
YOU'RE ON YOUR OWN, MAN!
YOU INVOKE THE WRATH OF THE COOPER AT YOUR OWN PERIL!
HAD ENOUGH, YOU BEANIE-WEARING WEIRDO?
WAH! I CALL A CEASEFIRE!
APOLOGIZE?
YES! **YES!**
STOP WITH THE HITTING!
EXCELLENT! PEACE IN OUR TIME!
LET US FEAST ON THE CEREMONIAL **MOZZARELLA STICKS OF PEACE!**
WITH A SIDE OF HEALTHY **AMITY SALAD!**
YOU WILL ALWAYS REMAIN OPAQUE TO ME!
Uh, GUYS...?

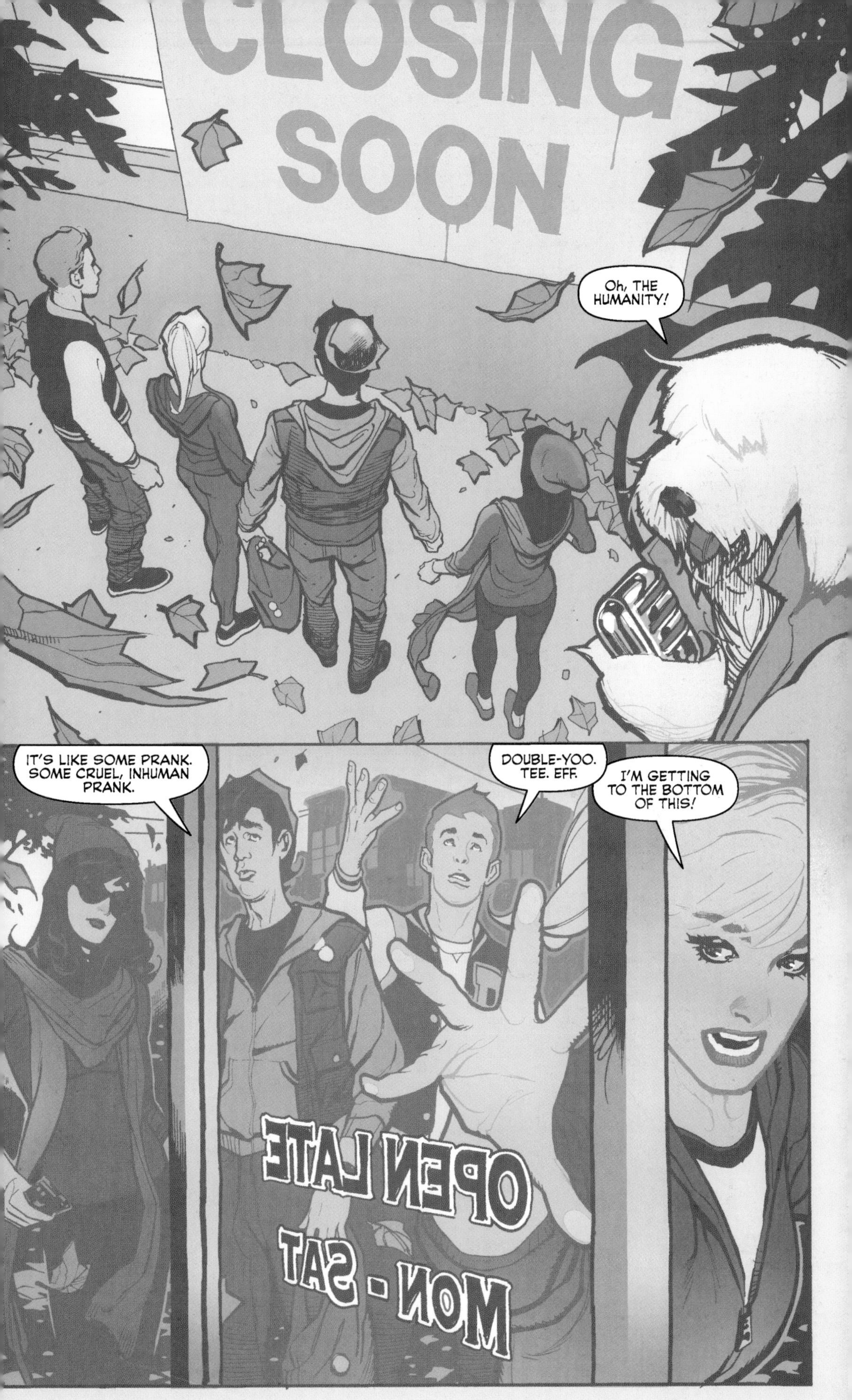
CLOSING SOON
Oh, THE HUMANITY!
IT'S LIKE SOME PRANK. SOME CRUEL, INHUMAN PRANK.
DOUBLE-YOO. TEE. EFF.
I'M GETTING TO THE BOTTOM OF THIS!
OPEN LATE
MON - SAT

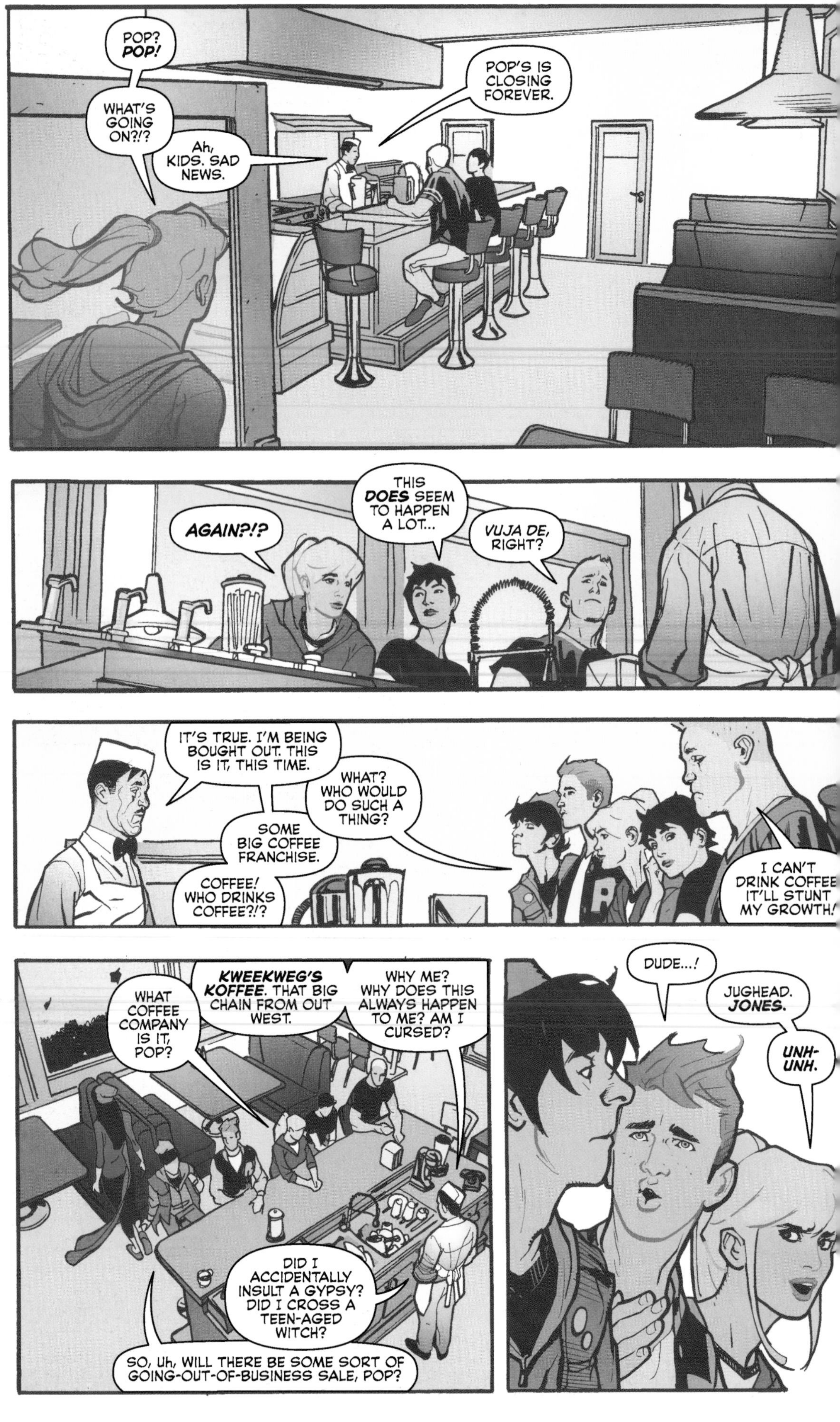
POP? POP!
WHAT'S GOING ON?!?
Ah, KIDS. SAD NEWS.
POP'S IS CLOSING FOREVER.
AGAIN?!?
THIS DOES SEEM TO HAPPEN A LOT...
VUJA DE, RIGHT?
IT'S TRUE. I'M BEING BOUGHT OUT. THIS IS IT, THIS TIME.
WHAT? WHO WOULD DO SUCH A THING?
SOME BIG COFFEE FRANCHISE.
COFFEE! WHO DRINKS COFFEE?!?
I CAN'T DRINK COFFEE IT'LL STUNT MY GROWTH!
WHAT COFFEE COMPANY IS IT, POP?
KWEEKWEG'S KOFFEE. THAT BIG CHAIN FROM OUT WEST.
WHY ME? WHY DOES THIS ALWAYS HAPPEN TO ME? AM I CURSED?
DID I ACCIDENTALLY INSULT A GYPSY? DID I CROSS A TEEN-AGED WITCH?
SO, Uh, WILL THERE BE SOME SORT OF GOING-OUT-OF-BUSINESS SALE, POP?
DUDE...!
JUGHEAD. JONES.
UNH-UNH.

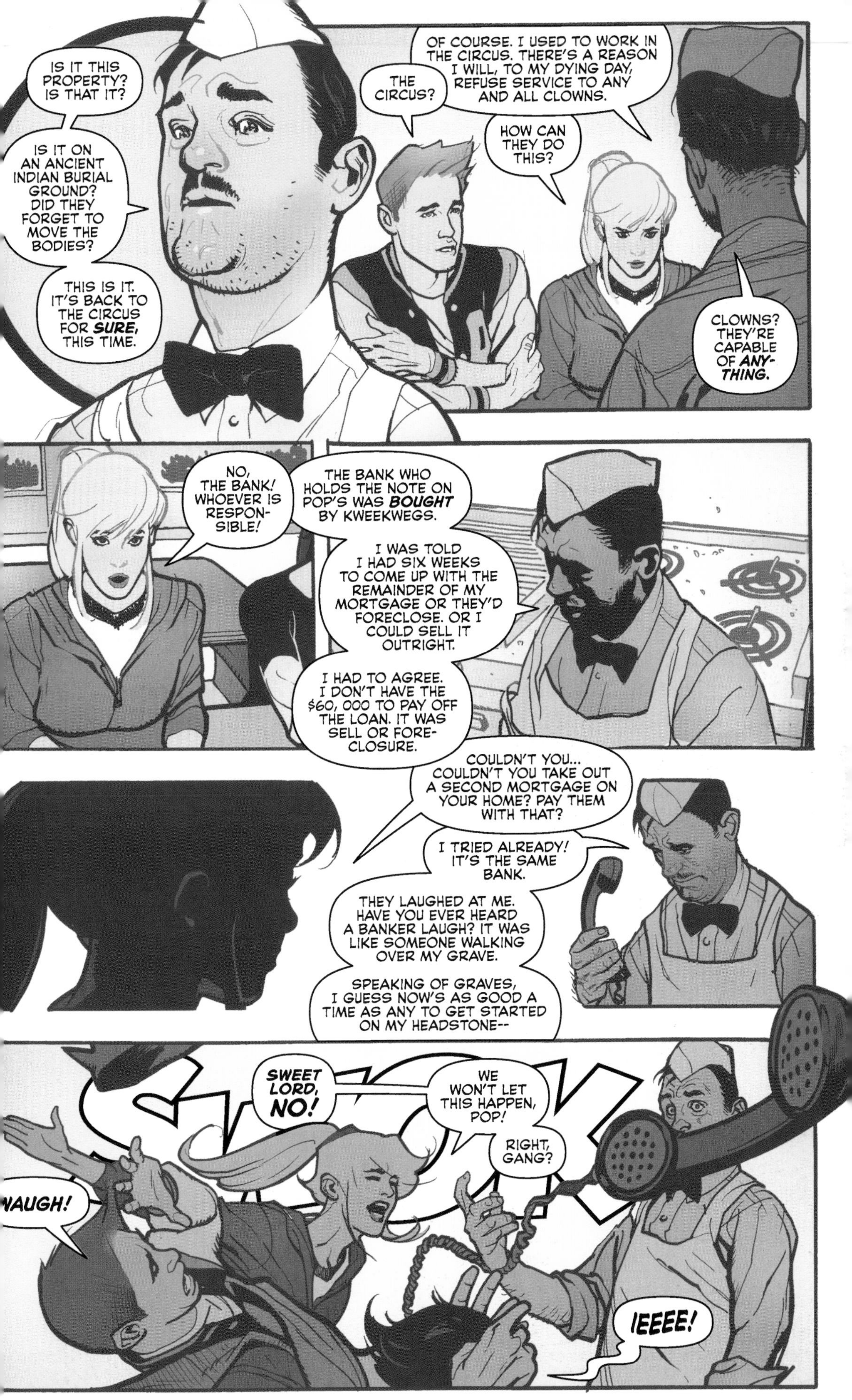
IS IT THIS PROPERTY? IS THAT IT?
IS IT ON AN ANCIENT INDIAN BURIAL GROUND? DID THEY FORGET TO MOVE THE BODIES?
THIS IS IT. IT'S BACK TO THE CIRCUS FOR **SURE,** THIS TIME.
THE CIRCUS?
OF COURSE. I USED TO WORK IN THE CIRCUS. THERE'S A REASON I WILL, TO MY DYING DAY, REFUSE SERVICE TO ANY AND ALL CLOWNS.
HOW CAN THEY DO THIS?
CLOWNS? THEY'RE CAPABLE OF **ANY-THING.**
NO, THE BANK! WHOEVER IS RESPON-SIBLE!
THE BANK WHO HOLDS THE NOTE ON POP'S WAS **BOUGHT** BY KWEEKWEGS.
I WAS TOLD I HAD SIX WEEKS TO COME UP WITH THE REMAINDER OF MY MORTGAGE OR THEY'D FORECLOSE. OR I COULD SELL IT OUTRIGHT.
I HAD TO AGREE. I DON'T HAVE THE $60, 000 TO PAY OFF THE LOAN. IT WAS SELL OR FORE-CLOSURE.
COULDN'T YOU... COULDN'T YOU TAKE OUT A SECOND MORTGAGE ON YOUR HOME? PAY THEM WITH THAT?
I TRIED ALREADY! IT'S THE SAME BANK.
THEY LAUGHED AT ME. HAVE YOU EVER HEARD A BANKER LAUGH? IT WAS LIKE SOMEONE WALKING OVER MY GRAVE.
SPEAKING OF GRAVES, I GUESS NOW'S AS GOOD A TIME AS ANY TO GET STARTED ON MY HEADSTONE--
SWEET LORD, NO!
WE WON'T LET THIS HAPPEN, POP!
RIGHT, GANG?
WAUGH!
IEEEE!

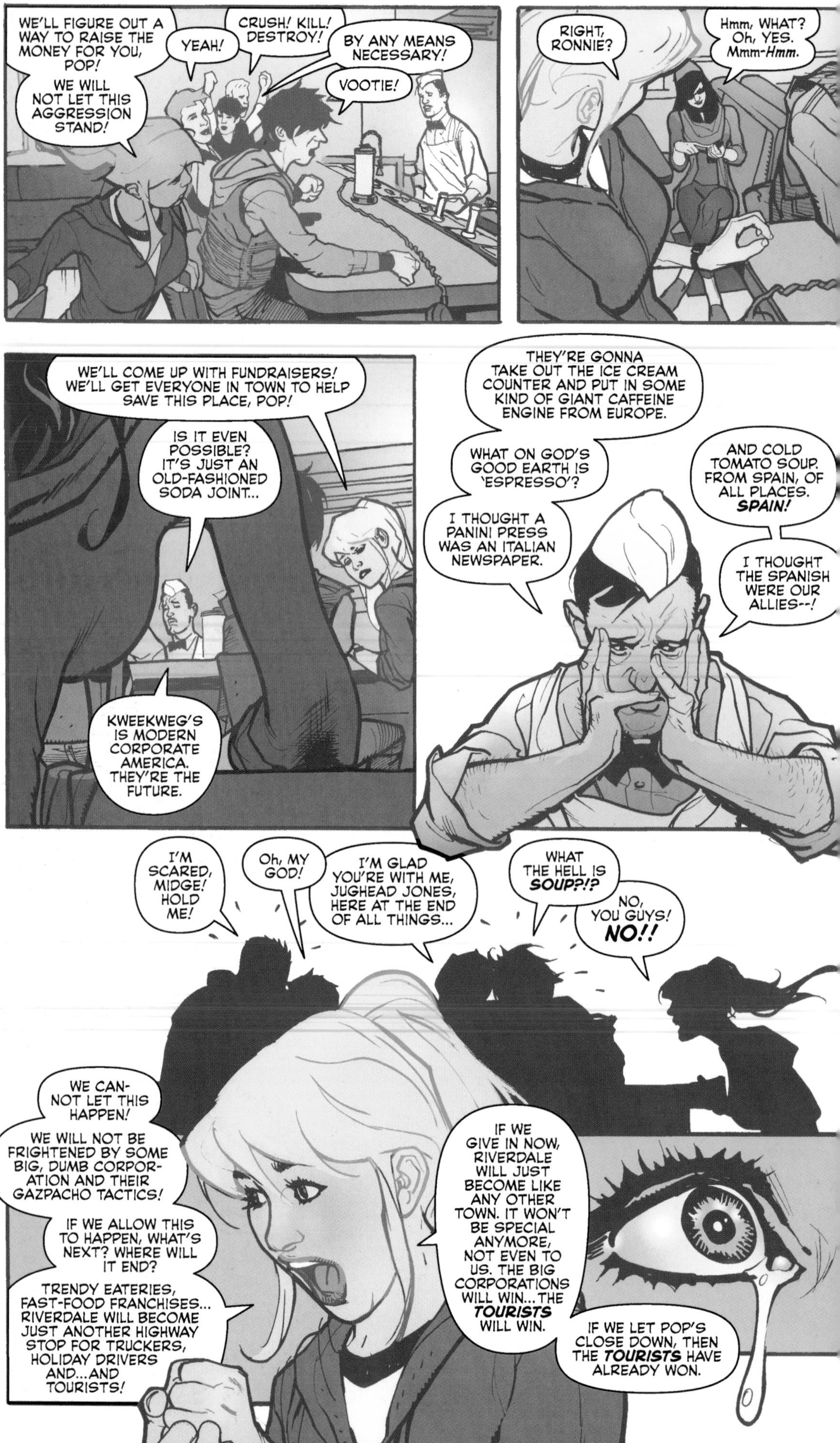

WE'LL FIGURE OUT A WAY TO RAISE THE MONEY FOR YOU, POP!
WE WILL NOT LET THIS AGGRESSION STAND!
YEAH!
CRUSH! KILL! DESTROY!
BY ANY MEANS NECESSARY!
VOOTIE!
RIGHT, RONNIE?
Hmm, WHAT? Oh, YES. Mmm-*Hmm*.
WE'LL COME UP WITH FUNDRAISERS! WE'LL GET EVERYONE IN TOWN TO HELP SAVE THIS PLACE, POP!
IS IT EVEN POSSIBLE? IT'S JUST AN OLD-FASHIONED SODA JOINT...
KWEEKWEG'S IS MODERN CORPORATE AMERICA. THEY'RE THE FUTURE.
THEY'RE GONNA TAKE OUT THE ICE CREAM COUNTER AND PUT IN SOME KIND OF GIANT CAFFEINE ENGINE FROM EUROPE.
WHAT ON GOD'S GOOD EARTH IS 'ESPRESSO'?
I THOUGHT A PANINI PRESS WAS AN ITALIAN NEWSPAPER.
AND COLD TOMATO SOUP. FROM SPAIN, OF ALL PLACES. ***SPAIN!***
I THOUGHT THE SPANISH WERE OUR ALLIES--!
I'M SCARED, MIDGE! HOLD ME!
Oh, MY GOD!
I'M GLAD YOU'RE WITH ME, JUGHEAD JONES, HERE AT THE END OF ALL THINGS...
WHAT THE HELL IS ***SOUP?!?***
NO, YOU GUYS! ***NO!!***
WE CAN-NOT LET THIS HAPPEN!
WE WILL NOT BE FRIGHTENED BY SOME BIG, DUMB CORPOR-ATION AND THEIR GAZPACHO TACTICS!
IF WE ALLOW THIS TO HAPPEN, WHAT'S NEXT? WHERE WILL IT END?
TRENDY EATERIES, FAST-FOOD FRANCHISES... RIVERDALE WILL BECOME JUST ANOTHER HIGHWAY STOP FOR TRUCKERS, HOLIDAY DRIVERS AND...AND TOURISTS!
IF WE GIVE IN NOW, RIVERDALE WILL JUST BECOME LIKE ANY OTHER TOWN. IT WON'T BE SPECIAL ANYMORE, NOT EVEN TO US. THE BIG CORPORATIONS WILL WIN... THE ***TOURISTS*** WILL WIN.
IF WE LET POP'S CLOSE DOWN, THEN THE ***TOURISTS*** HAVE ALREADY WON.

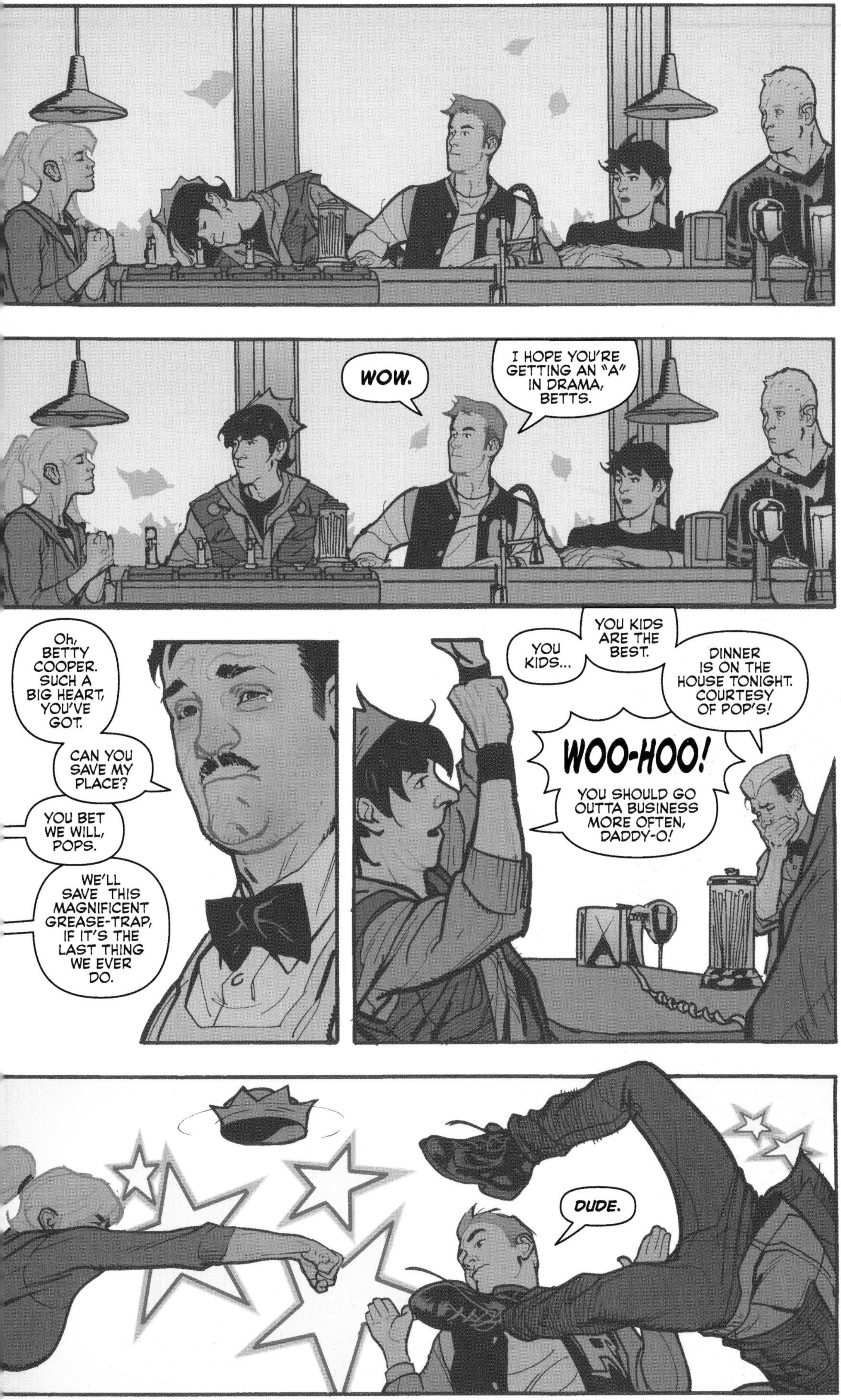
WOW.
I HOPE YOU'RE GETTING AN "A" IN DRAMA, BETTS.
Oh, BETTY COOPER. SUCH A BIG HEART, YOU'VE GOT.
CAN YOU SAVE MY PLACE?
YOU BET WE WILL, POPS.
WE'LL SAVE THIS MAGNIFICENT GREASE-TRAP, IF IT'S THE LAST THING WE EVER DO.
YOU KIDS...
YOU KIDS ARE THE BEST.
DINNER IS ON THE HOUSE TONIGHT. COURTESY OF POP'S!
WOO-HOO!
YOU SHOULD GO OUTTA BUSINESS MORE OFTEN, DADDY-O!
DUDE.

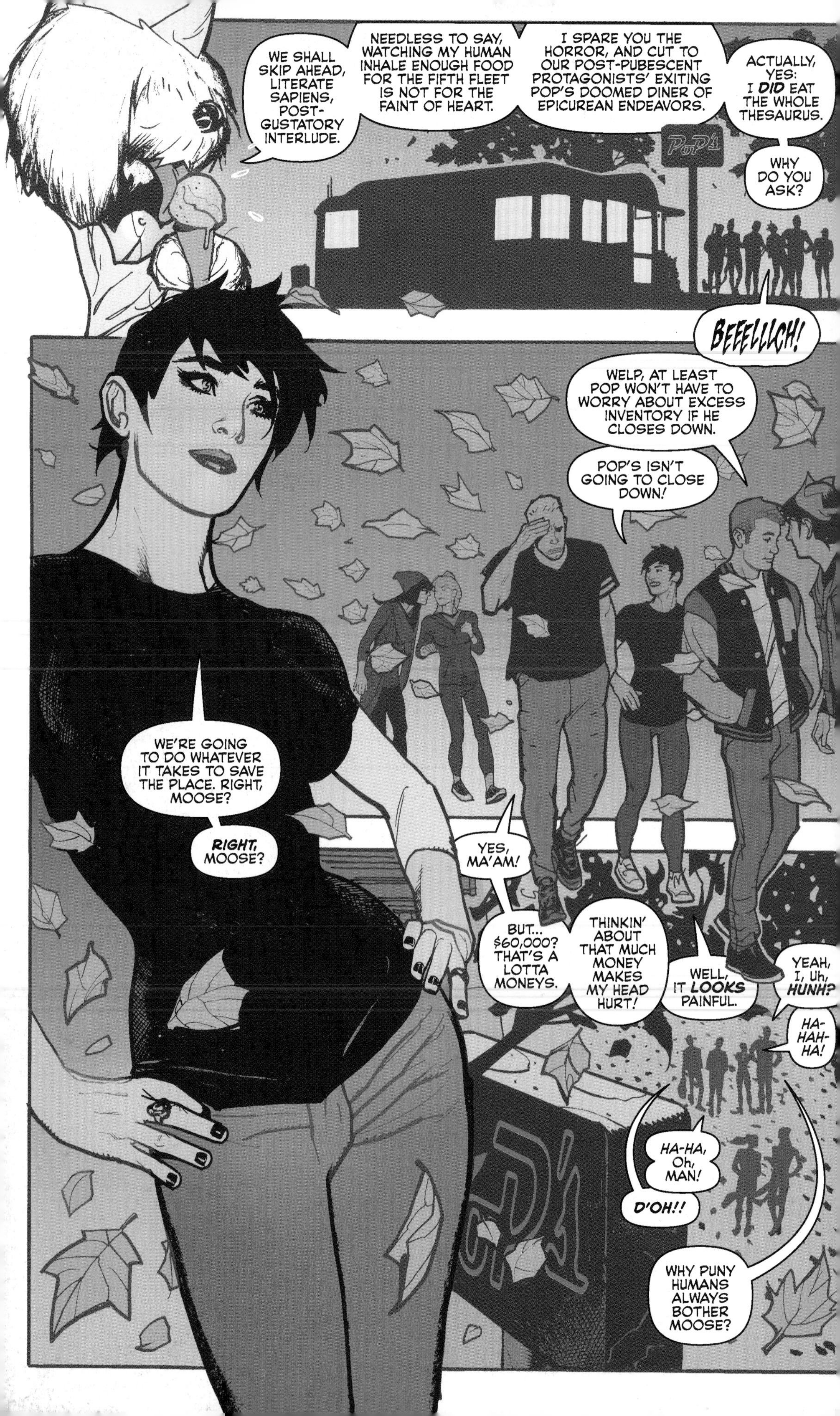
WE SHALL SKIP AHEAD, LITERATE SAPIENS, POST-GUSTATORY INTERLUDE.
NEEDLESS TO SAY, WATCHING MY HUMAN INHALE ENOUGH FOOD FOR THE FIFTH FLEET IS NOT FOR THE FAINT OF HEART.
I SPARE YOU THE HORROR, AND CUT TO OUR POST-PUBESCENT PROTAGONISTS' EXITING POP'S DOOMED DINER OF EPICUREAN ENDEAVORS.
ACTUALLY, YES: I DID EAT THE WHOLE THESAURUS.
WHY DO YOU ASK?
PoP's
BEEELLLCH!
WELP, AT LEAST POP WON'T HAVE TO WORRY ABOUT EXCESS INVENTORY IF HE CLOSES DOWN.
POP'S ISN'T GOING TO CLOSE DOWN!
WE'RE GOING TO DO WHATEVER IT TAKES TO SAVE THE PLACE. RIGHT, MOOSE?
RIGHT, MOOSE?
YES, MA'AM!
BUT... $60,000? THAT'S A LOTTA MONEYS.
THINKIN' ABOUT THAT MUCH MONEY MAKES MY HEAD HURT!
WELL, IT LOOKS PAINFUL.
YEAH, I, Uh, HUNH?
HA-HAH-HA!
HA-HA, Oh, MAN!
D'OH!!
WHY PUNY HUMANS ALWAYS BOTHER MOOSE?

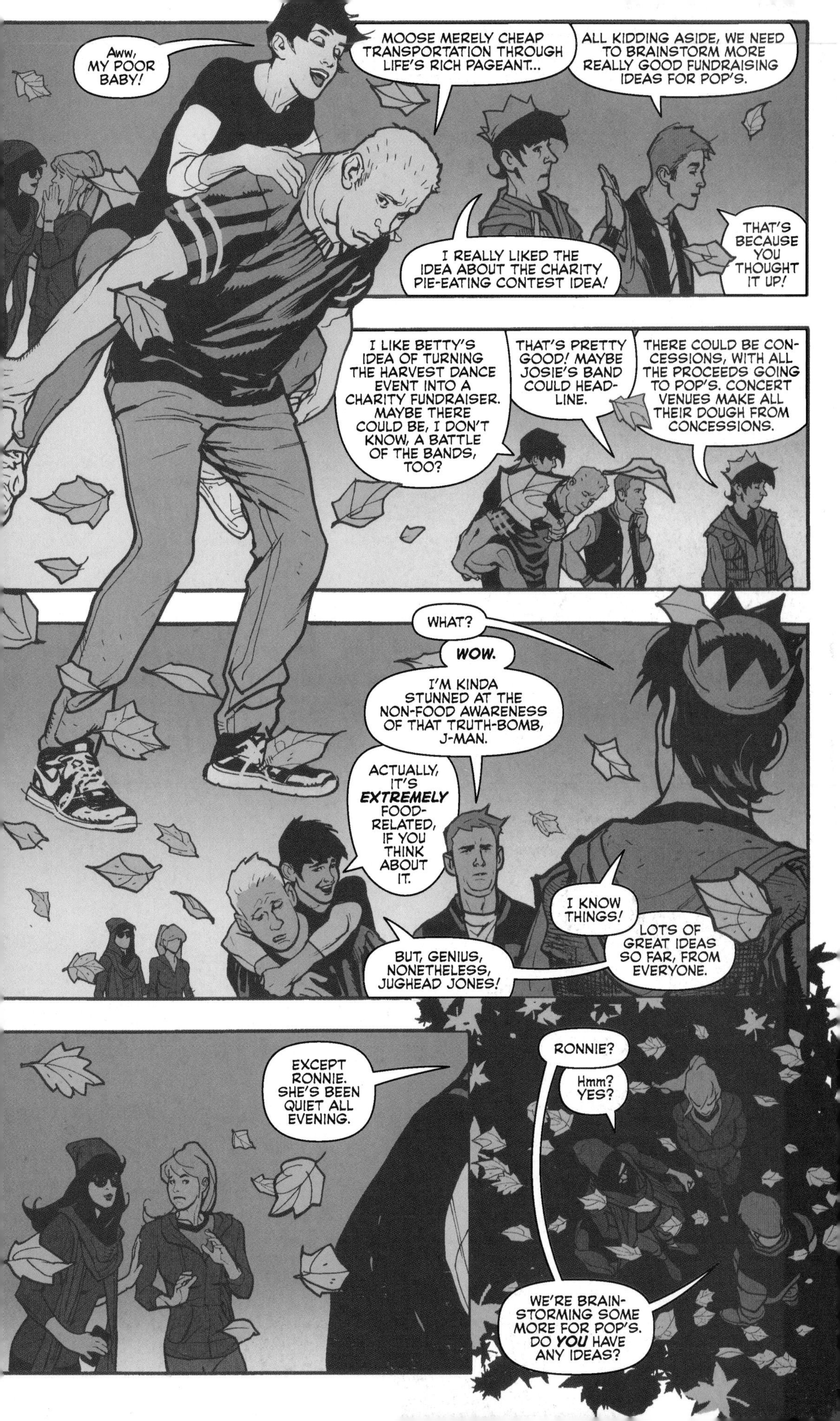

Aww, MY POOR BABY!
MOOSE MERELY CHEAP TRANSPORTATION THROUGH LIFE'S RICH PAGEANT...
ALL KIDDING ASIDE, WE NEED TO BRAINSTORM MORE REALLY GOOD FUNDRAISING IDEAS FOR POP'S.
I REALLY LIKED THE IDEA ABOUT THE CHARITY PIE-EATING CONTEST IDEA!
THAT'S BECAUSE YOU THOUGHT IT UP!
I LIKE BETTY'S IDEA OF TURNING THE HARVEST DANCE EVENT INTO A CHARITY FUNDRAISER. MAYBE THERE COULD BE, I DON'T KNOW, A BATTLE OF THE BANDS, TOO?
THAT'S PRETTY GOOD! MAYBE JOSIE'S BAND COULD HEAD-LINE.
THERE COULD BE CON-CESSIONS, WITH ALL THE PROCEEDS GOING TO POP'S. CONCERT VENUES MAKE ALL THEIR DOUGH FROM CONCESSIONS.
WHAT?
WOW.
I'M KINDA STUNNED AT THE NON-FOOD AWARENESS OF THAT TRUTH-BOMB, J-MAN.
ACTUALLY, IT'S ***EXTREMELY*** FOOD-RELATED, IF YOU THINK ABOUT IT.
I KNOW THINGS!
BUT, GENIUS, NONETHELESS, JUGHEAD JONES!
LOTS OF GREAT IDEAS SO FAR, FROM EVERYONE.
EXCEPT RONNIE. SHE'S BEEN QUIET ALL EVENING.
RONNIE?
Hmm? YES?
WE'RE BRAIN-STORMING SOME MORE FOR POP'S. DO ***YOU*** HAVE ANY IDEAS?

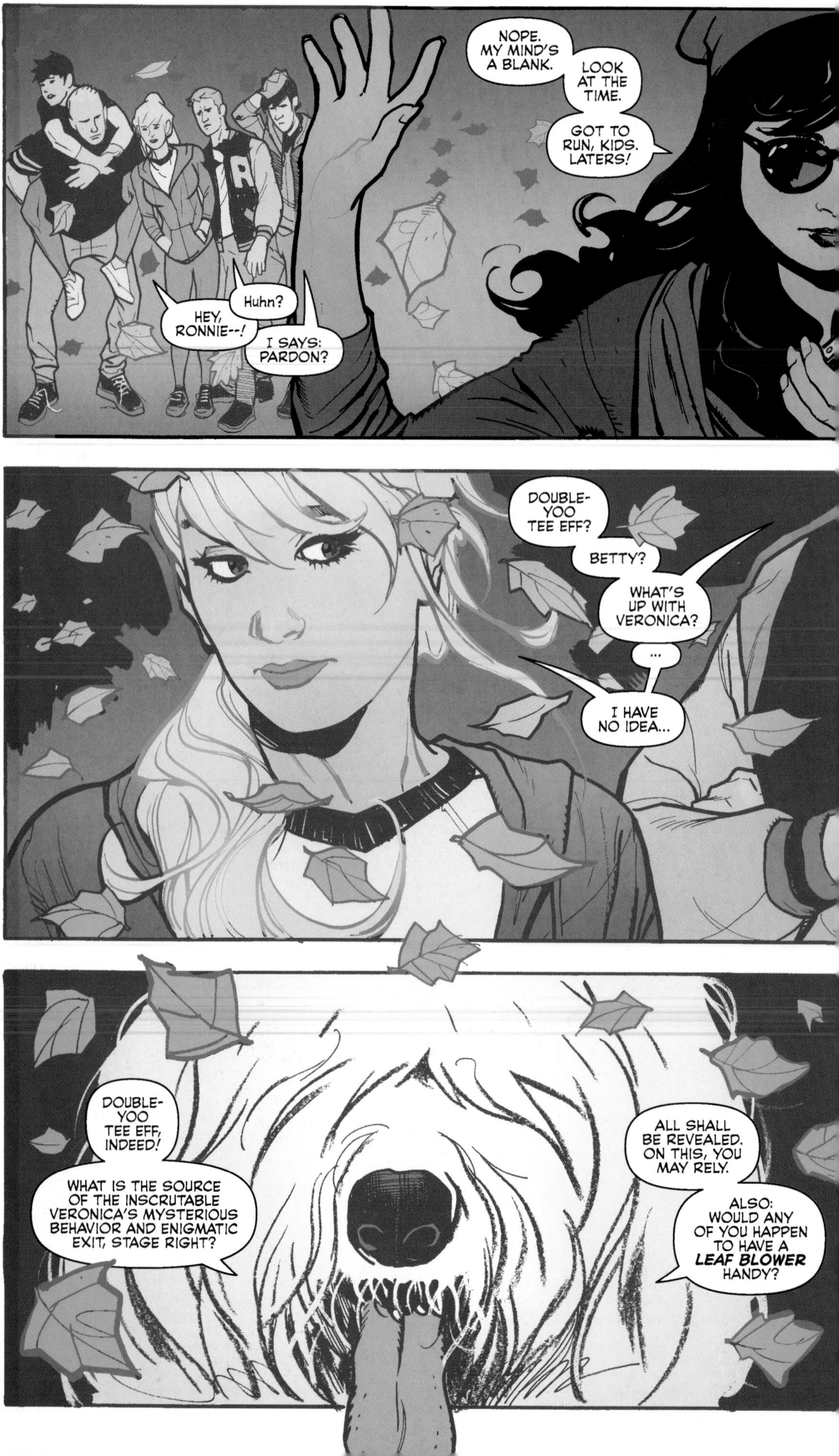
HEY, RONNIE--!
Huhn?
I SAYS: PARDON?
NOPE. MY MIND'S A BLANK.
LOOK AT THE TIME.
GOT TO RUN, KIDS. LATERS!
DOUBLE-YOO TEE EFF?
BETTY?
WHAT'S UP WITH VERONICA?
...
I HAVE NO IDEA...
DOUBLE-YOO TEE EFF, INDEED!
WHAT IS THE SOURCE OF THE INSCRUTABLE VERONICA'S MYSTERIOUS BEHAVIOR AND ENIGMATIC EXIT, STAGE RIGHT?
ALL SHALL BE REVEALED. ON THIS, YOU MAY RELY.
ALSO: WOULD ANY OF YOU HAPPEN TO HAVE A LEAF BLOWER HANDY?

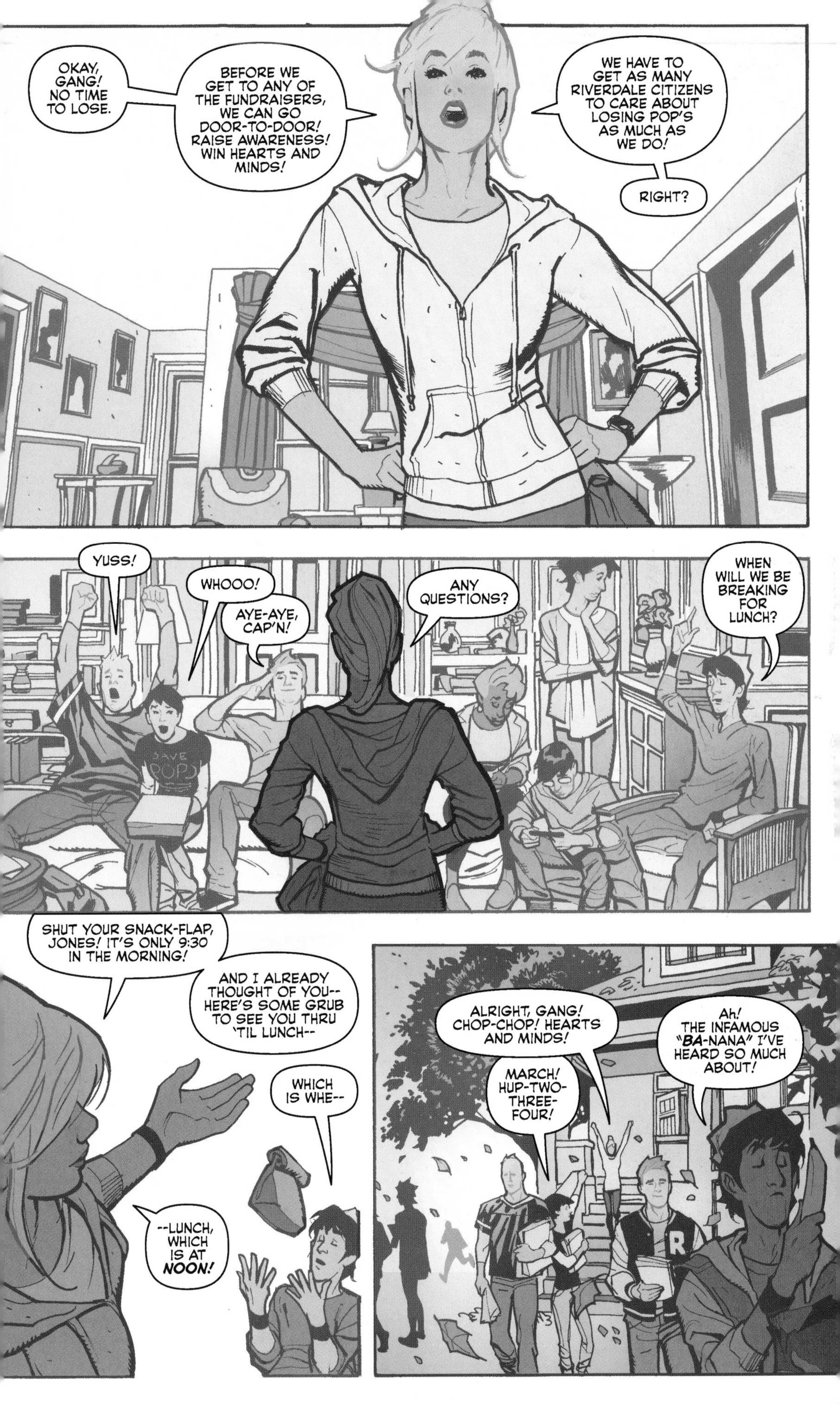
OKAY, GANG! NO TIME TO LOSE.
BEFORE WE GET TO ANY OF THE FUNDRAISERS, WE CAN GO DOOR-TO-DOOR! RAISE AWARENESS! WIN HEARTS AND MINDS!
WE HAVE TO GET AS MANY RIVERDALE CITIZENS TO CARE ABOUT LOSING POP'S AS MUCH AS WE DO!
RIGHT?
YUSS!
WHOOO!
AYE-AYE, CAP'N!
ANY QUESTIONS?
WHEN WILL WE BE BREAKING FOR LUNCH?
SAVE POP'S
SHUT YOUR SNACK-FLAP, JONES! IT'S ONLY 9:30 IN THE MORNING!
AND I ALREADY THOUGHT OF YOU-- HERE'S SOME GRUB TO SEE YOU THRU 'TIL LUNCH--
WHICH IS WHE--
--LUNCH, WHICH IS AT *NOON!*
ALRIGHT, GANG! CHOP-CHOP! HEARTS AND MINDS!
MARCH! HUP-TWO-THREE-FOUR!
AH! THE INFAMOUS "*BA*-NANA" I'VE HEARD SO MUCH ABOUT!

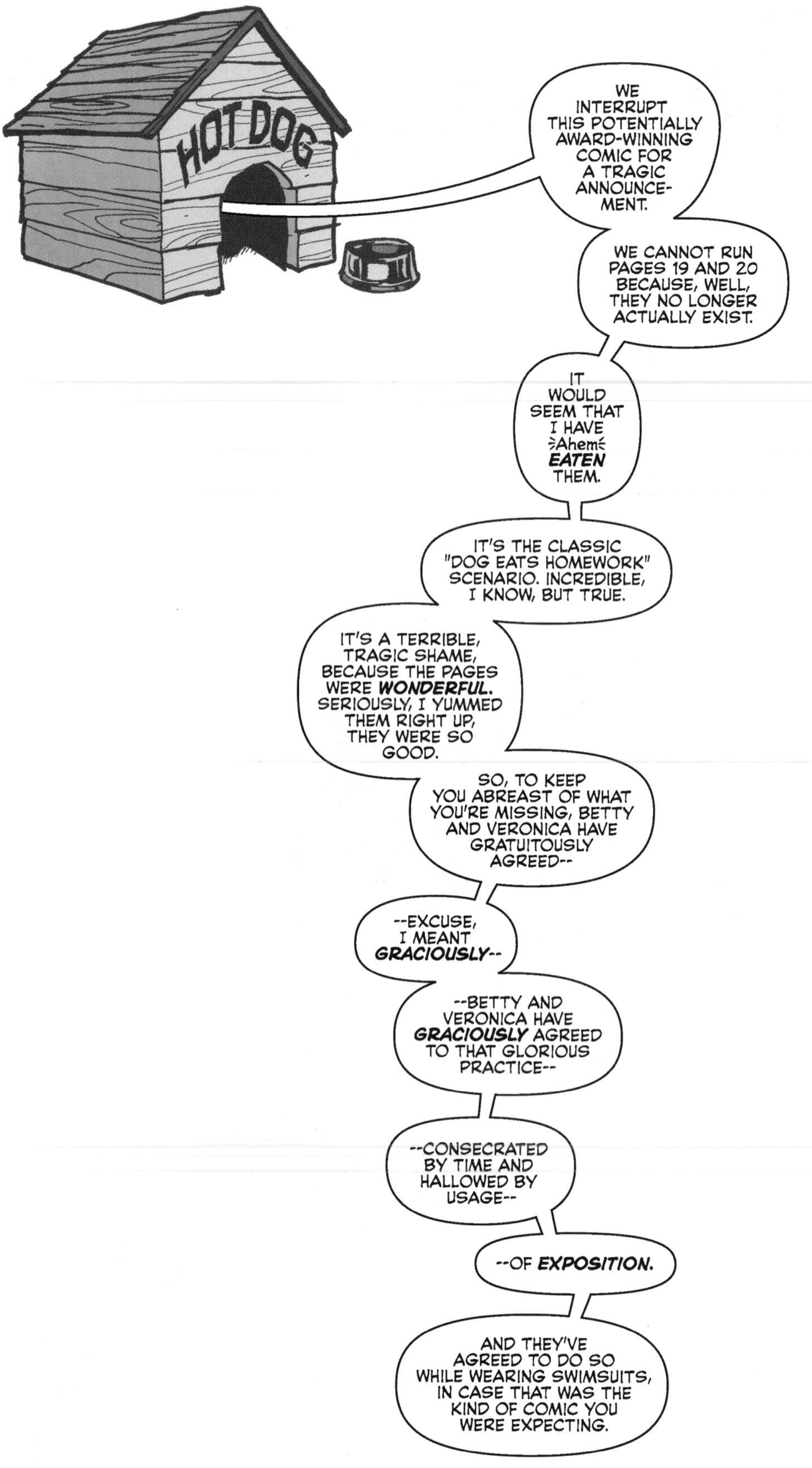
HOT DOG
WE INTERRUPT THIS POTENTIALLY AWARD-WINNING COMIC FOR A TRAGIC ANNOUNCE-MENT.
WE CANNOT RUN PAGES 19 AND 20 BECAUSE, WELL, THEY NO LONGER ACTUALLY EXIST.
IT WOULD SEEM THAT I HAVE *Ahem* ***EATEN*** THEM.
IT'S THE CLASSIC "DOG EATS HOMEWORK" SCENARIO. INCREDIBLE, I KNOW, BUT TRUE.
IT'S A TERRIBLE, TRAGIC SHAME, BECAUSE THE PAGES WERE ***WONDERFUL.*** SERIOUSLY, I YUMMED THEM RIGHT UP, THEY WERE SO GOOD.
SO, TO KEEP YOU ABREAST OF WHAT YOU'RE MISSING, BETTY AND VERONICA HAVE GRATUITOUSLY AGREED--
--EXCUSE, I MEANT ***GRACIOUSLY***--
--BETTY AND VERONICA HAVE ***GRACIOUSLY*** AGREED TO THAT GLORIOUS PRACTICE--
--CONSECRATED BY TIME AND HALLOWED BY USAGE--
--OF ***EXPOSITION.***
AND THEY'VE AGREED TO DO SO WHILE WEARING SWIMSUITS, IN CASE THAT WAS THE KIND OF COMIC YOU WERE EXPECTING.

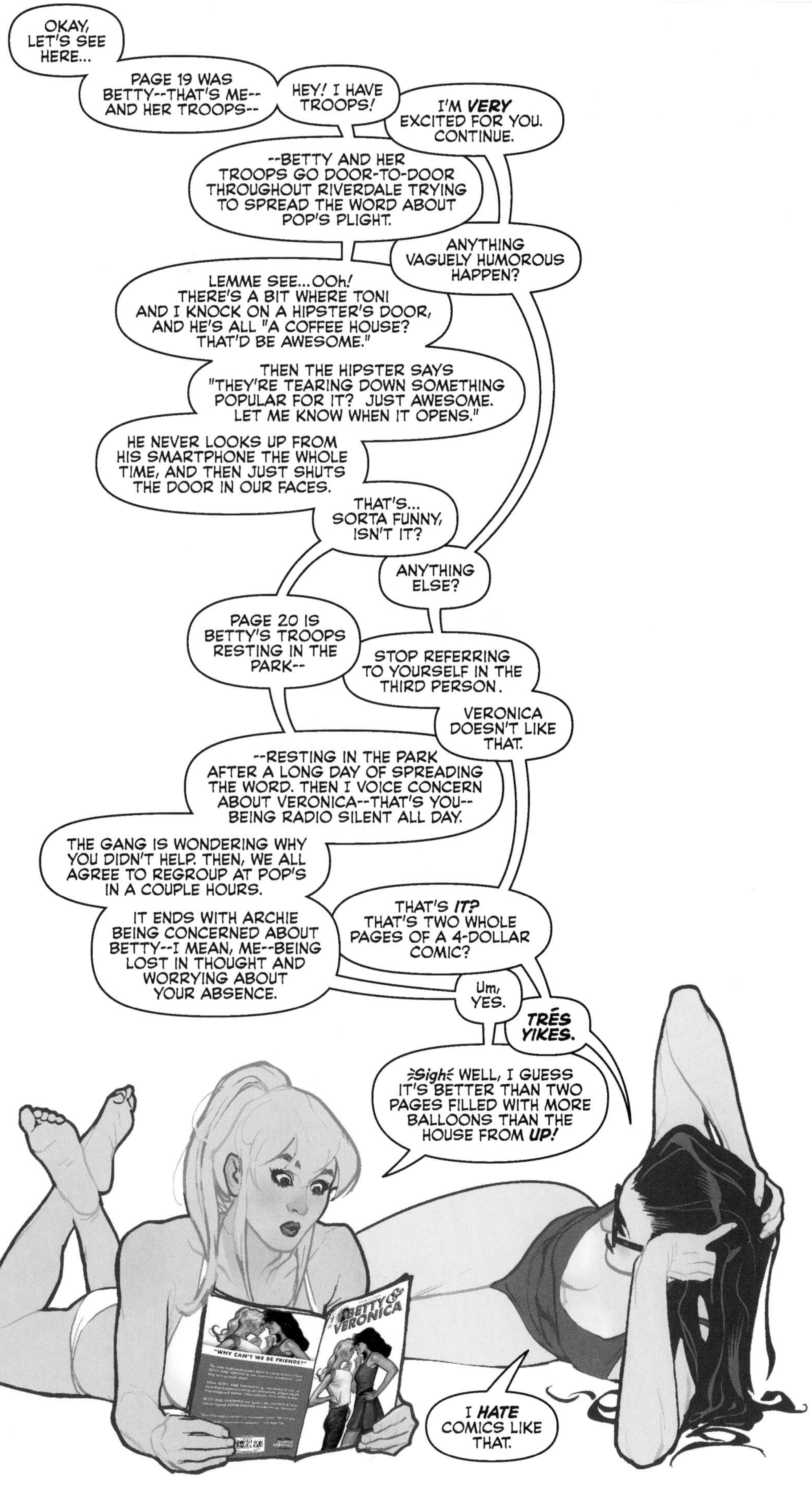

OKAY, LET'S SEE HERE...
PAGE 19 WAS BETTY--THAT'S ME--AND HER TROOPS--
HEY! I HAVE TROOPS!
I'M **VERY** EXCITED FOR YOU. CONTINUE.
--BETTY AND HER TROOPS GO DOOR-TO-DOOR THROUGHOUT RIVERDALE TRYING TO SPREAD THE WORD ABOUT POP'S PLIGHT.
ANYTHING VAGUELY HUMOROUS HAPPEN?
LEMME SEE...OOh! THERE'S A BIT WHERE TONI AND I KNOCK ON A HIPSTER'S DOOR, AND HE'S ALL "A COFFEE HOUSE? THAT'D BE AWESOME."
THEN THE HIPSTER SAYS "THEY'RE TEARING DOWN SOMETHING POPULAR FOR IT? JUST AWESOME. LET ME KNOW WHEN IT OPENS."
HE NEVER LOOKS UP FROM HIS SMARTPHONE THE WHOLE TIME, AND THEN JUST SHUTS THE DOOR IN OUR FACES.
THAT'S... SORTA FUNNY, ISN'T IT?
ANYTHING ELSE?
PAGE 20 IS BETTY'S TROOPS RESTING IN THE PARK--
STOP REFERRING TO YOURSELF IN THE THIRD PERSON.
VERONICA DOESN'T LIKE THAT.
--RESTING IN THE PARK AFTER A LONG DAY OF SPREADING THE WORD. THEN I VOICE CONCERN ABOUT VERONICA--THAT'S YOU--BEING RADIO SILENT ALL DAY.
THE GANG IS WONDERING WHY YOU DIDN'T HELP. THEN, WE ALL AGREE TO REGROUP AT POP'S IN A COUPLE HOURS.
IT ENDS WITH ARCHIE BEING CONCERNED ABOUT BETTY--I MEAN, ME--BEING LOST IN THOUGHT AND WORRYING ABOUT YOUR ABSENCE.
THAT'S **IT?** THAT'S TWO WHOLE PAGES OF A 4-DOLLAR COMIC?
Um, YES.
TRÉS YIKES.
Sigh WELL, I GUESS IT'S BETTER THAN TWO PAGES FILLED WITH MORE BALLOONS THAN THE HOUSE FROM **UP!**
BETTY & VERONICA
"WHY CAN'T WE BE FRIENDS?"
I **HATE** COMICS LIKE THAT.

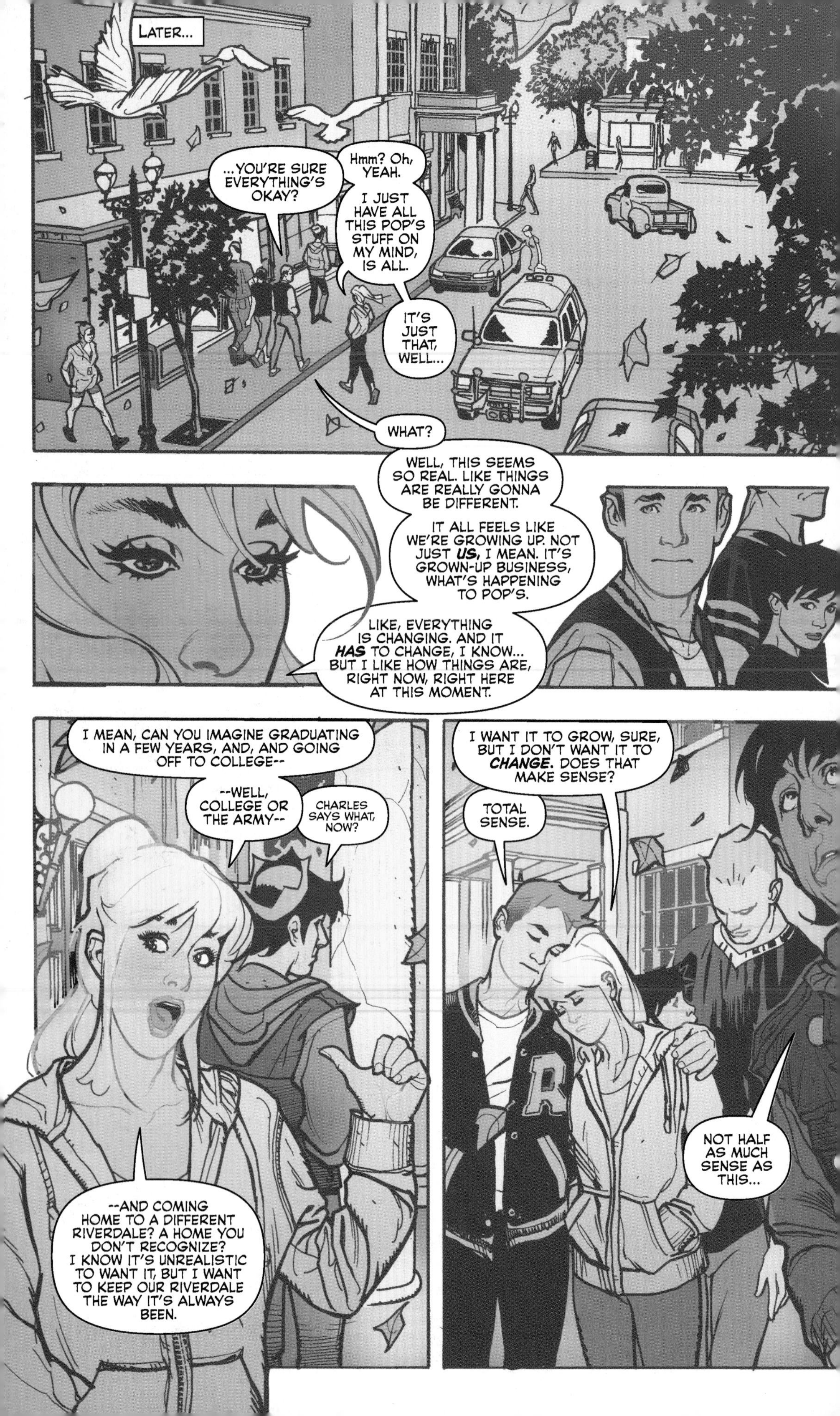
LATER...
...YOU'RE SURE EVERYTHING'S OKAY?
Hmm? Oh, YEAH.
I JUST HAVE ALL THIS POP'S STUFF ON MY MIND, IS ALL.
IT'S JUST THAT, WELL...
WHAT?
WELL, THIS SEEMS SO REAL. LIKE THINGS ARE REALLY GONNA BE DIFFERENT.
IT ALL FEELS LIKE WE'RE GROWING UP. NOT JUST US, I MEAN. IT'S GROWN-UP BUSINESS, WHAT'S HAPPENING TO POP'S.
LIKE, EVERYTHING IS CHANGING. AND IT HAS TO CHANGE, I KNOW... BUT I LIKE HOW THINGS ARE, RIGHT NOW, RIGHT HERE AT THIS MOMENT.
I MEAN, CAN YOU IMAGINE GRADUATING IN A FEW YEARS, AND, AND GOING OFF TO COLLEGE--
--WELL, COLLEGE OR THE ARMY--
CHARLES SAYS WHAT, NOW?
--AND COMING HOME TO A DIFFERENT RIVERDALE? A HOME YOU DON'T RECOGNIZE? I KNOW IT'S UNREALISTIC TO WANT IT, BUT I WANT TO KEEP OUR RIVERDALE THE WAY IT'S ALWAYS BEEN.
I WANT IT TO GROW, SURE, BUT I DON'T WANT IT TO CHANGE. DOES THAT MAKE SENSE?
TOTAL SENSE.
NOT HALF AS MUCH SENSE AS THIS...

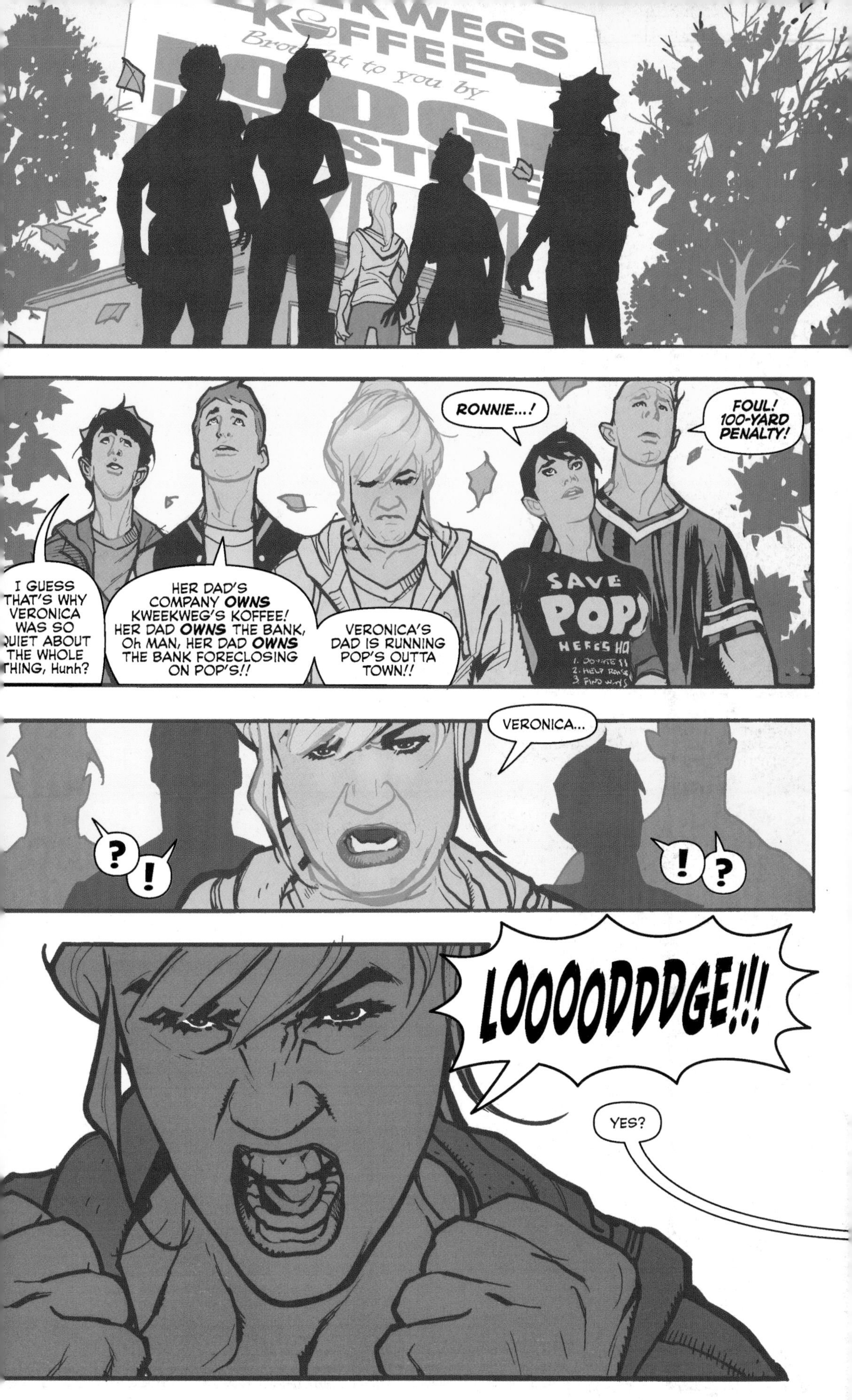

KWEGS KOFFEE
Brought to you by
RONNIE...!
FOUL! 100-YARD PENALTY!
I GUESS THAT'S WHY VERONICA WAS SO QUIET ABOUT THE WHOLE THING, Hunh?
HER DAD'S COMPANY OWNS KWEEKWEG'S KOFFEE! HER DAD OWNS THE BANK, Oh MAN, HER DAD OWNS THE BANK FORECLOSING ON POP'S!!
VERONICA'S DAD IS RUNNING POP'S OUTTA TOWN!!
SAVE POPS
VERONICA...
?!
!?
LOOOODDDGE!!!
YES?

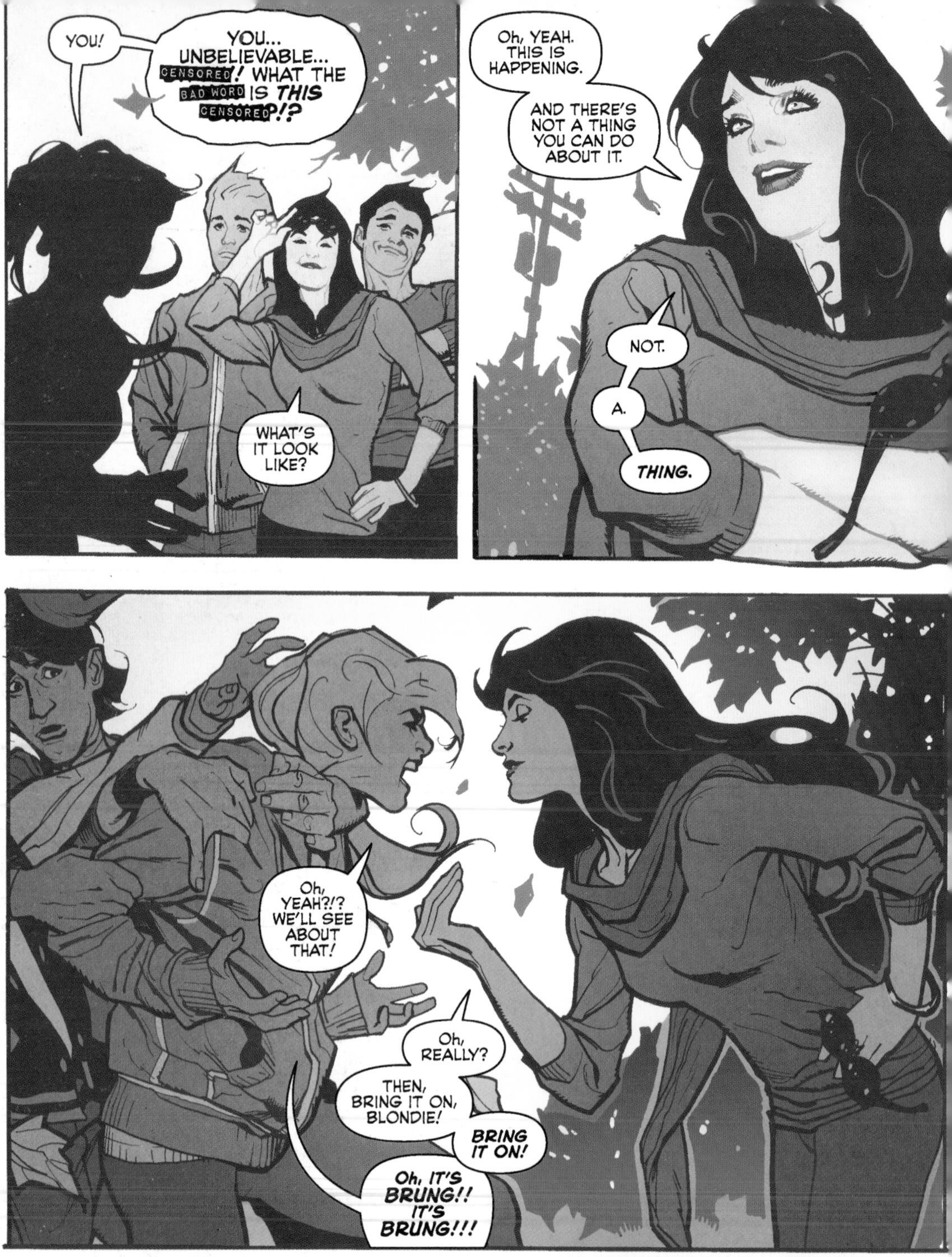
YOU!
YOU... UNBELIEVABLE... CENSORED! WHAT THE BAD WORD IS *THIS* CENSORED?!?
WHAT'S IT LOOK LIKE?
Oh, YEAH. THIS IS HAPPENING.
AND THERE'S NOT A THING YOU CAN DO ABOUT IT.
NOT.
A.
THING.
Oh, YEAH?!? WE'LL SEE ABOUT THAT!
Oh, REALLY?
THEN, BRING IT ON, BLONDIE!
BRING IT ON!
Oh, IT'S BRUNG!! IT'S BRUNG!!!

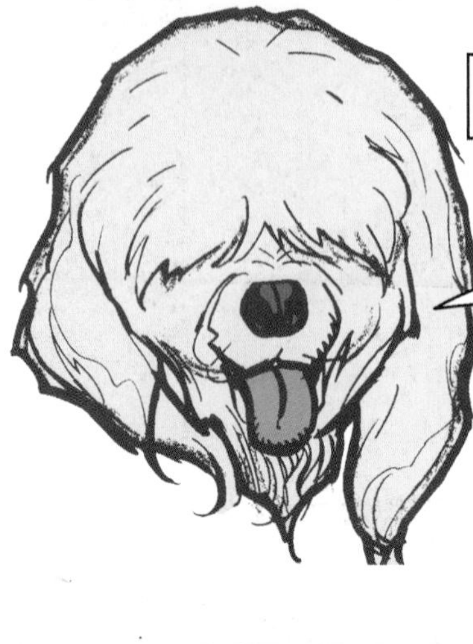
COME OUT FROM UNDER YOUR COVERS; REMOVE YOUR PAWS FROM YOUR EYES. WE PAUSE OUR CALAMITOUS CONFRONTATION, FOR THE NONCE.
BUT WHEN WE RETURN NEXT TIME, THINGS WILL HAVE GOTTEN MUCH, *MUCH* WORSE.
NOW, COULD SOME-ONE KINDLY LET ME OUT, PLEASE? I'VE NEEDED TO USE THE YARD FOR THE LAST 9 PAGES.

NEXT: The MISSES of OCTOBER

CATCH UP WITH THE ONGOING BETTY & VERONICA SERIES ON SALE NOW!